For Cathy and Norborn Felton

with best wishes from

Alicia and Wayne Kime

Jan. 2001

The
Indian Territory Journals
of
Colonel Richard Irving Dodge

Colonel Richard Irving Dodge, 1881

The Indian Territory Journals of Colonel Richard Irving Dodge

Edited by Wayne R. Kime

University of Oklahoma Press : Norman

Other Works Written or Edited by Wayne R. Kime

Pierre M. Irving and Washington Irving: A Collaboration in Life and Letters (Waterloo, Canada, 1978)

(ed.) *Raising the Wind: The Legend of Lapland and Finland Wizards in Literature* (Newark, Del., 1981)

(ed.) *Miscellaneous Writings, 1803–1859*, by Washington Irving (Boston, 1981)

(ed. with Andrew B. Myers) *Journals and Notebooks, Volume IV, 1826–1829*, by Washington Irving (Boston, 1984)

Donald G. Mitchell (Boston, 1985)

(ed.) *The Plains of North America and Their Inhabitants: A Critical Edition*, by Richard Irving Dodge (Newark, Del., and London, 1989)

(ed.) *The Black Hills Journals of Colonel Richard Irving Dodge* (Norman, 1996)

(ed.) *The Powder River Expedition Journals of Colonel Richard Dodge* (Norman, 1997)

This book is published with the generous assistance of the Wallace C. Thompson Endowment Fund, University of Oklahoma Foundation.

Library of Congress Cataloging-in-Publication Data

Dodge, Richard Irving, 1827–1895
  The Indian territory journals of Colonel Richard Irving Dodge / edited by Wayne R. Kime.
    p.   cm.
  Includes bibliographical references and index.
  ISBN 0-8061-3257-4 (hc : alk. paper)
    1. Dodge, Richard irving, 1827–1895—Diaries.   2. Indians of North America—Indian Territory.   3. Cheyenne Indians.   4. Arapaho Indians.   I. Kime, Wayne R.   II. Title.
E78.I5 D63 2000
976.6'04'092—dc21
  [B]   00-027413

1   2   3   4   5   6   7   8   9   10

Contents

Illustrations

Maps

Preface

THE EIGHT JOURNALS PUBLISHED IN THIS VOLUME, with entries dated between September 18, 1878, and December 18, 1880, are Lieutenant Colonel Richard Irving Dodge's personal record of an eventful period in his career as a United States Army officer. Of the twenty Dodge journals now housed in the Everett D. Graff Collection of Western Americana at the Newberry Library, Chicago, Illinois, these are chronologically the eleventh through the eighteenth. The first six, written between May and October 1875, comprise a record of Dodge's experiences as commander of an eight-company Army escort to a geological surveying expedition in the Black Hills of Dakota Territory. My edition of these journals was issued by the University of Oklahoma Press in 1996 as *The Black Hills Journals of Colonel Richard Irving Dodge*. The next four, written between October 1876 and January 1877, detail Dodge's activities as commander of the infantry and artillery battalions in General George Crook's Powder River Expedition against the Sioux and Northern Cheyenne Indians. Also edited by me, these were published in 1997 as *The Powder River Expedition Journals of Colonel Richard Irving Dodge*. The final two journals, as yet unpublished, record Dodge's observations between June and September 1883 during a valedictory tour of military posts and major cities of the West by the General of the Army, William T. Sherman.

Taken as a group, the twenty journals encompass a period of eight years, but they do not comprise a continuous chronological record, nor do they portray a common set of circumstances. The unifying feature is their authorship by Dodge, an articulate career officer whose rank gave him some access to top-level commanders like Crook, Pope,

Sheridan, and Sherman and whose duty with an infantry regiment kept him in contact with junior officers, enlisted men, civilians, and the Plains Indians whose cultures had interested him for many years. A soldier-author, Dodge published three books during this period: *The Black Hills* (1876), *The Plains of North America and Their Inhabitants* (1877), and *Our Wild Indians* (1882). His private journals also merit publication, for they deal with matters of permanent historical interest and do so lucidly, suggestively, sometimes memorably.

The journals dated between 1878 and 1880 are all associated with Indian Territory, the expanse of land that later became the state of Oklahoma. Whether as the scene of events that necessitated his taking the field in Kansas, as the location of his regular duty station, or as the place from which he made excursions, during this period the region of the Cheyenne and Arapaho reservation in Indian Territory was the controlling center of Dodge's activity. However, unlike the Black Hills and Powder River Expedition groupings, this series of journals does not present a continuous record of the period it covers. Intervals from a few weeks to several months separate one journal from the next. Moreover, as military needs evolved and priorities shifted, Dodge and his men were ordered from place to place. Each of his postings and assignments was in response to a problem with its own origin, history, underlying issues, and cast of characters. The historical contexts of Dodge's multiple missions are described and discussed in commentaries between the journals and in a concluding chapter. Fortunately, a range of published and unpublished material is available to shed supplementary light on Dodge, his contemporaries, and his times.

The coverage of Colonel Dodge in the journals and commentary sections constitutes a relatively thorough biographical study of him at this stage of his career. The accounts of his official duties yield a varied portrait of him as a military man, and two additional dimensions of his identity are also visible. The journals record landmark events in his family life, as father, husband, and son, and they document experiences that were to serve him soon afterward as an author. For in December 1880, Dodge completed the manuscript of his best known book, *Our Wild Indians*, a classic of its era.

The history of Dodge's activities between 1878 and 1880 naturally features Cantonment North Fork Canadian River, the six-company military post he established and commanded during those years. Dodge identified himself with Cantonment to such an extent that for many months his personal history and the early history of the post were in effect one. The present description of his experiences in Indian Territory therefore incorporates a history of this little-known military installation, the last one to be established in the territory prior to its achieving statehood.

Throughout the Indian Territory journals, the personality of their author is implicit. Dodge writes as a man upwards of fifty years of age, a soldier proud of his profession but with strong ties to his loved ones and life outside the service. He is confident of his involvement in actions of historical importance, playing his part in them thoughtfully and energetically yet with a wry sense that, after all, the course of history is not his to determine. His capacity for hard work, amusement, boredom, joy, anger, and missionary fervor all manifest themselves, as do his mental poise, gregariousness, and zest for life. One senses the justness of the characterizations later made of him, as "a gallant and very popular officer" and "a duty officer second to none."

For courtesies and assistance extended to me as I prepared this work, I am indebted to many persons and organizations, not all of whom are mentioned here. Financial support came from the sabbatical leave program at Fairmont State College, the Fairmont State College Foundation, the West Virginia Humanities Council, the National Endowment for the Humanities, and the Newberry Library, to all of which I express sincere thanks. For their support of my applications for research aid, I am grateful to Professors Ralph M. Aderman and Richard D. Rust and to Robert G. Masters, former library director at Fairmont State College. Wallace and Sue Jungers, Kathleen Moyne, Eleanore Hofstetter, Jude Olsen, Gene and Kate Rosselot, Peggy Wolivar, and Stan and Pat Hoig were gracious hosts during my expeditions in search of information. Once again, Robert Heffner Jr. provided expert assistance with the maps and John Piscitelli with photography. I am happy to thank Bazil Layman for his painstaking work in preparing a pen-and-ink sketch of Cantonment North Fork Canadian River. I also owe thanks to Stan Hoig and an anonymous reader for their careful study of the manuscript and suggestions for improving it. My son Evan R. Kime helped me minimize the consequences of certain mishaps with my computer program, and from first to last, as usual, my wife Alicia assisted me with my work in many ways.

Institutions whose facilities and personnel have assisted me in my research include the Newberry Library, Chicago; the National Archives, Washington, D.C.; U.S. Army Military History Institute, Carlisle Barracks, Pa.; Oklahoma Historical Society, Oklahoma City; Western History Collection, University of Oklahoma, Norman; Kansas Historical Society, Topeka; Beinecke Library, Yale University, New Haven, Conn.; New York Public Library, New York City; New-York Historical Society, New York City; Columbia University Library, New York City; Rutgers University Library, New Brunswick, N.J.; University of Pennsylvania Library, Philadelphia; University of Delaware Library, Newark; Towson State University Library, Baltimore, Md.; Johns Hopkins University Library, Baltimore, Md.; History Library, Museum of New Mexico, Santa Fe; Northwestern University Library, Evanston, Ill.; West Virginia University Library, Morgantown; Vermont Historical Society, Montpelier; and Fairmont State College Library, Fairmont, W.V. I am especially grateful to the staff of the Fairmont State College Library for their helpful services. Sharon Mazure, in charge of interlibrary loans, obtained for me scarce material that proved of considerable value.

For permission to quote from unpublished or copyrighted material and to reproduce photographs I thank the following: Newberry Library, Chicago; U.S. Army Military History Institute, Carlisle, Pa.; Western History Collection, University of Oklahoma; Oklahoma Historical Society, Oklahoma City; Columbia University Press, New York City.

Finally, I extend grateful thanks to Patricia Heinicke, Jr., the copy-editor of this volume, to Alice Stanton, who supervised the editing and production of the work, and to the able staff of the University of Oklahoma Press.

WAYNE R. KIME

Fairmont, West Virginia

Note on Editorial Policy

THE GENERAL AIM IN PRESENTING THE TEXTS OF Dodge's journals written between 1878 and 1880 is to coordinate the realization of two not always compatible goals: fidelity to what the author actually wrote and utility for the reader. Dodge compiled his journals under a variety of circumstances: indoors and outdoors, at leisure and in haste, in comfortable conditions and in awkward or trying ones. Not surprisingly, the character of his entries varies widely, from considered, relatively finished discourses to disjointed "telegraphic" notes. Yet despite the variations in their style, the manuscript texts all exhibit Dodge's tendency as a journal writer to take liberties with the standard practices of written expression. For example, he freely abbreviated words and names, and at some points he almost dispensed with punctuation. At times he seems to have regarded the shift of his pen from one line to the next as a sufficient substitute for whatever terminal punctuation one might ordinarily expect.

Presenting Dodge's manuscript journals in printed form clearly necessitates certain adjustments in order to render them accessible to a modern reader. The procedures I have followed in editing these texts are identical to those detailed in editorial notes to two volumes previously issued by the University of Oklahoma Press, *The Black Hills Journals of Colonel Richard Irving Dodge* (1996) and *The Powder River Expedition Journals of Colonel Richard Irving Dodge* (1997). For fuller discussion of the matters summarized here, the interested reader is referred to either of those volumes.

Except to correct spelling errors that are so serious that they might baffle or so odd that they might distract, I have allowed Dodge's variant spellings and even misspellings to stand. Where confusion seems possible, it is obviated either by an editorial interpolation within square brackets or by a footnote. For proper names that Dodge spells in more than one way, the correct spelling is indicated in an identifying note at the point where the name is first mentioned.

Abbreviations employed by Dodge appear here, with few exceptions, just as he wrote them. Abbreviations that may be problematical are filled out within square brackets or explained in notes at the points where they appear. Superscript letters written in connection with abbreviations are brought down to the line except in datelines, for which a standard format is used. Ampersands and "&c" (for *et cetera*) are allowed to stand.

Dodge's habits of capitalization, generally conventional though far from consistent, are respected. He did adopt quite often the traditional practice of capitalizing for emphasis, but his intention in doing so is clear and presents no difficulty. No effort is made to regularize his capitalization, except that the first letters in proper names and in daily entries are always capitalized.

The inconsistent punctuation and formatting of Dodge's journal entries requires some editorial regularization, for to present it unchanged would result in frequent ambiguity and pervasive distraction. Thus, for example, the sometimes irregular spacing between his paragraphs and entries is made uniform unless it seems to carry a special significance, such as to mark a place for information he expected to receive in the future, or to signify text written at a new sitting.

A few rules of thumb are adopted to govern the representation of Dodge's terminal punctuation. If a sentence at the end of a paragraph or a day's entry concludes without a punctuation mark, none is supplied. If, within paragraphs, a sentence concludes without punctuation and the one that follows it begins with a capital letter, no punctuation is supplied. If, as occasionally occurs, a sentence concludes with a comma, semicolon or colon, the error is corrected and the change noted. Question marks and exclamation marks are supplied as called for when Dodge concluded sentences without punctuation, but otherwise his terminal pointing is left essentially as he wrote it.

Dodge liked to record colorful and characteristic dialogue, but in doing so he often failed to complete pairs of quotation marks or to insert them at all. Thus, when necessary, omitted quotation marks are supplied within brackets. Parentheses and dashes, whether single or in pairs, are treated similarly.

Within sentences, distinguishing between what Dodge may have regarded as commas, hyphens, or something else can be quite difficult. Fortunately, once one recognizes the effective interchangeability within sentences of Dodge's commas and his dashes, or as I call them, "extended dots," problems of interpreting his meaning become rare. In transcribing the journals, I have recorded as dashes only those marks that clearly justify the identification; they appear in the edited text with a space between them and what precedes them. In more doubtful situations I have interpreted the marks as commas.

Cancellations are relatively infrequent in Dodge's journals, and on the whole they are not especially significant. Most often he deleted matter, not to censor himself, but to correct errors, insert afterthoughts, and revise for style. However, in the interest of completeness all canceled matter is included here, except that deleted words and phrases that he immediately rewrote are ignored. Mere slips of the pencil and cancelled fragments of illegible letters are also ignored.

Dodge often employed the caret (∧) to indicate placement of inserted matter. Here the caret is used to denote interlineated material, which is shown in a free space above the printed line (see the list of editorial symbols and abbreviations below).

Dodge assigned no page numbers in any of his journals. Ordinarily he wrote his entries straightforwardly—more or less filling each page, writing first on the front and then on the back of each leaf, and passing from front to back in a journal. No systematic numbering of pages is supplied here, but in order to facilitate the location of drawings, blank pages, reversed text, and other variations from the norm, page numbers are shown within square brackets at the points where that information is called for. The page numbers given are designated *R* for *recto*, the first or front side of a sheet on which Dodge ordinarily wrote before turning it over, or else *V* for *verso*, the reverse side. Thus

[*38V*] means the reverse side of the thirty-eighth manuscript page. Page numbers given without *R* or *V* denote both sides of a sheet.

Dodge began almost all his entries with a dateline, but in doing so he adopted several formats, providing varying amounts of information. Some consistency is imposed here on these diverse practices. Making use of all the information Dodge included in any particular dateline but presenting at a minimum the month and date, the information is given in the following format:

> *Designation of day (e.g., Thanksgiving), day of the week, month, date, year. Place, camp number*

Any ordinals appearing in the manuscript dateline, as in *March 23rd*, are presented as cardinal numbers, so that in this case the date would appear as *March 23*.

Editorial Symbols and Abbreviations

[roman]	Editorial additions
[*italic*]	Editorial explanations
< >	Restorations of canceled matter. Cancellations immediately written over are shown next to the letters or numerals written over them, without intervening space.
? ? or [?]	Doubtful readings. The question marks are used within square or angle brackets. A single doubtful word is followed immediately by a question mark within square brackets, without an intervening space.
unrecovered	Unrecovered word
∧	Interlinear insertions.

Editorial situations not covered by these symbols are explained at the points where they occur.

The
Indian Territory Journals
of
Colonel Richard Irving Dodge

Abbreviations

The following abbreviations are employed in citations throughout the volume:

AAAG	Acting Assistant Adjutant General
AAG	Assistant Adjutant General
AG	Adjutant General
AGO	Adjutant General's Office
ANJ	*Army and Navy Journal*
BHJ	*The Black Hills Journals of Colonel Richard Irving Dodge*
C&A	Cheyenne and Arapaho agency
CNFCR	Cantonment North Fork Canadian River
C.O.	Commanding Officer
DMO	Department of the Missouri
G.O.	General Order
I.T.	Indian Territory
LR	Letters Received
LS	Letters Sent
MDM	Military Division of the Missouri
OIA	Office of Indian Affairs
OWI	Dodge, *Our Wild Indians*
PNA	Dodge, *The Plains of North America and Their Inhabitants*
PREJ	*The Powder River Expedition Journals of Colonel Richard Irving Dodge*
RID	Richard Irving Dodge
SI	Secretary of the Interior
S.O.	Special Order
SW	Secretary of War
USAMHI	United States Army Military History Institute, Carlisle Barracks, Pa.

Commentary on Journal One
The Northern Cheyenne Outbreak

ON THE NIGHT OF SEPTEMBER 9, 1878, A BODY OF 353 Northern Cheyenne Indians slipped away from their encampment not far from the Cheyenne and Arapaho agency, in Indian Territory, beginning a desperate journey away from reservation life and toward their ancestral homeland in the northern plains and mountains.[1] These Indians represented about one-third of their tribespeople, who had arrived at the agency a year before under escort by United States Army troops under First Lieutenant Henry W. Lawton, Fourth Cavalry. Demoralized, and with most of their possessions destroyed in fighting during the recent Sioux War, in the spring of 1877 the Northern Cheyennes had agreed to peacefully occupy the reservation lands earlier set aside for them by treaty. However, on their arrival in Indian Territory, they were disappointed with their new home and soon became dissatisfied with the treatment they received there. They resented the rationing system imposed upon them by the agent, which deprived chiefs and head men of authority to distribute goods to members of their bands.

---

1. The best known account of the Northern Cheyennes' effort to return to their homeland is Sandoz, *Cheyenne Autumn*. Others include, from the Cheyenne point of view, Grinnell, *The Fighting Cheyennes*, pp. 403–17; Powell, *Sweet Medicine*, 1:198–210, and *People of the Sacred Mountain*, 2:1160–76; and Stands in Timber, *Cheyenne Memories*, pp. 232–35; see also Carriker, *Fort Supply*, pp. 120–28; Chalfant, *Cheyennes at Dark Water Creek*, pp. 174–75; and Wright, "The Pursuit of Dull Knife," pp. 144–54. Much detailed testimony by persons involved in events leading up to the outbreak and by participants on both sides in the escape and pursuit was published in the Senate *Report . . . on the Removal of the Northern Cheyennes*, pp. 45–47, 53–152. See also the report by General John Pope in House, *Report of the Secretary of War* (1878), pp. 39–51. Berthrong, *The Cheyenne and Arapaho Ordeal*, pp. 33–37, deals primarily with causes and consequences of the outbreak.

They did not mix well with the Southern Cheyennes already enrolled at the agency. They felt betrayed, for they had understood from senior military officers like Brigadier General George Crook, commander of the Department of the Platte, that they would be free to return north if they wished;[2] but now that option was denied them, and they were effectively imprisoned. Unaccustomed to the southern climate, they grew ill with malaria and other diseases, and in the absence of adequate medical treatment many died. They were homesick, and gravest of all their afflictions, they were hungry.

The potential for all these causes of discontent had been recognized and reported on within weeks of the Northern Cheyennes' arrival in Indian Territory. Under orders from his regimental commander, Colonel Ranald S. Mackenzie, on September 30, 1877, Lieutenant Lawton revisited the Cheyenne and Arapaho agency and the adjacent army post, Fort Reno, to ascertain the condition of all the Indians enrolled there. In an interview with the post commander, Major John K. Mizner, he was informed that the agent, John D. Miles, seemed to be doing all he could, faithfully issuing to the Indians their rations from the supplies made available to him by the Office of Indian Affairs, known more familiarly as the Indian Bureau. However, the quantities Miles had for distribution were in Mizner's view "entirely insufficient and inadequate to their wants." On the next day Lawton observed a weekly issue of rations. The sugar distributed was of inferior quality, he later reported, and the beef "not . . . merchantable for any use." In all, the food allotted the Indians amounted to no more than two-thirds the legally authorized provision, evidently owing to the failure of the Indian Bureau to make available sufficient supplies. Lawton sensed the frustration of the Indians but regarded them as peaceably disposed unless driven to violence "as the alternative to starvation." His report received strong endorsement from Mackenzie, who warned that any future outbreak by the Northern Cheyennes would be the fault of the

2. General Crook denied that the Northern Cheyennes had received such a promise; see Senate, *Report . . . on the Removal of the Northern Cheyennes*, pp. 224–25. Nevertheless, the Indians clearly believed they had been assured of their freedom to return to their homeland if they chose.

federal government and would be caused by starvation. Brigadier General John Pope, commander of the Department of the Missouri, forwarded the report to Army headquarters with the observation that its contents were worthy serious consideration by officials of the Indian Bureau.[3]

The Lawton report, which became known within the Department of the Interior as the "Lawton charges," had little practical effect except to intensify hostility between the Army and the Indian Bureau. Accusations of dishonesty were levelled against Lawton, as the federal organization under criticism rallied to protect its good name. On October 20, 1877, Carl Schurz, secretary of the interior, reported to the secretary of war that the administrator who oversaw Indian Bureau operations in the Indian Territory had assured him there was "no scarcity of supplies at that agency," though the Indians would need to supplement their rations by hunting or farming. His informant suggested that, as a precaution, additional Army troops should be moved to Fort Reno from Fort Sill, approximately seventy-five miles south. The small size of the garrison at Fort Reno tended to embolden the already warlike Indians and could bode trouble.[4]

In November 1877, Indians attached to the Cheyenne and Arapaho agency were permitted to leave their reservation in order to hunt buffalo, as they had done with success in recent years. However, this year the hunt was an abject failure, for the buffalo herds were seriously depleted and not to be found. Destitute and in danger of starving, the hunting party was issued emergency rations at Camp Supply, on the north fork of the Canadian River 130 miles upstream from the agency, to enable it to return home.[5] Meanwhile, General Pope and other

3. Lawton to Post Adjutant, Fort Sill, October 11, 1877, with endorsements (OIA LR, C&A). A brief visit and report by Lawton in early September had prompted Mackenzie to order a more detailed inquiry. See Lawton to Adjutant, Fourth Cavalry, September 12, 1877, with endorsements (AGO LR, C&A).

4. Schurz to SW, October 20, 1877 (AGO LR, C&A). Schurz was quoting from a letter of September 18 from William Nicholson, of the Central Superintendency at Lawrence, Kansas, to the Commissioner of Indian Affairs. The Office of Indian Affairs was under the aegis of the Department of the Interior.

5. Carriker, *Fort Supply*, pp. 117–18.

concerned officials warned of an imminent outbreak. Earlier in the year, Pope had expressed dismay that the Army was expected to force the Indians to remain on their reservations and "starve peaceably." William T. Sherman, General of the Army, agreed. It was "simply useless," he wrote, "for the Army to capture and compel Indians to live on a reservation if they must starve by remaining thereon."[6] By law, Army officers in Indian Territory were to exercise forcible control over Indians only upon request from representatives of the Indian Bureau. Yet the officers found it distasteful to bear responsibility for sufferings they had no legal power to alleviate. Thus Colonel Mackenzie directed Mizner to use no force whatever against Indians at the Cheyenne and Arapaho agency unless in extreme situations, lest the Army "be placed in a position of assisting in a great wrong."[7]

Against this background of disputed facts and jurisdictional jealousy, the Northern Cheyennes suffered and grew desperate. Dull Knife, one of their leaders, had earlier expressed to Lawton his will to remain on the reservation and follow a course of gradual adjustment to American ways, according to the policy of the Indian Bureau. Yet as more of his tribespeople fell ill during the oppressive summer of 1878, the chief's resolve lost its strength. Some of his young men were restless and inclined to violence. In a statement often heard, they expressed their own resolution: "We are sickly and dying here and no one will speak our names when we are gone. We will go north at all hazards and if we die in battle, our names will be remembered and cherished by all our people."[8]

Acting on a report that some Northern Cheyennes had left the reservation, on September 6, 1878, Major Mizner ordered his whole cavalry force, Companies G and H, Fourth Cavalry, under Captain Joseph Rendlebrock, to encamp within sight of the Northern Cheyennes, who had moved their village to a location further than usual from the agency. Rendlebrock's orders were not to interfere with the

6. Pope to AAG MDM, July 11, 1877, with endorsements (AGO LR, C&A).
7. Mackenzie to Mizner, September 15, 1877 (AGO LR, C&A).
8. John D. Miles to Mizner, September 20, 1878 (AGO LR, C&A). Among his own people, Dull Knife was known as Morning Star.

Dull Knife, Northern Cheyenne (Western History Collections, University of Oklahoma Libraries)

Indians unless they moved still further away from the agency offices, where Agent Miles wished to re-enroll them all in order to ascertain whether in fact any were absent. Ordered to return, the Indians delayed the move for two days, offering one excuse or another, but it was understood that on the morning of September 10 they would comply with the agent's demand.[9] However, with Rendlebrock's pickets in distant view, Dull Knife and his party slipped away unnoticed the night before, leaving their campfires burning and their tipis standing outlined against the dark sky. Early the next morning their departure was discovered, and at 8:00 a.m. Rendlebrock set out on their trail with orders to overtake them and return them to the agency. If at all possible, he was to accomplish this object without resorting to force, for Mizner feared hostility from Cheyennes still on the reservation who were sympathetic with their fellow tribespeople.[10]

Moving with difficulty through the rough country north and west of the agency, Rendlebrock and his men pushed hard, traveling sixty miles on their first day out. That afternoon he sent a courier to Camp Supply with a request for reinforcement, and by noon the next day Company I, Fourth Cavalry, under Captain William Hemphill was moving north on the ninety-mile wagon road between that post and Fort Dodge, Kansas. Rendlebrock continued to march rapidly on September 11 and 12, and midmorning of the following day he met the Northern Cheyennes. They had doubled back on their own trail and fortified a position at Turkey Springs, Indian Territory, thirty-five miles east of the Dodge-Supply road and a few miles north of the Cimarron River. In response to a demand to surrender and return to the agency, their spokesman, Little Wolf, refused, indicating their willingness to fight.[11] Skirmishing began at once and continued through most of the next day. By that time, after thirty-six hours without water, the soldiers were suffering from thirst, and after managing to break

9. Miles to E. A. Hayt, Commissioner of Indian Affairs, September 10, 1878 (OIA LR, C&A).

10. Senate, *Report . . . on the Removal of the Northern Cheyennes*, p. 113.

11. Carriker, *Fort Supply*, pp. 122–23; Wright, "The Pursuit of Dull Knife," pp. 147–48.

the Indians' position and put them to flight, Rendlebrock retreated to find fresh water and sent his wounded soldiers under escort to Camp Supply. Three of his men had been killed and three wounded. Shortly after this interchange, Chalk, the Arapaho scout who had parleyed with Little Wolf, died of wounds he received.[12]

News of the Northern Cheyenne outbreak reached General Pope at departmental headquarters, Fort Leavenworth, Kansas, on September 11.[13] Pope at once began marshaling his forces to intercept the fleeing Indians, ranging troops along the Atchison, Topeka and Santa Fe Rail Road, which crossed southern Kansas from east to west, and also along the Kansas Pacific Rail Road approximately one hundred miles north. Along the Kansas Pacific he ordered one hundred mounted infantry to Fort Wallace, in western Kansas, to head off the Indians if they crossed the railroad in the vicinity. Two other infantry companies at Fort Hays he ordered to take station at points between that post and Fort Wallace, 131 miles west of it by rail. To the south, one infantry company from Fort Dodge, Kansas, began patrolling the region west of that post and south of the Atchison, Topeka and Santa Fe Rail Road. Troops at Fort Lyon, Colorado, were alerted to watch the country east of them and to move at once along the railroad once the route of the Indians was determined. Should the Northern Cheyennes reach the vicinity of Fort Dodge, Lieutenant Colonel William H. Lewis, Nineteenth Infantry, would assume command of the pursuit force. To ensure stability at Fort Reno in the absence of troops regularly posted there, Pope ordered one company of cavalry from Fort Sill to reinforce the garrison. Pope was taking what precautions he could, but in proportion to the large tracts of country involved, the resources available to him were quite limited. On September 12 he suggested to his immediate superior, Lieutenant General Philip H. Sheridan, commander of

12. Carriker, *Fort Supply*, pp. 123–24; Senate, *Report . . . on the Removal of the Northern Cheyennes*, pp. 127–28. Powell gives the name of the Arapaho scout as Ghost Man (*People of the Sacred Mountain*, 2:1163). For a detailed account by Second Lieutenant Wilber E. Wilder, Fourth Cavalry, of the movements immediately afterward by the troops under Rendlebrock, see the Senate *Report*, pp. 128–29.

13. Mizner to Pope, September 10, 1878 (AGO LR).

the Military Division of the Missouri, that preparations for action should also be made in the more northerly Department of the Platte.[14]

In the days that followed, the Northern Cheyennes held their own against the troops under Rendlebrock, proving themselves both elusive and formidable. They seemed in no hurry to make their way north through Kansas. On September 18 Captain Hemphill with his troop of cavalry managed to locate them along Sand Creek, south of the state line, but he was badly outnumbered and after a brief engagement withdrew to Fort Dodge. Three days later, acting on information that the Indians were still in that area, Hemphill's company and an infantry unit under Captain Charles E. Morse, Sixteenth Infantry, joined the cavalry under Rendlebrock and, commanded by Rendlebrock as senior officer, fought the Indians inconclusively that afternoon and all the next day.[15] On the morning of September 23 the troops marched northwest in pursuit of the fugitives toward the Arkansas River, approximately fifty miles distant.

The Indian outbreak had by this time received nationwide attention, and the Army's obvious inability thus far to control and capture the Northern Cheyennes was giving concern to military authorities. Pope reported to Sheridan on September 18 that he had reinforced the troops available to Lewis, who should soon have three companies of cavalry and five of infantry. If Lewis did not stop the renegade band at the Arkansas River, he would follow them toward the Kansas Pacific where Lieutenant Colonel Richard Irving Dodge, Twenty-third Infantry, had also been sent reinforcements by railroad. "The want of cavalry is severely felt," Pope concluded, "but I will do all possible with the force I have."[16] Sensing Pope's fragile confidence, the next day Sheridan telegraphed General Crook, urging him to do everything possible to cut off the fugitives. Should Dull Knife and his band succeed in returning to their homeland, their feat would endanger the uneasy peace then prevailing with Indians of the entire northwest. Moreover,

14. Sheridan to AGO, September 12, 1878 (AGO LR). This communication transmitted Pope's report on his disposition of troops.

15. Wright, "The Pursuit of Dull Knife," pp. 148–49.

16. Pope to Sheridan, September 18, 1878 (AGO LR).

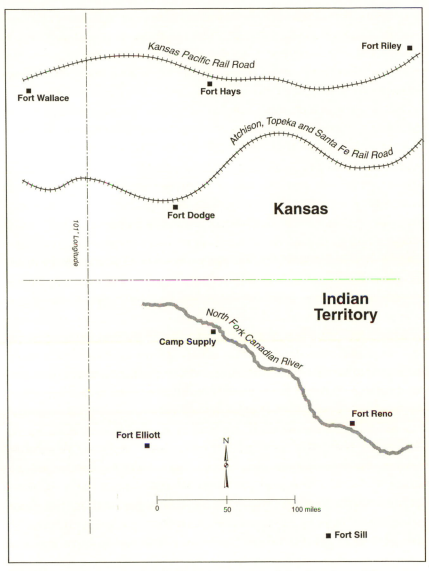

Region of military activity during the pursuit of the Northern Cheyenne, September 1878

it would surely destabilize the reservation system in Indian Territory, encouraging disaffected bands there to make more trouble.[17] On September 19 Sheridan assured his own commander, General Sherman, that "every effort will be made" to capture Dull Knife and so help preserve the peace.[18]

News of the outbreak had reached Fort Hays, Kansas, on September 11, when Pope ordered the post commander, Lieutenant Colonel Dodge, to select points along the railroad west of him where two companies from his garrison could be placed on alert.[19] As days passed, a steady stream of reports and new orders reached Fort Hays by telegraph. Citizens in the region were alarmed, and dire rumors and calls for special assistance abounded. Dodge received reports from soldiers and civilian scouts in the field and was in frequent communication with Lieutenant Colonel James Van Voast, Sixteenth Infantry, his counterpart at Fort Wallace, to share information and make provisional arrangements. However, in the absence of developments within reach of his post, he could do little more.

The Northern Cheyenne Indians under Dull Knife were of longstanding interest to Dodge, from several points of view. In his most recent field service, as commander of the infantry and artillery battalions of the Powder River Expedition under General Crook, he had participated in decisive operations against this very tribe. Colonel Mackenzie's pre-dawn raid of November 25, 1876, on the village of Dull Knife had badly weakened the warlike Northern Cheyennes, hastening their surrender a few months later.[20] Like Mackenzie, Dodge admired this brave people, not only as adversaries but as worthy exemplars of a mode of human life other than his own. In his recent book, *The Plains of North America and Their Inhabitants* (1877), he had dealt at length with the Cheyennes, designating them "the best

17. Sheridan to Crook, September 19, 1878 (AGO LR).
18. Sheridan to Sherman, September 19, 1878 (OIA LR, C&A).
19. AAG DMO to C.O. Fort Hays (Fort Hays LR).
20. For Dodge's description of the Mackenzie–Dull Knife battle, see *PREJ*, pp. 85–90, 92–96.

specimens of man and womanhood on the plains."[21] He sympathized with their recent plight—removed from their homeland, denied rations and other considerations guaranteed them by treaty, and, he believed, victimized by corrupt traders and the contractors who supplied substandard goods and services to the Indian Bureau. Nevertheless, Dodge understood the Cheyennes to be savages and in need of discipline by force. Like most military men of the era, he believed the Army potentially a far more effective body than the Indian Bureau to help prepare the aboriginal peoples of the plains and mountains to assume the rights and responsibilities of United States citizenship.

As a professional soldier, Dodge welcomed the opportunity to take the field if necessary against the Northern Cheyennes, whose abilities as a fighting force he regarded as second to none.[22] Unlike some of his Army contemporaries, he was not consumed with ambition for glory in battle or for obtaining a generalship. Nevertheless, he valued the good opinion of his colleagues, and he knew that for an officer of the line like himself, performance in the field was the high road to respect and possibly even preferment. A graduate of West Point in the class of 1848, Dodge had served for thirty years in a variety of roles—among others, as adjutant, quartermaster, provost marshal, instructor, inspector, post commander, mustering and disbursing agent, and member of a board to revise the code of Army regulations. He was a seasoned veteran, and despite bouts of rheumatism aggravated by exposure during the severe plains winters, at the age of fifty-one he was still in good physical condition. The prospect of distinguishing himself as a commander of troops in the field excited him

21. *PNA*, pp. 238–39 n. This work has been issued under three titles. The earliest, bearing a title assigned it by Dodge's editor, William Blackmore, was the English edition, *The Hunting Grounds of the Great West* (London: Chatto & Windus, November 1876). This was followed by an American edition printed almost entirely from the same plates and bearing a title recognizably similar to Blackmore's but more in accordance with the author's wishes: *The Plains of the Great West and Their Inhabitants* (New York: G. P. Putnam's Sons, January 1877). A recent edition, based on the author's manuscript and given the title he wished, is *The Plains of North America and Their Inhabitants*, edited by Wayne R. Kime (Newark: University of Delaware Press, 1989), cited here as *PNA*.

22. See *PREJ*, p. 96.

as he awaited further reports about the Indians, still more than one hundred miles away.

On September 18 General Pope ordered Dodge to proceed to Monument Station, 101 miles west of Fort Hays by railroad, and to assume command of all troops east of that point along the Kansas Pacific line.[23] Pope believed that, should the Northern Cheyennes manage to move this far north, they would attempt to cross the railroad at some point where one of the old Indian trails intersected it. These were at or near Monument and the two railroad stations immediately east, Grinnell and Buffalo. Dodge would thus be placed where his commanding general thought troops were most likely to see action. As had become his custom when given military assignments likely to be of special interest, on this day Dodge began a journal—presented in the pages that follow—describing his experiences in the campaign to come. For professional purposes, he would make of this small pocket notebook a repository of memoranda about daily marches, observations, and communications that would serve him as the basis for a report at the end of the action. For reasons more personal, he would also include in it much other matter—expressions of opinion, accounts of conversations, descriptions of scenery and personages, speculations, anecdotes. Dodge enjoyed expressing himself in writing, and the days to come promised much to write about. His journal would record the preparations, strenuous efforts, observations, and ruminations thereon by one senior officer caught up in the Army's attempt to intercept and capture Dull Knife, Little Wolf, and their band of escaping Northern Cheyennes.

23. AAG DMO to RID (Fort Hays LR). On the same day Pope addressed a letter to Dodge apprising him of the information then available about the Northern Cheyennes and directing him to call upon Van Voast at Fort Wallace for assistance as necessary (Fort Hays LR).

Journal One
September 18–
October 13, 1878

September 18. Fort Hays, Kansas[1]

Recd telegraphic order to go to Monument Station, & assume Comd of all the troops east of this station.[2]   Packed up at once.   Took Shob, one of Goodales men to cook for me.[3]   The train was 2 hours late.   Trout stayed with me, & we played billiards at O'Briens[4] until

1. The manuscript journal, manufactured by Reynolds and Reynolds of Dayton, Ohio, measures 3 5/8 by 6 11/16 inches and consists of brown flexible cardboard covers at front and back, secured to the pages between them by a strip of tape at the top. Its fifty-six pages, designed to be flipped up from the bottom, are of cream-colored paper lined horizontally on both sides with pink ink. Near their top edge, the sheets are perforated to permit easy tearing away. On the front cover Dodge has written in black ink "No. 1 [/] Sepr 18th 1878 [/] to [\] Novr 3rd 1878 [/] [*space*] [/] Cheyenne Campaign." Also written in ink are the text on pages [1R], [4V]–[13R] (through "Stern chase"), and [36R] ("There is") to the end. Pages [1V], [18V], [19R], and [48R]–[54V] are blank. The pages following [47V] are written with the notebook in reversed position.

Page [1R], written in blue ink, is a postage account showing amounts paid for letters sent between September 19 and 26 to several persons: Van Voast (4 letters), Pope (2), Trout (5), Hinton (1), Dallas (2), and Saxton (1). The text begins on page [2R].

2. Dodge was to assume command of troops east of Monument Station, not east of Fort Hays as his statement suggests. Also on September 18 he received a telegram from General Pope containing general instructions. The Indians were expected to cross the railroad at the "usual places," between Monument and the two railroad stations immediately east of it—Grinnell and Buffalo—and "must be stopped at all hazards" (Fort Hays LR).

3. Private William Schob of Company K, Twenty-third Infantry, commanded by Captain Greenleaf A. Goodale.

4. First Lieutenant John F. Trout, Twenty-third Infantry, was post quartermaster and commissary of subsistence at Fort Hays. He had served ably under Dodge for several years. See *BHJ*, pp. 72, 107, 134, 185, 197; *PREJ*, pp. 147–48, 179. Michael O'Brien, Acting Assistant Surgeon at Fort Hays, was a civilian physician employed by the Army. He resided in Hays City, one-half mile north of the post.

train time – 2 am   Trout got my horses on freight, very promptly and well.   Take Tomlinson along as scout, &c[5]

Got sleeper –   Telegram that 1 compy from Ft Riley ordered to report to me

September 19, 1878. Monument Station

Capt Hale 16th Infy with Compy, on same train with me.[6]   Arrived here 6 a.m.   Pollock & all up to see me.[7]   Telegram from Lewis saying that Hempill attackd Indians on breaks of Bear Creek yesterday. They are more than 100 miles from me yet, & Lewis ought to get them before they reach here.[8]   Telegram from Eskridge who is at Sheridan with 25 mounted men.[9]

Turned very cold about 11 am   Went to bed under a Buffalo robe. At about 3 pm a terrible storm of rain came on – lasting till near sunset.   Spent the evening before a good coal fire in the station – and enjoyed it.   Very cold & windy at night.   Have slept most of the day.

5. Boon H. Tomlinson, twenty-five years of age, was a civilian teamster employed in the post quartermaster's department.

6. Captain Clayton Hale commanded Company H, Sixteenth Infantry, the unit from Fort Riley that had been ordered to report to Dodge.

7. Captain Otis W. Pollock commanded Company C of Dodge's regiment, one of two units that on September 11 he had ordered to points along the railroad for observation. Pollock took station at Monument, and the other unit, Company B under Captain James Henton, at Grinnell, twenty-two miles east. Dodge consistently misspells Henton's surname as "Hinton."

8. Lieutenant Colonel William H. Lewis was at Fort Dodge, Kansas, awaiting the arrival of three companies of cavalry from Camp Supply and Fort Elliott, posts to his south. Upon their arrival, he was to command them and infantry troops from Fort Lyon, Colorado, pursuing the Indians northward toward the Kansas Pacific Rail Road. Captain William C. Hemphill's Company I, Fourth Cavalry, from Camp Supply, was one of the three cavalry units. After engaging the Northern Cheyennes in a brief skirmish on September 18, Hemphill withdrew, being badly outnumbered. He and his men arrived at Fort Dodge at 3:00 p.m., September 19.

9. Captain Richard I. Eskridge commanded Company H, Twenty-third Infantry, one of three mounted infantry units that had been sent from Fort Leavenworth on September 12 under Major Alexander H. Dallas of the same regiment. The force under Dallas had reported at Fort Wallace, thirty-nine miles west of Monument. Sheridan, a railroad station, was midway between Monument and the village of Wallace, which was located along the railroad two miles northwest of the fort.

Wrote to Genl Pope, Van Voast,[10] Trout & Hinton –
Tomlinson got an antelope.

September 20

Bad stormy night, wind & rain –   Slept under 2 heavy blankets &
Buffalo robe.   Taken short in the worst part of storm & had to get up
– "Sich is tent life" —
Telegram from Genl Pope, giving instructions also one from Van
Voast asking information.   Wrote to Van Voast & to Dallas.   Tele-
graphed to Genl Pope asking him to organize a pack train   Wrote to
Trout for forage & other things –
Much pleasanter today – wanted to go hunting but dont dare leave,
lest important orders come in my absence.   Citizen – unknown – fell
from train & killed near here today.
Seems as if I had been here a month.   Forgot to mention that I
yesterday sent Lt Vinal 16 Infy to Carlisle, 12 miles east.[11]
Indians not yet across the Arkansas.[12]   Compy C men got 2 antelope
today.[13]

10. Lieutenant Colonel James Van Voast, post commander at Fort Wallace, had
charge of troops west of Monument Station. He and Dodge had been instructed to
exchange information and assistance as necessary, so a steady stream of messages
passed between them.
11. First Lieutenant William H. Vinal was attached to Company H, Sixteenth
Infantry.
12. The Northern Cheyennes had now been at large for eleven days, and their
exact location was unknown. On September 20 General Pope assured General
Sheridan of his determination to use "every effort and all the means I have to stop the
Indians and capture them. Lewis has at his disposal two hundred and fifty men, one-
half cavalry. On the Kansas Pacific Road between Buffalo Station and Wallace and at
Wallace are two hundred and fifty men about one hundred of them mounted infantry.
Lewis & Dodge are as you know competent and active officers familiar with the
country and the Indians. . . . They are impressed with the necessity of the case and
each has force quite ample to deal with these Indians. If they cross Arkansas [River]
Lewis will follow them closely so that they may be placed between Dodge and
himself. The misfortune is that we have no sufficient cavalry force" (MDM Cheyenne
Outbreak Special File).
13. Beginning with the entry for September 21, on p. [4V], Dodge wrote in blue
ink.

Saturday, September 21, 1878

Telegraphed to Hinton to hire 4 scouts – also ∧ wrote to Dallas to hire 4 for me.   Wrote long letters to Van Voast & Dallas about transp[ortatio]n.   Telegraphed to Genl Pope, & to Lewis.   Letter to Pope & one to <P>Saxton about scouts wagons &c.   Recd telegrams from Hd Qrs Hinton, Van Voast, & Dallas.   Quite busy all morning – Sent Tomlinson over to Smoky after a said-to-be good scout named Sam Schaik.[14]   Wrote letter of instructions.   Not a word of Indians today. No letters.   Miserable place for mail – no post office.   Played cribbage with Pollock until 10 pm & went to bed –   Before the storm is the calm –

Sunday, September 22

Not an Indian to be heard of.   Tomlinson returned & reported that Schiack declined to be employed as scout, but would carry out my instructions & send in a runner in case he found the Indians.   He is engaged in "rounding up" his cattle.   About 20 other men are engaged in same business & their duties take them exactly where I want them as scouts   In enlisting his good offices I have 20 scouts, where I would have had only four.

In answer to my letter of yesterday about organizing the transportation, Van Voast telegraphed me today "If a pursuit is to be made & if I have my way, will turn it over to you, &c".[15]   I answered "if you dont want the Comd. of the pursuit telegraph the fact to Genl Pope. I cant do it."   He telegraphed back "I want the Comd. as much as you –" &c.[16]   I had at one time visions of the Comd. wherever the Indians

14. Elsewhere Dodge spells this man's name as Schiack and Schrack. See the journal entry for September 22 and RID to AAG DMO, October 12, 1878 (DMO LR).

15. Van Voast telegraphed: "If the Indians are to be pursued, if I <can> have my way, will turn it over to you. Send Trout, your Quartermaster to me, give him your instructions." He then described what wagons and other transportation he had available for use (Enclosure, RID to AAG DMO, October 12—DMO LR).

16. Clarifying his earlier message, Van Voast now telegraphed: "I am as anxious to command pursuit as you are but my offer was to let you organize transportation to please you, not myself. Better let this matter stand where it is. I will pursue if they cross [the railroad] within my lines, and you if they cross within yours" (Enclosure, RID to AAG DMO, October 12—DMO LR).

might cross, but all is now as before –   I wrote to him tonight & told him if he didn't want it more than I, he didn't hanker after it.   Telegram from Genl Pope telling me that 50 pack saddles had been shipped to Wallace yesterday.   Recd. a large lot of stuff from Trout today – rations &c – also a letter from Father, from Trout, Miss Anne V.V., Mrs Kammerer of Harrisburg & some papers.   Wrote to Father & Mother – to Julia, Trout & Mrs Kammerer,[17] also to Van Voast & Dallas.

A man of Pollock's Co went out hunting today & killed 2 antelope at a shot.   When they were brought in each had 2 bullet holes in him.   On asking an explanation he said that on getting near after they were down he thought they might attack him & so he put another bullet into each.   This is worse than the man who killed a sheep for fear it might bite him.   I have raided[18] Pollock on the courage of Co C

Monday, September 23

Long letter from V. V. whose feelings are much hurt by my telegram in regard to the Comd. of the pursuit.   I wrote a soft answer – & have I hope turned away his wrath.   How he expected me to do otherwise than I did I cant conceive.   He proposed to turn over the Comd to me.   We both have our orders   He cant "turn over" nor I accept comd. except by orders of Genl Pope.   Unless his offer was mere

17. James R. Dodge (1795–1880) and his wife Susan Williams Dodge resided on a farm in rural Yadkin County, North Carolina. Dodge, the eldest of their four children, kept up a regular correspondence with them. "Julia" was Dodge's wife, Julia Rhinelander Paulding Dodge. The other two ladies mentioned are unidentified. "Annie V.V." is likely the "Annie V. Vleck" in the journal entry for September 23. Miss Kammerer's city of residence, Harrisburg, Pennsylvania, was Dodge's duty station during much of the period 1862–1864, when he was the Army's mustering and disbursing officer for the states of Pennsylvania and Maryland.

18. Likely Dodge meant "railed at" or "rallied." Witty observations often passed between Dodge and Pollock. For example, in a dispatch of September 17 the latter referred to Captain Joseph Rendlebrock, the German-American cavalry officer who had engaged the Northern Cheyennes four days before, as "Reglebrock (if you know who he is)." In a dispatch the next day he designated the battle as "What-you-call-em's fight" (Fort Hays LR).

gas[19] I cant see why he should be so hurt, when I ask him to take the only step which can make that offer effective

Pope telegraphs that 50 pack saddles were shipped to Wallace yesterday.   Recd. a long letter from Dallas about the V. V. imbroglio yesterday & answered it today.   Not a word of the Indians today. Am satisfied they have kept south of Arkansas & gone west.[20]   Lewis must be after them as nothing has been heard of him.   Wrote letters to Joe & Laura[21] – Annie V. Vleck.   Telegraphed a clincher to Van Voast about pack animals.   Asked Pope to order Trout to Wallace for 2 days to organize pack train.   Played cribbage with Pollock at night.   P. went up by 10 Oclk pm freight to visit Eskridge at Sheridan

Tuesday, September 24

A box arrived this a.m. bringing our mail, some stationery, horse brush & comb some butter from Laura – all very welcome.   Blowing a stiff gale from South all day, making out of doors unbearable, & inside of tent unendurable.   You pays your money & takes your choice.   Telegram from V. V. asking for saddles pistols &c.   Telegraphed to Trout to send them from Hays.   Sent Trout D/L. Also ration returns.[22]   Ordered all my troops rationed to include 10th Oct. Recd. several letters & plenty of papers by mail.

10 pm.
        ∧   It has been a terrible day the worst in some respects of the summer.   A gale blowing outside so stiff that one cant see or walk or do anything but hold to his hat & scud for shelter, & so hot inside that a tent or room is like the door of a furnace.   I am parched

19. Slang for "empty or boastful talk . . . humbug, nonsense" (*Oxford English Dictionary*). More often Dodge uses "gas" or "gassing" to denote informal conversation accompanied by whisky.

20. Like Dodge, Van Voast expected the Northern Cheyennes to move westward. On September 19 he had telegraphed that, if not captured along the Arkansas River, they would probably cross the Kansas Pacific in the vicinity of Fort Wallace (Fort Hays LR).

21. Dodge's domestic servants, a young black man and wife.

22. A D/L or "descriptive list" was an itemization of military stores and equipment, and a ration return described foodstuffs used and on hand.

through. At this present time near 10 pm it is just beginning to be comfortable. Telegram from Platt<e> authorizing me to order Trout to Wallace –[23] Another just recd. from Hinton reporting 4 Indians on Smoky 28 miles from him Ordered him to send scouts tomorw early, investigate fully & report promptly.

Wednesday, September 25

A lively day. Positive news of the Indians at last. After I went to bed, the operator brought me a dispatch from Col Lewis that the Indians had crossed the Arkansas, & at least four or five telegrams have come today reiterating this news.[24] One of the earliest dispatches recd. was from Platt, informing me that 2 more Cos of 23d were ordered to report to me from 11 Worth.[25] I immediately telegraphed to Trout to ship light wagons mules &c. Telegraphed & wrote for rations yesterday. Then telegraphed order to Trout to report by first passenger train to Comdg Officer Ft Wallace – to turn over his duties at Hays to Goodale – also telling him what to bring.[26] Was greatly surprised to receive a tel[egra]m. in reply, saying he "didnt see how I could expect him to &c.["] I also recd. telm. from Goodale saying he had no authority to order Trout to Wallace. Answered both very curtly & to the point – directing them to obey

23. Major Edward R. Platt, assistant adjutant general of the Department of the Missouri, was the officer through whom all General Pope's orders and official communications were sent.

24. At 8:30 a.m. on September 25, Lewis reported that a trail seventy-five yards wide, showing tracks of about 150 ponies, had been discovered nine miles northeast of Pierceville, a railroad stop thirty-nine miles west of Dodge City. He set out in pursuit, having with him one company of infantry under Captain James H. Bradford of his own regiment and two companies of cavalry, just arrived from Fort Elliott, under Captain Clarence Mauck, Fourth Cavalry. Lewis hoped to make junction with the battalion under Captain Rendlebrock, which he assumed was on the Indians' trail (AAG DMO to Sheridan, September 25—MDM Cheyenne Outbreak Special File). The substance of this telegram was widely distributed.

25. These were Company F, under Captain Joseph T. Haskell, and Company G, under Captain Charles Wheaton.

26. Dodge's message concluded: "If I command pursuit you will go. Tent & mess with me. Bring bedding &c. and have it here. Send up my Saddle . . . also two pistols belts holsters & 100 rounds ammunition" (Enclosure, RID to AAG DMO, October 12—DMO LR).

orders.[27]   All was right at once, & they came down.   I believe I am
all ready now for work & good work.   The Indians ought to be on
line of this Road tomorro if they do not cross it tonight.   The only
question is where will they cross.   The pursuing Comd. will be first
rate, & if the Comdr. is the right sort of man he will capture them,
unless something very unforeseen occurs.   I want the Comd. badly,
& V. V. dont want it at all – yet we are so ordered, that chance will
decide.

Have been busy all day writing up telegrams – vouchers for Tel
Compy's a/c.[28]   Saw some objects far off this afternoon, which from
their action I took to be Indians   Sent Tomlinson to see, & soon after
he left my horse broke his lariat & went after him.   T. saw & caught
him & soon came back reporting cattle.   If Trout does his work, & I
dont doubt him – for he is the very best Qr Mr[29] I ever saw, I will be
fixed early tomorro for a prompt & vigorous pursuit.   I am not
"spilin" for a fight, but I want the Comd. of this exp[editio]n.

There will be six Cos Infy, three of Mounted Infy under Dallas & at
least two Cos of Cavy under Lewis, who I hope will overtake me.[30]

27. Captain Greenleaf A. Goodale, who was left in command at Fort Hays, telegraphed Dodge on September 25: "I have no authority from Dept. Headquarters to
send Trout. Have you?" He informed the departmental adjutant at Fort Leavenworth
of Dodge's order and, adding that the services of Trout were required at Fort Hays,
asked, "Shall I send him?" Both Platt and Dodge quickly set him straight. The adjutant
wrote: "Your doubt of obeying orders of Col Dodge to send Lieut Trout is not
understood. Comply with the order at once and report when you have done so. By
command of Genl Pope." Dodge telegraphed: "I have full authority. Obey my orders"
(Fort Hays LR, LS).
28. Between September 18 and 25 Dodge had sent eleven telegrams to officers
under his command and at least as many to Van Voast, Platt, and Pope.
29. Quartermaster.
30. Although consistent with the information he had received, Dodge's summary
of the combined pursuit force was optimistic in regard to the number of units that
would comprise it and in the assumption that they would be able to operate in
coordinated fashion. In fact, the state of affairs south of the Kansas Pacific Rail Road
was doubtful. On September 24 Lieutenant General Sheridan had reported to the
Adjutant General in Washington that the information received from the Arkansas
River region had been so meagre he had not thought it worth passing along. He
added, incorrectly, that the Northern Cheyennes had not yet crossed the river (MDM
Cheyenne Outbreak Special File). They had crossed it unopposed on September 23.
See Powell, *People of the Sacred Mountain*, 2:1167.

He is now on the trail, but he is awfully slow.   I cant understand how he let the Indians remain 11 days right under his nose without doing anything.   They were within 40 miles of Dodge from 13th to 23d inclusive.   After the storm last night, it has been lovely, though cool.

Thursday, September 26, 1878

Trout passed before daylight this a.m. leaving his bedding & a bundle of warm clothing &c for me.   Train with the stock wagons &c arrived 3. 1/2 p.m.   No news of Indians up to that hour.   Wrote to V. V. & to Trout.   All the things sent for & about the supply of which Trout was troubled came in good order.   At 8 pm Smith's & Brady's (Stillé Comdg) Cos arrived 60 strong.[31]   Everything is now ready, wagons mules rations all   We can pull out in two hours.   Not a single word or rumor of Indians   They will probably cross the R.[32] tonight that is if they cross east of here.

Genl Davis & the Regl Staff go to Wallace[33] – arriving tomorro morning –   I dont know what to make of this new move of Pope's though I *think* I know.   He ∧ goes to Wallace.   If the orders are left as before, all right, but if he has come to Comd pursuit after Van & I have done all the work, I shall ask to be sent back to Hays.   Wrote again tonight to V. V. & Trout.   Asked Van to send Trout to me tomorro, as I need him & he has large amount of property here.   Complimented Trout on his success in doing the work I ordered.   Ordered some more edibles.   Monument appears quite lively tonight.   Nothing like it ever occurred before –

31. Company D, Twenty-third Infantry, commanded by Captain Thomas M. K. Smith, and Company E, commanded by First Lieutenant Louis R. Stillé, were both stationed at Fort Leavenworth. Captain George K. Brady, the regular commander of Company E, was on leave of absence.

32. Probably Dodge meant "River," not "Railroad." The Smoky Hill River, eighteen miles south of Buffalo Station, ran further south of the railroad at points to the east.

33. Colonel Jefferson C. Davis, whom Dodge refers to by his brevet rank of major general, commanded the Twenty-third Regiment of Infantry. On September 26 he and his adjutant, First Lieutenant Patrick T. Brodrick, and his quartermaster, First Lieutenant William F. Rice, left Fort Leavenworth by railroad for Wallace Station. On the day before, General Pope had directed Davis to assume general charge of operations to intercept and capture the fleeing Indians (DMO LS).

Friday, September 27, 1878

Nothing of Indians today.   Recd. telegram from Davis announcing that he had assumed Comd. at Wallace.   I think most officers would feel hurt that a senior should be put in charge, just after the junior had got everything ready   I am very sure that Pope did not aim this blow at me.   He has been very friendly & appreciative always.   Van, is fussy & weak and somebody was wanted there.   I could'nt be sent for he ranks me.[34]   Pope would be foolish to put me aside for Davis if he could help it.   I know all this country, the Indian trails & where they are likely to go.   Davis knows nothing but what he learns from day to day from guides &c.[35]   I am vain enough to believe I am a better Comdr. here than Davis, & I am very sure I would have it did my rank warrant it.   They dont seem to want to send Trout back to me.   I have written & telegraphed.   If he dont come tonight I'll telegraph to Pope tomorro.   Windy – Windy day – & not feeling at all well.   I need exercise, & cant leave this confounded job for a hunt or anything.   Eskridge ordered to Beaver Ck.[36]   Played cribbage with Pollock at night & sent him home in a bad humor.   Trout arrived 11 pm. with orders to concentrate my forces.

Saturday, September 28, 1878

Sent orders to Hinton to be ready to come to me on arrival of train.[37] Reported to Davis, that he could send his train for the troops.   Trout is getting everything in order for our move.   He states that Jeff pro-

34. Of the twenty-five lieutenant colonels of infantry regiments in the U.S. Army, Van Voast was fourteenth in lineal rank; Dodge, seventeenth (Official Army Register, 1878, p. 230).

35. Between 1867 and 1873 Dodge had served almost continuously in this region, known as "the Republican country" after the Republican River to the north. He had commanded at North Platte Station and at Forts Sedgwick, Fred Steele, Lyon, Larned, and Dodge, and had seen much service in the field. Colonel Davis was a relative newcomer to the region. After the Civil War he had been assigned through 1873 to posts in northern California, Oregon, and Alaska, and thereafter he served chiefly in the recruiting service and in other sorts of desk duty.

36. Captain Eskridge, at Sheridan Station with his company of mounted infantry, had been ordered south on a reconnaissance mission.

37. Captain Henton, with Company B, mounted infantry, had been posted by Dodge at Grinnell.

poses to send this Comd. to the Smoky or south of it.   If so he will commit a fatal error, & will not see an Indian   They must have passed west & ought now to be on or near Big Sandy.[38]   Our only chance is to watch the R.R. all ready for a move.   As soon as the Indians cross, the whole Comd. should be taken by Rail to that point & put on the Trail.   We ought to be on trail within 6 or 8 hours of their crossing. If Jeff sends his Comd. away from the R.R. he will, when he hears they have crossed have to send out for the Comd. & it will have to march to R.R. losing two three or more days – entirely too much to be made up on a stern chase.[39]

The above had hardly got dry before a telegram was recd, directing me to march at once with 4 Cos. due south to a point on Poison Ck, &c.   Orders were at once given to get ready.   All tents & heavy baggage were taken down & stored under the water tank, & at 4 pm I started with 3 comps, leaving orders to Hinton to push on & join me as soon as he arrived.[40]   I intended to go about 8 miles, but my guide was unacquainted with the route & as darkness overtook us we missed the water.   I pushed on looking for it, but as it came very dark I feared the Comd. would not be able to follow the trail   I started back for it, but both I & my sharp-eyed guide Tomlinson lost the trail – nor could we find it anywhere   We kept on however travelling by the North Star   After a while I saw a light for an instant We went in the direction an apparently interminable time, & gave it up as an hallucination <until> when I saw another.   Again we went for it – again to travel a long time without seeing or hearing the Comd.   At last I got tired of this & halting fired my rifle in the air. In a few moments the welcome answering shot came & we soon rejoined the Comd.   After a hard march, we at 11.30 came to the

38. Dodge places the Indians to the west even of Fort Wallace. Big Sandy Creek flows southeast through eastern Colorado until it joins the Arkansas River there.

39. In naval usage, a chase from astern is proverbially a long one. At this point, on p. [13R] in the manuscript journal, Dodge began writing in pencil.

40. Dodge was marching south with Companies C, D, and E of his regiment. Company B, under Henton, boarded a train east from Grinnell to Monument and marched from there. Poison Creek, the destination named in Colonel Davis' order, was approximately forty-five miles south of Monument.

Smoky[41] & went into camp, <After> making fully 16 miles.   I sent one of the guides back to bring up Hinton, who, I knew, could never find his way to us.   I was soon asleep & in a short time all seemed to be so except the Sentinels.   Trout announced his intention of setting up for Hinton

Sunday, September 29

Reveille just before sunrise, to enable the men to get a good rest. Just at 7, when all ready to move, Guild came up at a gallop bearing a telegr from Davis.   It announced the fight & death of Lewis - the pursuit by Mauck of the Indians to Chalk Ck - & ordered me to move up the Smoky towards Sheridan.[42]   I started at once up by the old stage road sending my scouts to follow up the river on S. side & 2 or 3 miles away, as I thought the Indians would scatter at the river & road.   About a mile above camp I saw 2 fresh traks of unshod ponies, but thought they must be Cowboys - the whole country being full of cattle.   Marched slowly but persistently, & at 6 pm, arrived at Sheridan.   Went to telegraph office at once, & to my very

41. The Smoky Hill River, whose course in the territory between Forts Hays and Wallace roughly paralleled the Kansas Pacific Rail Road.

42. Elsewhere Dodge identifies Guild as "the Geological collector at Monument" (RID to AAG DMO, October 12, 1878—DMO LR). The force under Lewis joined two cavalry companies under Rendlebrock and one under Hemphill and overtook the Northern Cheyennes the afternoon of September 27. Later that day Lewis was seriously wounded in an engagement on Punished (or Famished) Woman's Fork of the Smoky Hill River, and the fighting soon tailed off. The Indians resumed their march that night, and the next morning Captain Mauck, now in command of the pursuing force, set off on their trail. He detached Second Lieutenant Cornelius Gardener with a surgeon and twenty-five cavalry to escort Lewis and two wounded men to Fort Wallace. The party arrived at the fort at 1:00 a.m. on September 29, but Lewis, whose femoral artery had been severed, had died on the trail of blood loss. Gardener bore a dispatch from Mauck describing the fight and speculating that the Indians would cross the railroad the night of September 28. Upon receipt of this information, Davis telegraphed to Pope: "I now know where the Indians are and can begin to operate intelligently. Prospects good for capturing the Indians. Dodge's command must be in close proximity to them. He will move at daylight for them. Dallas' command is thirty miles south of this place but has been ordered back" (MDM Cheyenne Outbreak Special File). Dodge's orders were to move west along the Smoky Hill River toward the railroad at Sheridan, scanning the country for signs of the Indians.

intense disgust learned that the Indians had crossed the RR last night at Carlisle – only 12 miles east of Monument, where I was stationed.[43] Had it not been for Jeff's foolish order sending me away from the R.R. I would now be at least 20 miles North of the R.R. on the track of the Redskins & if Pope had not sent Davis to command, I would have been there with 6 Cos Infy & 3 Cos M[oun]t[e]d Infy. – better for a fight than any Cavalry.[44]

I telegraphed my report to Davis – shortly after I sent another, urging that I be ordered to strike direct from here to the old Indian Crossing of the Sappa, & a third asking for a Surgeon.   Have a very nice camp.   Water yesterday & today badly alkalied – have nearly drowned my insides with it, without quenching my intolerable thirst.

About 8 pm recd. telegram from Davis directing me to move on the line I proposed.   It is an unusually familiar & pleasant telegram,

43. Moving rapidly eastward, the Northern Cheyennes had carefully concealed their tracks as they crossed the railroad the night of September 28. See Dodge's journal entry for October 11 and Powell, *People of the Sacred Mountain*, 2:1171. Captain Mauck with his force did not reach the railroad until 11:00 a.m. on September 29. He spent the remainder of that day being outfitted for the move further north. Davis had ordered him to begin "pursuit to the utmost" the morning of September 30 (Pope to AAG MDM, October 1—MDM Cheyenne Outbreak Special File).

44. Dodge repeats his summary of forces in the journal entry for September 25, omitting only the cavalry companies under Mauck. His belief that infantry troops were superior to cavalry in a fight against Indians was unorthodox but deeply held; see *PREJ*, pp. 17-18, 31, 57, 85 n, 173, 175. In the recent operations against the Northern Cheyennes, cavalry had been ineffective. On October 10 Pope expressed his disappointment to Sheridan: "I had the hope that the Cavalry companies, of which five were in pursuit under Colonel Lewis . . . would be able to deal with the Indians or at least delay their movements so that the Infantry could meet them or come up with them. The Cavalry had four skirmishes with them with indecisive and unsatisfactory results. . . . The Indians have the long range arms and plenty of ammunition, and the Cavalry is armed with the Carbine, which is no match. . . . As soon as the Indians make a stand, they put themselves in rough country and in rifle pits where the Cavalry cannot charge them, nor with their Carbines fighting on foot drive them from their defences" (Pope to AAG MDM, October 10—MDM Cheyenne Outbreak Special File). Shortly afterward Pope recommended that cavalry troops in his department be armed with .50 caliber Springfield rifles, which was done.

indicating I think that the Old Man feels that he has made a mistake & is desirous to conciliate.[45]   Issued stringent orders about baggage, & proposed to leave Smith & some other offs. & men behind – but Smith came to me afterwards & was so manly about the affair, that I shall take him along if I possibly can.[46]   Am trying to make arrangements to get horses for the officers.

Rice came in for a moment.   He had been down to see Mauck, who is encamped tonight at Carlisle.[47]

All my changes will delay my movement tomorro a.m. but I will gain by that.   <My> The very first water is 35 miles from us, & I will do better to start at 10 Oclk, letting my animals take a good drink before I start.   Poor Lewis, he was a noble fellow, & died a noble death, the death of all others that a soldier should desire —[48]

Monday, September 30, 1878

Had all extra baggage sent to station for transportation to Wallace. One Sergeant & 8 men reported sick & unfit to make the trip. Ordered them to Wallace & telegraphed to Davis to send transpn for them by Rail.   Cowles went back 7 miles to try & hire horses.   Trout succeeded in hiring a wagon & team of 2 horses & one extra saddle

---

45. Davis' telegram began: "Your three telegrams received. Am pleased with your day's work. Owing to the news received this afternoon from Captain Mauck, I was afraid that you were left out in the cold in the pursuit, but now I think you are fully abreast of the other commands. . . . Mauck starting from Carlyle tomorrow morning, trailing the Indians will be on your right [to the east of Dodge]. You will not delay in order to communicate with him, but push. I wish you and your command had the fabled seven-league boots" (Enclosure, RID to AAG DMO, October 12—DMO LR). By "the Old Man" Dodge refers to Davis as his Army superior; in fact, at fifty-one years of age he was a year older than Davis.

46. Captain Smith, who commanded Company D, did accompany Dodge.

47. Rice, the regimental quartermaster, was making arrangements for the supplies Mauck required for his move north the next morning.

48. In the official announcement of Lewis' death, General Pope wrote: "Calm in judgment, courteous and refined in bearing, active, firm, and upright in the discharge of every duty . . . Lieutenant-Colonel Lewis had won the respect of all who knew him" (G.O. 11, September 30, 1878—DMO). The *Army and Navy Journal* also warmly praised Lewis (October 5, 1878, pp. 136-37). Fort Lewis, Colorado, established in 1880, was named after this officer.

horse.   Cowles got 2 horses and a mule.[49]   All was ready a little earlier than I expected & I pulled out at 9.30.   We were delayed nearly half hour in crossing the R.R. the crossing being blocked by trains.   At last however all was clear, & we started.   The road or trail ran up a divide for 4 miles, landing us at last on a high dry prairie. After 6 or 7 miles the trail became so hard to follow that I cut loose from it & took the course that comparison of the ideas of Tomlinson – my guide – & the rather imperfect map I have led me to believe the correct one.   I have never seen so generally level & apparently interminable a piece of prairie.[50]   I had a great many sore-footed men, & was compelled to impose on the animals, by letting these ride on the wagons – for some distance nearly half the Comd. was riding.[51]   I found towards evening that this was telling on the mules & stopped it.

At dark we had got into the head breaks of the Sappa but could find no water & had to make a dry camp.   The men with a soldiers usual improvidence had drunk up all the water finishing nearly a gallon to the man.   I sent Tomlinson down the Creek & after an hour or two he came back & reported water 2 1/2 miles down the Creek.   A man of each Compy was mounted, & sent with all the canteens of the Compy   They returned at 8.30 pm with a good supply.   I then ordered Trout to send all the animals down, & they are just starting now.   This will enable the animals to feed properly tonight & save my laying up for a couple of hours tomorro morning.   Shortnose, the

49. In a "Diary of Events" that accompanied his letter of October 12 to departmental headquarters, Dodge wrote in the entry for September 30: "All sick and foot sore men ordered left behind. One Sergeant and 8 men ordered to Wallace. Hired a wagon & 2 ponies, as the ambulance for sick. . . . I propose a hard march, & cannot possibly carry sick & foot sore on the light two horse wagons, already overloaded with 10 days' forage and ammunition" (DMO LR). Second Lieutenant Calvin D. Cowles was attached to Company B, which had accompanied Dodge from Fort Hays.

50. Pages [18V] and [19R], which follow, are blank, probably having been skipped over inadvertently.

51. Dodge later reported complaints by men on this march about their footwear, known as Cable Screw shoes: "It appears that the action of walking tends to force the screws inwards. It is difficult to get at these projections inside the shoe, to break or bend them, and some of the men had their feet dreadfully lacerated" (RID to AAG DMO, October 31, 1878—Fort Hays LS).

running fork of the Sappa is only 6 miles from us.   I shall reach it by
8.30 as I have ordered reveille very early.   I ought to strike the trail
of the Indians by or before 12 tomorro anyhow.   Mauck must be
encamped within 5 or 6 miles of me & I hope to catch him tomorro.
I have made about 2<1>2 miles today, & if I can get on at the same
rate I will be up with the Indians or across the U.P. RR by Friday night
or Saturday am[52]   I killed a nice antelope today   It ran up to the
column.[53]   I am perfectly well & enjoying myself, but my Comd is
very dilapidated, nearly all the Offs being sore footed.

Tuesday, October 1, 1878

Had reveille at 5 am & broke camp at 6.10.   Had a wretched night,
pain in bowels, & had to run 3 times in face of cold & wind.   Tomlinson was certain that we would strike good water & plenty of wood
in 8 miles on a N.E. course.   <Str>Took a N.E. course & followed it
with scarcely a deviation for 17 miles.   Here Tomlinson found a
puddle or two of dirty water – nearly a mile to the northward.   I
turned off the whole comd. & men and animals were permitted to
slake their thirst.   I tasted it & found that though muddy & thick it
was quite palateable.   Here I gave up[54] my N.W. course as from the
appearance of the country there was no water to my left.   I therefore
stuck to the arroyo which I had crossed at the 15th mile of my march.
These arroyos, that on which I camped last night & the one I am on
tonight, I believe to be the S & N branches of the Sappa.[55]   If not I
dont know where we are & Tomlinson is even more out than I.   I
followed down until 4.15 p.m. & there being no appearance of water
or wood, I went into camp, after a continuous march of ten hours –

52. The Union Pacific Rail Road, immediately north of the Platte River, was
approximately 120 miles north of Dodge's present position.
53. At the end of the manuscript journal, following a record of game he and others
had taken, Dodge wrote: "On the Indian Expedition many antelope & much other
game were killed by the Offs & hunters, but I had to play guide & had no chance to
hunt. My only antelope ran up on me – & paid the penalty."
54. Dodge wrote "gave it," probably with the preceding sentence still in his mind.
55. The branches of Sappa Creek flow north-northeast through north central
Kansas, joining the Republican River in southern Nebraska.

Fortunately the day was cool a brisk wind blowing from north & the men & animals stood the march wonderfully well.   After we got into camp, the Wagon Master, Manning[56] asked for a horse to go & look for water.   In a short time he returned having found a pool containing a barrel or two.   A wagon was immediately sent down with all our kegs and canteens, & it is now just returned 7.30 pm, & the whole camp is in a delighted uproar.   There is not a stick of wood but great hot fires of buffalo chips, are giving a ruddy & comfortable glow to the camp.   I shall give up the Sappa tomorro and strike directly North for Beaver Ck.   I will not strike the Indian trail so soon, but I'll strike it further north.   A heavy smoke sprung up about 3 pm – some miles to the South – which looked like an Indian signal – though I can hardly believe any are yet South of us.   It has been a hard day, but all are cheerful & certainly enjoying themselves at present –

Distance 25 miles.   Total distance marched 82 miles.   Country almost a level – dry, barren & uninviting – but will make fine farms some day when advancing civilization has brought rain[57]

Pollocks Compy. averaged yesterday one & one half gallons of water to the man.   No matter how little thirst a soldier habitually has for water – just tell him that he is to make a dry camp & may need it, & he at once proceeds to drink up all his own, & everybody else's he can get hold of.[58]

Tomlinson got an antelope – & I ought to have got several but shot badly.   Two men not in when I go to bed.

Wednesday, October 2

Broke camp 6.15.   The 2 men left yesterday not having got in, I sent one of the guides back after them with an extra horse.   Marched due north.   The men suffered greatly yesterday there not being enough water.   Some have not had coffee for 2 days.   A few miles

56. A civilian employee of the quartermaster's department.
57. Dodge here expresses the contemporary belief that "rain follows the plow." See Miner, *West of Wichita*, pp. 42–43.
58. Dodge wrote "hold it," an obvious error.

from Camp passed a great draw & down it we could see large trees & a herd of cattle. Some of the men started for it I brought them back & saw that while actually obedient they were really mutinous. I gave them a sound rating for effect – for I recognize that entire discipline can only be maintained, by the utmost show of authority, when men are desperate either by reason of hunger or thirst. But shortly after, I turned the head of the column towards the supposed water.

I intended to camp on Beaver anyhow, & as I could reach it by an afternoon march I determined to give the Comd. a three hours nooning, & then go to Beaver. We found sufficient water. I directed Trout to kill and distribute to the Comd. one of the Beeves. In a time[59] all were happy & all cooking & eating. At 1.20 started north again everybody in good condition. To my great astonishment I did not get away far from the ravine at which we lunched. Soon the breaks of another large ravine appeared on our left, & to keep the divide I was forced to a N.E. course. By 4.30 pm these ravines had approached until we could see timber & lovely camping places on each – & I soon turned to the north – crossed & camped on the most northerly in one of the most beautiful & convenient camps I have ever seen. Wood & water in abundance & grass enough. I dont know where I am. Tomlinson is completely at fault. The maps are wrong. I think I am on little Beaver.[60] There is a ranche near this Camp – a man named Gaumer. <His house I> He & his family evidently left on the first alarm – The house has been gutted by the Indians – a small party of whom have been here within a day or two – A trail of 3 wagons passed by here probably this afternoon. I suspect they are Maucks If so I will probably overtake him in a day or two.

The Indians are not far ahead of me – in fact we ought to have them pretty well cornered if all the Comds. have marched as fast as I have.

59. This is the first word on p. [23V]; probably on turning over the leaf Dodge forgot to write a word like "short."

60. Beaver Creek, and to its north Little Beaver Creek, were both north of the Sappa. In fact, Dodge was encamped on Little Prairie Dog Creek, near the South Sappa.

I caught a few sun fish after getting in.   I think I will camp on the Republican tomorro night, but am so muddled with the uncertainty of the maps that I'm certain of nothing   Made each Compy march by itself today – with an Officer at its head – with marked improvement
        Distance 1<8>9 miles.
Total   "   10<0>1   "   in 96 hours

Thursday, October 3

I have had a horrible day & have neither time nor inclination to put the details in a diary.   After leaving our lovely camp of last night we marched nearly due North west 7 1/2 miles & reached a lovely Valley, which I hoped & believed was the Driftwood.   A ranch was directly before us, & more were visible here & there – while fields of corn & wheat gave a curious variety to the characteristically wild landscape. Riding up to the Ranch I asked a man if he had heard anything of Indians.   "Yes,["] he replied, ["]we have heard seen & felt them. Our whole valley is in mourning & we are not yet through burying the dead."   To add to my mortification & sorrow at this news, I now found that we are on the South Sappa – almost exactly where I was

                        East &
ordered to go – but   ∧   <far> South of where I hoped to be.
    This valley was pounced upon by the Indians at 9 am on Monday – before I had yet left Sheridan.[61]   <I am n> Mauck passed in hot pursuit on Tuesday a.m.   The Indians camped on Monday night on the top of a high plain – only two miles from North Fork of Sappa – & but about 20 miles from where Mauck camped the night before. My camp last night was on *little* Prarie Dog, & my lunch yesterday on Prarie Dog.   I spent two hours listening to the heartrending stories of outrage – then marched   Crossing North Sappa & pushing on Camped in a draw, or tributary of the Beaver.   Mauck camped only

61. After crossing the Kansas Pacific Rail Road on Saturday, September 28, the Northern Cheyennes had moved north rapidly, securing fresh horses and supplies by raids on settlers. Despite their numbers and the presence among them of many women and children, the Indians carried few impedimenta and were able to outdistance their pursuers by regularly securing new mounts. See the Senate *Report . . . on the Removal of the Northern Cheyennes*, p. 136.

a short distance down.   He marched very fast but the Indians do not seem to have feared him in the least.   They scattered out in small parties, & harried the whole valley – killing fourteen men, wounding others.   Every house has been sacked, every female over 10 years of age captured was ravished.   Fortunately the thickets along the stream were dense – & all who escaped did so by concealing themselves in this thicket.

I have never seen such a horrid picture of devastation –   A lovely valley laid waste, horses, food, bedding, clothing all gone.   Not a family but has to mourn a father or brother killed – or mother or sister ravished.   One family had Father & three sons killed – Mother & two

daughters raped.   The Mother & \<some> ∧^(two) younger children were then put on a bed, & the house set on fire.   The fiends left, the Mother got herself & children out of the burning house & escaped to the brush.   I rode up to the burned house today.   The ruin was complete – every thing about the house had been cut to pieces – trunks opened & ransacked, &c &c – \<ther> everything taken that pleased the fancy of the Indians – all else destroyed or burned —

While I was examining the wreck, a poor little half grown kitten came running from under a wood pile with the most frantic demonstrations of delight, & climbed at once to my shoulder —   I can write no more. I am disappointed – & stricken with horror that in a civilized country such things as I have seen & heard today are fostered & encouraged by people who think themselves Christian & humane –[62]   I would wipe every Indian off the face of the earth, sooner than allow it.

62. Dodge expresses the frustration of an Army officer who believed that the Bureau of Indian Affairs bore ultimate responsibility for outrages of this sort by Indians. In his view, the Indian Bureau, by its policy of pacification, failed to curb the Indians' impulses to violence by the threat of force and thus effectively permitted them to do whatever they pleased. He had complained in *PNA* that persons infected by a "sentiment of humanitarianism" ignorantly idealized American Indians, decrying efforts by the Army to make them accountable for their crimes: "Indians murder a family of settlers with all the usual horrors. It touches no sympathetic cord in the philanthropic breast. Troops pursue, overtake and kill some of the murderers. At once there is a storm of indignation against the assassins of the 'Noble Red Man'" (pp. 364–65).

Distance 24 miles
Total   125   "

Friday, October 4, 1878

In four miles from camp of last night we struck the Beaver.   It is a rather pretty valley, ranches & fields scattered over – but not a sign of life anywhere except the grazing cattle –   Directly in our front was a rather imposing looking settlement & we thought from its appearance at a distance that the inhabitants had been able to stand

off the Indians.   On arrival however ^we found our error.   In front of the door lay the body of a large dog which had evidently <sold> given

^ its life in defense of its Master.   The house, stables &c were in themselves intact but more complete destruction I never saw visited on any place.   The whole inside of the house was torn out, everything valuable & portable taken away – everything else utterly destroyed. The beds & pillows had been ripped open, & the feathers covered the garden or were piled by the wind in masses against the fence.   Dead geese, ducks & chickens were lying around, killed in mere wanton- ness.   While we were examining the wreck <3>4 women & <2>a man came up to us.   The women were a Mother <& 2 daughters> 1 daughter a daughter in Law & a neighbor who had come with them to interpret   The people were Bohemians   The Indians had come to the house in a very friendly way, shaken hands all round tried to talk, then bade good by & appeared to be going off.   In an instant & without a word they turned & shot the unarmed men.   The women were seized, taken into the house & all repeatedly violated.   The house was then plundered –   The poor women told their pitiful story with many tears, <&>   To add to their miseries they are left entirely without food, clothing, bedding, everything.   Thirteen men were killed and 1 missing on the Beaver – 25 men killed and 2 missing

on the Sappas –   Every <woma> ^female   over ten years of age that fell into their hands was violated   These statistics come from a very reliable gentleman from Mendota[63] – who with a party has gone all around to bury the dead, & care for the indigent.

We made only a short stop & pushed on.   Just before arriving at the breaks of the Driftwood I met a party of Citizens who were returning from the front with a number of Indian ponies that had been abandoned.   They informed me that Mauck had left the Republican on a N.W. course <of>on Wednesday am   Dallas & Vance left on Thursday am – Vance's men all in wagons.   This information convinced me that I am entirely out of the race.   If Vance was on foot I would follow for I can march 3 miles to his two, but I cannot possibly overtake men provided as they are.[64]   I went on to Driftwood & while nooning, thought the matter over very carefully & decided to return –

Turned back, & marched to Beaver in 3 hours & campd.   It is hard to have to give up but it would <be>simply be foolish to march my men down for nothing.   I never recovered from the first unfortunate order of Davis.   Men in good condition.   Distance 22 miles   Total 147 miles.   Caught a fine mess of perch for supper –

Saturday, October 5

Continued my journey south, making one of the straightest trails for a whole days march I ever made.   Found that the N. Fork of Sappa

63. A village in Trego County, Kansas, immediately east of Hays County, where Fort Hays was located.

64. On October 2 Mauck reported from his camp on the Republican River that the main body of the Northern Cheyennes had crossed the river at 9:00 a.m. that day. He anticipated that they would cross the Union Pacific Rail Road on the night of October 4–5 (Pope to AAG MDM, October 3—MDM Cheyenne Outbreak Special File). However, the Indians moved more rapidly than he expected, crossing the railroad five miles west of Ogallala, Nebraska, at 1:30 p.m. on October 4. Troops in the Department of the Platte, under Major Thomas T. Thornburgh, Fourth Infantry, and Major Caleb Carlton, Third Cavalry, set out in pursuit (R. Williams to AAG MDM, October 5—MDM Cheyenne Outbreak Special File). Mauck reached the railroad at 6:30 p.m. on October 4 and continued north. Official information about the progress of Dallas and his mounted infantry troops had not yet reached any headquarters. If the reports received by Dodge from citizens were accurate, the command under Mauck was well over two days in advance of him, those of Dallas and Vance more than one day. Meanwhile, Pope reported to Sheridan on October 5 that Dodge was "not heard from" (MDM Cheyenne Outbreak Special File).

joined the Middle fork at least 8 miles further west than the map puts it.   Soon after starting I was overtaken by a courier from Vance, bearing a duplicate of a letter from Davis ordering me to take Comd. of Dallas' Column.[65]   As that was impossible I kept the Courier with me, & at night wrote a report to Davis, which I will send to Wallace tomorro.

Camped on Middle fork of Sappa – no running water & pools very scarce.   It & the N. fork join a mile below my Camp.   Bough[t] a Beef butchered & distributed it to the Comd.   There are a good many cattle hereabouts, and a few settlers, nearly all of whom are packing up to leave so dangerous a country.

Very pretty camp – wood & grass abundant – water enough.

Distance 16 miles

Total   163   "

Sunday, October 6

Struck S.E. intending to strike the Prairie Dog at the Water holes where we nooned on 2d.

I am taking it easy, & a very roundabout course to Monument – because of the scarcity of water.   From here to the RR & West there is scarcely a pool which can be relied on.   Got into camp about 12 – No antelope – no nothing   The Indians appear to have devast[at]ed even to driving off the game

65. On the morning of October 3 Captain Duncan M. Vance, Sixteenth Infantry, in command of a column from Fort Wallace numbering seventy-five infantry and twenty-five cavalry troops, received while in camp along the Republican River a dispatch of October 2 from Colonel Davis addressed to Dodge. Not knowing Dodge's whereabouts, Vance opened the envelope, copied the substance of Davis' order, and sent a courier bearing the copy in search of its addressee. This was the "duplicate" Dodge received. Its chief points were: "The indications are that the Indians are pushing for the Whiteman's or Frenchman's fork of the Republican, with one day's march ahead of Mauck. Yet it is possible they may retreat in the direction of Fort Macpherson [northeastward]—in either case on receipt of this you will assume command of Major Dallas' Column, as soon as possible, and push forward in pursuit without regard to Capt. Mauck's movement as far as the U. P. R. R. at least, and report to both Genls. Pope and Crook" (Enclosure, RID to AAG DMO, October 12—DMO LR).

The Courier went off this am with my report to Jeff Davis.   Now that it is gone, I am sorry I did not take more pains with it - as I've no doubt it will go to the papers.[66]   However it was written in pencil on my knee, & the surroundings were not favorable to composition. So it may go -

Distance 14 miles

Total   177 -

Strike direct for Monument tomorro, with probably a dry camp - A Stranger in camp.   Gave him supper hope he wont steal my horse.

Monday, October 7

Our guest of last night went off without Breakfast this am, cursing us all.   I have not yet found out his cause of complaint, either that I did not invite him to share my tent - or that Trout & I sat down to breakfast without asking him, which was a necessity in as much as we had plates cups &c only for two.   He is a blackguard anyway or he would have shown some thanks for a good supper, & several extra blankets.

Marched S.S.W. continually with a "little deviation" south.   Crossed North Solomon - no water - South Solomon - dry as a bone.   Everybody hunting water, but no water.   At last when I had given it up & determined to go into camp - in fact was in camp, the animals partly unhitched, when Tomlinson came in with the welcome information

that he had found water enough for the animals - <Tomli>   ^ about half a mile from camp.   Tomlinson killed 2 antelope at one shot today.

66. No published version of Dodge's report has been located. However, Davis attached it to a report of his own dated October 17, 1878. Dodge first summarized his activities between September 30 and October 4 and the information he had received from citizens on the latter date, then recounted his inferences that Mauck was almost three days ahead of him, Dallas one day, and Vance only slightly less: "I was yet fully twenty miles behind Vance, with no possibility of overtaking him, his men being mounted [and] in wagons. Finding myself thrown utterly out of the race, and being unwilling uselessly to break down my men, I determined to return, and marched back to Beaver the same day. On the morning of the 5th, I was overtaken by a courier from Vance, bringing me a copy of your letter directing me to take Dallas' command and march as far as the U. P. R. R. &c. It being impossible to overtake Dallas' column and comply with the order, I continued my march to the K. P. R. R.— and if nothing happens, will reach Monument on Tuesday 8th" (DMO LR).

Distance 20 miles
Total   197   ″

Tuesday, October 8

Passed a good night

Studied out my course last night, and this am took <S.S.W.> SW by W.   After I had made about five miles altered to SSW – for fear of going too far to right   Struck the RR in 10 miles – 6 miles east of Monument, got in in good condition 2 p.m.

No news – Letter from Haskell who had seen Julia and Fred in N.Y.[67] All well – Wrote to Father & Mother, also to Julia.   Telegraphed report of my arrival to Pope also to Van Voast to send my men & baggage. All arrived promptly by first train.   Sent a sick man to Hays.   Played "Cinch" at night with the Officers – & had a pleasant evening.   Got into my wall tent, & a mattress under me & feel bully.

Distance 16 miles
Total   214   ″

Wednesday, October 9

Slept well.   Had a pleasant enough day with the Officers, loafing, gassing & playing "Cinch" –   Received a telegram from Platte telling me to remain here until further orders.[68]   Everybody excited as to

67. Captain Haskell, Twenty-third Infantry, had relinquished command of his company on September 12 to begin a tour of recruiting duty at David's Island, New York. While in the city he had seen Dodge's wife, Julia, and their only child, Frederick Paulding Dodge, who both resided there.

68. On receipt of Dodge's telegram reporting his arrival at Monument Station, Pope telegraphed that news to Sheridan, noting that "why he returned instead of pushing on to U. P. R. R. is not yet explained" (MDM Cheyenne Outbreak Special File). Pope asked whether Dodge and his men should be sent by rail to the Department of the Platte to rejoin the pursuit, but Sheridan, who already had fifteen companies in the field north of the Union Pacific Rail Road, was concerned that posts to the south might be undermanned should further outbreaks or other Indian troubles occur in Texas and the Indian Territory. Pope had the same concern; see House, *Report of the Secretary of War* (1878), p. 43. Thus on October 10 Dodge received orders to return to Fort Hays (W. T. Sherman to Sheridan, October 7—AGO LS; Pope to AAG MDM, October 8—MDM Cheyenne Outbreak Special File).

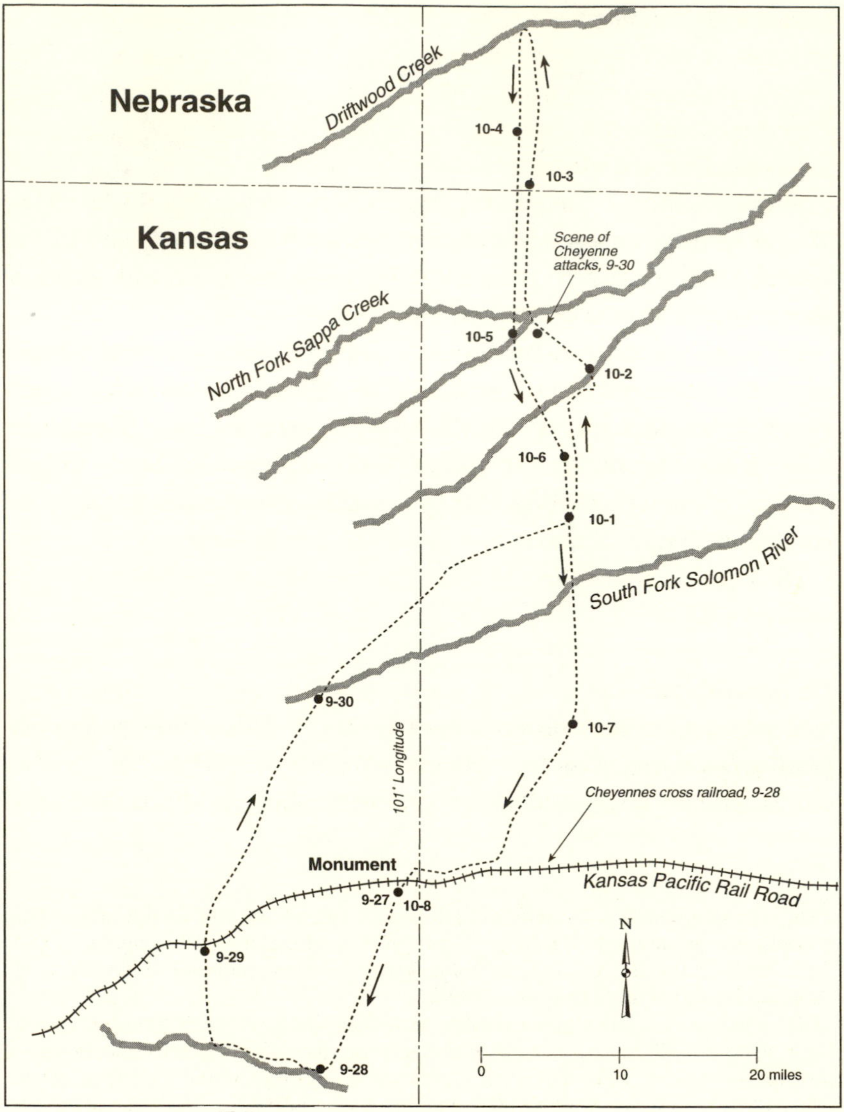

Nebraska
Kansas
Driftwood Creek
North Fork Sappa Creek
South Fork Solomon River
Kansas Pacific Rail Road
Scene of Cheyenne attacks, 9-30
Cheyennes cross railroad, 9-28
101° Longitude
Monument
10-4
10-3
10-5
10-2
10-6
10-1
10-7
9-30
9-27
10-8
9-29
9-28
N
0
10
20 miles

Dodge's itinerary, September 27–October 8, 1878

what it means.   Ordered Stillé to Ft Leavenworth & Trout to Ft Hays. Both left by midnight train on which was Hale's Co 16 Infy.[69]

No news of any sort –

Wrote to Laura & ordered things for a months trip.[70]

To bed at 12 pm

Thursday, October 10, 1878

Soon after breakfast recd the hoped for telegram to return to Ft Hays – breaking up my Comd. here.

All necessary orders were given & arrangements made.   We leave on the express tonight – 11.30.

Loafed, gassed & played "Cinch" –   Capt. Widdemeier 16th camped at Monum[en]t tonight enroute to the scenes of massacre, to gather statistics[71] – to be used I suppose in payment of damages.   Got on train at 11:30 with Comd.

Friday, October 11, 1878

Arrived Ft Hay[s] 3.30 am all right.[72]

There is but little to add.   The campaign was an utter failure, not an Indian having been seen by any soldier on the line of the K.P.   I

69. Company E, under First Lieutenant Stillé, together with Company D, arrived at Fort Leavenworth at 8:30 p.m. on October 11. Captain Hale's company had arrived at Fort Riley earlier the same day.

70. Dodge expected to be absent from Fort Hays on court-martial duty at Fort Sill, I.T. However, the general court-martial originally scheduled to convene on October 15 was postponed to November 15. See below, pp. 63–64, 76–77.

71. Captain William G. Wedemeyer, Sixteenth Infantry, had received orders to report on the depredations by the Northern Cheyennes along the valley of North Sappa Creek. His report was incorporated in James Van Voast to AAG DMO, October 29, 1878 (DMO LR). Estimates of the number of persons killed, women and girls raped, and property stolen or destroyed by the Northern Cheyennes on September 30 and October 1 varied widely. According to two twentieth-century scholars, Peter J. Powell and William Y. Chalfant, nineteen men died on the first day alone (*Sweet Medicine*, 1:206; *Cheyennes at Dark Water Creek*, p. 174). Another student of the Indian Wars, Peter M. Wright, observed that "people of Kansas had this raid burned into their minds and it engendered a fear of the Cheyennes that lasted for years" ("The Pursuit of Dull Knife," p. 152).

72. Beginning at this point on p. [36R] and through the end of the notebook, the text is in black ink.

still believe that my plan, to sit on the R.R. every thing in readiness &

when the Indians cross concentrate & pursue with vigor $\wedge$ best[73]
$$was$$
- but Jeff thought differently & he was in position to decide -

As it turns out, & with the knowledge of the action of the Indians that we now have - I do not believe that anything could have changed the result.   It was anticipated that the Indians might move slowly, as they did below, but they went like the wind.   On the night of their

passage of the R. R. they $\wedge$ travelled for nearly 24 hours at a stretch,
$$had$$
& stopped for necessary rest at least six hours on the Saline & within six miles of Carlisle where they crossed.   Could they have been jumped then something might have been done.   But there was the rub.   We had no proper persons to watch the line of R R & had to depend on the reports of section hands.   These I understand discovered the tracks on the morning of Sunday - went back to the station & reported.   Davis got the news, about noon of Sunday[74] - too late to have caught the Indians on the Saline, even had all the troops been on the R. R.   So well had the Indians disguised & covered up their trail in passing the R. R. that though Mauck reached the R R at Carlisle at 11 am on Sunday, his Indian guides had not at 12.30 been able to trail the enemy across, nor did they succeed until late in afternoon.[75]

With the white guides we had, it would have taken at least a whole day.   Another thing - I have had ample experience of trails, in a long

---

73. Dodge's ideas were in accord with the orders he had received from General Pope prior to Davis' assuming command; they were also consistent with orders given by General Crook to commanders at points along the Union Pacific Rail Road. The use of railroads to transport troops and supplies to the scene of their need was becoming standard military practice. For Pope's views on the subject, see House, *Report of the Secretary of War* (1880), p. 83; for Sheridan's, see p. 53; for Sherman's, see pp. 4-5.

74. September 29. Davis' order to return north toward the railroad reached Dodge at 7 p.m. that day.

75. Elsewhere Dodge commented on the great difficulty of discerning the trail of the Northern Cheyennes, observing that, though white scouts were utterly at fault, one "invaluable Pawnee Indian" with Mauck "never hesitated a moment" as he crossed the railroad (*OWI*, pp. 572-73).

service, & have never seen such an Indian trail as this.   They did not move in a compact body as usual – but singly or abreast – no two (2) ponies went out behind the other.   They covered a broad space of from 3 to 8 miles – & except when they crossed streams or fire guards, there was no trail to be seen.   I have never yet seen a white man who could have followed that trail, at a rate of more than 5 or 6 miles a day   My guide acknowledged that he could not have followed it at all –

The Indians left their resting place on Saline, about 3 or 4 pm, that night they committed some depredations on Solomon & next morning (Monday) at daylight commenced killing & pillaging on Prairie Dog, & at 7 am were on South Sappa – not less than 45 miles from the R. R.

They had gained a whole day on Mauck, & placed themselves, for some days at least, beyond danger of being overtaken.

On the Sappas & Beaver they secured 60 or 80 fresh horses.

If this escapade succeeds & there seems little doubt but it will, there will be others – & if the thing is going to continue it behoves the powers not only to put some Cavalry on this line, but to keep pack trains always ready.   Even then nothing will be done unless each post is furnished with one or more first class Indian Guides.   As I before said not a white man I ever saw could have followed the trail across the valleys of the Sappas & Beaver.   Maucks Indian crossed at a trot, never being out even for a moment.

The Indian troubles will never be settled until we learn to use Indian against Indian.[76]   In a fight the Army will almost always beat the Indians – but you cant make people fight who dont want to fight & can outrun you.

76. In this view Dodge agreed with his former department commander General Crook, whose success using Indian scouts he had observed at first hand. See PREJ, pp. 7, 14, 15, 65–66, 132, 174. However, a wide divergence of opinion existed within the army over the reliability and usefulness of Indian scouts and auxiliaries. For a survey, see Dunlay, *Wolves for the Blue Soldiers*, pp. 59–69. Dunlay observes that employing Indians for reconnaissance and trailing was "a prerequisite to any effective military action against hostile Indians" (p. 90).

Sunday, October 13, 1878. Fort Hays, Kansas

I thought my last entry closed the record of my portion of the Great Pursuit of the Cheyennes.   It seems that there is to be another Chapter.

On yesterday I recd. a Com[municatio]n. from Dept Hd Quarters calling upon me "to give such explanation as you are able to make of your failure to obey the orders that Col Jeff C. Davis reports he gave you to follow the Indians to the U. P. R R" —[77]

I dont know when I have been quite so mad as when I recd. this letter.   I however wrote an explanation, & sent a copy of Davis' order to me.   The "order,"[78] or the substance of an order came to me from Vance, by a Courier who overtook me on the route between Beaver & N Sappa Creeks, after I had turned back.   It directed me to "assume command of Dallas Column, & push the Indians as far as the U.P.R.R.["]

I had never been nearer than 30 miles to Dallas.   The party of Citizens met by me on head of Driftwood, told me that Dallas had left

the Republican in pursuit that morning – ∧ 4th   I was yet nearly 30 miles from the Republican & could not hope to reach it before the evening of 5th.   The utter hopelessness of an effort to overtake Dallas, was what induced me to turn back.   At the time I recd. the order I had already turned back, & was fully ten or twenty miles further from him, than I had been when I gave up the pursuit of him. Dallas was at least 60 miles away, on horse back.   My Comd. was on foot, & to overtake Dallas before he got to the R. R. was simply impossible.   I might as reasonably have been ordered to catch a R. R. train ∧ in motion .   The order was undoubtedly given in good faith, & in the belief that Dallas & I were together, or near each other.   But at the time of its reception by me, it was simply an impossible order,

---

77. Dodge quotes almost exactly from Major Platt's letter of October 10 (DMO LS). On October 9 Platt had directed Davis to forward to departmental headquarters all orders and communications he had sent Dodge in relation to the movements of his command. Evidently Dodge's conduct as a field commander was to be reviewed.

78. Dodge wrote two beginning quotation marks, one before "The," and the other before "order."

& I did not even try to obey it.[79]   Had the order been received the day before, I would have pushed on with my own Comd. to the U. P. R. R. though I could have had no hope of overtaking Dallas.

I would have liked the trip.   It would have been a pleasant one. I had rations & forage sufficient, & there was no reason for my turning back except that I thought I might be needed back, & that I did not want to run down my already over-worked command.   Also that I was perfectly aware that my going on would have been simply a piece of buncombe[80] without any use whatever.   There is nobody to blame for not catching the Indians   With the means we had it was simply impossible.   There is no doubt that Davis feels badly.   He took Command with his usual good opinion of himself.   He knew it all, & would take advice from no one.   His egotism & desire *to do*, led him to make the only real mistake of the Campaign[81] – not that he would

79. This paragraph duplicates the rationale for not obeying the order of October 2 given by Dodge in a letter of October 12 to departmental headquarters. Characterizing Davis' order as "impossible of fulfillment and therefore of no effect," he defended himself vigorously, forwarding with his explanation "all the orders, telegrams &c" he had received while at Monument and in the field and with them a selected extract from his "diary," the journal reproduced here. That documentation included forty-two items, and it was supplemented by copies of thirty-two telegrams he had himself sent. He concluded: "From these papers it will be seen by the Dept. Comdr. that I and my Command did all that men could possibly do, and that no shadow of blame for the non-capture of the Indians can fairly be attributed to us" (RID to AAG DMO, October 12, 1878—DMO LR).

80. Or *bunkum*: "Stuff, nonsense, humbug, often with reference to legislative action to satisfy or impose upon public opinion" (Mathews, *Dictionary of Americanisms*).

81. Though harsh, Dodge's angry judgment of his regimental commander was based upon several years of close contact and on familiarity with the checkered military career of Davis. Colonel James B. Fry, who had known Davis since youth, wrote that he considered himself a "born military chieftain." Fry recalled him in 1852, then only twenty-four years of age, expressing perfect confidence in his ability to direct an invasion and capture of Cuba. Summarizing the diverse elements that coexisted in Davis's character, Fry described him as "brave, quiet, obliging, humorous in disposition, and full of ambition, daring, endurance, and self-confidence" (*Military Miscellanies*, p. 397). Fry offered a riveting account of the incident on September 29, 1862, wherein Davis, then a brigadier general of volunteers, shot and killed his commanding officer, General William Nelson, after an argument. Davis was never tried by court-martial for the homicide, and civil charges were presently dropped, but his act of violence against a fellow officer made him the subject of quiet but unresolved controversy thereafter. He served with credit during the remainder of the Civil War, and at its close he was rewarded with the brevet rank of major general and the

likely have done better in any event, – but our only hope was in sticking to the R. R.

He felt his mistake, when he found the Indians had crossed, while his Comd. was in advance of the R. R.   His telegram to me at Sheridan indicates this.   He did what he could & failed, with no blame to be fairly attached to him – as after all, it was a mere difference of opinion, & at the very worst, an error of judgment.

But the Great *I*, which solely composes the man prevents him from accepting the situation.   He was necessarily right, & somebody else must be wrong.   He looks around for a scape-goat, some one on whom he can throw some suspicion of blame, which he absurdly hopes may cover up his own fault, & rushes off to Pope & reports me for disobedience of his orders.   And suppose I had obeyed his orders

Suppose that Dallas had been by – how could that in any ^ way have affected the result.   Of all ^ the Commanders to pitch on me – who had a foot command solely, who was already far behind in the race – (although I marched tremendously, sending one poor fellow to his grave)[82]

He is a huge Ass – worse than an Ass, or he would have had sense enough to keep quiet.   I do not believe anything will result or any further steps be taken in this matter – but if they force me on a

colonelcy of the Twenty-third Infantry. Nevertheless, he was bitter because he had not attained the rank of brigadier general in the regular army, to which he felt himself entitled. He hankered after duty that would bring him renewed glory in combat. In 1873, for example, he sought unsuccessfully to displace then Lieutenant Colonel George Crook as commander of operations against the Apaches of Arizona Territory. See William D. Whipple, AAG , to Davis, February 5, 1873 (U.S. Army Headquarters LS). Thereafter Davis, a slight man of sallow complexion whom Fry described as "dyspeptic-looking" (*Military Miscellanies*, p. 389), was in uncertain health. In the pursuit of the Northern Cheyennes he elected not to take the field, but directing Dodge and other field commanders from Fort Wallace offered him a rare opportunity to confirm his early reputation as a soldier.

82. On October 8 Private Thomas Selwor, Company B, Twenty-third Infantry, was transported by train from Monument to Fort Hays. He died in the post hospital on October 12. The cause of death was given as erisypelas of the left lower extremity (Fort Hays LR, LS; Twenty-third Infantry Regimental Return).

defence, I will very easily show that the only mistakes made were by Pope & Davis - Pope in sending Davis to command, & Davis in sending the troops away from the R. R.[83]

Van Voast & I had the thing all right, & we understood the situation & each other.   At least we were agreed in what ought to be done. Had we been left alone I would have had my whole Comd. with Dallas, & all the Infy at Wallace at Carlisle on Sunday, & on the trail early Monday am at latest.

Jeff came & busted up the whole thing.

My men made a foolish & objectless march of 40 miles in 24 hours

          north
- & then started ∧ from the R. R. already footsore & tired out. Could that vigor & effort have been expended on the trail, it would at least have saved many lives & outrages on the Sappas and Beaver.

Dallas was 40 miles from the R R, south, when he got orders to return for the pursuit.   Could his Comd have started fresh on the trail

---

83. Dodge clearly sensed that a military court of inquiry or even a general court-martial was a possibility, absurd as such a prospect might seem. His confidence in being able to mount a decisive defense of his behavior and a exposure of Pope and Davis as the responsible parties was well founded. He had been disappointed when, on September 26, he learned that Davis would command the pursuit from the Kansas Pacific Rail Road. However, he speculated at the time that Pope had had no real choice in the matter, since as the ranking officer then available Davis had a claim on the command if he wished it. Documentary evidence supports that idea, for prior to September 25—that is, during more than two weeks of frequent communication between departmental headquarters and various other posts and commands—the name of Davis never once occurred in messages to or from Pope and his adjutant. Suddenly, on September 26, Pope placed Davis in charge of operations in the field.

Upon his arrival at Fort Wallace, Davis ordered troops to scout south of the railroad, rather than remaining there as Pope had directed. Moreover, he ordered Dodge to concentrate his command at Monument rather than, as Pope had also directed, placing them at several stations along the road. Subsequently he sent Dodge and his men on a march south from the railroad. His orders may have been well considered in view of known circumstances, but they departed from Pope's earlier strategy. As events transpired, they rendered impossible the effort by troops in the Department of the Missouri to overtake the Northern Cheyennes once they had crossed the Kansas Pacific Rail Road.

Dodge's explanatory letter of October 12, with its enclosures, reached departmental headquarters two days later. It was marked "file," and no further action was taken.

at Carlisle he would with less effort have been on the Sappa in time to prevent the Indians from doing as they did.

Had my plan been carried out, (to which Van V. was fully agreed,) we might not have caught the Indians, but we would have been so close behind them, that they could have done little or no damage.

Jeff changed it all – He is responsible for the result, except in so far as Pope is responsible for Jeff.[84]

84. At this point Dodge wrote "See other end of book" with a flourish underneath, and below that a brief notation, dated November 3, which is reproduced below, p. 62. Pages [48R]–[54V], which follow, are blank. The remaining text, not included here, is a record of hunting and fishing results between early August and November 2, 1878. It is written with the notebook reversed, beginning on the last page, p. [56V], and ending on p. [55R] in the original sequence.

Commentary on Journal Two
The Aftermath: Explanations, Accusations, and Trials

THE NORTHERN CHEYENNES CROSSED THE UNION Pacific Rail Road five miles east of Ogallala, Nebraska, at 1 p.m. on October 4. At approximately the same time, more than one hundred miles distant, Dodge abandoned his pursuit of them. Within three hours they were being followed from the railroad by troops under Major Thomas T. Thornburgh, and when Captain Clarence Mauck reached the point of crossing he was directed to push ahead on Thornburgh's trail. Major Caleb H. Carlton at Fort Robinson set out with five companies of cavalry to head off the fugitives, and posts yet further north were placed on alert. General Crook had deployed what forces he had available, but a successful outcome remained far from certain. Meanwhile, on October 14 all pursuit troops from the Department of the Missouri except those under Mauck received orders to return to their stations.

Not long after crossing the railroad, the Northern Cheyennes separated into two parties—the larger, under Little Wolf, moving toward the Powder River country and the smaller, under Dull Knife, toward the former site of the Red Cloud agency near Fort Robinson. Little Wolf and his people managed to elude the authorities for several months, camping through the winter in the sand hills of western Nebraska and points north. The following spring they were persuaded to surrender at Fort Keogh, Montana Territory, where they remained, many serving with credit as scouts under Colonel Nelson A. Miles, Fifth Infantry. The band under Dull Knife, numbering about 150, were less fortunate. Discovered in the sand hills seventy miles southeast of Fort Robinson, they at first prepared to fight, but after tense negotiations and the arrival of cavalry reinforcements, they agreed to surrender. They were

then disarmed and dismounted, and on the evening of October 24 they
and their military escort reached Fort Robinson.[1] What should be done
with them remained a matter for debate. Dull Knife's people vowed to
die rather than return to the reservation in Indian Territory. Crook
favored permitting them to remain in the north, but Sheridan regarded
such a course as a threat to the stability of the reservation system. The
"ringleaders," he thought, should be sent to Florida for training in
civilized customs, as had been done in 1875 at the close of the Red
River War.[2] The Indian Bureau took no position for the present.

With the escaped Northern Cheyennes brought thus far under control, attention turned to analysis of the Army's failure to capture more
than a fraction of them despite a month's intense effort. Pope attributed the poor results within his department to the insufficient number
of cavalry troops stationed there. As to the infantry, he wrote, "There
is no doubt that they did all that it was possible for them to do."[3]
Sheridan, who never tired of pointing out the inadequacy of funds
made available by Congress for him to ensure order in the Military
Division of the Missouri, explained in his next annual report that the
supply of 2,988 officers and men in the Department of the Platte and
the 3,350 in the Department of the Missouri averaged out to one man
for each seventy-five square miles to be made secure.[4] "It is hard," he
wrote the adjutant general on November 19, 1878, "to head off or
overtake Indians in an open country well known to them, with two
or three fresh horses for each Indian to ride on, as relays, the horses
unencumbered by baggage of any kind, while the pursuing force has

1. A lucid account of the Army's foray into the Nebraska sand hills, written
before the Northern Cheyennes had yet been discovered, is First Lieutenant John G.
Bourke, Third Cavalry, to AAG, Department of the Platte, October 15, 1878 (MDM
Cheyenne Outbreak Special File). For a report of the capture, see Crook to Sheridan,
October 26, 1878, with enclosures (MDM Cheyenne Outbreak Special File).

2. Endorsement, Crook to Sheridan, October 26, 1878 (OIA LR, C&A). Some of
the correspondence between bureau heads concerning the capture and imprison-
ment of the Northern Cheyennes under Dull Knife is summarized item by item in a
Senate document, *Letter . . . in Relation to the Escape of the Northern Cheyennes
from Fort Robinson*, pp. 2–6.

3. Pope to Sheridan, October 10, 1878 (MDM Cheyenne Outbreak Special File).

4. House, *Report of the Secretary of War* (1879), p. 42.

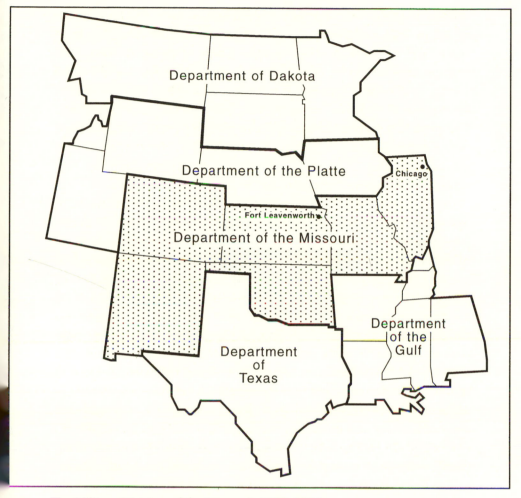

The Military Division of the Missouri, 1878–1880

only the same horses loaded down to some extent by rations for the man and forage for the animal."[5] The root of the problem, in Sheridan's view, was the present system wherein troops had no authority to attack Indians until they had already escaped from their reservation.

5. Sheridan to AG, November 19, 1878 (AGO LR).

Pope, Sheridan, and Sherman differed in their ideas about a solution to the problems faced by the military in Indian Territory, but they agreed that the weight of responsibility heaped upon the Army was unconscionable. On October 12 an angry citizen of Kansas addressed a letter to President Rutherford B. Hayes, demanding that protection be extended to settlers like those who had suffered on Sappa Creek. The president forwarded this letter to Sherman, who brushed aside the demand as posing "a physical impossibility . . . for the few troops we have available." He deplored the attacks on settlers but noted that similar cases had occurred annually in the past ten years.[6]

Inquiries within the Department of the Missouri into the conduct of individual officers during the Northern Cheyenne outbreak led General Pope to authorize general court-martial proceedings against three, all of Colonel Mackenzie's Fourth Cavalry: Captains William Hemphill, Sebastian Gunther, and Joseph Rendlebrock. In proceedings at Fort Supply on March 10 and 14, 1879, Hemphill and Gunther were both acquitted of charges brought against them for their activities in the early stages of the chase.[7] However, on March 24, a court at the same post found Rendlebrock guilty on several specifications connected with his field duty between September 14 and October 13. He was sentenced to dismissal, but on recommendation of the court and subsequently the General of the Army, the punishment was remitted in view of his long and creditable service and poor physical condition. On June 30, 1879, Rendlebrock was ordered to appear before a Retiring Board, and a short time thereafter he was removed from active duty.[8]

The proceedings against these three officers concluded the public allocation of blame within the Department of the Missouri for the failed efforts of the previous September and October. However, other

6. Endorsement, A. M. Claflin, Salina, Kansas, to Rutherford B. Hayes, October 3, 1878 (AGO LR).

7. *ANJ*, April 12, 1879, p. 632; April 19, 1879, p. 652; April 26, 1879, pp. 671–72. The presiding officer at both courts-martial was Colonel Jefferson C. Davis.

8. *ANJ*, July 12, 1879, p. 884; AGO, General Court Martial Order 36 (1879); Fort Reno Post Return, August 1879. For a summary of Rendlebrock's career, see the notice of his death in *ANJ*, May 18, 1889, p. 779.

accusations had reached Fort Leavenworth that might have resulted in further inquiry or judicial action had General Pope chosen to authorize it. Colonel Jefferson C. Davis had been displeased with Dodge's failure to obey his order of October 2, and upon learning of the lapse, he had at once reported it to departmental headquarters. Dodge's detailed explanation reached the adjutant's office on October 14, and three days afterward Davis incorporated a response to it in a report of his own activities on September 26 and after. Handsomely inscribed by a clerk on thirteen pages of heavy paper and followed by enclosures labeled A through I, this document comprised a summary review of the campaign from the Kansas Pacific Rail Road. Taking no blame to himself for its failure, Davis briefly praised the efforts of Major Dallas and Captain Duncan M. Vance, then condemned those of Captain Mauck and Lieutenant Colonel Dodge bitterly and at length. Mauck, who was then at Sidney Barracks, Nebraska, and about to begin another punishing march across country, came in for the harshest attack. Davis ridiculed his "utter failure" to keep pace with the Indians as they passed north. In his view, the cavalry officer was "satisfying himself with merely herding the Indians . . . and was not intent on pushing and bringing them to an engagement as he should have done." Mauck had failed to give timely notice to troops at Fort Wallace of the engagement in which Lieutenant Colonel Lewis was mortally wounded. Had he sent the necessary message, reinforcements from the post might have intercepted the band as they fled their pursuers. Instead, he permitted the Indians to outdistance him and then "murder citizens, and steal stock at pleasure in his front." Davis pronounced his allegedly lax performance of duty "highly censurable,—so much so, as to demand a thorough investigation."

Turning to Dodge, he shifted his tone from censure to contempt. Commenting on Dodge's report from the field, he quoted the phrase "thrown utterly out of the race," following it by three exclamation marks to register amazement at its frivolity. He faulted Dodge for failure to stay in contact with field headquarters at Fort Wallace, for want of energy in not marching further, and for want of purpose in marching with no particular object in view. "He was out nine days,

Jefferson C. Davis (Luther P. Bradley Collection, U.S. Army Military History Institute)

marched 25 miles a day, and accomplished nothing so far as I can see." Davis did not address Dodge's rationale for not attempting to comply with the order to take command of Dallas's column, but he implied that a more able and energetic officer could have done so. The statement by Davis reached departmental headquarters on October 18 and was quietly buried, being marked "file" with a cross-reference to the communication received from Dodge four days earlier.[9]

Within days of the Northern Cheyennes' escape from their reservation, a debate broke out at higher organizational levels over the conditions at the Cheyenne and Arapaho agency that had precipitated the outbreak. In essence, this controversy pitted adherents of the Army against those of the Indian Bureau, each side seeking to lay blame on the other. On September 19 Major Mizner at Fort Reno forwarded to Pope a report, based upon information supplied him by Agent Miles, demonstrating that the food and supplies furnished to the agency in the current fiscal year amounted to only two-thirds of what the Indians required. Recent events made clear how important it was that the government live up to its treaty obligations, he warned. Indians continued to suffer much from hunger and were forced to eat dogs, coyotes, and horseflesh in order to survive.[10] Five days later Agent Miles reported to his own superior, Commissioner of Indian Affairs Ezra A. Hayt, with a fuller set of reasons for the outbreak, noting however that noncompliance with treaty stipulations was one of the problems.[11]

What might have become a disagreement in good faith over the points for emphasis rapidly changed character when a third report, by Lieutenant Colonel Lewis at Fort Dodge, reached Washington, D.C., and became public. While Hemphill's company of cavalry was detained at his post awaiting further action, Lewis had discussed the Northern Cheyennes with Amos Chapman, the interpreter at Camp Supply, who was accompanying the troops as a scout. Chapman, married to a Cheyenne woman, said he had been at the agency a short time before the breakout. From what he had been told by Indians and also from

9. Davis to AAG DMO, October 17, 1878 (DMO LR).
10. Mizner to AAG DMO, September 19, 1878 (DMO LR).
11. Miles to E. A. Hayt, September 24, 1878 (OIA LR, C&A).

his own observation, he knew the Northern Cheyennes were suffering from want of food, for they were driven to eat horseflesh cut from animals that had died of disease or natural causes. In his view, they had fled in order to reach a place where they could feed themselves and their families.[12] Lewis's report of this interview, dated September 15, made its way up through the Army's chain of command, then between departments from the secretary of war to the secretary of the interior, and finally back through that organization to Agent Miles, who received it on October 2, five days after Lewis had received his mortal wound.

Miles at once denounced the Lewis report as "false in every particular," and the more offensive as originating with an individual like Amos Chapman, "known throughout the country as a squaw man."[13] The matter received wide circulation on October 15, when the *New York Times*, drawing upon Lewis's report, accused Miles of failure to provide full rations to the Northern Cheyennes and therefore of responsibility for their outbreak. Likening the Indians to Oliver Twist and Miles to the niggardly Mr. Bumble, it held up the image of famished Indians devouring diseased horseflesh as proof that the agent's contention of their having no real cause for complaint from hunger was absurd.[14] The imputation of dishonesty stung Miles to a heated rebuttal, obviously intended for publication, in a letter of November 1 to the Commissioner of Indian Affairs, Ezra A. Hayt. While he spared the late Lieutenant Colonel Lewis from rebuke, Miles did point out that an officer at a post like Fort Dodge, many miles distant, could have no direct knowledge of conditions at the Cheyenne and Arapaho agency. The real problem was the unreliability of Chapman, who Miles claimed had visited the agency for only one day and spent that short time in "carousing at Fort Reno" and bargaining with Indian women

---

12. Lewis to AAG DMO (MDM Cheyenne Outbreak Special File).
13. Miles to Hayt, October 2, 1878 (OIA LR, C&A). The term *squaw man* denoted a white man married to an Indian woman, but it carried connotations of lawlessness, opportunism, and moral degeneracy.
14. "The Refractory Cheyennes," *New York Times*, October 15, 1878, p. 4.

"for purposes of prostitution." On the horseflesh question, Miles denied that any Indian had been "*compelled* to eat decayed or any other kind of horse meat."[15]

Presently Commissioner Hayt entered the fray, lending it a tone of greater dignity while suavely putting the Army on the defensive. Transmitting to the secretary of the interior another report by Miles on the causes of the outbreak, Hayt corrected statements in the report of September 19 by Mizner, who "by his want of familiarity with the subject, is led into a serious error" in regard to the supplies called for by the treaty of 1876 between the United States and the Cheyenne Indians. Hayt suggested that Mizner was meddling in matters not his proper concern, and also that he and other "military authorities" were themselves to blame for the damage wrought by the outbreak. The Indians used their long-range rifles to great effect in the rampage that followed; had they been properly disarmed and dismounted, the assault on the settlers never would have occurred.[16]

The patronizing treatment by Commissioner Hayt provoked Mizner to a rejoinder, published in the *New York Herald* on December 8. Mizner's letter goaded Agent Miles to write a further statement of his own, citing a "determined effort" by the Army to attribute the escape of the Northern Cheyennes to their near starvation. Yet, he observed, they had not traveled like starved men, nor was hunger the cause of their Army pursuers being outwitted and ambushed. Perhaps further inquiry would fix responsibility for the escape on the laxity of "certain officers" whose duty it had been to prevent it. The habitual drunkenness of Army officers was surely a contributing factor.[17]

The controversy that raged in December 1878 over events three months earlier had taken on a life of its own. On December 17 Amos Chapman made affidavit confirming the accuracy of his statements to

15. Miles to Hayt, November 1, 1878 (OIA LR, C&A). In this communication Miles listed the names of all the Indians who had left the reservation.

16. Hayt to SI, November 16, 1878 (Senate, *Report . . . on the Removal of the Northern Cheyennes*, pp. 290–91).

17. Miles to Hayt, December 9, 1878 (OIA LR, C&A). Agent Miles was at this time in Washington, D.C.

Lewis.[18] Later in December Mizner wrote angrily to the adjutant general in response to yet another attack on him by Hayt. Mizner wished his new statement to be published in the New York papers, but to discourage further hostilities this was not permitted to occur.[19] The breach between the two federal agencies that shared responsibility for conditions in Indian Territory already seemed definitive. George W. Manypenny, an advocate of the much maligned Peace Policy toward the Indians and a longtime proponent of staffing Indian agencies with representatives of religious denominations, regarded the public imbroglio as a "hungry raid" by the Army to gain control of the Indian Bureau.[20] On January 2, 1879, General Sherman wrote a terse memorandum accompanying a document that was to be copied in the Adjutant General's Office and forwarded: "I doubt the wisdom of sending so many of these communications to the Secretary of the Interior. It seems labor absolutely wasted."[21]

The passage of the Northern Cheyennes through western Kansas had brought fear and panic to rural settlers, exposing the still fragile veneer of civil order in that region. As the extent of the depredations became known, Kansas citizens expressed their outrage and demanded protection from future attacks and redress for the one just experienced. Governor George T. Anthony asked General Sheridan to post additional troops at Forts Reno and Sill in order to restore public confidence and ensure safety.[22] However, Sheridan could offer no immediate satisfaction, for in his view all troops in the Military Division of the Missouri were stationed at points where the danger to citizens and their economic interests was as great as that in Kansas. He suggested moving Colonel Mackenzie with six companies of his regiment to Indian Territory from the Rio Grande River in Texas and perhaps also transferring the Eighteenth Infantry from its station at Atlanta, Georgia, but General Sherman demurred. The recent surrender of Dull Knife

18. AAG MDM to AG, December 17, 1878 (AGO Register LR).
19. AAG MDM to AG, December 30, 1878, with enclosure (AGO Register LR).
20. Manypenny to Hayt, December 19, 1878 (OIA LR, C&A).
21. Sherman to AG, January 2, 1879 (AGO LR).
22. Anthony to Sheridan, November 11, 1878 (AGO LR).

ought to deter other Indians from rash efforts to break away, he thought, and meanwhile the troops in Indian Territory would need to rely on "vigilance and increased activity."[23] General Pope was thus left to deal with the tense state of affairs as best he could. On December 10 Mauck reported from Fort Elliott, Texas, that Indians in his vicinity were "very discontented" at the rations being allotted them and were determined to feed themselves. Should they come into contact with cattlemen, violence could ensue, for "it needs but the touch of the match to light the blaze of an Indian war on this frontier."[24]

The desire of Kansans for legal redress against the Northern Cheyennes led to the initiation of proceedings against Dull Knife's entire band, then imprisoned at Fort Robinson. Despite public awareness that the Indians had cause for anger and frustration while at their agency, the list of treacherous shootings, rapes, temporary abductions, and slaughters of domestic animals apparently for vindictive sport was too long to be overbalanced by sympathy. Governor Anthony spoke for the people of his state when he asked the secretary of war to surrender to civil authorities for trial "the principal Chiefs" and other Indians who could be identified as participants in the acts of violence.[25] On February 17, 1879, seven Northern Cheyennes—Old Crow, Wild Hog, Left Hand, Old Man, White Antelope, Frizzly Hair, and Blacksmith—arrived at Dodge City to answer charges against them.[26]

As debates and discussions between generals, governors, and heads of government agencies moved forward, their subordinates sought to restore a fragile normalcy that approximated conditions prior to the outbreak of the Northern Cheyennes. At Fort Hays, where he had assumed command in July after a period of service at Fort Leavenworth, Dodge returned to what in official reports was termed "ordinary garrison duty." In response to the steady westward move-

---

23. Sheridan to AG, November 18, 1878, with endorsement by Sherman (AGO LR).

24. Mauck to AAG DMO, December 10, 1878 (OIA LR, Central Superintendency).

25. Anthony to SW, November 11, 1878 (AGO LR).

26. For a photograph of these men seated on the courthouse steps with their interpreter, George Reynolds, see Miner, *West of Wichita*, p. 117.

ment of settled territory and the rapid development of a railway system, the Army was abandoning some posts no longer strategically necessary and building up others adjacent to the railroads. For example, in the Fort Hays region, Fort Harker to the east and Fort Larned to the southeast were no longer occupied by troops, and their military reservations would soon be turned over by congressional action to the State of Kansas. On the other hand, a full garrison would be maintained at Fort Hays in case of need for their rapid deployment.[27] As commander of the post, Dodge bore responsibility for renovating its somewhat dilapidated buildings so as to ready it for its future function.

Assisted by his quartermaster, Lieutenant Trout, Dodge had earlier thrown himself into the assignment with a will. He enjoyed some reputation for ability in the laying out and construction of frontier posts, and supervising the process, however inglorious a duty, interested him. In the weeks prior to taking the field in September, he had assessed the needs for repair and renovation, arranged for the post bakehouse to be rebuilt by a master mason, and begun discussion with officials of the Kansas Pacific about a railroad loop that would connect the quartermaster's shed with the main line running through Hays City.[28] Upon his return, he took up where he left off, making arrangements for installation of a telegraph office at the post to save the trouble and delay caused by using the one in town.[29]

In moments of freedom from his official duties, Dodge was also engaged in a private undertaking that had occupied him at intervals since publication of *The Plains of North America and Their Inhabitants* almost two years before. That work had received enthusiastic praise from reviewers in England and the United States, and he was planning a sequel. As originally conceived, *The Plains* was to include five sections: on the plains environment, game animals, native inhabi-

27. AG to SW, February 3, 1879 (AGO LS). See also House, *Report of the Secretary of War* (1880), p. vi.
28. RID endorsement, August 9, 1878; RID to Chief Commissary of Subsistence, DMO, August 11, 1878; RID to J.T. Odell, Assistant Superintendent, Kansas Pacific Rail Road, August 27, 1878 (Fort Hays LS).
29. RID to J. T. Odell, November 3, 1878 (Fort Hays LS).

tants, frontiersmen, and the frontier Army. However, the manuscript had rapidly grown to the length of an ample octavo volume, and Dodge had elected to publish it without completing either of the two latter sections. The chapters on Indians alone made up fully one-half of the work, though even then he still had a good deal more to say on the subject. Reviewers had seized upon the Indian discussion with special interest, making clear the continuing public appetite for the sort of information he had to offer.[30] He now felt confident in beginning a new book focused on Plains Indians that would draw more fully on his years of study and observation. "Readers want *facts*," he wrote his friend William Blackmore in February 1877. "If those facts are worth knowing then I am justified."[31]

A few days after his return to Fort Hays, Dodge drafted a twenty-five hundred word narrative of the Northern Cheyennes' experiences from the Dull Knife battle of November 25, 1876, to their escape from the Cheyenne and Arapaho agency and journey northward. Only a small fragment of this account subsequently appeared in his completed book, *Our Wild Indians* (1882).[32] Although even the full account made no mention of the part he had played in the Army's pursuit, it captured the mixed reactions recorded in his journals during the experience. Based upon stories heard while in the field, on a letter from Captain Mauck,[33] and probably on telegraphed dispatches and newspaper reports, it registered his horror at the cruelties committed by the Indians at Sappa Creek. Yet its predominant tone was positive. He expressed sympathy for the sufferings of the Northern Cheyennes, both in the aftermath of the Mackenzie fight in 1876 and also after their removal to Indian Territory. He praised their courage and indomitable will, and he also paid tribute to their military prowess. In all, he

30. For a survey of the reviews in England and the United States, see *PNA*, pp. 26–30.

31. RID to Blackmore, January 31, 1877 (Blackmore Papers). Dodge was reacting to objections by some reviewers to the explicit sexual content of a few passages in the recently issued book. See Kime, "'Not Coarse . . . But Not Delicate,'" pp. 72–78.

32. See *OWI*, pp. 498–500.

33. See Dodge's journal entry for December 7, 1878.

ranked their desperate odyssey on a par with the most celebrated of human undertakings.[34]

Dodge's leisure for authorship was limited during these busy weeks, and for several months in the future it was to be still more limited. A few days after drafting his account of the Northern Cheyennes, he added a message to his journal of the recent campaign before putting it in the mail to his parents:

November 3

Keep this book until I come, then give it back to me. You may read such portions as you like to any person who will not publish it.

I shall keep a diary on my Fort Sill trip & expect to beat the hunting record at the end of this book hollow. Will send it to you when I finish it.

Have got all my work done & am nearly ready to start.

Lovingly

Rich.[35]

This notation marks a departure from Dodge's earlier use of his journals, for until now he had compiled them for his own eyes alone. By forwarding the recently completed journal through the mail, he was giving it a larger audience, and therefore a new function. He was perhaps placing in some peril his good name as an officer, since an unofficial account of a military campaign that found its way into print within one month of its conclusion would subject the author to military discipline.[36] However, he had confidence in his parents' discretion and knew that, after all, potential auditors and opportunities for publication were few in rural North Carolina. From this point on, anticipating that family members would read his journals, he modified his purpose in writing them. He kept in mind the special interests of his small audience—for example, his father's love of hunting and his mother's concern for family matters. He took a bit more care to write

34. See Appendix A for the text of Dodge's manuscript narrative.

35. This entry appears on pp. [47R] and [47V] of the journal.

36. "Private letters or reports relative to military marches and operations are frequently mischievous, and are strictly forbidden" (House, *Revised Army Regulations*, p. 65).

legibly, and he tended not to dwell on official matters so much as formerly. Probably he restrained somewhat his earlier inclination to set down whatever thought crossed his mind. At times, one senses his conscious awareness that he was addressing an audience.

The "Fort Sill trip" mentioned in the November 3 entry was to be a lengthy journey, first by railroad and then by military ambulance, to that remote post in Indian Territory, where a general court-martial was scheduled to convene on November 15. Once his duty as a member of the court was finished, Dodge had orders to return to Fort Hays by a different route, one that would afford him opportunity to indulge his lifelong enthusiasm for hunting and fishing. From Fort Sill, he and his escort would pass northward along the military road to Fort Reno, adjacent to the site of the Northern Cheyenne outbreak. From there he would travel upstream along the North Fork of the Canadian River to Camp Supply, passing through country little known except as a prime habitat for the wild turkey. The last leg of the return trip would be along the wagon road north to Fort Dodge, and from there to Fort Hays.[37] Dodge expected to be away from his post for about a month. Evidently he planned to emphasize hunting and fishing in his journal of travel, topics that would give satisfaction to some family members. Subsequently he wrote on its cover a title: "Turkey Hunting."

In the journal that follows, Dodge made almost no mention of the general court-martial that necessitated his extended absence from Fort Hays. Yet it was surely of much interest to him, even though, as he once admitted, "I do hate a Ct Martial of all things."[38] The defendant, Captain Philip L. Lee, Tenth Cavalry, stood accused of offenses that formed part of a perceived campaign by him and another officer to discredit their post commander. The object of their malice was Lieutenant Colonel John W. Davidson, Tenth Cavalry, a West Point graduate and an officer with a long and distinguished record of service. Captain Lee's name had come before the General of the Army so often that Sherman at last elected to make an example of him. The case involved

37. S.O. 197, DMO, October 30, 1878; Fort Hays Post Return, November 1878.
38. *PREJ*, p. 125.

issues of due discipline and subordination, topics essential to Dodge's understanding of himself as a career soldier and about which he would eventually write for publication.[39]

The campaign against Davidson by Lee and Captain Theodore A. Baldwin, his fellow officer at Fort Sill, began in May 1878, when Lee was ordered to appear before a general court-martial at Fort Concho, Texas. After initial meetings, this court was reconstituted and reconvened at Fort Sill in July.[40] Amidst continuing controversy, Lee was acquitted, but to secure revenge against Davidson for preferring the charges that had resulted in his trial, he began preparing a set of countercharges.[41] Meanwhile Baldwin, smarting from a written rebuke by Davidson for wearing unmilitary costume and for disrespectful conduct, transmitted early in August a request for official redress, followed in September by a set of his own formal charges.[42] The two men had begun collaborating in a vendetta through official channels against Davidson and a group of officers whom they considered his favorites and toadies. Their efforts suffered a reversal when, on September 14, in an argument with Davidson's adjutant, First Lieutenant S. R. Whitall, Lee struck Whitall repeatedly over the head with a cane and challenged him to a duel. As a result of the incident, Lee was placed under arrest and charges of conduct unbecoming an officer and gentleman were filed against him. This was the matter to be considered by the general court-martial of which Dodge was a member.[43]

During October the assault on Davidson's reputation and peace of mind pressed ahead, but with scant success. On October 10 Lee forwarded to departmental headquarters a set of charges and specifications again Davidson; these, however, were set aside by General

39. See RID to Julia R. P. Dodge, January 16, 1870, and August 14, 1870 (Dodge Papers, Yale Collection); RID, "The Enlisted Soldier," pp. 260–61, 279–80, 286, 288.
40. War Department, Office of the Judge-Advocate General, Registers of Army General Courts-Martial; *ANJ*, July 20, 1878, p. 805.
41. *ANJ*, August 31, 1878, p. 52; Division of Military Justice to Lee, July 31, 1878 (AGO LR).
42. Baldwin to AG, August 8, 1878, and September 22, 1878 (AGO LR).
43. Fort Sill Post Returns, September and October, 1878; AGO, General Court-Martial Order 22, April 10, 1879.

Pope as not worth pursuing.[44] The next day Sheridan forwarded to Washington his agreement with Pope that the request by Baldwin for redress against alleged unfair treatment was "frivolous." Sherman concurred, observing tartly that Davidson's handling of Baldwin was "mild under the circumstances."[45] On October 13 Baldwin's wife became a combatant, addressing a letter to the wife of President Hayes in which she accused Davidson of shameful conduct. According to her, Davidson had become so drunk at the post trader's store that he was unable to stand, being carried to his quarters "on the back of a young officer." Sherman, to whom the letter from Mrs. Baldwin was forwarded, bristled. He returned it to Davidson with the message that the lady's "meddling" with official matters could hardly benefit her husband, who "cannot shelter himself behind her petticoats."[46] Baldwin thereupon addressed a letter to General Pope, holding himself alone responsible for the claims his wife had made. When his defiant statement reached Washington, D.C., Sherman refused for a last time to order a general court-martial, "as a doubt remains which should be tried, Captain Baldwin or Colonel Davidson."[47]

At this point Baldwin prudently suspended his efforts, at least in public. Not so Captain Lee, who stepped up the offensive. Judged guilty in the encounter with Lieutenant Whitall, he was sentenced to be reduced to the bottom of the long list of captains in the Army's lineal ranking and to forfeit fifty dollars from his pay in each of the ten months that followed. However, President Hayes commuted the sentence generously, to a single forfeiture of fifty dollars.[48] Presently John H. Reagan, a congressman from Texas, addressed a letter to the president asking that the fifty-dollar fine also be remitted.[49] Lee now set about collecting new charges against his post commander. On

44. Lee to AG, October 10, 1878 (AGO Register LR).
45. A few days later Sherman also declined to authorize a general court-martial to consider Baldwin's formal charges. See AAG MDM to AG, October 11, 1878 (AGO LR); AG to C.O. MDM, October 12, 1878, and October 21, 1878 (AGO LS).
46. AGO, General Court-Martial Order 71, December 15, 1879, pp. 1–2.
47. AG to C.O. MDM, January 14, 1879 (AGO LS).
48. AGO, General Court-Martial Order 22, April 10, 1879.
49. SW to John H. Reagan, March 1, 1879 (SW LS).

February 1, 1879, he forwarded twelve specifications of alleged conduct unbecoming an officer and gentleman. These were disapproved
as lacking focus and specificity, and on June 27 he sent a new set,
detailing among Davidson's offenses drunkenness on duty, favoritism,
use of "deleterious drugs," suppression of charges filed against him,
giving the lie to Lee in public, using a sergeant as a spy on commissioned officers, wrongfully imprisoning a civilian, lying, and authorizing another officer to utilize public property for strictly private
purposes.[50]

Whatever General Sherman may have believed about the validity
of these charges from an officer whose motive was so obvious, at
this point he judged it proper to convene a general court-martial to
consider them. Davidson had just received promotion to the colonelcy of the Second Cavalry, but before he assumed command of his
new unit in Dakota Territory, it seemed wise that he be tried, lest he
be followed there by allegations that would discredit him. The result
was nomination of a blue-ribbon court, consisting almost entirely of
full colonels, to meet in October 1879 at Fort Riley, Kansas.[51] In
authorizing the trial, Sherman observed that if Davidson should be
found not guilty, his accuser ought to be tried in turn for having
caused the Army great expense and having done it grave moral
harm. In the proceedings that followed, Davidson was acquitted of
all charges.[52] On October 25 Sherman therefore ordered trial of his
foiled "persecutor." "If [Lee] escapes free now," he wrote, "every commanding officer will be assailed by every subordinate who is reproved
or feels aggrieved."[53]

50. General Court-Martial Order 71, December 15, 1879, pp. 2–17—AGO.

51. AG to General Pope, November 3, 1879 (AGO LS). The officers detailed for
the court were Colonel Israel Vogdes, First Artillery, President; Colonel Galusha
Pennypacker, Sixteenth Infantry; Colonel Franklin F. Flint, Fourth Infantry; Colonel
Henry B. Clitz, Tenth Infantry; Colonel H. J. Hunt, Fifth Artillery; Colonel Cuvier
Grover, First Cavalry; Colonel R. B. Ayres, Second Artillery; Major Robert H. Offley,
Nineteenth Infantry; and Major D. G. Swaim, Judge-Advocate.

52. *ANJ*, November 1, 1879, pp. 235–36; see also the issue for November 15, p.
276.

53. Sherman to Pope, October 25, 1879 (AGO LS).

The court reconvened on November 15 and found Lee guilty of conduct unbecoming an officer and gentleman for having maliciously made false charges against his commanding officer in each of the twelve specifications he had submitted.[54] The court sentenced him to be severely reprimanded in General Orders by the General of the Army, to be suspended from rank and command for one year, to forfeit one-half his monthly pay for that period, and to be confined to the limits of a post to be designated by General Sherman. In his published reprimand, Sherman named Fort Concho, Texas, as the place of detention and confined his remarks almost entirely to "a mere statement of the case [which] should be all the reprimand required, if Captain *Lee* possessed that delicate sense of honor and duty which should characterize every officer of the Army."[55] But Lee was deficient in just that article. He delayed until late February 1880 his arrival at Fort Concho to begin serving his sentence, and a few days thereafter he addressed a letter to the adjutant general complaining of the treatment he received there.[56] Letters to the secretary of war from Texas senators S. B. Maxey and Richard Coke asking remission of Lee's sentence made clear that he had not yet abandoned hope of escaping the punishment he had brought on himself.[57]

How closely Dodge followed the subsequent fortunes of Captain Lee after the court- martial at Fort Sill can only be guessed, but they came before the entire Army not only through printed General Court-Martial orders but in the military's unofficial weekly newspaper, the *Army and Navy Journal*. Coincidentally, the getaway hunting trip that followed Dodge's stay at Fort Sill was to include a "difficulty"

54. On the twelfth specification, Lee was judged not guilty of conduct unbecoming an officer but guilty of conduct to the prejudice of good order and military discipline.

55. AGO, General Court-Martial Order 71, December 15, 1879, pp. 18–20.

56. Colonel Benjamin H. Grierson, Tenth Cavalry, to AG, February 16, 1880; Lee to AG, March 1, 1880 (AGO Register LR).

57. SW to Maxey and Coke, July 15, 1880 (SW LS). Captain Lee served the remainder of his sentence as ordered and then returned to duty with his company. In 1886 he was again court-martialed but was acquitted (*ANJ*, August 14, 1886, p. 54). Still at the rank of captain, he retired from the Army on Christmas Day, 1889.

between Dodge and a junior officer that threatened to recreate the atmosphere of resentment and malice that surrounded Davidson and his subordinates. Altogether unexpected, this falling out between hunting companions was soon followed by an at least partial reconciliation, but it gave food for thought to both men. The journey to Fort Reno and Camp Supply brought other, more easily anticipated echoes of the recent past. At Fort Reno, Dodge would socialize with Major Mizner, who had been in command there at the time of the Northern Cheyennes' outbreak. At Camp Supply, Dodge would encounter Captain Mauck, his fellow campaigner north of the Kansas Pacific Rail Road.

The shadow of the future rested on Dodge as well, even as he diverted himself in search of game. Army officers of his era were officially encouraged to make hunting excursions in order to keep themselves in good physical condition, to maintain their skill as marksmen, and to familiarize themselves with country where they might one day see military action.[58] On this particular hunting excursion, Dodge can hardly have credited that the rationale to promote field sport would apply especially to himself; he had never been stationed in Indian Territory and had no reason to believe he ever would be. Nevertheless, such was to be the case.

At Sheridan's Roost, midway between Reno and Supply, Dodge exhausted himself with exhilarated effort one night in late November, attempting to bag some of the numberless turkeys that roosted in the scrub timber all around him. As he neared Camp Supply, he happened upon a large body of Northern Cheyennes, under escort by troops, who were nearing their destination at the Cheyenne and Arapaho agency after a long trek south from Sidney Barracks. At this time, the Indians were objects only of his curiosity and pity, but within a few weeks he would pass by this same spot on an urgent military mission

58. With the concurrence of the secretary of war, in August 1879 General Sherman directed that permission given officers to hunt should not be charged to them as leaves of absence. Being "in many ways so advantageous to the Service," hunting was to be encouraged. See G.O. 9, August 27, 1879, MDM; *ANJ*, September 4, 1880, p. 79.

and the Indians would become the focus of his professional attention. Without his suspecting it—and so far as can be determined, without General Pope's intending it—Dodge's turkey hunting expedition in Indian Territory proved to be a preliminary reconnaissance mission, providing a foundation for his duties in the two years to come.

Journal Two
November 5–
December 10, 1878

November 5[1]

Left post a few minutes after 2 am.   Train was on time, & I took it at 3.40 – went to bed.   Waked up in time for Breakfast & found Van Voast & Baird on cars.   Arrived Junction City [12]:30.[2]   An ambulance was sent down for us & we went up to Post & spent an hour with Pennypacker.[3]   Took M K & T R R at 2.30.   Senator Plum was on the train & we talked to him & were talked to by him all the way to Emporia.   Capt Rose 16 Infy joined our party at Junction.   Plum is [r]emarkably posted on & has kindly feelings

1. This manuscript journal, of a size and variety identical to Journal One, includes fifty-seven unnumbered pages, several of which have been torn loose along the perforated cut near their top edge. On the front cover Dodge has written in black ink, "No. 2 [/] Novr. 5th 78 [/] to Decr. 10th 78 [/] Turkey Hunting." Except for this identification and the text on p. [57V] and part of p. [57R], the notations are entirely in pencil. Following p. [54V], three sheets—pp. [57V]–[55R] in the original sequence—are written with the notebook in reversed position. The text begins on p. [1R].

2. Here and following "Plum is" a few lines below, the manuscript is torn and bits of text have been lost. The hour is supplied hypothetically from the context.

3. Lieutenant Colonel Van Voast was also en route to Fort Sill as a member of the general court-martial. Lieutenant Colonel Absalom Baird, Assistant Inspector General for the Military Division of the Missouri, was on an inspection tour. Junction City, Kansas, was adjacent to Fort Riley, where the three officers paid their respects to the post commander, Colonel Galusha Pennypacker, Sixteenth Infantry.

for the Army -[4]   Supper at Emporia.   Remington joined us there <−−−>[5]

Arrived at Parsons 11.30, & had to wait until 2 for train.   Got sleeping berths but did not sleep well.   A consumptive man kept up a continuous coughing under me.   The car was full close & dirty. Rose & I had an Oyster Stew in Parsons.   This is a lovely country. The Neosho Valley is a garden spot.[6]

November 6

Was roused early, & found Gibson & his clerk on Bd.   Learn that a large party is to go from Cadoo to Sill − 16 persons

Arrived at Cadoo at 2.30 p.m.   No transpn. from Sill.   We hoped to find it here, so we could go out a few miles, camp & wait for balance of party.[7]   Stopped at Hotel − R.R.   Towards evening we went out to look for Chickens.   I found none, but Rose got one.

November 7

Good nights rest.   Wanted to go hunting, but waited for the transpn.   Gibson, who got off yesterday to pay Ft Gibson arrived in

4. The Missouri, Kansas and Texas Railway, the only railroad that passed north to south through Indian Territory, ran 577 miles between Hannibal, Missouri, and Denison, Texas. Dodge and his fellow officers boarded a branch line that ran southeasterly from Junction City to Parsons, Kansas, where they would change trains. Preston B. Plumb (1837–1891), their companion, was a United States senator from Kansas. A former soldier, Plumb was a member of the Committee on Military Affairs. Captain Thomas E. Rose, Sixteenth Infantry, was stationed at Fort Riley and also en route to attend the court-martial.

5. Captain Philip H. Remington, Nineteenth Infantry, was another member of the general court-martial; he was stationed at Fort Dodge.

6. Elsewhere Dodge dilated on the beauty and agricultural prosperity evident in this region, contrasting it with the "scarcely inhabited solitude" just south of the line separating Kansas from Indian Territory. See RID, *A Living Issue*, pp. 25–26.

7. Major William R. Gibson was one of seven paymasters in the Department of the Missouri who passed from post to post paying the troops. He was stationed at Wichita, Kansas. Following a stop at Fort Gibson, his itinerary in coming weeks would duplicate Dodge's (ANJ, October 29, 1878, p. 183). In the journal entry for November 10, Dodge identifies Gibson's clerk as "Hunt." Members of the court had earlier been informed that transportation for the 160-mile wagon journey to Fort Sill would be at Caddo Station (misspelled Cadoo by Dodge) on November 7.

the night, but owing to his going off to other Hotels – went without a bed all night.   Rose had a D—l of a nightmare & roused the house. Last night I called on Mrs Marchand formerly Miss Young of Leavenworth, now a wife & mother of two children.   She & husband invited me to dine today but I declined on a/c of the hunt.   At 2.30 pm Mrs Davidson & 2 other ladies arrived – also Genl Smith & Capt Taylor[8]   We are now all ready & start tomorro a.m, 11 Offs & 3 ladies.   The transportation under Lt. Lassiter arrived at about 12. m   Mrs D. had tents pitched for herself & the other ladies, & went into camp.   I suspect she has spent all her money east & cant afford the Hotel Bill.

Just at nightfall saw a chicken light in a corn field, & went after him. Found six or eight but so wild, I could get only the longest shots. Fired 3 times, wounded all but bagged only 1 bird.   Gave it to the ladies for breakfast   Wrote to Father and Mother.   Bought bread beef sausage apples eggs &c for mess.

Went to bed 10 p.m.

November 8, 1878

Started about 8.30 am.   There is always some trouble & delay in getting started.   Van, myself, Remington, & Rose in one amb[ulan]ce. Gave a Negro man transpn & food to Sill for his services.[9]

A couple of Indians in front of us frightened up a flock of Turkeys, we followed.   They lit in a thicket but all ran except one which squatted & which V. V. was fortunate enough to stumble on & bag.   I saw none.   Rose saw three, but got no shot.

---

8. Mrs. Davidson was the wife of Lieutenant Colonel John W. Davidson, Tenth Cavalry, post commander at Fort Sill. The other named arrivals were Colonel Charles H. Smith (referred to by his brevet rank of major general), Nineteenth Infantry, from Fort Lyon, Colorado, and First Lieutenant Daniel M. Taylor, ordnance officer for the Department of the Missouri. These two officers were to serve, respectively, as president and judge advocate of the court-martial.

9. In later entries this man is identified only as George. He was paid four dollars for his services on December 4.

Arrived at Camping place 1.30 p.m.   Took a nap but was so shaken up with the miserable side seated ambulance that I did nt go out to hunt.   Delightful day & pleasant evening –

18 miles

November 9

Got out of camp soon after daylight to get ahead of Mrs Davidson who in pure perversity will go ahead & drive the game away.   It was no use.   She overtook us in an hour.

Stopped at the Blue 10 miles, a lovely stream clear as chrystal – can plainly see the bottom in 6 feet water.   Tried very hard to get some fish but got not even a bite.   Van & Rose went hunting   V. saw nothing.   When I was tired fishing, I went back to ambulance & he & I had lunch.   Shortly after Rose came in, in a great state of excitement & said he had mortally wounded a deer, & wanted us to go help him find it.   We went & we looked but found no deer.

Rose also claimed to have seen a large flock of Turkeys, & some ducks.   He brought in 4 quail.

We then hitched up & came on to camp on Pennington Creek – getting in to find all our tents pitched & every thing prepared for a rain which soon set in – & continued all afternoon.   Had an excellent dinner in spite of all – & enjoyed ourselves, but failed to have our afternoon hunt.   Played 5 cent poker with Van & others until 9 pm took a drink, turned in, wrote this & am now on the sleep.   It has cleared off beautifully.   Distance today claimed to be 22 miles is really about 1<8>7 or 18.

Sunday, November 10

Up early.   Gibson being evidently a man of bad conscience – cannot sleep in the morning.   The morning was murky & threatening, but cleared off & we had a lovely day.   Finding we are to pass a post office today, I wrote to Father & Mother a short note.   The rain made the roads heavy and <we> our mules are very poor   The distance is called 22 miles, & we were six hours.   Camped on Rock Creek – a beautiful stream clear as possible, the bottom being perfectly seen at 6 or more feet.   There are many bass in it, but the disgust I have this day contracted for the Bass family, I hope will be avenged on it by my family to its latest Generation.[10]   I saw a low bank, under which was deep water.   Creeping on hands & knees, I got position & silently dropped my line with two hooks each hidden by a tempting grass-hopper.   There was a dash & a swirl, & in a moment I could see some 15 or 20 bass & almost as many sunperch, surrounding the baits at <a> distances never less than 2 feet.   They evidently held a coun-cil – for after a few brief moments, the leaders a pair of bass of at least 1 1/2 to 2 lbs. each quietly turned away, & sailed off taking all the rest.

By hard & careful work I got 6 perch, & 1 Ch. Cat.   Only 3 quail. Rose reports shooting at another deer.   A poor day for hunting or fishing.   Hunt, Gibsons clerk got 1 small bass & 1 cat.   Distance 22 miles

November 11

Started 7 a.m.   Had a hard time today with dysentery.   Could not hunt or do anything but gripe & run.   Beautiful country.   Crossed Wachita & camped 3 miles beyond in Paul's Valley – a lovely & fertile place.[11]

Here is a large store kept by a man named Green.   Bought some chickens – wrote postal card to Father.

Saw 2000 acres corn in one field.   The party got some quail.   I went to bed – was sick all day, but better tonight   Distance 24 miles.

10. The personification of animals and use of vaguely biblical language were features of Dodge's comic parlance for the amusement of family members.

11. In *A Living Issue*, a pamphlet excoriating federal Indian policy and calling for reform, Dodge characterized Paul's Valley as "one of the garden spots of earth." However, he added, the enormous crops of corn grown there by Chickasaw Indians could be sold only to the authorized Indian trader. He paid them fifteen cents per bushel in goods, whereas the product was worth over one dollar per bushel in cash (p. 16). Dodge misspells the name of the Washita River.

November 12

Lovely day & quite good luck hunting the party getting 17 ducks and 8 grouse.   Beautiful country   Tried fishing but tho' there were plenty of bass they would'nt bite.   Pleasant camp.   26 miles –

November 13

Sick in night, & sick all day.   Killed 4 grouse & 1 quail, in spite of sickness.   Party got 7 grouse 3 quail, 2 ducks, 2 snipe.   Had I been well we would have got much more, as twas the best hunting ground we've had.

November 14

Rainy bad morning – growing worse all the time.   We determined to make the whole distance, 28 miles, & got in by 2 pm after a very hard drive.[12]   Went at once to the Post Traders, where we had secured rooms,[13] as we intend to mess together at Sill, instead of staying with the Officers.   Smith, Taylor & the Pay Dept are provided for at the Post   Our mess, Van, Remington Rose & myself take care of ourselves & are very comfortable.   Davidson has done everything to make us as comfortable as possible pitched tents for our mess & cooking &c, &c.   Rained hard at night, but Remington & I went to the saloon & played a few games of billiards.

Went to bed early.

12. Established in 1868 as Camp Wichita and completed in 1875, Fort Sill was a relatively large post, with barracks capable of housing ten companies. It was remote, being 123 miles north of Fort Richardson, Texas, 75 miles south of Fort Reno, and 190 miles southeast of Camp Supply. The stage line that regularly traveled between it and Caddo made the trip in four days, but supply trains took longer. For description of the post and vicinity as they appeared in this era, see Nye, *Carbine and Lance*, pp. 277–83; early photographs and drawings follow p. 77. See also *ANJ*, December 15, 1888, p. 307.

13. Dodge had been informed on October 31 that members of the court-martial would need to make their own arrangements for mess and bedding at Fort Sill (Fort Hays LR). The firm of Rice and Beyers held the post tradership; W. H. Quinette, who later held the office for many years, was at this time their employee (Nye, *Carbine and Lance*, p. 290).

November 15

Payed my respects to Davidson this a.m. before the Court met.[14] Sat on Court from 10 to 2.35 on the trial of Capt. Lee 10th Cavy. Tedious work.[15]   Wrote to Father & Mother – also to Joe and Laura. Played billiards & received visits in evening –

November 16

Still at work on Court.   Prosecution closed today.   Spent evening at Genl Davidson's.   Received lots of letters, one from Julia, Father &

Mother, both Kates,[16] &c.   To bed about <10> $\wedge$ 11 pm   Have almost entirely recovered from my dysentery.

Sunday, November 17

Went up to look at G[uar]d Mounting.   Spent an hour pleasantly in Davidsons office.   Then took a ride to the Indian farm, to the Agency & School.

---

14. According to the *Revised Army Regulations* of 1873, "Officers arriving at any military headquarters on duty will, if inferior in rank to the commanding officer, report personally; if superior, by writing or otherwise, as may be convenient" (p. 103). Dodge and Davidson were both lieutenant colonels, but the latter had seniority.

Owing to Senate inaction, the *Revised Army Regulations* of 1873 did not carry the force of law. The Army continued to be guided by the outdated *Regulations* of 1861, as amended through 1863. Nevertheless, the regulations of 1873, which Dodge had helped formulate, presented a detailed image of the post–Civil War Army as it then functioned and understood itself. Greatly expanding the earlier document, they laid a basis for further revision in the *Regulations* of 1881. The above quotation, from an article entitled "Military Obligation and Etiquette," has no precedent in the 1861 *Regulations*. However, the articles of the 1873 document referred to in all subsequent citations of *Army Regulations* do have exact counterparts in the earlier code.

15. The proceedings of a general court-martial were elaborate, and for its regular members, somewhat confining. For example, only the presiding officer could ask direct questions of witnesses. For further description, see House, *Revised Army Regulations*, p. 196.

16. One of the Kates was Catharine ("Kate") Chambliss, a cousin; the other was probably Catharine Paris Frothingham (1832–1914), another cousin. For the latter, see Aderman, *A Genealogy of the Irvings of New York*, p. 15 and entry 95.

Got a drink or two of very fine brandy from the Indian Trader.[17]

Good dinner, thanks to Davidson who sent us a young wild Turkey. Visitors & plenty of gass in evening.[18]   To bed at 10 pm

Wrote to Julia.

November 18

Court Martial again.   Slow & very tedious.   Wrote to Gilman on the important potato question[19]   Also a note to Cath.   With Van & Remington paid visits to all the people who have called on us, except the Doctors.[20]   We will do them tomorro.

Lovely day, too beautiful to waste on a Court.   I ought to have been fishing

Letter from Father & Mother – all well.

November 19

At last we have come to an end of the Court.   The defense having stopped short in its witnesses.   <The> Many Offs & Ladies in the Court room to hear the Arguments of Counsel.[21]

---

17. This was John S. Evans, formerly post trader, an old-timer at the fort. See Nye, *Carbine and Lance*, pp. 100, 201, 291; E. Townsend to Messrs. J. S. Evans & Co., December 9, 1878 (AGO LS). Fort Sill was adjacent to the agency for Kiowa, Comanche, and Kiowa-Apache Indians (Frazer, *Forts of the West*, p. 124). The Indian agency was under the direction of James M. Haworth.

18. The presence at Fort Sill of several senior officers from outside the garrison was a social event, whatever their official business. The *Revised Army Regulations* prescribed suitable behavior: "Officers are, of course, expected to maintain among themselves the courtesies and amenities of social life as observed between gentlemen. Officers arriving at posts or military stations on visits of convenience or pleasure have a right to expect that the officers at the post visit them socially, and render such offices of courtesy as the occasion may demand" (p. 103).

19. The ironic phrase refers to an official squabble in which Dodge had become engaged with Captain Jeremiah H. Gilman, chief commissary of subsistence of the Department of the Missouri, over a shipment of potatoes sent from Fort Leavenworth to Fort Hays. See below, pp. 107–13.

20. Acting Assistant Surgeons A. T. Fitch and C. T. Gibson, medical officers at the post (DMO *Roster*, November 1878, p. 5).

21. After witnesses had been examined and further documentary testimony read to the court, the accused person had opportunity to present his defense. The court was then closed for discussion and a series of votes on the charges and specifications, the majority determining the verdict (*Revised Army Regulations*, p. 196). For the verdict in the present case, see above, p. 65.

Invited to a hop – & went to find only three Ladies.[22]   Everybody
is quarrelling at the Post.   It is in a most wretched condition socially.
Faults on every side.   Wrote to Mizner on 17th asking if he will give
me escort & transpn from Reno to Supply[23]   Have to wait here until
I hear from him.

November 20

After breakfast Remington & I started with Davidsons son Ed to try
fishing.   We had no bait, & had to catch it on minnow hooks.   After
immense effort I got 10 little minnows – which were gone in no time,
the bass biting well.   We got 5 very nice fellows – R 3 & I 2.   I also
got 4 good perch.   If we had had plenty of minnows I think we
would have taken a large number of bass.   They were quite plenty
& bit well on live bait –   The snags & branches interfered greatly with
us, & we lost more than we caught.

Mrs. Davidson gave the Court a very pleasant little party at night –
cards & dancing, champagne & gas, & a very nice supper.   Van V.
claimed that he was just properly gentlemanly drunk.   I was about
40 pr ct. behind him.[24]   Made arrangements for another fishing frolic
tomorro with Jewett.   Remington goes to the mountains with the
girls –[25]

November 21

Was waked up this morning by a Colored Sergeant, who reported
himself in charge of a party to escort me to Reno.   Almost immediately after recd postal card from Mizner telling me that he would
give me everything I wanted.   Jumped out of bed & gave dir-

22. A hop was a formal dance, often followed by refreshments.
23. The distance from Fort Reno to Camp Supply was approximately 130 miles
along a military wagon road that roughly paralleled the North Fork of the Canadian
River.
24. Apparently, on the passage toward a drunken state.
25. Dodge refers to Second Lieutenant James S. Jouett, Company I, Tenth Cavalry,
a unit commanded by one of Lieutenant Colonel Davidson's persistent enemies,
Captain Theodore A. Baldwin. The Wichita Mountains, north and west of the post,
were a favored destination for social excursions.

ections to get ready to start.   After breakfast went up to see Davidson.   He was thoroughly disgusted, somebody having ordered my transpn & escort for today instead of tomorro.   It was an accident – a blunder really – such as should not occur at a well regulated post – but I was delighted, as it enabled me to get off a day sooner.

Got some Com[missar]y Stores bade Mrs D & the girls good by, packed up & got the baggage wagon off at 10 am.   Went to the store & wrote a letter to Father & Mother, & one to Trout, telling him to have ambulance & wagon at Ft Dodge for me on 6th Decr.[26]

Remington Rose & myself got off at 11 am.   Smith & Van V, left earlier, going to Cadoo.   We went nearly west, & camped 2 pm on Cache Creek, making what is here called 16 miles tho its not so much –   Real nice camp.   No game too many Indians –   Passed many camps and houses.   Tried fishing – only 2 perch.   Sat up late gassing with Remington.   Courier from Davidson informing me that the Cheyennes have broken out again.[27]   Lovely day –

26. By S.O. 40, December 2, Fort Hays, Second Lieutenant Calvin D. Cowles, with two privates and a wagon, was ordered to Fort Dodge, where he would report to Dodge. Cowles would traverse a seventy-five-mile wagon road between the posts that had been in existence since 1867. Completion of the Atchison, Topeka and Santa Fe Rail Road to Dodge City in 1872 eliminated military necessity for the wagon road, since troops and supplies at Fort Hays could be transported more rapidly to Fort Dodge via railroad connections at Salina and Junction City, Kansas. Dodge planned a few days of hunting along the now little-used road to his post. For a description of the road and its history, see Clapsaddle, "The Fort Hays–Fort Dodge Road," pp. 101–12.

27. This unfounded rumor caused alarm at military posts in the Indian Territory and Texas. On November 1 Little Robe, a Southern Cheyenne, had been given permission to go with many of his people to his farm, about sixty miles from the Cheyenne and Arapaho agency, in order to hunt there. He interpreted the permission liberally, and three weeks later, with three hundred men organized as a war party, he was ranging far south of his authorized destination. He had found buffalo and killed many, but at the end of the hunt he showed no inclination to return. Lieutenant Colonel John P. Hatch, Fourth Cavalry, believed Little Robe was demonstrating to all concerned that he was not to be kept from hunting or otherwise treated lightly (Enclosures, SW to SI, December 2, 1878—OIA LR, C&A). The Army kept discreet watch over his activities, and within a few weeks he returned to his farm, then to the agency.

November 22

Started 7.30.   On top of divide found a crazy lot of quail. Remington & Rose potted the whole covey, 26.   The foolish birds would neither hide nor fly.   At the Wachita River the geese were abundant & all tumbled out of the ambulance to get a shot.   I got 4 shots but only 1 goose wounding one or two others.   We intended to camp at some ponds, but found them miserable mud puddles & went on to Sugar Creek, 3 miles from the Agency.   The Indian Agency for the Cadoos Keechees &c is at the crossing of the Wachita on North Bank.[28]   There are a good many houses.   The farms of the Indians are large and look well.   These Indians are as civilized as the average southern Cracker, live in the same kind of houses & are quite as well educated.[29]   The country is very lovely but sandy & I think poor. <B>Camped on Sugar Ck, 2 p.m.   Gibson & Taylor passed in stage just as we finished dinner.   They came up & took a drink with us.   I went out after they left & bagged 2 more quail.   Rose was terribly annoyed at not getting a goose, & while I was after ducks in the pond he took a horse from the escort that here overtook us, & went back. He returned at 8 p.m. with nothing, & very much put out.   He is oddity itself, & the hugest "blower" I have ever met.   He claims to be a first class shot, when really he is no better than I - & to be an expert on hunting matters while he is really very ignorant.[30]   Beautiful

---

28.   The Caddo and Wichita tribes occupied a designated but as yet informal reservation between the Washita and Canadian Rivers. Their agency, manned by representatives of the Society of Friends and Baptist missionaries, was established in 1872. The Kichai Indians, formerly confederated with both Caddos and Wichitas, had lost many of their people to cholera in an epidemic of 1867. The remnant were among the affiliated tribes on the Wichita-Caddo reservation (Wright, *A Guide to the Indian Tribes of Oklahoma*, pp. 52, 164-65, 259-60).

29.   The comparison reflects Dodge's personal background, for he was reared in rural North Carolina. For a vivid description of his childhood surroundings, see A. H. Guernsey, "Surry County, North Carolina," *Harper's New Monthly Magazine* 25 (1862): 178-85.

30.   Dodge was an excellent marksman and a skillful hunter. See *BHJ*, pp. 119, 155, 194, 203 *et passim*; *PNA*, p. 438. One of the three sections of *PNA*, entitled "Game," was comprised of essays on the habits and distinctive characteristics of animals indigenous to the plains, with suggestions on the best methods for hunting them. As late as 1883, Dodge qualified to wear the Army marksman's buttons, satisfying rigorous standards for shots at 200, 300, and 600 yards (Dodge Papers, Graff Collection).

weather – could not be finer.   Davidson & Gibson have the Cheyenne "escape" very much mixed.   22 miles.

November 23

Got a long shot at geese that flew over camp before breakfast, but got none tho' I hit a fellow badly.   Started 8 am.   Got a long shot at a prarie chicken but did'nt get him.   Marched to the Ranche of a Caddo Indian who calls himself Geo. Washington very pretty and thriving farm.[31]   The road was very sandy & bad today so I determined to Camp at Washingtons – as there is no wood or grass on other side of Canadian & only the river water which is very alkaline and bad A very good & comfortable camp.   Took a nap in afternoon. Gibson & stage party stuck in river & got everything wet.[32]   Had to be taken out & carried to Reno in ambulance sent for them.   Gibson came near drowning.

The above was written just before I laid down to take my nap, & I expected that a very few words more would end the diary for this day. A singular adventure however awaited my waking.

Just before I laid down Rose fired his gun off at a tree.   Soon after both he & Remington came into my tent.   I told them that I was going to take a nap, & said "Now Rose if you go popping off your gun any more, I'll fill your bottom with No 4 shot, & Remington, if you go making any noise around this camp I'll put that foot on you" at the same time holding up my foot.[33]   They soon after left the tent, everybody apparently in a good humor.

31. According to Wilbur S. Nye, Caddo George Washington had passed a colorful career, driving an illicit trade in liquor and guns to local Indians while professing friendship with the whites at Fort Sill (*Carbine and Lance*, pp. 51, 115, 130; see also Nye, *Plains Indian Raiders*, p. 386). A full-length photograph of Washington is reproduced in *Carbine and Lance*, following p. 74; another photograph, a bust portrait showing him carefully groomed and attired in city-style clothing, is in Wright, *A Guide to the Indian Tribes of Oklahoma*, p. 53.

32. The party was crossing the Canadian River. See also the journal entry for November 24.

33. Dodge was a large man, well over six feet tall and weighing more than two hundred pounds. He was accustomed to accompanying jocose threats by allusions to his size. See *PREJ*, p. 127.

George waked me up with call to dinner.   I soon got ready & went out to find Rose walking up & down near the tents, and Remington gone down to the corn field   Calling to Rose to come I sat down to dinner.   He still walked about uneasily, but he is so odd that I paid little attention to it.   Soon I called to him again, saying, "Rose why dont you come to dinner[?]"   He answered, "I'm not hungry" –   While eating I sent George to fix my bed, & after he got through I saw him & Rose at work on Rose['s] bed.

As I rose from the table I was met by Rose, who had his overcoat on, his gun in one hand & India Rubber boots in the other.   He said "Colonel I think I will walk into Reno tonight" –   I said very much astonished, "What on earth do you want to do that for[?]"   "Well,["] said he "You dont seem to like my popping my gun around & I think I'd better go"   "Why Rose" I said "you are acting very foolishly, my remarks about your popping were only in fun, & its very absurd in you to act in this way" –

I then went to my tent for my pipe leaving him standing just in front, some ten paces off.   As I came out again advancing towards him, he said, "I am used to have people speak out when they dont like what I do, & I dont like these insinuations.   I dont seem to suit you people & I think I'll go in." –   The remark about insinuation made me lose my temper, & I replied rather hotly, "Capt Rose I do not use insinuations.[34]   When I want to say anything I say it.   If you want to leave this party, you can do so as soon & in any manner you wish.["]   He made some reply, to the effect that he intended to go at once.   I told him, that ["]he was making a fool of himself but that he might go just as quick as he <——> pleased"   Whereupon he turned on his heel & went off without another word, taking the road to Reno –   Remington came back just as the last passages between us were given, & heard all that passed after I came out of my tent with my pipe.

I am very sorry that this thing occurred.   Rose is a dogmatic, illiterate ill informed man, uncouth in manner dirty in person, & the

34. The change in Dodge's form of address, from "Rose" to "Captain Rose," is a clear signal of the senior officer's angry scorn. See Knight's discussion of military forms of address in *Life and Manners in the Frontier Army*, pp. 101-02.

most infamous "blower," as to his own prowess & exploits I have ever met.   He is the oracle on hunting in his Regt. & claims to know everything so positively that he has evidently been accustomed to put down every difference of opinion.   Remington & I dont think much of his shooting, & take him up on his "blowing" assertions not disagreeably, but enough to show him his own absurdity.   For instance today in conversation with me about crossing the river in front of us, he asserted that "at 19 years old he knew more about quick sands than any man in Kansas -"   I said, "Now Rose, wer'nt you brought up in the east[?"]³⁵["]Yes,["] he replied.   "At 19 years old had you ever seen a quick sand," I asked.   "No" he replied, ["]<——>

               I was a very smart boy.
but   ∧   ["]   ["]Well,["] I continued, ["]what an absurdity for you to make such a statement as that just made."

This kind of "taking up" has been of almost daily occurrence, & though all has apparently been pleasant they have evidently rankled in him.   Added to this he has been about two thirds drunk ever since we left Sill.   He has "blowed" about his skill as a shot, & success as a hunter, but has brought in very little game, & when hunting with Remington or I has not beat either of us.   He "blows" about his wood-craft, & knowledge of country.   Both of us know far more than he does.   He brings in a lot of Spoon bills, & calls them Mallards & we

                       really
laugh at him - & while not one single   ∧   unpleasant thing has

---

35. Born in Pennsylvania, Rose had thus far served an honorable career in the Army. Through much of the Civil War he was active in volunteer regiments from his state, earning for his services the brevet rank of brigadier general, U.S. Volunteers. For gallantry at the battles of Liberty Gap, Tennessee, and Chickamauga, Georgia, he also won brevets as major and lieutenant colonel in the regular army. His best-remembered accomplishment was in February 1864, as leader of the forty-nine Union soldiers who dug a lengthy tunnel and escaped from Libby prison in Richmond, Virginia. See *ANJ*, October 20, 1883, p. 224; September 3, 1887, p. 99; January 5, 1889, p. 367. Promoted to captain, Eleventh Infantry in July 1866, Rose was unassigned in April 1869 as part of the Army's postwar reduction in force. In February 1870 he was reassigned, now to the Sixteenth Infantry, and he served in that capacity thereafter (Hamersley, *Records of Living Officers*, pp. 308-09). Rose retired in 1894 at the rank of major, Eighteenth Infantry.

occurred, the accumulation of mortification at his want of success as a hunter, & his ignorance as a man, has driven him to the desperate resolve to seperate from us —

I am sorry because I'd rather have had all pleasant on the trip -.   I am not sorry to get rid of him, but I am sorry for the manner of the riddance.   It is at least 12 miles to Reno & a nasty river intervenes.[36] I would willingly have given him a horse, had he asked it, but I would'nt offer it.   He has acted like a fool, but I doubt not he has repented it $\overset{\text{before this is written}}{\wedge}$.   Whether so or not he has punished himself worse than any court would have punished him. Verily, the folly well punishes the fool.

Distance 24 miles.   No game.   Exit Rose -

I forgot to say that Rose had rolled & packed his bedding & everything before he came to speak to me.   Remington says that all the time I was asleep, he sat outside, evidently deeply cogitating something.   He has undoubtedly had this in his mind for the last day or two.   I believe that *my* killing the goose yesterday instead of *him* had much to do with it.

Sunday, November 24

Cold, blustery & disagreeable.   Got off soon after 8 am   Gave a man a dollar to show us the best ford over the Canadian.   Arriving at that stream I mounted one of the spare horses.   The ambulance & horsemen got over beautifully, though the channel was quite deep, but narrow.   We got into no quick sand but we saw our danger in a stage & buck board hopelessly stuck.   Sent back the leaders of ambulance team, hitched them on to our baggage wagon, & it came

36. The Canadian River, not the North Fork of the Canadian, which lay twelve miles further north. A contemporary observer characterized the river as "a most treacherous stream, liable to rise at any moment, and whose channel changes from hour to hour" (*ANJ*, December 3, 1881, p. 381). John Homer Seger, who lived for many years near the Cheyenne and Arapaho agency and worked there in several capacities, also described the Canadian as "a treacherous stream" that could rise suddenly, "leaving me in great anxiety on the wrong side" (*Early Days Among the Cheyenne and Arapahoe Indians*, p. 109).

1884

Thomas E. Rose (Massachusetts Commandery, M.O.L.L.U.S., U.S. Army
Military History Institute)

across beautifully without a stop.   I confess to being a little uneasy as to Rose.   We found his boots on the bank.   I asked our guide if he had heard anything of a man who had crossed on foot the night

before.   "A man with a gun", he <asked>   ^ exclaimed -, ["]why he came near being drowned.   He stood on the sand in the ^ river & directed the buck-board how to go.   When it stuck, he abused the driver for being stupid, & started to reach the further bank.   In a moment he went down completely out of sight – but got out with a thorough wetting."

We came on against a stiff cold norther,[37] & about 11 am arrived at Ft Reno.   We were met by Capt Clapp who invited me to his house.   Arrangements had also been made for Remington & as the weather was exceedingly bad we accepted the invitation.   On going in, Rose came out of the bed room, & in a half smiling half sheepish way held out his hand[38]   I took it, & said, "Well Rose I am glad to see you have got safely out of your foolish scrape" –   He made no intelligible reply.   After taking a drink & getting my things unloaded I went over to see Mizner, at his adjutants office.[39]   He met us very cordially.   We also found Gibson & Taylor & rallied them on their ducking.   Gibson really had a very narrow escape. Everything they had was thoroughly soaked and on getting to the bank they built a fire, unlocked their trunks, took out everything &

37. In his chapter on "Climate" in *PNA*, Dodge stressed the destructive power of a "norther," a winter storm on the plains whose "icy wind cuts like a knife; no clothing seems to keep it from the person, and penetrating to every point it drags out every particle of vital heat, leaving but a stiffened corpse of him who is so unfortunate as to be exposed to it" (p. 83).

38. Rose was a guest in the quarters of Captain William H. Clapp, his fellow officer in the Sixteenth Infantry.

39. The chief administrative center of the post, the adjutant's office was adjacent to that of the post commander and a natural gathering place. For early photographs of Fort Reno and an artist's bird's-eye sketch of its layout, see W. Edwin Derrick, "Fort Reno: Defender of the Southern Plains" in Faulk, et al., eds., *Early Military Forts and Posts in Oklahoma*, pp. 113–21.

hung them up to dry.   They did not reach the post until 12 m. (23d) & would not then had not Mizner thoughtfully sent an ambulance for them.

From the Adjts Office we all adjourned to Mizners house met the madam, took a drink & had a good time.   They invited us to dinner, & gave an account of Rose.   About 10 p.m the night before there came a ring at the door.   Gibson was nearest & open<ed>ing it was surprised to see Rose looking dazed and wandering.   He was invited in, but he was either crazy or feigned to be so.   He accounted for leaving my camp by saying that he & I had had a difficulty & that he had got the worst of it.   He had got thoroughly soaked in the river, & had walked near 12 miles in the teeth of a stiff norther.   He said he got along very well until within 5 miles of the post, when he fell & remained partially unconscious for some time.   He was fed & condoled with & Clapp was sent for, & took him off and put him to bed.   He could give only the most incoherent account of his nights wanderings, or of the cause of them. Clapp thought he was somewhat demented (& he certainly acted so.)   On being asked if he had had a very serious quarrel with me, he replied "No, only a little one - & I have no feeling in the matter. I got punished for it" —

After we left Mizners, I went back to Clapps & dressed for dinner. Had a most excellent dinner & good wines.   Enjoyed it immensely. About <7>6 ock I went back to Clapps and held a levee almost all the Officers of the Post calling on me.   Had a very pleasant evening and did'nt get to bed until after 1 am.

Of course I let Rose understand that he could not go on with us, & he will remain here until well, & then go home by stage.

Mizner ordered all I need for trip to Supply & I get off tomorro. Weather very disagreeable   Cold & windy - a regular Norther. Distance 13. 1/2 miles.

Monday, November 25, 1878

The wagon reported at 8 am & was soon loaded & started off. Directed the Sergeant to go with wagon & escort to Ravin

Springs.[40]   The day was cold & blustery, looking like continuous bad weather.   Clapp gave me a most excellent breakfast, after which I wrote a short note to Father & Mother & a postal card each to Julia & to Trout. Went over to the Post Traders store & walked about with Mizner.[41]   At 10 1/2 went & bade good by to Mrs Mizner.   Dr. Chase[42] & several of the Officers came to see us off & at 11 am we go<o>t into our ambulance & turned our backs on Reno.   Poor Rose looked badly & disconsolate enough, but I did not invite him to come with us, as I do not propose to be bothered with & have the responsibility of such a man.

Had a cold ride up the river, in view of numbers of Indian Villages.

We are now at the Cheyenne & Arrapahoe Agency.   Twelve miles from the post we passed the sand hills made famous by the escapade of Dull Knife.   Here were their fortifications wonderfully well constructed, which they held while getting ready for their flight to the North[43] –   I did not go to see them, as the day was so disagreeable, but I had seen a plan of the defenses.

Just before 2 pm we came up with the wagon & escort & passed, arriving at Ravin Springs about 2.30 pm.   Soon after I went out after quail which were very plenty but the weeds were so high & the thickets so dense that I had poor success, getting only 5 birds.   I never saw birds so wild, or fly so fast, & I did really well to get a bird for every 2 shots.   The wagon a 6 mule team, arrived late, & we did'nt get supper until after dark.   It is now clear tho' still cold & windy & we hope for a good day tomorro.   Remington saw some Turkeys but didn't get a shot.

Excellent camp.   Distance 20 miles.

Only 7 quail all told.

40. The sergeant and his men were to set out ahead of Dodge and Remington, who would follow in an ambulance at their own pace. Ravin Springs (or Raven's Spring) was twenty miles from Fort Reno on the road to Camp Supply.

41. The post trader at Fort Reno was Neal W. Evans. The ambulatory tour of the post seems to have been a feature of military etiquette.

42. Acting Assistant Surgeon T. B. Chase, medical officer of the post.

43. Upon moving their village further from the agency prior to the outbreak, the Northern Cheyennes had encamped among low hills. Anticipating pursuit and possibly interference by troops from Fort Reno, they secretly dug trenches and erected breastworks in case violence should break out.

Tuesday, November 26

Broke Camp 8.30 am   Remington & I went ahead on foot & worked hard for a chance to kill something.   After a 3-mile tramp the horses overtook us, & we then worked harder.   I at last found a flock of some 25 turkeys but got none.   Remington had a like fate.   I fired twice, but far off.   All the ground between the river & road has been burned. About 12 we went back to the ambulance tired & mad, & took a drink for pure spite.   The day was very cold & windy up to 2 pm, then cleared off very prettily.   Made a nice camp on the North Fork, at which we in ambulance arrived <at>before 2 Ock.   <P>After putting the ambulance as a starter for camp, R & I started to see what we could see, & after an absence of an hour & a half we returned to camp, I with one poor quail, he with nothing.   I had however found a small Turkey roost.[44]   He claimed to have found the paradise of deer & Turkeys. We got dinner & by a little after 4 pm R started for his deer & Turkey stand.   I waited till dark & then with Shob[45] went to my little Turkey Roost.   It was an awful thicket but we worked with a will.   The trees were tall, the night was dark.   How I hated myself for not bringing my field glass.   The turkeys were much scattered not more than 2 or 3 in a tree.   I shot & shot – sometimes a turkey would fall, sometimes the dead silence would proclaim that I had fired at a bunch of leaves or dead branch.   Sometimes a fluttering commotion, & disappearance would indicate that I had only wounded my game.   Twas pitch dark below in the thicket & I could only get along by feeling – one moment I'd run into a brush pile or lap of a dead tree – the next my eyes were assailed by numberless twigs of willow, & other small underbrush.   A grape vine would tangle my legs, at one step – at the next a bamboo brier would catch me around the neck and try to throttle me.   One limb would take my hat, another seize my gun another lay hold on my coat.   I looked to Heaven so constantly & earnestly that like many

44. Dodge ended this statement with a hyphen followed by a semicolon; but the capitalized "He" which follows clearly indicates a new sentence.

45. Private William Schob, who had been ordered to accompany Dodge from Fort Hays as orderly, also served as cook to his mess. On December 4 he received six dollars in payment.

other good people I became dizzy, lost my head & tumbled around indiscriminately.   Oh, I had a glorious time, & came in by 7.30 wet to the skin with perspiration, to find the water in camp so frozen that I had to thaw it out to get a drink – but with 5 splendid Turkeys.[46]

I fired 14 shots, killed 5, mortally wounded <3>2 that got away – fired 5 times at bunches of leaves or branches that looked like Turkey, & missed two.   They wer[e] on large branches, & I think were in this way protected.   My shot were I think too large.   With smaller shot I would have fired at the heads.

Remington has this moment got in – 9. pm – having bagged 9 Turkeys, after a longer & harder tramp than I had.

Distance <20>17 miles – 17[47] – 14 Turkeys 1 quail – 1 duck – Clearing up — —

Wednesday, November 27, 1878
Started 8 am.   Went after my turkeys which I had hung up in a tree last night.   Found & took them to wagon.   Found a pond & bagged a duck.   Chilly for horseback riding & we got into ambulance. About 1 pm arrived at a place which the Sergt & men of the Escort said was Sheridans Roost.[48]   Remington got on his horse & went to look. At once he pronounced it *not* Sheridan's Roost.   While looking about

46. In February 1878 William E. Strong was a member of a hunting party along the Canadian River that included Generals Sheridan and Crook, both experienced turkey hunters, and other dignitaries. Strong, himself a lifelong hunter, later described the experience, including his efforts one moonlit night to shoot into an enormous flock of turkeys roosting in blackjack timber. Like Dodge, he was both frustrated and exhilarated, pronouncing his time in the turkey roost "more exciting, more exhausting, and more enjoyable, withal, than the labors of a full day of ordinary hunting" (*Canadian River Hunt*, p. 23). For a description of another turkey hunt in this vicinity during the fall of 1879, see Aldridge, *Life on a Ranch*, pp. 162–66.

47. Dodge rewrote "17" because his first, corrected notation of the mileage was virtually illegible.

48. Reputed as a prime site for turkey hunting, Sheridan's Roost took its name from the exploits of General Sheridan there in March 1869. De Benneville Randolph Keim, who witnessed the hunt, recounted it in his *Sheridan's Troopers on the Borders*, a classic account of that winter's military campaign against the Cheyennes and allied tribes. According to Keim, in one night's shooting the general's party bagged sixty-three birds, Sheridan himself claiming eleven (pp. 303–04).

I came on to a large flock of Turkeys.   In a moment I was off my horse, & in another knocked over 2, when there arose such a cloud of Turkeys that I was utterly disgusted that my second barrel got only one, instead of a dozen.   R. got one with each barrel as they flew.   Following them up I got 8 in a very few moments.   R got 4.

R thought that Sheridan's Roost was only about 4 miles on, so I came on.   <S>After a mile or so the driver called to me that there were Turkeys ahead.   Mounting my horse I went for them & soon returned with 3.   We found it a long & very tiresome march to the Roost.   The road was deep sand, & at 4 pm I went into camp at a water hole east of the Roost –   Everybody tired and worn out, & I especially disgusted that I did not camp at the Marsh where we killed the Turkeys.

I walked out with my gun from camp, saw lots of ducks, but did not fire as I wanted a deer.   Just before getting back to Camp I came upon an Opossum & nailed him – the only one I ever saw in the Indn. Tery.   I had my gun to clean & shells to load, & was too dead tired to go out, though there are beautiful looking trees near us.   About 8 pm R. tho' tired, summoned resolution to try it.   He is out yet –   Had I camped at the Marsh (as known on the Map) I would have had a delightful day, & probably got lots of Turkeys tonight.   I was too greedy – made a labor of pleasure marched too far <s>– tired every-body out, & got nothing – Wont do it again.   Have really had a delightful day <eve> in spite of all – I have bagged 11 Turkeys, 1 duck, 1 rabbit & 1 possum, & could have got a great deal more small game. I saw immense flocks of ducks –

Good camp 1 1/2 miles east of Sheridans Roost.   The country is very wild & broken, full of Sand Hills & black jack timber – a very Paradise for Turkeys & deer.   I shall make only a very short march tomorro.

Distance today 23 miles & the road very heavy – 15 Turkeys, 3 quail, 1 duck, 1 rabbit & 1 possum.   Weather very fine.   Total Turkeys 29 –

Thanksgiving, Thursday, November 28, 1878
Went out early to get some ducks.   The slough was too wide & miry – only got 3.   Took rifle, shot gun & orderly and went for a deer.

Hunted hard & well – saw two – one a magnificent Buck, but got no shot.   At last came on a small flock of Turkeys – only 10.   They were not wild – gave me a rake with No 6 shot, which bagged 5 & I got another with second barrel.   Soon after I discovered another lot of 4.   Got 3 – 2 with first barrel & 1 with second – felt pretty good – 9 Turkeys with 4 shots   Coming on found another flock, from which I got only 2 with 4 shots, wounding 3 others mortally but they got away.   Struck the road at upper Sheridan's Roost to find that the wagons had gone on –   I followed & at 2 pm came into camp at Cottonwood Grove.   Remington had been unable to find water at Sheridan's Roost & was forced to come on –

Took a nap on getting in for I was very tired.   After dinner a flock of Turkeys came down to water just at our camp.   I fired at them, but got none.   I then went out to get some ducks – great flocks flying about – but they were very wild.   I gave that up, but as I was about to return to camp, I saw a large flock of Turkeys fly into the trees about the camp.   In a few moments they were banged at from all sides by the men & driven out.   I went off onto the prarie, & fired several long shots, bagging only one.   After lugging it awhile I saw another flock ahead and threw my turkey down putting my white handkerchief on the grass to mark the spot.   When I came back I could find neither handkerchief nor Turkey, but I had driven a large flock or two into the trees around camp & R. was plugging into them manfully.   I came in only on the tail of the affair but got <8>7 – making 19 for the days work.

Numbers were in the Black Jacks half a mile from Camp, but I was too tired to go after them.   R. bagged eleven (11)   So that in spite of the fact that we have lost the shooting at Sheridan's Roost, the best place in the country we have done pretty well.   R says he saw thousands in the upper Roost, but would not shoot as he expected the night hunting.   He is terribly disgusted at not finding water there. All were in by 6.30 pm.   Water poor – Wood & grass abundant.

I got 19, R 11 Turkeys –
I got 3, R. 1 duck –
R got 8 quail at a shot –

Total 30 turkeys, 4 ducks 8 quail.   Weather beautiful.   Total
Turkeys 59 — (64) One of the men killed 5 Turkeys with
Carbine –   Distance about 10 miles[49]

Friday, November 29, 1878

Our unlucky day of course.[50]   Started at 8 1/2 am   I went to look
after my handkerchief & Turkey.   I found the former, but the latter was
gone.   I expected he would be, as the wolves were thick, but he was
not eaten.   He had evidently recovered & gone off on his own account.
This was pretty good for Turkey – after being killed & carried by the
head for 200 yds.   He was a polite Turkey, for he left his card.   I got
a long shot at Turkey, but failed to get him.   Also shot with Carbine at
the head of a deer, standing in the tall grass 150 yds off.   I think I
touched his neck as he appeared to fall, but he went off at a great rate.
Just before reaching our camping place I went off to look for deer.   All
along the river to our left is a<n> range of huge sand hills.   Between
that & the river lie immense level bottoms, with tall grass, heavy
thickets & sloughs running in all directions.   I went into these
bottoms.   After a long tramp on horseback, a splendid buck jumped
out of the grass & went off, when about 75 yds I gave him a dose of
buckshot.   He disappeared at once & I thought I had killed him – but
soon after my Orderly saw[51] him going over a sand hill.   I found no
blood, & dont know whether I hit him.   He was a glorious fellow.
Came back to Camp.   After dark tried the Turkeys, but found none.
R. is out yet, but I have not heard his gun.   Lovely camp, & fine day –
About 18 miles.   No game   Saw no turkeys except those we
frightened last night

49. The notation of distance is written in the right margin, from bottom to top of
the page.
50. Friday has traditionally been regarded as a day of ill omen, being the day when
Adam was created, when he and Eve were expelled from Paradise, when he repented,
when he died, when Christ was crucified, and when the dead will rise for the Last
Judgment. During the Powder River Expedition, Dodge once expressed skepticism
about the mystical power of Fridays but noted that others, including "My little wife,"
were more credulous (*PREJ*, p. 136).
51. Dodge wrote "say."

Saturday, November 30

"Who can tell what a day may bring forth"?[52]   Yesterday was lovely – & we all went to bed with the full assurance of a delightful morrow. In the middle of the night I was awakened by what appeared to be rain & sleet.   I feared our Turkeys might be spoiled, but was too wedded to my blankets to get up, & soon went to sleep.   When George came in to make my fire this morning I noticed that his boots were covered with s<l>now – & on further investigation found at least 3 inches already fallen, & it continuing as if there never would be a let up.   There was a terrible old Norther   We have a beautifully sheltered camp, but the wind howled in the branches of the trees overhead & the whole air was thick with falling snow.   No move in such weather – so I gave orders.   The morning dragged along wearily enough.   R & I played Cribbage until we got tired.   About 12 m the snow ceased – & by 2 pm the sun was out smiling.

Though full 6 inches of snow covered everything we ordered our horses and went out.   We had a long & tiresome tramp – the snow in the grass being nearly to the knees of the horses   I saw 2 deer but got no shot, & returned at sundown with one Turkey.   R got 2 – Played cribbage & gassed until near 11 pm –   It has cleared off beautifully & is now cold.   We will make a move tomorro.

3 Turkeys 2 quail – Total Turkeys 62 – & all in splendid condition yet

Sunday, December 1, 1878

The sun rose bright & clear with every prospect of a lovely day.

Gave orders to march but it <was> ∧ is a cold and tedious business to break a camp in 7 inches of snow.

At 9 am all were off.   The road, a mere wagon trail was greatly blocked with drifted snow, & my intention was to keep ahead of the wagons & break the road for them.   Near Taylor's Creek however the deer & Turkey tracks got so thick that I could'nt stand it.   Went off to the left.   Came on to a flock of Turkeys but in so dense a thicket

52. An adaptation of Proverbs 27:1b.

that though I could see twenty I could'nt hit one.   At last a big fellow gave me a show & I bagged him.   The others flew in every direction. Noting the direction of some that went on open ground, I followed, found the tracks, pursued on horseback started them up from the grass in which they squatted & bagged 3 more – all beautiful shots at long range & from a horse that had not been shot off of before.

I could'nt spare much time to hunt as I expected a long march. Overtook the wagon in 3 or 4 miles, <&> put my turkeys in, and went ahead.   Crossed the river at what is called the 22 mile crossing.[53]   Camped at Cedar Bluffs said to be 1<7>6 miles from Cp Supply.   Splendid camp.   Cleared off the snow, & made ourselves comfortable.   Wagon arrived 2.30 p.m.   Good dinner & pleasant evening.

Wolves around us in great numbers.   Distance 1<6>7 miles – called 20 by the people here.   R got no game.   Total turkeys 66 of which I have bagged an even 40 —

The foregoing is not to be read by my Mammy as she will be shocked at the idea that her boy baby hunted on Sunday.[54]   Thats a mistake, he only protected himself from the Turkeys that attempted to bite him –   Being a soldier he has always to guard himself against the enemy.   The weather today has been lovely, & but for the snow-covered ground one could not believe it the first day of winter.   We camped in a Cedar Br<k>ake & had roaring camp fires.

December 2, 1878

Started 8.15 a.m.   Beautiful day –   About 4 miles from camp I met Capt Gunther with 2 Cos Cavy, in charge of the Cheyennes who surrendered to Miles last winter.   There were only about 40 fighting

---

53. Here the party moved from the north to the south side of the river, gaining easier access to Camp Supply. That post was located one and one-half miles above the junction of Wolf and Beaver Creeks, which combined to form the North Fork of the Canadian River.

54. Dodge occasionally poked fun at the Episcopalian beliefs of his mother, and also at the Roman Catholic beliefs and practices of his wife and son. For an example of the latter, see the journal entry for April 10, 1880.

men, & possibly 150 women & children.[55]   They left Supply on the
day before the storm – 29th & were delayed by it until 1st.   When
about to break camp Mauck came in with 2 Cos, & an order from Pope
to disarm the Indians & take away their war ponies.[56]   These Indians
had surrendered voluntarily nearly a year ago, & had been employed
by Miles as soldiers & scouts.   They had done excellent service
against the Nez Perces, & were provided with excellent characters &
discharges in writing from Miles, & with the promises of both Crook
& Miles that they should keep their Arms & Ponies.   When they
understood that they were to be disarmed they went to their Teepees
painted themselves & put on a war aspect.   Mauck talked, & urged.
The Indians pulled out their papers, <sai>insisted that they had the

55. These Northern Cheyennes, under escort by Captain Sebastian Gunther,
Fourth Cavalry, with Companies G and H of that regiment, were en route to the
Cheyenne and Arapaho agency. The Indians numbered 186 persons and consisted of
bands under Little Chief, Crazy Mule, Ridge Bear, Iron Shirt, and Black Bear. They had
not accompanied the 937 of their tribespeople who arrived at the agency in August
1877 but remained in the north, serving as scouts under Colonel Miles in operations
against the Sioux and Nez Perces. However, they were subsequently ordered by
Sheridan to join the other members of their tribe in Indian Territory; and though this
course was against their wishes, they agreed to do so. At the time of the outbreak
under Dull Knife, they were at Sidney Barracks, Nebraska, technically as prisoners of
war since they were in custody of the Army, but under no special restraint. At that
time they still had possession of their arms and ponies, having been promised the use
of them on their journey south. Care was taken lest the Indians under Little Chief
should learn of Dull Knife's attempt to return north and complicate the situation by
making an effort to rejoin him.
    On October 14 Captain Clarence Mauck, still in command of troops from the Fourth
Cavalry and Nineteenth Infantry, received orders at Fort Robinson to take charge of the
Indians at Sidney Barracks, known as the "friendly Cheyenne prisoners," and conduct
them to Fort Wallace, where he would receive further orders. He did so, and on
November 17 he left Fort Wallace for Camp Supply, where the party arrived ten days
later. He remained encamped near Camp Supply until the morning of November 29.
    56. On November 29 General Pope's adjutant telegraphed the commanding
officer at Fort Dodge the following order, which was to be delivered to Mauck by
courier: "Capt. Mauck—The Department Commander directs that on receipt of this
dispatch, wherever en-route it may reach you, you are at once to seize and retain in
your possession all arms the Indians with you may have with them, and to take
measures to be certain that you get possession of all arms. All war ponies are also to
be immediately taken possession of. When the Indians reach Fort Reno they are to
be turned over to the agent dismounted and disarmed" (OIA LR, C&A). The message
reached Mauck, still in camp near Camp Supply, the evening of November 30.

promises of big Chiefs &c, &c, & finally tore their papers to shreds & stalked back to their tents still keeping their Arms.[57]   The Indians were greatly outnumbered, & surrounded by the troops, but stubbornly refused to surrender.   About 2 pm Mauck told <s>them that at 3 he would commence to fight, that all Indians disposed to obey orders & give up arms should come to his tents, all determined to fight were to remain in their own Camp   This was too much. The Women & Children & peacably disposed men came in & by 3 p.m. all, led by the force of example had surrendered.

Mauck, whom I met a short time after at the Post told me it was the most disagreeable duty of his life.[58]   The Indians were in the right, &

57. The Indians had in fact been promised by Miles and subsequently Sheridan that upon reaching Indian Territory they would be permitted to keep the guns and ponies that had been issued them. Ben Clarke, their interpreter, attempted to make this clear to Mauck, but without avail (Senate, *Report . . . on the Removal of the Northern Cheyennes*, p. vi). In official documents and in correspondence, the surname of Clarke appears sometimes with, sometimes without the final *e*.

58. In a report on his completed assignment as commander of the military escort to Little Chief's people, dated December 24, 1878, at Fort Elliott, Mauck made no mention of the incident's tense character (DMO LR). However, two officers who were part of his command left accounts of their impressions. One, Second Lieutenant Wilber E. Wilder, Fourth Cavalry, described the scene in which Mauck, accompanied by his scout and interpreter Amos Chapman, walked the few rods between the soldiers' camp and that of the Indians to sit down with them in council: "The proposition was laid before them; was received with true Indian imperturbability, and rejected with dignity and decision. Chapman argued and protested with them a few minutes, until seeing the wrath of the bucks getting hotter, he said to Mauck that if they were going to get away alive they must be about it. So Mauck got up slowly and quietly moved toward the entrance, with Chapman after him. Not a moment too soon. He had scarcely risen from his place, when a knife slit down the canvass of the teepe from the outside, and a furious young buck sprang through the opening, crying: 'Let me kill —— thief! Let me kill him!' And he would have killed him if Mauck had not moved when he did. But that instant peril passed, the other chiefs restrained the hot head and Mauck and Chapman got back to camp and the protection of the troops" (*The Papers of the Order of Indian Wars*, p. 91).

Another officer, Second Lieutenant Heber W. Creel, Seventh Cavalry, had been assigned to live with the Northern Cheyennes in Indian Territory while learning their language and preparing an English-Cheyenne dictionary. Creel was in the Indians' camp when they learned of the order from General Pope. For several hours, he wrote, "the camp was in a wild state of confusion and excitement. My tent in the midst of the encampment was filled to its utmost capacity with women and children—guns cocked, arrows drawn. I remained in the midst of these Indians, which they still remember" (Creel to Major Barbar, June 5, 1879—OIA LR, C&A).

an attack on them would simply have been a massacre.   They had only about 14 Rifles all told & were not at all dangerous.   From all I can gather the whole affair was a strong commentary on the miserable inefficiency of a Govt, whose promises are not binding.[59]

Arrived at Camp Supply abt 1 pm, & went to Capt. Lyster, Comdg. He & wife are very kind & hospitable.   After dinner got a box & sent 14 Turkeys to Hd. Qrs. by stage.[60]   Wrote to Taylor about them – also a short note to Trout & to Comdg. Off[icer] Ft Dodge. Played a few games billiards.   Had a pleasant evening, & went to bed 11.30 pm. We have to remain here 3 days.

Distance 17 miles – 1 quail

December 3. Camp Supply

Nothing to add.   Spent the day very quietly   Played billiards at night for the delectation of the Offs & Ladies of the Post.   Beat the Post Champion every game very easily.[61]

Only a few Officers here & the Post extremely dull.   Wrote note to Father & Mother also one to Julia –

A quail hunt is proposed for tomorrow –

December 4

Intended to go out hunting quail today, but felt too tired & good for nothing.   Lyster & Remington went, but got only 8, after a hard days work.   Played several games of billiards, & bought some little presents

59. On December 19 Pope explained his reason for issuing the order of November 29. He had just learned that, on instructions from the Commissioner of Indian Affairs, the acting agent at the Cheyenne and Arapaho agency, Charles E. Campbell, refused to receive the Indians under Little Chief unless they were first disarmed and dismounted. Thus, even though he was then unaware of the promises made by other Army officers, Pope had no choice but to order them broken (Pope to AAG MDM, December 19, 1878—SW LS).

60. Captain William J. Lyster, Nineteenth Infantry, had assumed command at Camp Supply on October 22, his predecessor Major Henry A. Hambright of the same regiment having been transferred to Fort Dodge to fill the vacancy created by the death of Lieutenant Colonel Lewis. Freight on Dodge's turkeys, which were sent to the chief commissary of subsistence at Fort Leavenworth, was three dollars.

61. Dodge was a superior billiards player, rarely beaten. See BHJ, pp. 40, 41, 238, 244, 246; PREJ, p. 167.

Clarence Mauck (U.S. Army Military History Institute)

for Joe & Laura.[62]   Took a nap in afternoon, & wore the day away after
a weary fashion.   Only one day more here if it please the Powers.

Dined with Lieut. Ives son of Ives of Engrs. (resigned Rebel & dead)

December 5

Just a month since I left home.   To look back on it, it seems like
half a year.   Went around with Lyster & looked at his Post.   It is large,
badly constructed, illy situated.   That he cant help.   It is dilapidated
& dirty, which he could help at least to some extent.[63]   Played a few
games of billiards with Lt. Bud,[64] in the morning.   Took a nap in afternoon, during which Mrs. Lyster's brother arrived with the transportation we have been impatiently waiting for.

Returned all my calls – first on Lieut Vance, who is a bachelor,
then on Lt Ives, whose mother arrived today   Found her very
pleasant, & we had many memories in common.   Her husband
was hardly a friend, as we were not much together, but I knew &
liked him.   She is a rank Catholic, & came near embracing me
when I told her I was ba<b>ptised by Bishop Ives.[65]   Next on Dr.
[blank] and wife.   They leave for NY in a few days.[66]   We leave

62. The presents for Dodge's servants cost eight dollars, no inconsiderable sum.
His mess bill for the entire month from November 8 to December 8 was $29.04.

63. A spacious installation with barracks for six companies that were occupied
by only three, Camp Supply was exposed to almost constant winds from the south
and west. All its buildings had been erected or rebuilt since 1872 (MDM, *Outline
Descriptions*, pp. 70–71). Photographs of Camp Supply during this era are in Carriker,
Fort Supply, following p. 112.

64. First Lieutenant Otho W. Budd, Fourth Cavalry, the post quartermaster and
commissary of subsistence.

65. Dodge called first on First Lieutenant Richard Vance of Company A,
Nineteenth Infantry, then on Second Lieutenant Edward Ives of Company B. See the
journal entry for December 4. Ives' father, Joseph C. Ives, was West Point graduate
in the same class as Dodge. He served in the Confederate Army and died in 1868. Levi
Silliman Ives (1797–1867) was elected Protestant Episcopal bishop of North Carolina
in 1831. In the years that followed he was influenced by the Tractarian Movement in
England and came to favor Roman Catholic teachings and practices, developments
in his spiritual life that spawned much controversy. In 1852 Bishop Ives deposed
himself as bishop and converted to the Roman Catholic church. His *The Trials of a
Mind in Its Progress Toward Catholicism* appeared in 1854.

66. Acting Assistant Surgeon T. A. Davis was bound first to Fort Leavenworth as
a witness before a Retiring Board (*ANJ*, December 7, 1878, p. 283).

tomorro.   Spent the evening pleasantly at Lysters.   He is an excellent kind hearted hospitable man, & his wife is a very agreeable & pretty woman.   I have been most kindly & pleasantly entertained. Gave orders for the wagon to get an early start.   We will go leisurely after breakfast –

December 6

Wagons reported late & that for baggage proved too small.   Another was ordered, & we got off with flying colors 10 am[67]   Day cold & a biting wind directly in our faces –

Soon after getting to Buffalo Springs all the mules gave evidence of playing out, & it transpired that the 3 teams were all new, & had not before been driven in a trot.   By hard work we got to the Cimarron Ranche at 5.30 p.m. almost dark, without accident.   The mules were not broken down, but only leg weary from being driven at an unaccustomed gait.

Got a tolerable supper & a passable room.   To bed early –

Distance 36 miles

December 7

Sent baggage off very early.   Started, ourselves at 8.30.   Cold raw & very disagreeable day, threatening snow or rain.   Our team is an aggravating one – looks as if it were working tremendously, but all its efforts are up & down.   However I wont abuse it, as we came into Bluff Ck Station at a quarter past 2 p.m. "in good order & well conditioned."[68] 30 miles in 5.45 hours –

Ranche full of the wild element of the frontier.   Might draw a picture or make a story of it.   At least 30 men, good bad and indifferent. Respectable men, sat cheek by jowl, in amiable conversation with horse thieves & train robbers.

67. A map of the wagon road between Camp Supply and Dodge City, with a cutoff to Fort Dodge at Mulberry Creek, a few miles south of the city, is in Haywood, *Trails South*, pp. [18]–[19].

68. Formula phrases used in reports to describe troops, horses, stores, or equipment on arrival. See also the journal entry for May 10, 1880.

Until quite late, numbers were added to our party.   One hard looking case came in, looking for prisoners escaped from the Dodge jail.   Later two, half & half, might be anything from preachers to train robbers came in looking for a horse thief.   R & I had all to ourselves the only good room of the house – each with a large double bed. When bed time came we went & had a good nights rest (this being written in the morning).   Where the other 20 guests are stored is a question – but they all seem to acquiesce in the arrangement, & to admit our right to the room.   All sat together in the bar room after supper & discussed the subjects of Indians & horse thieves.   They were well posted in the Dull Knife affair, & gave many particulars of the escape, which if true would go very far to d—— the 4th Cavy. as a nest of cowards.   Several were with Lewis when he was killed & say that there was but a single Cavy. Captain with his Compy in that

fight.   All   ∧   were safely collected at the wagons.   Mauck comes
                Capts

in for charges not only of incompetence but cowardice.   One of his principle guides, here last night, saying publicly that whenever Mauck came in sight of the Indians he always halted to lunch, or something else.   He says M caught the Indians several times.   He further states that M did *not* stop at Carlisle <for> because the guides could not take the trail over the R.R. (as M told me in his letter)[69] that the trail was taken over to the Saline by 12 m. & that the Indians were not over 2 or 3 hours ahead.   On the Sappas M. came in sight of the Indian rear G[uar]d., & on Frenchmans the whole Comd was in good charging distance of the Indians – in plain view – & stopped 2 hours to lunch. I dont believe these stories fully, but they are worth investigating.

December 8

Got off soon after 8 a.m.   Miserable day cold & very windy. Crossed Arkansas without accident & arrived Ft Dodge 12 m - 18 miles.

---

69. Dodge must have heard from Mauck before leaving Fort Hays, for in his manuscript account of the Northern Cheyennes' outbreak he described Mauck's Indian scouts as requiring much of the afternoon on September 29 to locate the trail leading north from the Kansas Pacific Rail Road.

Went to Remington's house.   Soon after call on Maj Hambright, the Comdg Offr.

Found Cowles here with ambulance, wagons my horse, &c – but the weather is so bad that I determined to take cars.   Cowles recommended me to do so as there is no game on the road across.   All the Offs & some of the ladies came to see me.   Tremaine is not at the post[70]   Played several games of Billiards with Vernou one of the Crack young players of the present age, & beat him easily.[71]   I played

in good luck however.   He ought to have beat me, as ^{he was used to} <T>the table <he> & the light very poor for my old eyes –

Cowles went to Dodge[72] with me, & saw me off.   Got a berth & soon went to bed – bound for Topeka.

December 9

Woke up on time & had a good breakfast.   Arrived at Topeka after 12 & it was a question if I could catch the west-bound train on the K.P. Got my trunk out with all expedition, took a hack offering the driver double fare if he would make the connection.   That "fotch" him & I arrived just in time – but missed my dinner which I wanted badly. Got supper at Aberline[73] – a good one & made up for the lost dinner. Got into conversation with a man named Fitch, on the cars, & had a pleasant talk.   He is about to settle at Russell.

Arrived at Hays City 1.15 am of the 10th.   Had telegraphed to Trout to send for me, & was met by an ambulance.   Got over all safe – found fires & lights but nobody to meet me.   Shall bully them all

---

70. Dodge's old friend Assistant Surgeon William S. Tremaine was at Fort Leavenworth, appearing as a witness before the retiring board in session there.

71. This was First Lieutenant Charles A. Vernou, Nineteenth Infantry.

72. Neither Dodge City nor Fort Dodge was named after Richard Irving Dodge. The former took its name from Grenville Mellen Dodge (1831–1916), engineer and Civil War general, who after the war became chief engineer for construction of the Union Pacific, the Texas Pacific, and other railroads. Fort Dodge was probably named for Colonel Henry Dodge, First U.S. Dragoons (Frazer, *Forts of the West*, p. 52; Roberts, *Encyclopedia of Historic Forts*, p. 294).

73. Abilene—spelled in the nineteenth century *Abeline*—was about 120 miles east from Hays City.

tomorro for their laziness.   Dont feel a bit sleepy, though it is now near 2. a.m.

Have been absent just five weeks, & had take it all in all a most delightful trip.

Cowles brought me two or three letters to Ft Dodge & I hope to find some here but I dont see anything of them yet.

December 10

Up late – sent word to Capt Hinton to do the Office work as I was too late for it.[74]   After Breakfast went all over the Post, & inspected everything.   <It>All is in admirable condition & the Amount of work done by Trout during my absence is really wonderful.

He actually surprised me with the quantity & quality of his work The stables & cowsheds of all the Officers are completed as I ordered. The men's Qrs ceiled & partitioned, & the ice house, which was my bug bear, is ready for ice, though not yet done.   Another month of good weather & I'll have the prettiest cleanest & best arranged post in this Dept –

The Hospital fence is done, & the whole building painted inside & out.   Looks first rate.

I had all these works cut out & started before I left, & I ordered the work to go on during my absence.   It is a great satisfaction though a rare one to be able to go away for a month or two & return to find that everything has gone on according to your wishes, & as rapidly & well as if you had been present.

That I can do here.

And now you see dear Dad & Mam, what constitutes a real good time on a hunt – for I have had a "real good time" & enjoyed every moment of the outdoor life.   We could of course have bagged much more game, by working harder, & hunting at night, but we got as much as we could get along with.   We took into Camp Supply nearly 60 turkeys, & would have brought them to our posts, but for the

---

74. During Dodge's absence Captain James Henton was post commander.

unfortunate delay of 3 days there.   As it was I sent a box containing 14 by stage to Dodge City to be shipped to Dept Hd Qrs.   Remington sent about the same number to his post Ft. Dodge.   The remainder we divided among the Offs & men of Supply.

Joe & Laura tell me I am as thin as a rail, but I weigh 200 lbs yet, though my pants & drawers are a "world too wide"[75] at the waist.   I have not had a moment's sickness since I arrived at Fort Sill

I thought you might like to know what we live on in the woods so I leave the Mess account just as it is.   You will see that we nearly starved as we went along –   I took all my Mess outfit, which is very complete, & we had everything about as nice & comfortable as if we had been at home & a deal cheaper.

I have not entered in my diary into any description of Country. That would take too much time & labor.   The Indian Territory is however one of the most beautiful & fertile portions of our vast Country, perfect for the growth of cotton, & it is a sin & shame that so magnificent a country, capable of well sustaining 10 millions of people should be set aside for 50 thousand red vagabonds, about on a par with the white corn-crackers of the South.

It will not last long, however.   Sentimental foolishness will not be allowed to stand much longer in the way of the advance of civilization.[76]

Keep this book with the other – until I come[77]

75. An apt quotation from *As You Like It* II.vii.59–60, describing "His youthful hose, well saved, a world too wide / For his shrunk shank."

76. An unusually harsh comment by Dodge, except for its characteristic impatience with the "sentimental foolishness" of those who idealize Indians, valuing their interests above those of the progressive American citizenry. See below, pp. 419, 430.

77. The text that follows, on pp. [57V]–[55R], is omitted here. Written with the notebook in reversed position, it consists of two itemized lists, one for a mess account, the other for other expenses. The initial heading and a long account entry for November 4 are in ink; the remainder is in pencil.

Commentary on Journal Three
A Controversy, Consultations, and a Winter Mission

THE RETURN TO FORT HAYS WAS GRATIFYING TO Dodge both personally and professionally, for not only had he enjoyed "a real good time" on his fall hunt, but he found improvements moving ahead just as he wished. The discord at Fort Sill and the sense of imminent violence in that region seemed far distant as he resumed activity in his local sphere. The post trader, Hill P. Wilson of Hays City, had abruptly resigned, and a council of administration now had to meet to select a successor. Company commanders reported complaints that bread from the new bakehouse was inedible; a board of survey should meet to consider the matter. Space was at a premium in the officer's quarters, and some of the younger men were jealous of the living arrangements others enjoyed. To alleviate the latter problem, Dodge recommended to the departmental adjutant that the post chaplain and one of the two post surgeons be assigned elsewhere.[1] He stood fast against an appeal regarding his dismissal of Mrs. O'Keefe, a "troublesome woman," from her position as an authorized laundress.[2] He convened a garrison court-martial to try men accused of minor infractions.

1. Hill P. Wilson to C. O. Fort Hays, October 30, 1878 (Fort Hays LR); S.O. 42, December 18, 1878, Fort Hays; Second Lieutenant Calvin W. Cowles to Post Adjutant, Fort Hays, November 27, 1878 (AGO Register LR); RID to AAG DMO, December 12, 1878. Dodge wrote on December 12 that the presence of the post chaplain, David White, was "of little importance" since various religious denominations held services regularly in Hays City (Fort Hays LS).
2. Endorsement, November 2, 1878 (Fort Hays LS). Mrs. O'Keefe, who had been discharged for bad conduct, was the wife of a private who had been transferred from Fort Leavenworth to Fort Hays without consultation with his new company commander at the latter post. Dodge suspected that authorities at Fort Leavenworth had arranged the transfer as a means of "getting rid of a troublesome woman."

In general, he attended to problems that arose from day to day within the garrison, maintaining only general oversight of the improvements being completed under Lieutenant Trout. Dodge was accustomed to performing the duties of a post commander and enjoyed his role. Though not without its bickerings and dissatisfactions, Fort Hays was on the whole a comfortable place to be.

As a post commander, Dodge was solicitous for the welfare of the men under his charge but took seriously the injunction in the *Revised Army Regulations* that "the duty of every officer . . . [is] to exercise a rigid economy in the public expenses."[3] Jealous of the prerogatives of his office, he was quite willing to engage in debate over matters of military procedure that he thought material,[4] and although capable of expressing himself with considerable subtlety, when aroused he was not disposed to mince words. These traits of character were all displayed in a confrontation between Dodge and a departmental staff officer in November and December 1878. Conducted according to official protocol and involving multiple bills of lading, receipts, affidavits, endorsements, official and unofficial correspondence, and two reports of board of survey proceedings, each done in triplicate, this incident of friction between staff and line was a manifest waste of time and public funds. Its seriocomic character was heightened by the officious self-importance of the offended party, the departmental commissary of subsistence. Throughout the difficulty Dodge kept his temper and exhibited a wise sense of proportion, even though some loose words of his own had helped fan the initial flames. What he termed in private "the important potato question"[5] was hardly an earthshaking matter, but it did involve real issues of official responsibility and the proper conduct of government business.

3. *Revised Army Regulations*, p. 98.
4. For example, earlier in the year he had drawn attention to a conflict between paragraphs in the *Revised Army Regulations* of 1873 and Lieutenant Colonel Emory Upton's *A New System of Infantry Tactics*, then in use as a military textbook. See AG to RID, July 11, 1878 (AGO LS).
5. See the journal entry for November 18, 1878.

The trouble began on October 25 with the shipment to Fort Hays of 123 sacks of peach blow potatoes by Captain C. A. Woodruff, post commissary of subsistence at Fort Leavenworth. The potatoes had been purchased in the public market at Leavenworth, Kansas, at a price of sixty-three cents per bushel. Even before they had arrived at Fort Hays, Dodge expressed alarm to Woodruff at their "exhorbitant" price. Enclosing slips cut from recent issues of Leavenworth newspapers that showed potatoes offered there on October 24 at twenty-five cents per bushel,[6] he noted that in requisitioning the shipment he had wished it furnished as reasonably as possible. Even in the vicinity of Fort Hays, potatoes were for sale at thirty cents a bushel. Dodge wondered whether Woodruff's invoice price was an error. If not, "I must, in justice to the officers and men of my Command protest against it. They should not (and shall not if I can help it)" be required to pay extra for foodstuffs available at Hays City for half the price. "The potatoes you sent," he concluded, "are likely to be a dead loss to the government."[7]

To complicate the matter, on the arrival of the potatoes Trout reported that they weighed less than the gross amount shown on Woodruff's invoice, 16,668 pounds, and that they were very dirty. Accordingly, on November 1 Dodge convened a board of survey to report on their condition and quality. The next day three officers, Captains Henton, Pollock, and Greenleaf Goodale, weighed all 123 sacks and, selecting three at random, emptied their contents onto the storeroom floor. The gross weight was only 16,283 pounds, and each of the three emptied bags was found to include stones, coal clinkers, pieces of mortar, and dirt. Factoring the amount of foreign matter in the three bags, the board determined that a tare of 586 pounds, 13 ounces should be deducted from the shipment, leaving 15,696 pounds, 3 ounces of potatoes as the amount for which, as post commissary of

6. In its "Home Markets" section, the *Leavenworth Times* quoted the current local price of potatoes at twenty-five cents per bushel between October 20 and 26. Peach blow potatoes were not listed as for sale until November 1, when they were quoted at fifty cents per bushel.

7. RID to C. A. Woodruff, October 31, 1878 (Fort Hays LS)

subsistence, Trout should be responsible. It noted, too, that potatoes for sale at Hays City and recently advertised at Leavenworth were much less costly than these, which were of "average" quality.[8]

Dodge's letter about the price of the potatoes reached Captain Woodruff on November 2. Forwarding it at once to his superior, Captain Jeremiah H. Gilman, chief commissary of subsistence of the Department of the Missouri, Woodruff contented himself with observing that the market reports Dodge had enclosed were "a most unreliable guide."[9] But Gilman took the matter more seriously. That same day he telegraphed Trout, directing him to return the potatoes at once. Even before the written proceedings of the board of survey at Fort Hays reached Gilman on November 5, he had taken steps to vindicate himself against offensive statements made by Dodge. A few days earlier Dodge had written him an unofficial letter in which, assuming that he had employed a purchasing agent, he asserted that the agent "was undoubtedly guilty of fraud, or most gross neglect of duty."[10] This incensed Gilman, for he had been his own purchasing agent. He resented the imputation of dishonesty or incompetence and at once wrote a reply which reached Dodge at Fort Sill on November 18. Dodge responded that same day, withdrawing the charge of fraud but reiterating his objection to the high price.

A board of survey such as the one at Fort Hays had no power to dispose of property. Its function was simply to establish data through which questions of administrative responsibility could be answered and the adjustment of accounts made possible. Its work was complete upon approval of the commanding officer who had convened it, though that approval could be set aside and another board ordered by higher authority.[11] On November 6 Gilman recommended to General Pope that the Fort Hays proceedings be set aside and another board

8. "Proceedings of a Board of Survey, Convened at Fort Hays, Kansas [November 2, 1878]" (Fort Hays LR).

9. Endorsement, November 2, enclosed with Jeremiah H. Gilman to RID, December 18, 1878 (Fort Hays LR).

10. The quotation is from RID to AAG DMO, December 19, 1878 (Fort Hays LS). Dodge explained here that he had lost the first letter he wrote Gilman.

11. *Revised Army Regulations*, pp. 101–02.

convened. His one thousand–word statement seethed with anger, not so much at the board members as at Dodge. Gilman deemed it his *"duty, just* and *proper,"* to report Dodge's objectionable actions: first, in requisitioning for potatoes from Leavenworth when he could get them cheaper at Hays City; second, in writing to Captain Woodruff in a manner that reflected on Gilman and in basing his remarks on a mere newspaper quotation; and third, in ordering a board of survey about a matter—the price of potatoes at Leavenworth—he could not pretend to know from direct experience, and in denying Gilman "(whose efficiency or integrity . . . [was] apparently called in question)" or any other competent person an opportunity to appear before that board.[12]

The potatoes having been received back at Fort Leavenworth on November 9, Pope agreed to convene a new board of survey to examine them, especially with regard to the foreign matter alleged by the officers at Fort Hays to have been sacked with them. This body, consisting of Major D. G. Swaim, judge-advocate general of the department, Captain William McKee Dunn, Jr., Pope's senior aide-de-camp, and First Lieutenant Stillé, Twenty-third Infantry, met at 11:00 A.M. on November 12 in the quartermaster's shed. The board weighed the potatoes and supervised as they were emptied sack by sack onto the storehouse floor. Members picked up some "clinkers and small stones" but found that these impurities totaled only sixteen pounds for all 123 sacks. The 747 pounds net that had been lost by the shipment since first being sent to Fort Hays two weeks before they attributed to shrinkage and the numerous times the potatoes had since been handled. In all, board members judged it "an exceptionally fine lot of 'Peach Blow' potatoes, of uniform size, apparently entirely free from disease, or decay, and unusually free from dirt."[13] Writing in the absence of Gilman, Woodruff recommended in his endorsement of the board's proceedings that the

12. Endorsement, November 6, 1878, with "Proceedings of a Board of Survey Convened at Fort Hays, Kansas [November 2, 1878]" (Fort Hays LR).
13. "Proceedings of a Board of Survey Convened at Fort Leavenworth, Kansas [November 12, 1878]" (Fort Hays LR). On November 11 two employees of the Subsistence Department had made affidavit that on handling the potatoes for shipment they had found them in good condition and as free from dirt as usual when shipped in the fall. These affidavits were attached to the proceedings of the board.

potatoes be sold at cost price to officers and employees at Fort Leavenworth, and on November 23 Pope approved that course.

Captain Gilman had now officially cleared himself and his office from blame, but the points at issue between him and Dodge had not yet been completely resolved in his favor, for the proceedings of the Fort Hays board of survey had not yet been disapproved by the commanding general. That delay may have been owing in part to Gilman's absence for consultations in Washington, D.C.[14] The more probable cause was Pope's unwillingness to perform any official act that might then be countermanded by a junior officer such as Gilman. Recently, despite a threat of court-martial leveled against him, Pope had declined to take action on two boards of survey that had been convened at Fort Leavenworth to condemn certain ordnance stores. General Sherman supported him in his stand, pointing out to the secretary of war on December 7 that as the Army was then constituted, approval or disapproval even by a general officer like Pope was liable to be overruled by a junior officer attached to one of the staff departments—the Commissaries of Subsistence, the Engineers, the Signal Corps, the Ordnance Department, and others. Sherman cited a comment by General William H. Harrison, later president of the United States, that military commanders, not staff officers, must rule the Army—a view with which Pope heartily agreed.[15] In the present case,

14. See *ANJ*, November 23, 1878, p. 247; November 30, 1878, p. 267.

15. Sherman to George W. McCrary, Secretary of War, December 7, 1878 (AGO LS). In a letter of January 2, 1878, on the proposed reorganization of the Army, Pope offered an example of the inconveniences that could occur as the result of authority over staff officers being vested in departments centralized in Washington, D.C. Even though an arsenal, a unit governed by the Ordnance Department, was located at Fort Leavenworth, Pope had no authority as department commander to procure even a single cartridge there. He needed to forward "a requisition for it to division headquarters in Chicago, to be thence forwarded to the Adjutant-General of the Army for the General-in-Chief; and as neither of these officials had any more authority than I to order its issue, the requisition went to the Secretary of War, from him to the Chief of Ordnance, and thence back to me through the same channel" (House, *Report . . . Relating to Reorganization of the Army*, p. 28). Exactly one year later, Pope used the same example in a letter to Sherman on a reorganization bill then before Congress. See *ANJ*, January 18, 1879, p. 409. For a general discussion of the strained relations between staff departments and the regular command structure of the Army during these years, see Utley, *Frontier Regulars*, pp. 28–33.

should he approve the Fort Hays board of survey, his action might well be reversed by a captain. Of course, he recognized that except for its real organizational implications, the whole affair was much ado over next to nothing. On December 16 he concluded his involvement in the matter by disapproving the Fort Hays board of survey "and so much of the order convening it as directs it to report on the invoice price of the potatoes."[16]

Gilman was now in a position to declare triumph over Dodge, who appears to have taken no interest whatever in the potato shipment since being reminded of it at Fort Sill. On December 18 Gilman addressed Dodge a lengthy letter, enclosing a copy of the board proceedings at Fort Leavenworth and emphasizing that the board "saw *Every sack* emptied, examined the *entire lot*, sack by sack and found the potatoes to be in excellent condition." He and his family had since tried these potatoes at his own table, he wrote, and he judged them the best he had eaten that year. He ended by observing that the peach blows Dodge had objected to were the finest available variety, the quality of the original shipment excellent, and its price appropriate given market conditions.[17]

The peach blow incident was concluded with two letters by Dodge, one addressed to General Pope through his adjutant, the other directly to Gilman. To Pope he wrote that from his point of view the problem had been solved by the return of the potatoes from Fort Hays. Contrary to the early objections of Gilman, Dodge argued, "I believe that my action has been right and proper and but justice to my command." As to his having convened a board of survey whose proceedings Pope had disapproved, he offered no apology. In fact, he addressed the very topic that Pope himself had made an issue of not long before—the power of staff officers.

> I beg to remind the Department Commander that every post is to some extent at the mercy of the Department Staff, and that "Boards of Survey"

16. Endorsement, December 16, "Proceedings of a Board of Survey, Convened at Fort Hays, Kansas [November 2, 1878]" (Fort Hays LR).

17. Gilman to RID, December 18, 1878 (Fort Hays LR). The last statement was doubtful at best; see note 6 above.

are one of the means by which a Post Commander may protect his Command.

If I have no power to order a Board to inquire into the invoice price of Articles sent for the purchase and use of my Command, I have no power to protect that command from any excessive (or even fraudulent) charge that the invoicing officer might make. The Staff Officer rises above investigation, & the troops suffer.

Earlier, Dodge had not seen Gilman's long endorsement objecting to his letter of October 31 and the original board of survey proceedings, but he rebutted that endorsement now, reasserting his original claims. He made no personal reflections on Gilman, except in regard to his taste in potatoes: "I doubt if one man in fifty can tell the difference in taste between peach blows and other potatoes. Assuming therefore the truth of Captain Gilman's statement that this particular variety were so extravagantly high priced as compared with others, his obvious course would seem to have been to buy the other Varieties. He might have invoiced the same fancy potatoes with the same right and the same argument in his favor."[18] The letter to Gilman was briefer and, though confined to the matter of potatoes, not unfriendly. Quoting a word and a phrase from Gilman's recent letter, he was "glad to be able to say that, 'while I yet regard the price of the potatoes as exhorbitant,' I am satisfied there was no intent to defraud or 'swindle.'"[19]

Several years before, Dodge had confided to his wife that he possessed "something of a bump of obstinacy, & a *suspicion* of vanity. I think I can run a post as well as any man who has not been half as long . . . in service as I have been."[20] In recent weeks he had confirmed both parts of this playful self-analysis, for while not hesitating to call into question Gilman's practices and not backing down when his action had been objected to and even officially disapproved, as a post commander he had done his duty and given general satisfaction.

18. RID to AAG DMO, December 19, 1878 (Fort Hays LS).
19. RID to Gilman, December 21, 1878 (Fort Hays LS).
20. RID to Julia R. P. Dodge, November 21, 1869 (Dodge Papers, Yale Collection). Dodge was comparing himself to Captain William H. Penrose, Third Infantry, his immediate predecessor as post commander at Fort Lyon, Colorado.

Meanwhile affairs at Fort Hays went ahead smoothly, and awareness of events elsewhere within the region came more or less at random, from telegraph messages, newspapers, magazines, correspondence, and the reports of travelers. Dodge can only have guessed that conditions in Indian Territory would soon require his return there.

On December 19, explaining to General Sheridan the circumstances that had dictated his ordering the "friendly" Northern Cheyennes under Little Chief to be disarmed and dismounted, General Pope wrote that the Army's unintentional reneging on promises made earlier was not the sole cause of their hostility and disposition to make trouble. So long as the Indian Bureau failed to supply sufficient food, violence was inevitable. By statute the Army was forbidden to issue rations to Indians unless they were categorized as prisoners of war, and then only until they could be turned over to their lawful custodian, the Indian Bureau; thus, the Army was all but powerless to lessen the Indians' desperate resentment. Pope warned that he considered affairs in Indian Territory "critical" and the available military force, especially cavalry, "entirely inadequate" to protect the frontier should more Indians break away.[21]

In recent weeks post commanders at Forts Elliott, Reno, and Sill and Camp Supply had all voiced their concerns to Pope. Although midwinter was not ordinarily a season when military action was made necessary by Indian unrest, the winter of 1878–1879 seemed a likely exception to that rule. Pope forwarded to Sheridan the reports of his men in the field, urging that something be done soon. The latter comprehended fully the difficulties faced by field officers who were expected to give orders that could result in annihilation of their command by a superior foe, and he shared Pope's belief that the number of troops in Indian Territory was insufficient to meet a crisis.[22] The question he faced was where to position his forces given the constantly changing number and seriousness of trouble spots along a frontier that extended for more than a thousand miles. Ultimately, of

21. Pope to AAG MDM, December 19, 1878 (AGO LR).
22. Sheridan to AG, November 19, 1878 (AGO LR).

course, that question was the responsibility of the General of the Army and the secretary of war to answer.

On December 23 General Sherman responded to the expressed concerns of his department and division commanders by directing Pope to send troops from Forts Leavenworth and Riley to the Indian Territory. The six companies then at Fort Leavenworth were all of an infantry regiment, the Twenty-third, and the three at Fort Riley were also infantry, the Sixteenth Regiment. Sherman was willing to commit almost a full regiment to the region as a deterrent force, but the problem of where to place them remained. On December 24 Sheridan telegraphed him that the posts in the most dangerous section of Indian Territory had no quarters for more troops but that the reinforcements could go into camp somewhere, living in tents as they had done in far colder regions in the north.[23] On December 27 Sheridan modified his plan, reporting that ten companies from Fort Leavenworth and "other posts" would go to Camp Supply and Fort Reno. He had directed Pope, he informed Sherman, to send the whole of the Twenty-third Infantry to those two posts.[24]

Most of the frequent communications during these days passed between Sherman and Sheridan by telegraph, but on December 26 Pope sent a written letter to Sheridan that addressed the present initiative in a thoughtful fashion and strongly influenced the military policy then taking shape. Observing that deep snow and cold weather made travel away from main roads impossible for a time, Pope assured Sheridan that the Twenty-third Infantry would move "as soon as it can be done, without unnecessary hardship and exposure." He proposed to send four companies to Camp Supply but to establish the other six in a temporary winter cantonment along either the North Fork of the Canadian River or the Cimarron River a few miles north of it, midway between Camp Supply and Fort Reno. He thought this course prudent

23. Sheridan to Sherman, December 24, 1878 (AGO LR).
24. Sheridan to Sherman, December 27, 1878 (AGO LR). In fact, Camp Supply did have space for three more companies than the three already stationed there; Fort Reno, with a garrison of four companies, could accommodate no more troops in its barracks.

both in a military view and because the troops could make themselves more comfortable during winter in the timber of that country than in an exposed camp near one of the posts. The cantonment would be a suitable site "for one of a cordon of posts which must soon be established around the Indian Territory if the present divided jurisdiction over the wild tribes be kept up." The proposed new installation would have obvious strategic advantages, being situated near the line of journey traditionally followed by the Cheyennes and Arapahos as they moved north and south across land now forming part of the state of Kansas. Without the deterrence promised by the cantonment, "this whole frontier is in constant danger."

In Pope's opinion, the troops that could best protect surrounding states from incursions by Indians were cavalry, but given their unavailability, it was necessary "to do the best we can with the Infantry." Although of little value for forced marches or rapid evolutions in the field, infantry troops "would accomplish a most important task" if posted in "immediate contact" with the Indians and given power to control their conduct. Exactly how the infantry were to exercise this control given the limitations imposed on the Army by law was a matter that Pope did not address. "What we need here is Cavalry," he concluded. "Without it there is always danger of unavailing pursuit."[25]

Sheridan agreed wholeheartedly with Pope's assessment. He inquired of Brigadier General O. C. Ord, commander of the Department of Texas, whether six companies of cavalry could be spared from that organization. Ord proposed posting them within his own territory, the Llano Estacado region of northern Texas. However, on December 31 Sheridan telegraphed to Sherman that he preferred posting the companies at Forts Sill and Elliott. He would do so, he added, if Sherman thought conditions in Texas warranted the reduction in force there.[26] But Sherman was satisfied with his own first determination. "The true policy," he responded, "is for Genl Pope to reenforce the Posts in the Indian Country, viz Sill, Elliott, Supply, Dodge &c, with his

25. Pope to Sheridan, December 26, 1878 (AGO LR).
26. Sheridan to AG, December 31, 1878 (AGO LR).

Reserve viz the 23rd Infantry, and not call for help till he has used every man subject to his orders. Meantime," he concluded, "the Indian Bureau will be asked to keep their Indians at home."[27]

Neither Sheridan nor Sherman commented in these exchanges on the proposal by Pope to establish a cantonment, except perhaps for Sherman's "&c" at the end of his listing of posts. The issues they had in view were whether to send infantry or cavalry troops, from what postings those troops would be transferred, and how many men would be redeployed. However, Sherman continued to reflect on Pope's letter of December 26, which he thought stated the case "fully and well." In an endorsement of January 8, 1879, he contrasted the notion of a establishing a line of posts along the frontier of Indian Territory with neighboring states—Pope's "cordon of posts"—with another idea, of placing troops well within the territory, near the agencies. The latter would be the more economical plan. "It will require ten or twenty times as many men on the Circumference, as it would at the Center, to control these or any other indians liable to become hostile, from provocation, hunger, desperation or any other cause."[28] A cantonment located as Pope had suggested would enable the Army to stay in reasonably close touch with the Indians in their accustomed places of residence but would also permit troops to be sent to the frontiers of neighboring states with little delay.

Left free to pursue the plans he had outlined to his superiors, Pope followed that course. Suddenly the Twenty-third Infantry, Dodge's regiment, was at the center of emerging events. On December 26 the departmental adjutant informed Dodge that the regiment would take post in Indian Territory at "quite an early day" and that preparations for the move should begin.[29] Three days later he learned that Pope had entrusted to him the responsibility of selecting a site for the new cantonment. Except that the assignment was to be completed "without undue delay," the letter of instructions he received included only general guidelines. Given the remoteness of the post, troops there

27. Sherman to Sheridan, January 1, 1879 (AGO LR).
28. Sherman was endorsing Pope's letter of December 26, 1878 (AGO LR).
29. AAG DMO to C.O. Fort Hays, December 26, 1878 (Fort Hays LR).

would need to provide shelter for themselves from whatever resources might be found in the vicinity. The temporary site might possibly become that of a permanent garrison, so questions of year-round healthfulness should be considered. Dodge was to examine carefully a particular section of country, but the specific position within that region was for him to determine.[30]

The receipt of these instructions prompted a rapid flurry of activity by Dodge. He contacted the post commanders at Fort Dodge and Camp Supply to bespeak transportation and escort troops, emphasizing that he was on urgent business. He telegraphed the departmental engineer officer for a copy of the latest maps. He packed his winter clothing. Ready to take the field, at 2:00 A.M. on December 31 he set out on the circuitous railroad journey to Dodge City, and aboard the train later that day he began compiling a daily journal of his experiences on this official errand.[31]

Although not without intervals of delay owing to poor train connections, snowdrifts, difficult terrain, and similar causes, in the month to come Dodge's schedule of activity was demanding. The journey from Camp Supply to study the terrain around Barrel Springs on the North Fork took him through deep snow, often in wind and chilling cold.[32] The country between that point and the Cimarron River, the vicinity of which he likened to a compartment of Dante's Hell, was the most difficult he had ever passed through with wagons. Winter weather made the selection of a specific post site impossible, but he succeeded in determining an approximate location and was confident that in better conditions making a final choice would be a simple matter. The return to Camp Supply, across terrain made treacherous by thawing ice and boggy soil, required exquisite caution and also a measure of luck. More than once Dodge admitted in the journal that he needed rest. Yet despite the challenging physical difficulties he faced, he clearly enjoyed the assignment. Reduced to reliance upon

30. AAG DMO to RID, December 27, 1878 (Fort Hays LR).

31. On the front cover of the journal he wrote a title: "Site for New Post."

32. On January 30, 1879, a correspondent from Fort Dodge informed the editor of the *Army and Navy Journal* that "Our weather for the past two months has been the most severe known for years on the Plains" (February 15, 1879, p. 492)

his own skill, he took positive pleasure in dealing with the obstacles that confronted him. The mission also brought with it a genuine social satisfaction, for it placed him in close contact with Amos Chapman, the scout and interpreter at Camp Supply. Dodge was to share many experiences with Chapman in the two years to come, but from the first he recognized in him "a remarkable man."[33]

Dodge returned to Fort Hays on January 21, well satisfied with what he had accomplished, but exhausted. Later that day he was summoned by telegraph to Fort Leavenworth for an interview with the department commander. "If ever a poor fellow was pushed about its me," he remarked in his journal, only half humorously. The visit to Fort Leavenworth was itself filled with activity. It included a series of lively greetings from "the boys," his fellow officers, but its chief feature was a three-hour conversation with Pope, on matters official and otherwise, that each man seems to have found delightful. The meeting raised to a new level the mutual esteem between the two officers. Pope approved Dodge's report, and probably at this time he confirmed his intention to designate him the commander of the new post. Dodge was now free to return to his station and prepare his command for departure. The final words in his journal entry for January 31, 1879, written after his return, are "Nothing new"—words in utter contrast to the impression of burgeoning eventfulness conveyed by the entire text preceding them.

For a short time after Dodge's departure from Fort Hays on December 31, preparations for the regimental change of station had continued apace. On January 2 a request reached the adjutant general's office in Washington, D.C., for authority to purchase eighty mules for use on the march from Fort Dodge to Camp Supply and in service there and at "Cantonment."[34] On January 3 Lieutenant Trout received orders to prepare estimates at Fort Leavenworth of the supplies that would be needed at the new post.[35] However, within a few more days the mood of urgency began to abate. On January 8 Sherman

33. From Dodge's journal entry for January 6, 1879.
34. AAG MDM to AG, January 2, 1879 (AGO Register LR).
35. AAG DMO to C.O. Fort Hays, January 3, 1879 (Fort Hays LR).

John Pope (Massachusetts Commandery, M.O.L.L.U.S., U.S. Army Military History Institute)

telegraphed to Sheridan that conditions in Indian Territory did not seem so pressing as to require Pope to send out the Twenty-third Infantry until the worst of the winter was over, perhaps in March. The next day Sheridan replied that he had directed Pope not to put the troops into the field until February 1, when the weather ought to permit it. Sherman answered that Sheridan and Pope could decide together when the time was right. However, he added, "I have raided in Kansas, and have experienced in March weather of fearful severity. The fact that the troops are to go to that frontier will produce the necessary moral effect."[36]

This was a sensible view, and in regard to maintaining the peace in Indian Territory in the coming weeks, it proved correct. Yet Sherman's reasoning failed to account for a disastrous sequence of events that was to commence that same night, January 9, at Fort Robinson, Nebraska. Undeterred by bitter winter weather and unbowed by the moral effect of their confinement under guard at the fort, a group of Northern Cheyennes under Dull Knife broke away from their locked barracks and fled into the night once again. They had refused to return to the Indian Territory, as the government now demanded they do. Their rations had been ordered cut off in order to force their acquiescence, but they would not submit to starvation. They were determined to return to their ancestral hunting ranges or else to die in the effort.

Unaware of this new outbreak and its tragic results in the days that followed,[37] four hundred miles south Dodge pursued his strenuous

36. Sherman to Sheridan, January 8, 1879; Sheridan to Sherman, January 9, 1879; Sherman to Sheridan, January 9, 1879 (AGO LR).

37. Official documents relating to the incident, in which by January 13 thirty-five Northern Cheyennes had been recaptured and thirty killed, are in Senate, *Letter . . . Communicating Information in Relation to the Escape of the Northern Cheyenne Indians from Fort Robinson, passim.* On January 18 Sherman ordered an investigation and report on the circumstances surrounding the escape and pursuit from Fort Robinson of the Northern Cheyennes. The report, dated February 26, 1879, is in AGO LR but is also available on microfilm: Microcopy M666, Roll 429, National Archives and Records Administration. See also *ANJ*, February 1, 1879, p. 452–53; March 15, 1879, p. 571. Modern accounts include Grinnell, *The Fighting Cheyennes*, pp. 414–27; Sandoz, *Cheyenne Autumn*, pp. 194–230; Powell, *Sweet Medicine*, 1:241–77 and *People of the Sacred Mountain*, 2:1202–28.

task of locating the site for a new post that would exert a restraining effect on potentially rebellious Indians. Would a single temporary post in Indian Territory, manned by infantry, accomplish the ambitious aims Pope had attached to it? Perhaps so, perhaps not; the question was not for Dodge to answer. Confident foreknowledge was impossible to come by, even for experienced generals like those under whom he served. Had Dodge learned of the second Dull Knife outbreak while on his winter mission, he would perhaps have felt a vague alarm, but no real surprise, for he had gained some understanding of the Cheyennes. Meanwhile, he had his orders.

Journal Three
December 31, 1878–
January 31, 1879

December 31, 1878[1]

In obedience to orders to proceed to the Indian Terry. to select a site for a new Cantonment to be occupied by 6 Comps of 23d Infy I started at 2 a.m. for the Depot at Hays City, at 2.20 took the train & was in a few moments sound asleep.   Woke up in time for breakfast.

Just before arriving at Junction City, <it>we came to a dead halt, a freight train east of us having run off the track.   We had to wait about 3 hours – which brought us into Topeka after the train west had left. There was a bare chance to catch it, & I pushed across to the St Fe Road, but was too late.   There was nothing for it but to stop over – so I went to the Tefft House – kept by McMeekin.[2]   Had a tip top

1. This manuscript journal, of a size and type identical to Journals One and Two, includes fifty-seven unnumbered pages. On its front cover Dodge has written in black ink, "No 3 - [/] - [/] Dec 31, 1878 [/] Jany 31, 1879. [/] - [/] Site for [/] New Post." On the back cover he wrote, also in ink, "No 3 - [/] Jany 1879 [/] [*flourish*]." Except for these identifications, the journal is written entirely in pencil. Pages [1V] and [57R] are blank. Following p. [55R], two sheets and part of a third, pp. [57V]–[55V] in the original sequence, are written with the notebook in reversed position. On p. [1R] Dodge drew three fragmentary sketches of a route, shown by a dotted line, along a watercourse. The most detailed of these includes the labels "High Ridges," "Timbered Ridge," and "Bare Bend." Page [1V] is blank; the text begins on p. [2R].
2. Home of the general office and yard of the Atchison, Topeka and Santa Fe Rail Road, Topeka, Kansas, was the point of departure for many of the company's trains traveling south and west and a junction point with other railroads. See Bryant, *History of the Atchison, Topeka and Santa Fe Railway*, p. [xv]. 'The Tefft House, with 150 rooms ranging in price from two to three dollars per night, was the leading hotel in Topeka. Hayden W. McMeekin (1822–1895) was among the founders of several hotels in Kansas, including the Planters House at Leavenworth and the Hale House at Junction City (Wilder, *Annals of Kansas*, p. 1153).

dinner at 6 pm   Played a game or two of billiards, & went to bed about 9.30.   Was waked up by the Town Band playing Old Year out & New Year in, but I didn't stay to hear it.

January 1, 1879

Was waked by a long droning cry, like that of a man in sore distress, & it was only on<t> its repetition that I recognized that some unfortunate & undoubtedly hungry Negro was yelling Brekfu-u-st!   Got up & had a very good "brekfust."   Went out after & made some purchases.[3]   Met Peck, & some other acquaintances.[4]   Took several drinks & played a game of billiards with one of the champions of Topeka & beat him.   Got a good dinner & soon after went to the Cars.   Got a good berth & all right.   Between Scranton & Burlingame we stuck in a snow drift, where we are at this writing.[5]   We have only 3 passenger cars, yet we have 3 Locomotives & a snow plough in front of us –   We have not budged an inch for an hour, & as it is near dark we have every prospect of spending the night here. At this rate I get to Dodge some of these days –

Soon after the above was written we got out of the drift & as far as Osage City where we got supper – 9 pm & a very good one considering that 50 hungry men made a raid on one country Hotel.   Started again with 5 Loco[motive]s – 3 on the snow plough, & 2 on train.   In about 2 miles the plough ran off the track in a heavy cut, & after working a long time our train returned to side track at Osage, & I went to bed after a few games of whist in which 2 players knew nothing. Hard work all day and made 35 miles

January 2, 1879

Wakened by bumping of cars, & found we were off.   Slowly we worked along, & at 12 m arrived at Florence where we should have taken supper last night.   Here we got breakfast – they called it dinner.

3. A list of purchases at the end of the journal includes entries of $4.15 for "Boots & ex[tra] soles," $2.50 for "Over Shirt," and $.50 for "Suspenders."
4. George R. Peck was the U.S. Attorney for the District of Kansas.
5. Scranton and Burlingame were only a few miles south of Topeka, and the village called Osage City, mentioned later in the entry, was at the thirty-mile mark along the 310-mile route from Topeka to Dodge City.

Today is clear & still, the wind-storm of yesterday which closed the tracks to us, having ceased as suddenly as it came.

We abandoned our Snow Plough and its 3 Locos. at Emporia, & are now, 4 pm getting along finely – played several games of whist with unmitigated disgust – my partner having no more idea of the game than if he had never seen a card yet having the luck to hold hands, on which we should have skinned our opponents but losing everything by his ignorance —

Took supper at Kinsley & arrived at Dodge City 9.30 pm.   Went to Hotel where I met Dr. Wilcox, who with wife & children is en route from Supply to New York.[6]   After chatting a little while a man came up, & said he had an ambulance to take me to the post.   Got my baggage & started at once.   Arrived about 10.30 & went to Tremain's who I found in bed.[7]   He got up, made me very welcome, dressed, & we sat down to a regular old time "gas" –   He had no whiskey so I was obliged to provide that prime necessity to a good "gas" – & we had a pleasant time till 1 am of 3d – when I let him off.

January 3, 1879

A Sergeant reported to me before I was out of bed this morning.   I ordered all to be in readiness at 10 am   Got a tip top breakfast.   Remington Bradford & Vernou came in soon after.   Sent off baggage wagon on time.   Went over to the Office to pay my respects to Comdr.

me to give

He had telegrams for me from Platte – one asking ∧ name of Qr. Mr. of New Post.[8]   The other authorizing me to take Amos Chapman on my search after a post site.   I also recd. from

6. On orders from the Headquarters of the Army, Assistant Surgeon T. E. Wilcox had left Camp Supply for New York City on the morning of December 31.

7. In his telegram of December 29 to the commanding officer at Fort Dodge, Dodge had written: "Shall be at Dodge City morning of 1st January and wish to leave same day for Camp Supply. Please have ambulance and escort ready, and ask Tremaine to have bedding for me" (Fort Hays LS).

8. Dodge misspelled the surname of Major Edward R. Platt, adjutant general for the Department of the Missouri. As he indicated later in this day's entry, as his choice for quartermaster he named First Lieutenant Trout.

Ruffner[9] four bundles of cloth maps of Indian Terry.   I got off about 11 a.m.   Stopped in Dodge City to get a cover for my gun – also to telegraph my selection of Trout as Qr. Mr.   I found my escort in Town, tho' I had ordered the Sergt. not to stop.   Cleared him out – & followed.   All the party were more or less drunk.   One man lost his gun – another came near being left in the snow.   It was bitter cold, & though I was so bundled I could scarcely move, I was cold. The water froze in my canteen bundled up in my buffalo robes.   It is a long dreary road at any time, but with the whole vast expanse wrapped in white, it was desolate.   In some places the snow was very deep, but we made excellent time considering all the circumstances.

                                                          Ranche
    I thought I never would get to Bluff Creek   ∧   , but just at dark, it appeared.   It is not a very inviting looking place but it was very welcome to me.   My men were almost frozen, & I'm sure I would have been had I been exposed as they were.   Got supper, went out & took a look at the mules, & gave stringent orders to the Sergt. about the Guard.

    It must certainly be 30 miles to Ft D. by the Town.   My mules are all feeding well & I hope to have no trouble   Wrote to Father & to Genl Pope

January 4, 1879

    Had an attack of dyspepsia & dysentery combined, & was forced to get out twice in the night, which, with the thermometer at zero, & no sign of Modern Conveniences[10] was slightly disgusting!

    Had a pretty good breakfast & started 8.30 a.m.   A nasty, cold, miserable day.   Too cold to snow hard, but all day at intervals, a puff of wind would send the particles fine as frozen fog, into ones face & eyes – disgusting!!

---

9. First Lieutenant Ernest H. Ruffner was engineer officer of the department.
    10. According to the *Oxford English Dictionary*, the use of "convenience" to signify indoor plumbing was a recent extension of the word's meaning.

Met the stage on top of the high divide north of Bear Ck.   Was yelled at & in a moment Dr. O'Brien came crawling out.[11]   We were both sights to behold – bundled beyond recognition by our anxious Mama's, yet with red eyes & pinched noses, showing that it was cold.

After the Dr. started I was compelled, on the high divide – ther[momete]r. about 0, & wind cutting like a rag machine, to make obeysance to dysentery –   Very highly disgusting –

Per contra to these miseries almost all the snow seems to have stopped short at that high divide.   From there to Cimarron we have had but little, the road being bare & excellent.   We made splendid time arriving at Cimarron Ranche at a quarter to 2 pm 5 1/4 hours coming about 26 miles – maybe more.

This is not so comfortable or clean a place as Bluff Ck, but there is a stove in my room & I need not stay in the bar room for warmth. Took a little nap.   Had dinner at 4 p.m.   Read played solitaire, & went to bed – after giving orders for guard – & for tomorro's start –

January 5, 1879

Started 8 am –   The road was not so good as yesterday, yet not bad. It was much warmer & more pleasant, & tho' still cold, I did not suffer. Arrived at Camp Supply 3.15 pm – 35 miles – very good time, considering roads.

There is not nearly so much snow here as at Dodge.   Went to Lysters house & was hospitably received.   Made arrangements to start tomorro if possible – but they're rather slow here   Sent for Amos Chapman at once & he soon arrived.   He gave me such information regarding the South side of North fork as determined me to go down on that side as far as Cottonwood grove.   He rather dashed my hope

11. On December 16 Acting Assistant Surgeon O'Brien had been relieved from duty at Fort Hays and ordered to report to Camp Supply (G.O. No. 24—Fort Hays). He and Acting Assistant Surgeon C. H. Shriner, Jr., arrived at Camp Supply on December 29, relieving Assistant Surgeon Wilcox. On the morning of January 3 O'Brien had left the post on a leave of absence, his wife remaining behind in their new quarters. When Dodge met him he was a northbound passenger on the stage line to Dodge City.

of finding a good site on Eagle Chief Ck by informing me that there is little timber & of poorest quality.[12]   I shall see for myself.

Had a lovely dinner, to which I did full justice.   After several officers came in to see me, & we had a very delightful evening.   After all went, I started in to letter writing.   Wrote a six pager to Pope telling him my information & plans.   Another to Father & Mother, & another to Joe.   Ought to have finished all in an hour, but was so constantly talked *at* by, & was so constantly jumping up to talk to somebody, that twas nearly 1 ock when I finished.

Got a good hot bath, took a good drink, then lit my pipe, where I now am writing up this note.   No letters for me.

Monday, January 6, 1879

A sergt reported before breakfast.   I had made out my lists & set him to work.   Lyster was as kind & considerate as possible, furthering my interests in every way.

Last night was the coldest of the season at Supply - -13° - but the morning was bright.   Added a PS to letter to Mam & Dad & wrote to Trout.   Went to Qr. Mr. Com[missar]y.   Store & everywhere else getting ready, & finally got my wagons off at 1 p.m.   Of course I am not outfitted as I would have been had I started from my own post – but I am well satisfied.   I expect to have a rough time, but shall be comfortable unless some accident.

Called for few moments on Mrs O'Brien.   She is thoroughly disgusted with Supply.   Mrs Lyster gave me dinner at 1.30 pm & at 2.30 I started in the ambulance – proposing to camp at Reynolds Ranche.[13] Before starting I donned my warm clothing & was so uncomfortably hot before I got out of the house.   It has been blowing all day, increasing as the day wore on, & tho it was clear when I left the post, there was every indication of a storm, when I got to Camp – 2 hours

12. Chapman knew the territory around Camp Supply intimately, having served as scout and interpreter at the post since 1868.

13. Eight miles from Camp Supply, Reynolds Ranch was one of two ranches on the south side of the river from which Albert E. Reynolds and his partner W. M. D. Lee supplied hay and timber to the post.

later.   The Sergt & wagons had just arrived & were beginning to unhitch team preparatory to Camp, in an entirely exposed spot.   I made him hitch up & we ensconced ourselves in a thicket – rather to the disgust of the men who had to work harder.   By dark we were all ready & the storm struck us –   At this moment the wind is howling & roaring through the trees overhead, & once in a while a fiercer puff shakes my tent –   The cold outside is fearful – & a sort of misty snow fills the air.   I am lying on my back on my bed – (a big fire roaring in opposition to the storm) undressed & with no covering, the tent being really hot.   Amos Chapman the guide and interpreter of my expedition, spent the evening with me.   He is in many respects a remarkable man – a true frontiersman & Indian fighter.   He has lost a leg by an Indian bullet, but gets along first rate.[14]

I think my cook will suit me.[15]   My Mess outfit, is unique – my party seems to be composed of willing men.

If storm continues I will lie here tomorro – good camp – <9>8 miles.

Tuesday, January 7, 1879

Broke Camp 8 am.   The storm lulled about midnight, & the morning was cold, but still, & cloudy.   About 10 am the guide started up a lot of grouse.   A soldier, my orderly, who was on horseback

14. Chapman had won fame for his courage as an Indian fighter on September 12, 1874, when he and five other men bearing dispatches to Camp Supply from Colonel Nelson A. Miles at McClellan Creek, I.T., were attacked by Indians and forced to take refuge in a buffalo wallow, where they defended themselves under siege all that day. In a bold effort to rescue a disabled comrade, Chapman sprang from the depression, ran one hundred yards to the fallen man, and under intense fire shouldered him and returned with him to the place of safety. Only after reaching the buffalo wallow did he realize that during the excitement he had been badly injured. His lower leg was shot off just above the ankle joint, and he had made part of his return trip walking on the exposed bone. Chapman and four surviving comrades were rescued by troops late the next day. Shortly afterward the post surgeon at Camp Supply amputated his wounded limb below the knee, and he was fitted with a wooden prosthesis. (*The Papers of the Order of Indian Wars*, pp. 90–91; Carriker, *Fort Supply*, pp. 97–100; *OWI*, pp. 628–32). Dodge described Chapman in 1880 as "still in the government employ, as useful and as ready for a fight as any two-legged scout" (*OWI*, p. 632).
15. The cook, a Private Smith from Company I, Fourth Cavalry, and the waiter and orderly, Private Adams, had been assigned to Dodge at Camp Supply.

Amos Chapman (Courtesy Archives Division, Oklahoma Historical Society)

ahead, went to firing at them & scared them away before I could get on the theatre of action.   However one fellow gave me a chance & I nailed him.   In looking for the others I bagged 2 rabbits & 6 quail – soon after we came to Lee and Reynolds lower Ranch where I expected to get hay   It is a beautiful place, just between
two lovely little brooks which were as open, & purring along as merrily as if the spring had opened.   Some Mallards were enjoying the open water & though they got up very unexpectedly, I bagged a splendid drake.   I frescoed my wagons with huge bundles of hay, 'till they looked like overloaded pack mules, then went on.   In 8 miles more I struck the regular road,[16] which I followed for 4 miles.   I wanted to go on to Taylor's run – but about noon, the south wind of last night changed to a regular norther bitter & biting, & driving a furious snow storm before it.   I was snugly ensconced in the ambulance, not only not suffering, but not even cold, but Chapman began to show symptoms of weakening.   He evidently wanted to go into camp, & as my journey is not a matter of life & death, I told him to go into the first good place he came to –   So about 3 pm we turned off the road, & heading a little run, fringed with heavy timber we went in between it & the river, finding a most excellent camp.   I went out & amused myself tracking rabbits.   Didn't kill any, for the brush was so thick I could'nt see them, but they evidently thought I was a Fate.

After dinner sketched out my route so far, & wrote up an itinerary. I cant make a map as I have no means, but an Engineer who knows his business ought to make a good map from my description.[17]

16. In a narrative itinerary of the journey for use by the departmental engineer officer in drawing future maps, Dodge described this as a "blind, and not good road. . . . At least two miles . . . was across prairie – marshes impassable when not frozen" (Dodge Papers, Graff Collection).

17. Dodge was himself a skillful mapmaker. In 1875 he supervised preparation of a large map of the Black Hills showing the itinerary of his command through and around them. That map at once took precedence over all that had preceded it, being printed for public distribution and included as a foldout in Dodge's first book, *The Black Hills* (1876). A correspondent from the *Chicago Tribune* who accompanied Dodge on the mission wrote of him in August 1875: "Col. Dodge's greatest weakness is map-making and shooting, and he excels in these two accomplishments to a wonderful degree" (*BHJ*, p. 19 n. 28).

Chapman came in & spent the evening.   20 miles – 1 Grouse – 1 Mallard 2 Rabbits – 6 quail – all inside of half an hour

Wednesday, January 8, 1879

Hurra for Jackson!   Dad, I know you did today, for you always were a *tremenjus* Jackson man!!!(?)[18]

Broke Camp at a few minutes after 8.   Wanted to start earlier but my two (2) B[l]owers could'nt get the fire to burn – & there's no getting up in a tent without fire, & the thermr hugging zero – & zero ought to be ashamed of herself to let him do it so long.   Gave my Sergt. directions to push along as fast as possible, in obedience to which he was 3 hours making 7 miles.   He had an excuse ready of course, but I sat on him a little while.   I took to my horse at Taylors Run & went after Turkeys.   The ground was covered with tracks but I didn't see a turkey –

For about 7 miles from our last nights camp the country is good, well watered & with a good deal of timber.   From Osage Springs to Cottonwood Grove is a long 16 mile stretch of sand hill monotony – no water no wood, only sand & broom sage.   Waited at the Grove for the wagons.   They didn't get there until 3.30 p.m., but as I was willing to pay the Sergt & party for their slow gait in the morning, I determined to push on to Sheridan's Spring 9 miles further.   I got here at 5.15.   The wagons got in at 6.30.   It would have been dark, but for a most glorious full moon.

I am camped at the upper or west end of the famous Sheridans Roost.[19]   Here I am to begin to look for my site – & have already taken

18. January 8 was the anniversary of the Battle of New Orleans, in 1815, wherein Major General Andrew Jackson distinguished himself by repulsing an attempted invasion by the British. Dodge's father had served in the War of 1812, participating in the Battle of Brooklyn Heights against Major General Sir Edward Pakenham, who was later defeated by Jackson at New Orleans (Wheeler, *Reminiscences and Memoirs of North Carolina*, p. 394).

19. In his itinerary entry for January 8, Dodge further described this location: "'Sheridan's Roost' is the name given to a belt of tall timber extending for two miles. It is not on the river. From Taylor's Run to 'Naked Bend' the road is everywhere separated from the river, by from one half to four miles of distance, & by a heavy range of Sand Hills. Just here . . . the river is about a mile off" (Dodge Papers, Graff Collection).

a cursory glance.   I rode out with Chapman after <we>I had selected the Camp ground.   There are several springs.   The one I am camped on is quite large & will furnish enough water for the Post.   There are several very good sites quite together – & I doubt if I find any better.

The surface is everywhere covered with broom sage, an indication of sand, but Chapman says it is not sandy.   I'll dig in tomorro & see. We are just at the west end of the Roost a long stretch of heavy timber principally cotton wood, but elm, walnut, hackberry, the China tree, & Coffee bean intermixed.   North on the sand hills, is a dense growth of small oak – black jack.

I shall not move Camp tomorro, but Chapman I & my orderly will scout over the country on both sides of the river, & make as thorough an exploration as possible.   I see no stone nor any good building material   Saw a fox squirrel today, the first I have ever seen in the far west.   Saw also a fine flock of Mallards – got no shot.   Bagged 9 quail.   Perfectly clear tonight, but very cold – cold & cloudy all day. Indications of good day tomorro.   Distance 32 miles

Wrote my itinerary, & sketched up my map.   Did'nt get my supper until 8.30 – & it is now nearly midnight.

Had a long talk with Chapman, & laid out the work for tomorro –

This is the most famous Turkey Roost known in the west, yet there is not a turkey, not even a track.   Chapman says the Indians have driven them off.   At[20] any rate, I have not seen a single one – nor any sign of one near here ——

Thursday, January 9, 1879

Left the party in camp today, & with Chapman & an Orderly went to "View the Promised Land"

Were out 7 hours, travelled over a good deal of country crossed & recrossed the river.   Found 2 tolerable Post Sites.   The one just here would be first rate, but for 3 drawbacks.   It has not water enough. It is likely to be miasmatic & it is on the wrong side of the river for easy supply.   This last objection may be overcome by supplying the

20. Dodge wrote "It."

post from Wichita –[21]   The first may be obviated by pumps & wells, but the 2d. is insuperable   The site on the other side of river is inferior to this in almost every way, but it is likely to be healthy.   It is a beautiful country and a post here, anywhere will be far preferable to either Supply or Reno.

The Indian would say, I have had "bad medicine" today.   I saw considerable game – turkeys rabbits quail &c – but I always managed to stumble on them just wrong.   I worked hard, & have no doubt I have killed four Turkeys today.   I have bagged just one.

Came back from my unusually long horseback ride tired out, & took a nap.   After I got dinner I wrote out sketches of the advantages & disadvantages of the sites I have found.   Chapman came in & we had a gas on hunting.   Will move a few miles tomorro.

Day delightful – Just cool enough.

Friday, January 10, 1879

Got out of Camp at 8.15.   Cold raw wind from the South, though the sun shone brightly.   Got into ambulance & went ahead.   Looked up a camp near river about a mile south of Barrel Springs.   Leaving ambulance in camp, I mounted my horse & with Chapman & an Orderly, crossed the river to look at some fine rolling slopes on south side.   Rode a considerable distance & was much pleased with the prospect.   Here are in many respects the best sites for a post I have seen.   The slopes rise to 100 feet above the river, are near enough to it for water, are thoroughly drained, & must be perfectly healthy.

Being above the surrounding country there is a fine view.   There is no timber on them & the site will be cold in winter – but it will also be cool in summer.   Just above these slopes[22] the black jack timber comes down in a broad belt to the river.   I looked here carefully hoping to find a good site in the blackjacks, but the ground is too broken.

21. A military road 164 miles in length connected Wichita, Kansas, with Fort Reno, which was approximately equidistant with Camp Supply from Dodge's present position. The latter post received its supplies from Dodge City, 91 miles north of it.
22. That is, upriver.

There is very little timber on S. Side of river here,[23] & there is no first rate place for a Cantonment.

Saw several little flocks of Turkeys, but the Indians have made them very wild.   I got two. – Did'nt hunt much, for I was too anxious to get through my work.   Got back about 2.30 pm.   Took a little nap. Had dinner & then went out for half an hour on an old fashioned rabbit hunt.[24]   Saw 6 or 8, but the little rascals are very sharp.   They sit near a thicket, & when roused dash in as if the D—l was after them. All one can see is a momentary streak of rabbit, so momentary that it is impossible to get even a fair snap shot.   I fired 7 times & got 3 which I consider 1st class work.   My Cook, Smith, a Pvt. of Hempills Compy of Cavy, went out tonight & bagged 2 Turkeys.   A soldier got one, & a teamster one – 6 Turkeys & 3 rabbits all told.   Tried to dig out a Kangaroo Rat.   I have never seen one.   They dig a hole or holes in the ground, in a light sandy soil, always in timber, the roots protecting them greatly.   They then heap up a pile of sticks, at least 3 feet high, & sometimes 5 or 6 feet at base, over the mouth of their hole –   Some of the sticks are quite an inch in diameter, & 10 to 12 inches long, showing Mr. Rat to be an individual of considerable strength   I got a man to help, & we removed the sticks, & dug into the ground.   We found nest & store of seeds nuts &c, but the rat was not to be found.   He dug as fast as we could.   Distance 10 miles –

Saturday, January 11, 1879

Broke camp 8.10.   Marched due north.   Crossed road in a mile, & struck the timber 1 1/2 mile beyond.   Got along very well until we had made about 6 miles when we came to the head breaks of the branches of the Cimarron.   These would be in most cases impassable

23. Dodge meant opposite his present camp on the north side. The "fine rolling slopes" on the south side a short distance downstream were his eventual selection as the best approximate location for the post.

24. By "old fashioned" Dodge probably meant a hunt such as he recalled from boyhood. While on the Powder River Expedition, members of his command once started a rabbit, which ran and hid in a hollow log. "I twisted him out in North Carolina style with a forked stick – very much to the surprise of the officers with me who had never seen it done before" (*PREJ*, p. 69).

even if bare of timber, & with scrub oak growing as thick as possible we found it a terrible job to get along.   We cut & worked our way along for some distance – coming at last to a pocket from which we had to back out – not literally – but we turned around.   The day was cold, & cloudy with spits of snow.   I was tucked away among the buffalo robes & blankets of my ambulance, but the travelling got so bad that I took to my horse.   After a little distance we came to a high knoll, where we could see a long way.   On the left front was a series of steep hills, bluff banks deep Cañons.   On the right was an apparently smooth prairie leading down to a river.   "Thats our way" I said to Chapman.   "We can get along there easily".   "Yes, but Colonel,["] said C. ["]that is the North Fork you are looking at".[25]   I had'nt much to say.   I was turned around completely, but I was not the Guide. Chapman went on his way.   I had mislaid my compass, & he was supposed to know all about the country.   I therefore rode contentedly along side of him.   After an hour, he proposed that I should lead the wagons until he could go off to the left, & see how the land lay.   I did so, for some time, when I heard him call & saw him motioning to me.   He said he had found a route so we all went his way.   I however told him that I must be awfully turned round for I thought he was going wrong.   Not because he thought so, but to satisfy me he pulled out his Compass, took one look at it, & looked sick.   We were going nearly due South   I had been going nearly West Pulling around on our proper course, North, we stuck to it & the compass for near an hour, when we struck our own trail near the pocket we had turned out from 2 hours before[26]   That was too much for my endurance, so riding to a knoll ahead I selected a back bone, & made up my mind to get down it or break something –[27]   We got

25. Dodge wrote a quotation mark after "Yes" at the beginning of this speech.

26. The confusion of Dodge and Chapman, both experienced frontiersmen, bore out the remarks of the former in *PNA* that the "importance of always having a compass cannot be too strongly impressed on all who travel on the plains" (p. 101).

27. By "back bone" Dodge meant what in *PNA* he termed a "divide," the portion of upland that separates one ravine from another. The party's success this day in passing through broken terrain was a practical demonstration of the principles given in the book for maneuvering through broken country. See *PNA*, pp. 93–97.

down, but ambulance & wagons looked after it, as if they had been
throug[h] the wars.

I think it is one of the hardest countries on wagons I have ever
seen.   The hounds[28] of our wagon were broken – so after digging a
crossing of the Creek I went into Camp at 2.30 p.m. having travelled
six & a half hours, & made about 10 miles.   A good many Indians
are encamped in these breaks, which were full of game, deer &
turkeys, before they killed it off.   We passed about 50 going to
Agency, & several came visiting in our camp.   An excelent camp,
tho the water is sweet from Gypsum.   I hope to reach my destination, Eagle Chief Creek, tomorro, & will not likely make a long stay
there.   I have a huge joke on Chapman & he dont like it much.   He
says he expected to have a hard time getting through but he never
expected to strike his own trail.   This only proves further what I
said in my book, that these plainsmen are just as likely to get lost as
other people who do not use the Compass.   If Chapman had not
taken his out to show me that I was wrong, we would have gone
back to the North Fork.   He is very much disgusted, but takes it
quite well –   No game

Sunday, January 12, 1879

Got off in good time & struck up from Creek at once to get on
divide.   After two miles of twisting we got our back bone and
made chain sailing.[29]   The hills are very rough & the cañons impassable for wagons without work – but my strategy nullified them
completely.

The map is entirely wrong not only in the direction of the streams,
but in its topography.   The hills are about 4 miles from the Cimarron
on the route we came – passed "Glass Mountain" so called from its
Gypsum & Selenite glistening in the sun.   It is a portion of the 3d

28. *Hound*: "One of the wooden bars, of which there are two or more, connecting the fore-carriage of a springless wagon . . . with the splinter-bar or shaft; also
occasionally applied to supports of the connexion of the perch with the hind-carriage.
(U.S. and local Eng.)" (*Oxford English Dictionary*).

29. In general, rapid movement made possible by spreading sail in a brisk wind.

Plain.[30]   The top is level, sides abrupt & much torn by water.   I was not very close but estimate it to be about 600 feet above river.   It is nearly 2 miles long, perfectly level on top, apparently, & has several detached abutments – all together looking like a huge fortification. We struck the Cimarron just at the mouth of Glass Mountain Creek. The river is about half a mile wide – a dreary waste of sand.   The water is so salt that it freezes with difficulty, & we came very near getting a wagon stuck.   All the visible water could run in a ditch 20 ft wide by 2 deep – but the sand is full of water for the whole breadth. It is the worst stream to cross on the Continent, & in summer is impassable for wagons for many miles.   If it had not been frozen, I would have had to camp on other side.   Came out on this bank 6 or 800 yards below mouth of Eagle Chief Creek – my destination.

It is a stream of 60 feet water way, in which is now running, a cur-

rent 20 feet wide by 8 or 10 $\overset{\text{in.}}{\wedge}$ deep.   The water is clear & looks nice, but is impregnated with Gypsum so as to be unpalateable – which accounts for its not being frozen

The surroundings are miserable.   The West Side as far as the eye can reach is a jumble of sand hills.   The east side is a prairie, gradually rising to probably 100 feet at a mile from creek.   The soil is a loose mixture of sand, & red earth, & full of gopher holes.   There is very little Timber.   About a mile from Cimarron the Creek has one bluff bank, near 50 feet, from which come several springs of pure water. I am camped near those.   There is no decent place for a post on this stream so far as I can see, & Chapman says that this is the most

---

30. The term *Third Plain* came from geological speculations then current that postulated horizontal upheavals of country. Following a great vertical movement that formed the Rocky Mountains, these upheavals gave three sections of the plains to the east their distinctive character. As Dodge summarized them in *PNA*, the First Plain was formed earliest and is characterized by molten rocks and volcanic tufa that withstand weathering. The Second Plain, forming what became known as the "high plains," is of softer material through which streams have cut deep canyons. The Third Plain, "comprising all the portion from three or four thousand feet above tide water to the general level of the Mississippi Valley, appears to have been very recently formed of material brought from the mountains and upper plains and to have been slowly and gradually lifted or rather tilted out of the waters" (pp. 61–62).

favorable spot on the stream.   I shall not therefore waste time in going up it, especially as the weather is moderating & a thaw might force me to a long detour to get back to Supply.   I shall start back for the N. Fork tomorro.

The Cimarron, which my orders required me to examine,[31] is the worst possible place for a post.   From above the mouth of Buffalo, to below the mouth of Turkey Ck, a distance of nearly 100 miles it is a <b>sand bed from 1/2 mile to 4 miles wide.[32]   Quick sands almost everywhere.   The water is unfit for use, even for cooking, being full of Salt, Gypsum & every other nastiness –   There is scarcely any timber – the banks of the stream are either sand hill or swamp, it is the home of the mosquito, & in summer <the air> a cloud of acrid dust overhangs[33] the stream   If Dante had known of the Cimarron, he would have <cl>had it as one of his Compartments to Hell.   In all the world there is not a man I hate sufficiently to wish to condemn him to live on the Cimarron.   So I dont recommend it very highly to Pope.[34]

It has been rather a pleasant day.   Passed near several Indian camps, & saw the Noble Red Man in all the pride of his native dirt & dignity.[35]   Two who came into our camp last night told Chapman that they had come upon a <lot>party of 5 White hunters.   The Indians

31. Dodge's orders, conveyed in the letter of December 27, 1878, from Pope's adjutant, were to "examine the Country about Barrel Spring and Sheridans Roost . . and that on the Cimmaron about north from the points mentioned on the North Fork." However, in making his selection he was not to consider himself limited to the area within these points, which were "mentioned simply to indicate in a general way the Section in which it is desired to establish the New Post" (Fort Hays LR).

32. Dodge referred to territory as far west as to the Fort Dodge–Camp Supply road. In his itinerary, he wrote: "Except a few springs there is no good water north or south of Cimarron (tributaries) from Bluff Creek on N.W. to Turkey Creek S.E." (Dodge Papers, Graff Collection). Bluff Creek, further north than Buffalo Creek, flowed southeasterly into the Cimarron River.

33. Dodge wrote "overhands."

34. In his official report, Dodge omitted the comparison to Dante's Hell, but he wrote that so far as he could ascertain, there was "not a single spot on the Cimarron, below the mouth of Buffalo Creek, where it would not be simply inhuman to station troops" (Dodge Papers, Graff Collection).

35. A satiric jab at those who, as Dodge elsewhere expressed it, were possessed by "enthusiastic admiration for the 'noble Red Man'" (*OWI*, p. 41).

rode up to the Camp, when one of them put his hand into his pocket to get out his papers to show to the white men, when they imagined he was drawing a pistol, & jumping on their horses, all five took to their heels, leaving their Camp & all in it.   The Indians helped themselves to all the provisions in camp, & came away well satisfied. White men, are not allowed in the Territory, except on business - & these people had no right there.[36]   The Indians ought to have taken their arms & carried the men, prisoners to a Mil[itar]y. post, but I suspect, as there were 5 whites & only 2 Indians, the latter were well content with what they got.

Two wagons & several men passed our Camp this p.m, & there are immense herds of cattle wintering north of here in the Territory - All contrary to Law.[37]   A Post ought to be on this Creek, to stop all this, but the site is too bad.   What with Indians & whites there is very little game.   A fine black tailed deer came near camp.   Our bag today is 1 grouse.   Dist 13 miles –

The country is full of Wolves.   We came today to a spot where they had dug out some rabbits, which had made their home in a deserted prairie dog hole.   The ground was torn up wonderfully considering that it must have been frozen, & near the hole were 3 distinct spirts of blood, showing where 3 rabbits had been got away with.   One was caught within a few feet.   Another ran about 10 & the third about 30 yds.   The wolves struck a bonanza in that hole –

36. Section 2137 in the *Revised Statutes* of the United States provided that persons other than Indians who hunted in Indian Territory except for subsistence there were liable to confiscation of their supplies and peltries and a penalty of five hundred dollars. Section 2118 provided that settlers on lands belonging, secured, or granted by treaty to an Indian tribe were liable to a penalty of one thousand dollars and to be removed from those lands by military force. Section 2147 provided that representatives of the Bureau Office of Indian Affairs had authority to remove from the Indian country all persons found there contrary to law and to call upon military forces to effect the removal (*Revised Statutes*, pp. 373, 370, and 374, respectively).

37. Section 2117 of the *Revised Statutes* provided that any person who drove stock to range on land belonging to any Indian or Indian tribe without the consent of the tribe was liable to a fine of one dollar per animal (p. 370).

Monday, January 13, 1879

Off at usual time.   Found a fine pack of grouse just as we left camp, but they were on burned ground, & could not be forced or persuaded to get into cover.   I followed them a long distance, but they knew the range of a shot gun as well as I, & always got up too far.   I got one however – & wounded several.

Though it was cold last night, (the ther. must have got down to plus 15), the thaw which set in yesterday did not stop.   Consequently there was trouble.   The ambulance driver is a quick active knowing fellow, & gets along always.   The ice in the river was rotten,[38] & I gave directions for every team to go with all speed.   The ambulance passed all right.   Just as the first wagon was at its most critical point a half witted dutchman, (one of those who come over to teach us the art of war)[39] ran out on the ice to see how every thing went, & fell sprawling just in front of the leaders.   They stopped the others stopped, the wagon stopped, & in a moment the ice had given way & all were in the quicksands   Chapman seized the Dutch Gentleman, (a high Private tailor of Vance's Compy,) & threw him into the water.   I could'nt do justice to the subject, & rather than slight it I rode off.[40]   Came across the river, & went to taking Compass sights & sketching the Country. The Dutch – I mean German curiosity cost us an hour of delay, & a great deal of hard work.   I dont care how much of the latter falls on my men for a more utterly worthless party I have never been out with.   The Sergt would be a tip top private, for he works like a beaver himself, but he lets the six lazy privates stand by & see him work.

38. Permeated by water, weakened, and likely to give way if supporting heavy objects.

39. Equating the Dutch with Germans or Prussians, Dodge refers ironically to Prussian principles of military training and organization that had influenced Lieutenant Colonel Emory Upton, a respected Army theorist, in the years since the Franco-Prussian War of 1870–1871.

40. Dodge rode away from the incident because, so far as Amos Chapman was subject to military authority, his treatment of the soldier was a breach of discipline. Rather than make light of it by seeming to condone it, Dodge turned his attention elsewhere. Company A, Nineteenth Infantry, at Camp Supply was under command of First Lieutenant Richard Vance in the absence of its regular commander, Captain J. S. Wharton.

We got all over safe at last, & at 9.45 struck out on our trail of yesterday.   Followed it for about 10 miles, & then struck up the divide.   In going across from here we were going *down* the streams, & the divide was hard to find.   Coming back we were going *up*, & the divide finds itself – (See Dodge on the Plains)[41]   So in spite of the delay in crossing Cimarron, & the hard travelling in the melting snow, we made our camp on North Fork by a little after 4 pm.   Our return journey was a mile or two longer than the going over, in spite of all the turnings around on Saturday.   I could have made it shorter, but the travelling on the broken track was so much better than through the deep unbroken snow, that I stuck to the trail as long as possible. As soon as we had mastered the divide, we turned directly south, & in 2 hours, were through the bug bear, the Black Jacks.   I came on 2 miles west of Barrel Spring, & camped at a bend of the river called "Naked Bend," there being no timber where the road strikes it.[42]   By going up a little way we found a good Camp.   The day has been delightful – too much so in fact, for the snow is melting fast, & I fear that the ice on North Fork will be too rotten to bear us by the time we get to <it>the Crossing.   After getting to Camp, I went out to kill a rabbit, but could'nt find him.   Had dinner about dark.   Chapman came over, & we gassed until 9.30.   After he left I made a map of my trip over & back & I think a good one.[43]   It is now 11 pm very cloudy & I fear we are to have another storm.   I hope it may not rain Distance 25 miles – 2 grouse –

Tuesday, January 14, 1879

Got off at 15 minutes before 8 – the earliest start yet, but I am anxious to make Supply in 2 days if possible.   About 9 am it com-

41. Dodge alludes to his own discussion of travel by wagon in broken country, PNA, pp. 93–99.

42. In his itinerary Dodge further described this location: "All the country hereabouts is flat land, and though not subject to overflow from the river, becomes in the spring a huge lake or series of lakes" (Dodge Papers, Graff Collection).

43. In his itinerary entry for the day Dodge wrote: "Made a sketch at night, which I showed to Chapman, who pronounces it as good as if I had compass & chain, which is complimentary even if not quite true. At any rate it is much more correct than the map I am travelling by" (Dodge Papers, Graff Collection).

menced raining & is at it yet 11 pm & no prospect of a let up.   The snow is going like magic, & sloughs & swamps that we passed over with impunity on ice, only a week ago, now mire almost to the bellies of the mules.   I cant well complain of weather on this trip for I have had every variety, except good, & even of good I have had a specimen. I am very sorry that the cold did not continue.   I dont object to cold weather for one, by bundling up, can always be comfortable.   The cold congeals everything & for a trip like mine is just the thing.   I have crossed & recrossed the North Fork a dozen times on the ice in my search after sites.   If the river had been open I would have been greatly bothered.

Saw immense packs of grouse today, but they are very wild, & as it was raining I would not go after them.   Did'nt hunt at all.   Passed the finest turkey region known to man, without seeing a bird.   Wanted to hunt tonight & hoped to bag 20 or 30 from their roosts, to take in, but the rain, & impenetrable darkness kept us all in.

Camped at Osage Springs, one of my Camps on the Fort Sill trip.[44] Good camp.   Distance 31 miles —

Wrote up my itinerary for Ruffner, & gassed with Chapman until Bedtime —

Wednesday, January 15, 1879

The very worst morning of the trip.   The rain turned to sleet, slush & snow.   It was bitter & very raw, & tho' the actual temperature was not so low by many degrees as some days we have had, it was much more trying.   Got off at 8, & made a break for Camp Supply.   We arrived at my great bug-bear the river, at 10.30 & found it fast enough[45] to allow our teams to get over, though the water was running fast over the ice and it cant last long.   Pushed on over terribly bad road - deep in water & slush & arrived at Supply at 2 pm   6 hours trip - 33 miles, & the worst road out.

---

44. On the nights of November 29 and 30, 1878.
45. That is, the ice was strong enough.

Found letters from Father & Mother, Julia & others.   Old folks terribly worried that I have to leave Hays.   Julia wrapped up in her new found Theatre companions.[46] – Everybody wants <Trdder>

Trader
∧   ship of new post.[47]   Lyster & wife kind as possible.   Paid Comy. bill.   Could get no a/c from store.   All right – I can stand it.[48] No positive news   Jeff & 4 Co[mpanie]s is said to be going to leave 11Worth today.[49]   There is a rumor that I am to return to Hays via 11Worth.   I rather like the idea.   My Comd from Hays cannot start until the transportation gets back that takes Davis to Supply.   Not under 2 weeks.   Vance's Compy left yesterday for Ft Elliott, & Lyster is trembling in his boots.[50]   I shall probably meet Regl Hd Qrs at Dodge & also get orders there.   I start tomorro a.m.   Wrote a postal card to Father, telling him of my safe return.

46. Dodge's wife was becoming acquainted with persons in the New York theater scene through their son, who had adopted the stage name Frederick Paulding and hoped to become a professional actor. On February 17, 1879, he made his debut at the Lyceum Theatre as Bertuccio in Tom Taylor's *The Fool's Revenge*. In the weeks that followed, Fred performed in other New York productions, as Claude Melnotte in Edward Bulwer-Lytton's *The Lady of Lyons* and, especially, as Hamlet. See below, pp. 272–73, 297–303.

47. The information that a new post was to be established quickly became known through newspapers like the *Leavenworth Times* and the *Kansas City Times*, the latter of which regularly printed summaries of important orders issued from headquarters of the Department of the Missouri. In its issue for January 11, the *Army and Navy Journal* reported that Lieutenant Trout was at Fort Leavenworth making arrangements for quartermaster's supplies at a new post (p. 335).

48. The employee in the post trader's store would not accept payment from Dodge for goods he had bespoken. The post traders at Camp Supply, Lee and Reynolds, were energetic applicants for the tradership at the post soon to be established. See the journal entry for January 26.

49. "11Worth" was shorthand for "Fort Leavenworth." The rumor reported here by Dodge was inaccurate, as was another mentioned in the entry for January 16. The headquarters, staff, and band of the Twenty-third Infantry, with companies E, F, and H, left Fort Leavenworth under Colonel Davis ("Jeff") on January 27, arriving at Fort Dodge the next day. Company B left Fort Hays on January 26 and joined the other three companies en route at Topeka.

50. Lieutenant Vance's company was to take post at Fort Elliott, leaving Camp Supply with a garrison of only two companies at a time when the possibility of an Indian outbreak was being taken seriously.

Thursday, January 16, 1879

Sent for Smith & Adams who took care of me on trip & paid them. Also Tailor who fixed my overcoat[51]

Lyster & Wife were both very urgent in their efforts to persuade me to stay over one day, but though I need rest, <I>there is too much to do in front of me – & I determined to push on.   I do need rest greatly, I was so tired last night that I could'nt sleep well.   Mrs Lyster had breakfast for me at 8 1/2, & no sooner was it over than the ambulance came up – same vehicle torn & tattered in its combats with the black jacks, the same mules looking rough as Shetlands after their hard & cold journey of yesterday – & the same driver – a tough wiry little Swede, who never seems to feel cold – –   The weather is beautiful today, & we got off finally at 10 am with everything lovely.

Crossed Beaver & Buffalo without difficulty.   Had some little trouble at Cimarron (& be hanged to it for the meanest stream in the world) but got to the Ranche just at 5 Oclk – 35 miles in 7 hours. We did better yesterday, (33 in 6 hours) <but>and over most horrible roads, but we were then hunting shelter.   Today the road was excellent the weather delightful, & we made the trip, without turning a hair of our tired mules.   We have made 124 miles in 4 days, hunting route one day through dense thickets & deep snow.   News tonight is that the Regtl Hd Qrs do not move until 25, & that I have to wait until the transportation that takes it to Supply can return for me   All right.   I hope the fates will prevent any movement of my Comd until the middle of Feby.   Had a very good dinner at Cimarron Ranche – looked after my mules put out a sentinel & went to bed early. I fear we will have a bad day tomorro –   It is blowing heavily from the south –

Friday, January 17, 1879

Started at 8.30   Road good, & the day better than I expected though a Norther is blowing.   Very little snow until we got on top

---

51. Smith received five dollars, Adams two dollars, and the tailor—the "Dutch Gentleman" whom Chapman had thrown in the river—one dollar.

of divide about Bluff Creek.   Arrived at Bluff Ck Ranche in 5 hours –
27 miles which is good for the same old mules.

Saturday, January 18, 1879

Terribly cold night, & the morning unbearable a furious gale from
the North blowing directly in our faces.   Put off starting until near
10 Ock in hopes the wind would die down.   No use.   Shut myself
in ambulance & put for Dodge

Roads horrible.   Snow very deep – a track is broken but it has been
frozen in lumps, making the travel very bad & fatiguing.

My mules are excellent.   The[y] are not furiously fast but they
make about as good time on bad roads as on good.   Made my journey
of 31 miles at rate of 5 miles per hour.

Stopped at Tremain's.   Went over to Comdg Offr for my mail.
(The old fellow does not know enough of official courtesy, to be aware
that it is his duty to call on me.)[52]   Didn't go in.   Got several letters.
One from Fred, who is elated with his success, as he has a right to be.
Two from Father – &c, &c.   Several Off[icer]s called.   After dinner
packed up my war paint, & got civilized again.   Tremain goes east
with me.   No orders to go to 11Worth as I expected.

Got my transpn. Orders   Went up to town about 9 pm.   Had to
wait over until 12.   Knocked about – got several drinks – &c & just
before cars arrived <got>took an oyster stew.

Train an hour late.   Got sleeping berth & turned in.

Sunday, January 19, 1879

Slept delightfully –   Found on train Capt Bennet 9th Cavy &
Bride.[53]   They were going east on their Honeymoon –

---

52. "When an officer superior in rank to the post commander shall arrive on
official business at any military post, every commissioned officer on duty at the post
is expected to pay him an official visit in uniform" (*Revised Army Regulations*, p.
103). In May 1879 Major Henry A. Hambright, the post commander at Fort Dodge,
was found to be incapacitated owing to disability incident to his military service and
was retired (*ANJ*, May 10, 1879, p. 709).

53. Captain Frank T. Bennett, Ninth Cavalry, was stationed at Fort Wingate, New
Mexico.

Arrived Topeka about 3 p.m. too late for dinner & too early for supper.

Dr. stopped over with me.   (He is going to Atchison to attend Court as a witness.)   He met the Prosecuting Atty at Depot, & was told he could stay over here.   We went to Tefft House – & then adjourned to Poppendicks for a dish of Oysters.   Called on some of the Drs. friends, & had a pleasant afternoon of a stupid kind.   Am very sorry I missed connection here.   It is terribly stupid to be laid by in a country town, where you know few people, & care for less –

Monday, January 20, 1879

Slept tolerably considering how the Dr. snored.   Up at 8 1/2 and got a poor breakfast.   Don't think much of the Tefft House but I guess it is the best in town.   After breakfast went with Tremaine to call on Johnson of St Fe R. R.   He made us go up to see the Presdt. – Strong – a live man[54]   Had a pleasant call of a few minutes.   Gave me a yearly pass over his Road – which is a good thing to have.   Met many acquaintances.   Got a poor dinner at 12.30 & soon after went to cars Tremaine going with me to the Depot.   Met Bob Wright[55] & others. Took sleeper & got fairly off 2.30 p.m.   I hear the Regt is ordered to move this day week –

Tried to sleep at night but made a wretched failure of it.   Arrived Hays City 1.30 am & found Trout waiting for me.   Came home had a long talk & got to bed about 3.30 am.   Laura quite sick.

Tuesday, January 21

Waked up early by Joe & the baby.   Got up had breakfast & went to work.   Trout & Jo have done wonders in getting rid of my property, & <Trout> turned over to me about 400 dols.   The horses are

54. A. S. Johnson was acting land agent for the Atchison, Topeka and Santa Fe Rail Road, and William Barstow Strong its vice president and general manager (Poor, *Manual of the Railroads*, p. 878). Bryant describes Strong as "Dynamic, ambitious, highly competitive" (*History of the Atchison, Topeka and Santa Fe Railway*, p. 39).

55. Robert M. Wright, an old friend of Dodge, had been post trader at Fort Dodge since 1867 and was now active in other businesses and as a politician (Connelly, *A Standard History of Kansas and Kansans*, 3: 1219).

gone another 400 left & I am all right.   Letters from Julia, Father
Mother & lots of others.

Have been at work all day.   Made up my report of trip.

Went to see Mrs. Trout.   Recd telegraphic order to go to Ft Leavenworth without delay.[56]   If ever a poor fellow was pushed about its
me.   I am tired out now, yet have to start again tomorro –

Hinton & Compy leave here on 27th.   He is a selection for Regl
Hd Qrs.[57]

Wednesday, January 22, 1879

Up early, & have been hard at work all day.   Completed my report
& the maps to accompany it.   Pollock goes to Denver tonight taking
his wife that far on her journey to San Francisco.[58]   I gave him a list
of my securities connected with the D & R. G. R Wy to get from some
Banker an idea of their value.[59]   Also gave him coupons to amt. of
$38.67 to get cashed for me.   Wrote to Father & Mother.   Packed
up, & am all ready to start.   Had Dr. Comfort examine Laura today.
He says she will not be fit to travel or work for at least a month – so I
am obliged to give up the hope of taking her with me.   As she will
be entirely alone & helpless I have also to give up Joe – who will
remain behind to nurse Laura.   It is pretty hard, but may be for the
best.   They will stay here & come to me with the Officers families in
the spring.[60]

56. Dodge was quoting the order, received at 2:27 p.m.: "Dept Commander
directs that you report in person at these Headquarters without delay" (Fort Hays LR).

57. Captain Henton was in command at Fort Hays between December 31 and
January 24. On departing from the post, he and his company were to take post at
Camp Supply, where the regimental headquarters would be stationed.

58. On September 5, 1883, while accompanying General Sherman on an inspection tour, Dodge paid a call on the Pollocks at Alameda, California, pronouncing them
a "Nice family" (RID Journal, Dodge Papers, Graff Collection).

59. Two of Dodge's friends, William J. Palmer and the late lawyer-entrepreneur
William Blackmore, held large interests in the Denver and Rio Grande Rail Way, and
on their advice he had also invested. The railroad was at this time in danger of
receivership. See Bryant, *History of the Atchison, Topeka and Santa Fe Railway*,
pp. 45–53.

60. Laura had recently given birth to a daughter, Ida.

Sent word to my standby Shob to be ready to go as Cook, & Trout & I will take George to wait on us.[61]   Had quite a levee tonight, all the Offs being in to see me.   Shall write to Julia while waiting for train.

Thursday, January 23, 1879

Finished long letter to Julia about 1 a.m. & at 2.30 took cars.   Got a berth & turned in at once.   Was waked up near Abeline, the breakfast place.   Had a good breakfast.   At Lawrence I telegraphed to Hoyt,[62] for Ambulance & on my arrival at Depot at 11 Worth, took it & was driven to Post.   Went to Randall's house, then to Mess & had dinner.   All the boys appeared glad to see me.   Coppinger took possession of me sent to Randalls house for my baggage.[63]   After dinner I went over to call on Jeff Davis.[64]   After went to see Saxton.[65]   The old fellow let out that we were to be ordered to the new Post via Wichita.   I fought it with all my might but with little success, & went home disgusted with the prospect of having to march over such a country at this season, & determined to fight it out with Pope tomorro.

Friday, January 24, 1879

Soon after breakfast, I went over to see Genl Pope.   Handed in my report, had a most satisfactory interview.   Got the order for my

61. Apparently George was the Negro man whom Dodge had hired as a man-servant at Caddo, I.T., intending to retain him only until they reached Fort Sill.

62. Captain Charles H. Hoyt was depot quartermaster at Fort Leavenworth.

63. Captain George M. Randall, Twenty-third Infantry, an officer known for ability in managing Indian auxiliaries and scouts, was a valued colleague of Dodge. Captain John J. Coppinger of the same regiment had also impressed Dodge with his abilities.

64. This courtesy call was obligatory, yet Dodge appears to have held no lasting enmity toward his regimental commander, with whom on the whole he had a satisfactory working relationship. Nevertheless, Captain Charles King's remark that the lieutenant colonel of a regiment was "rarely, if ever, thoroughly en rapport with the colonel" was probably true in the case of Dodge and Davis (quoted in Knight, *Life and Manners in the Frontier Army*, p. 102).

65. Lieutenant Colonel Rufus Saxton, chief quartermaster for the Department of the Missouri, was a central figure in the debate on this day and the next over the railway depot from which supplies for the new post were to be transported.

march changed & fixed the time of my departure from Ft. Dodge.[66]
Explained to Genl Pope the character of the country – nature of
streams &c – showed & explained my maps (which accompanied
report) & I think satisfied him very fully.   He approved of my selection of site.[67]   Saxton having made a contract for the <ca>trans-
portation of some supplies by Wichita, is terribly worried at my
representations of the nature of that country, & the absence of roads,
he having been positively informed by his Wichita agent, & by the
Contractors that there is a good road nearer than that by Ft Dodge.

The Genl. directed me to designate an Officer to go to Wichita[68] &
examine, & I named Lt Heyl.[69]

After getting through with Genl Pope, I went to town & made
purchases of my hunting equipment &c.   Deposited some money in
Bank ($306.50[)] and attended to commissions of Offs.   Dined with
Clark.[70]   Did'nt visit at night as I wished, not feeling well.   Went to
bed rather early, after receiving many calls, & having a jolly evening.

Saturday, January 25, 1879
After breakfast went over to Hd Qrs.   Had a long & very pleasant
talk with Pope – a little on business, finishing up odds & ends, but

66. Dodge had earlier been to march from Wichita, along the military road south
to Fort Reno as far as Skeleton Ranch, twenty-eight miles into Indian Territory, and
from there southwest across country to the post site. The route was changed to an
established one Dodge knew much better, from Fort Dodge to Camp Supply and from
there to the site. His understanding with Pope about the date of the departure from
Fort Dodge was informal; he did not receive orders until February 15.

67. Dodge concluded his written report, dated January 22, 1879, as follows: "The
best site for the Cantonment and Post in my judgment, is some one of the high
plateaux south of Barrel Spring, on south bank of North Fork . I cannot recommend
any exact location. . . . As all are near together the future selection of the exact
location will be a simple matter of a few hours of survey and study" (Dodge Papers,
Graff Collection).

68. Dodge wrote "Wachita."

69. By S.O. 16, January 25, 1879, DMO, Second Lieutenant Charles H. Heyl,
Twenty-third Infantry, was ordered to proceed from Fort Leavenworth to Wichita
and from there to "a point . . . known as Barrel Spring, for the purposes of examining
into the practicability of the road between those points."

70. First Lieutenant William L. Clarke, Company G, Twenty-third Infantry.

& general

mostly personal   ∧   .   He is an exceedingly interesting man – well informed & a thinker.[71]   We differ on many points but agree in many more.   He has broad views on Army questions & talks well – & has the faculty of inciting me to talk.[72]   Not that I cant do quite my full share at any time, but I seem to myself to talk better to Pope than to any one else.   We had a 3 hours seige all alone by ourselves, & each was so used up that some stimulant was necessary.   I dont know what Pope's was but I went over to Taylor's[73] & got a drink of whiskey.

In this connection I will tell a little story, occurring before I left Leavenworth for Hays.   I was in temporary Command of the Post, & had occasion to write to Dept Hd Qrs on some business.[74]   A day or

71. General Pope's recent biographers, Wallace J. Schutz and Walter N. Trennery, portray him as possessing a retentive memory, an active curiosity, a lively sense of humor, and a capacity for hard work (*Abandoned by Lincoln*, p. 109). They note that since his defeat in 1862 at Second Bull Run, Pope had done much to repair his damaged reputation. After that controversial battle, "Pope spent twenty more productive years in the service in which he restored civil government to Missouri, took part in Reconstruction, was the army's chief expert in Indian affairs, advised on army re-organization and training, helped Western settlement, and wound up as a respected sage, public speaker, and even adviser to presidents" (p. 175). Pope's reputation as a thoughtful man underlay the description of him seated at a court martial in New York, looking "more like a savant than a General" (*ANJ*, April 12, 1879, p. 656).

72. A taste for conversation and facility in it were characteristics shared by Pope and Dodge. In 1862 a journalist had written of Pope that he "talks rapidly, and is rather fond of it, as an exercise or diversion" (Schutz and Trenerry, *Abandoned by Lincoln*, p. 169). Pope also enjoyed some reputation as an orator; see *ANJ*, November 22, 1879, p. 303. On the other hand, an admiring journalist wrote of Dodge in 1875: "He is a close student, a keen observer, and a fine conversationalist, and of course loves to talk; but, when a man can talk well, he is pardonable in any little display of vanity" (*BHJ*, p. 19 n. 28). Colonel Edwin P. Pendleton, who reported to Company I, Twenty-third Infantry, following his graduation from West Point in 1879, remembered Dodge as "a famous raconteur and brilliant conversationalist" (Shirk, "Military Duty on the Western Frontier," p. 121).

73. The residence of First Lieutenant Daniel M. Taylor, Dodge's companion on the Fort Sill trip.

74. Dodge was in temporary command at Fort Leavenworth December 18, 1877-January 21, 1878, February 3-May 18, 1878, and June 1-July 11, 1878. The post commander's building at the fort was two short blocks—perhaps 500 feet—from that of the commanding general (MDM, *Outline Descriptions*, p. 52).

two after I was in Pope's Office when he said, "Dodge I wish you would quit writing letters.   If you want anything or anything goes wrong, come over & we will talk about it" –   "No you dont" I replied, "you can beat me talking hollow, & I'd have no show to get anything that way, but I can beat you writing" –   There was quite a laugh at his expense & all passed off nicely, but it was an awful piece of vanity on my part, for Pope is one of the clearest, most logical & most forcible writers I know —[75]

Ordered a lot of things from Keeling.[76]   Didnt feel well.   Am malariously inclined.   Must take quinine when I got back to Hays. Took a nap in afternoon.   Dined with Pardee & wife   Nothing specially hilarious – not suited exactly.   Called on Mrs Pope & on Mrs Nichols at night[77] – On my return to Cops'[78] (who called with me) we found a lot of fellows – took a drink or two & gassed for an hour very pleasantly.   Went to bed rather early.

Sunday, January 26, 1879

Woke up early, packed my bag, & got all ready to start   Got breakfast, & pulled out after bidding good by to the fellows about me.

75. Pope's fluency and perspicacity as a writer was another quality he shared with Dodge. The flow of his letters and opinions was sometimes daunting to his superiors. Sheridan, who lacked this gift for expression, once implied to Sherman that Pope seemed more committed to carrying on discussions than to getting things done (Sheridan to Sherman, December 24, 1878—AGO LR). In March 1880 Sherman was attempting to obtain answers from the secretary of war to queries he had received from Pope, when to his alarm he received another set. He passed these along to the secretary but telegraphed to Pope, "please don't ask any more questions till the old ones are answered" (Sherman to Pope, March 6, 1880—AGO LS).

76. W. H. Keeling, the post trader at Fort Leavenworth. In 1884 Keeling also ran a hotel "opposite Infantry Barracks" at the fort (Schindler, *A Guide. Description of Fort Leavenworth*, p. 101). For a biographical sketch, see Morton, *Illustrated History of Nebraska*, 2:697.

77. First Lieutenant Julius H. Pardee was attached to Company D, Twenty-third Infantry, one of those that had marched with Dodge in pursuit of the Northern Cheyennes. Mrs. Nichols was the wife of Second Lieutenant William A. Nichols, Company H, one of the mounted infantry units that had marched under Major Alexander H. Dallas.

78. Coppinger's.

Met Reynolds at Depot & had quite a time with him.   He is a good fellow.   In 1869 he was the post trader at Ft Lyon under my Comd.[79] Since then, associated with Lee – as Lee & Reynolds – they have become a power in the land – the kings of the Indian Territory.   I have recd. many telegrams & notes from him asking for the tradership of the new Post – none of which I have answered.   He met me at Ft 11Worth & we had a square talk.   I told him that Keeling was my first choice for Trader not that I liked Keeling any better personally, but because I wanted Competition.   He & Lee were so big & had so much business & so many interests that I preferred to have a man who <c>would be willing to be small enough to attend to the wants of my Command &c.   Of course I cant give a conversation of an hour here. He was "busted", & today he went at me again.   We parted at Lawrence, good friends &, I believe, understanding each other perfectly. He will break Keeling (if he takes the position), or absorb him.   I rather think the latter.

So far as we, the Offs. can act Keeling will be our Post Trader, but Lee & Reynolds will be the power behind the throne.   I would prefer this otherwise but L & R. have money power business tact & a host of friends.   I also met Wilson, the Contractor who wants to put us all through via Wichita.[80]   I told him very frankly that I had broken up this arrangement.   He might have all the freight he wanted, but he could not with my consent, have my Command bumming around hunting a road through a new country for his benefit.   I told him that I wanted the road via Wichita – as competition to Lee & Reynolds – that I would as soon as possible open a good road, that he could go ahead on the contracts for freight, & I would help him all I could, but he could not have the transportation of my Command.   He acquiesced very neatly gave me some cigars took a dangerously big slug of my whiskey & got off at Topeka to help make a Senator.

79. Dodge was post commander at Fort Lyon between October 12, 1869, and February 23, 1871. George A. Reynolds, who ran a general store in Leavenworth, had obtained the post tradership at Fort Lyon in 1867 (Haywood, *Trails South*, p. 124).

80. This was B. C. Wilson, of Wichita, agent for Edward Fenlon of Leavenworth, who supplied beef to the Cheyenne and Arapaho agency.

I am very tired & worn out with all my labors, & was awfully bored by a man on the cars, who insisted on talking to me.   However he was intelligent polite, & seeking information, so I told him all about the Country, & branched off on many other subjects.   We got out at Abaline for Supper.   Just as I stepped out in the dark, this man (as I supposed) said, ["]Col[onel], would'nt you like to have a drink before supper?[81]   There is <a> very good liquor in a saloon near here"

Of course I said Yes.   When we got into the light of the saloon, I was much surprised to find that my entertainer was not the man I supposed but an entire stranger –

However as many people along the line know me by sight whom I dont know, I took it as all right.   I ordered some whiskey, & my new friend laying down a $5 bill called for something.   At the same moment another man came in, pulled out a huge roll of money & asking for a rum punch, tendered a $5 bill.   The bar keeper said "Gentlemen I can change one of those bills but not both."   Whereupon there was an amiable contest between the two, each asking the other to drink.   At last my friend said, "I'll tell you what we'll throw dice for it.["]   Agreed. The dice box was forthcoming.   "I tell you how we'll throw["] said my friend (?)   ["]We'll guess at the number of spots on top & bottom of the 3 dice, & the man who is furthest off shall pay" –   Agreed.   The stranger guessed 45, my friend 21.   The dice were thrown & 21 won. The stranger was petrified with astonishment that my friend should have guessed the exact number, & offered to bet $5 that he could guess nearer next time.   Each thrust a V[82] in my hand as stakeholder & guessed.   Stranger made a wide guess my friend 21 – & I passed the stakes over to him.   I was by this time open eyed in wonder how such a stupid fellow as the stranger, could have kept by him so much money. My friend said, "I'll bet you I can tell the number every time."   "Done for a hundred doll's,["] said stranger, & put up the money.   My *friend* whispered to me, "I hav'nt got a hundred dollars.   Have you got any money?   We've got a dead thing on this man & can win all we want." I smiled blandly, & replied, "I hav'nt got any money to bet on that little

81. Dodge added an unnecessary quotation mark after "supper."
82. A five-dollar bill.

game.   I've travelled too long & seen too many of your kind to invest in that sort of thing."   ["]What do you mean" said my friend.   ["]It's a dead thing, & you dont want to insinuate that there is anything wrong about this thing, do you[?]"   "Oh no," I said.   ["]I am sure its all right, & that you are a perfect gentleman, but I'll lose my supper if I stay here," & I walked out, leaving two as blank looking individuals, as I've seen in many a day –   The game was well played, & I did'nt suspect them until they wanted me to put up the money.   It was a very excellent performance for a little one horse western town & might have imposed on a novice very easily.   Hurra for the *live* West! – I am going hereafter to wear a white choker & plug hat.   My face & person must be very green, to warrant such people trying so transparent a game on me in my old age.   I enjoyed it hugely.[83]

After a tedious journey arrived at Hays City 1.30 am found Trout waiting for me.   Hintons Compy at Depot waiting western train. Got home & to bed as quick as possible, but the boys would'nt let me sleep till nearly 3 am

Monday, January 27, 1879

Found everything all right at Post.   Hinton & Company went last night, or rather this am[84]

Feel malarious & bad.   Have taken to quinine.   Part of the ill feeling, is due to indigestion.   Wrote several letters   One to Fred, it being his birthday.[85]   Laura still in bed very thin & weak.

---

83. A die is constructed so that the sum of the dots on its opposite sides is always seven. The sum of the dots on opposite sides of any three (honest) dice must always be twenty-one.

84. As ordered, Company B joined Companies E, F, and H at Topeka on January 27 and proceeded to Fort Dodge, where the battalion went into camp.

85. Born January 27, 1859, Frederick William Paulding Dodge had the distinction of being the first baby born in the quarters at West Point, where his father was then an instructor of infantry tactics. On September 29 of that year, Mrs. Dodge brought Frederick to the home of his great-granduncle, Washington Irving, near Tarrytown, New York, where according to an observer there were "Great demonstrations about the baby" (Kime, *Pierre M. Irving and Washington Irving*, p. 229). Colonel Dodge was a grandnephew of Washington Irving, and his wife's family was otherwise related to the Irvings by marriage. See Aderman, *A Genealogy of the Irvings of New York*, entries 4, 23, 85.

Tuesday, January 28, 1879

Commenced packing.   Letter from Chf Quarter Master saying that the money given the new post for lumber has been taken away ——[86] D— d— d— d—   Well I guess we can help ourselves.   I am taking everything I can from here, but unfortunately it is impossible to steal lumber enough to do any good.

Wrote to Father & Mother & others.

Wednesday, January 29

Have got through with my heaviest packing - two huge boxes, doing the job.   I take my side board & in it I have packed all my pictures - 2 comforters, 6 blankets <2>one quilt - 3 coverlets, 6 pillows, sheets, pillow cases, everything that would help to fill up. Another box has my sofa - (one is sold), 4 carpets, all the carpet paper, rugs, slips, &c &c &c —   The third has all my books, old papers (important enough to be lugged around -) Window shades, pieces of carpet & a pillow to keep all straight.   I also packed my china & glass (fine)   Not all, but most of it.   Tomorro ought to finish that Dept ——   It is a slow process, packing[87]

Thursday, January 30

Regular old fashioned rainy day - such as one might expect in North Carolina but entirely out of place on the *Plains*

---

86. On January 7, 1879, Colonel Rufus Ingalls, assistant quartermaster general for the Military Division of the Missouri, transferred to Lieutenant Colonel Saxton of the Department of the Missouri three thousand dollars, to be used for building the cantonment that had been authorized. However, on January 17 Saxton notified General Sheridan that, because of obligations created by contracts he had already entered into, he required those funds for other purposes. No more funds were available for use by Dodge. On January 27 General Pope did what he could by requesting of Sheridan "that the money can be furnished ($3000) for buying scantling and shingles for the Cantonment" (AGO LR). Eventually, after much delay, Dodge did receive some of the money he needed.

87. Dodge's living arrangements and furniture were clearly of better quality than the "crude but practical" items described by Knight as ordinarily to be found in officers' quarters. See *Life and Manners in the Frontier Army*, p. 120.

Finished packing my fine china glass, Lamps, shades & other break-able things that I wont need again until I get a house

Nothing new – A note from Randall tells me that Jeff Hd Qrs & the 4 Cos got off all right on 27th.

Friday, January 31, 1879

Woke up to find a furious snow storm raging.   It has snowed all day – with a cold fierce wind from the North.   I have been laughing to myself all day, at the terrific amount of swearing that Poor Jeff is getting off today.   In camp, little wood, & a long march before him.

Wrote a lot of letters.   Went to Hays house[88] to play whist & got wofully beaten.   I think whist is a very miserable game anyhow.   I play a pretty good game but of all games that I know, luck plays the greatest part in this supposing that the players have each a tolerable knowledge of it.

I played against two only ordinary players.   They made blunders, any quantity, but every blunder seemed only to help them.   I saw what I never saw before   Eight tricks taken on suit, before a trump was played.   Diamonds were trumps & I had 5.   One of my opponents led an ace of hearts, then King & Queen – all took.   He then led a small spade, his partner took it with ace, led King, then a small one, & then first took with Queen – then led ace & king of Clubs.   Every card except trumps was led out of my hand.

For 3 hours they held everything, & we were beat so mercilessly that I would'nt play longer & left disgusted with a game in which luck holds so prominent a position —

Nothing new.[89]

88. The home of First Lieutenant Charles Hay, Company C, Twenty-third Infantry, the post adjutant.

89. The text that follows, on pp. [57V]–[55V], is omitted here. Except for the first four lines, details about an investment in bonds, which appear right-side-up on p. [57V], it is written with the notebook in reversed position. The remainder, on pp. [56V]–[55V], is a list of Dodge's expenses between December 31 and January 24. A map on p. [57V] shows a watercourse curving to the northwest, ridges, a mountain, a reference "x," and indications of mileage from it. The chief notations are "Timber," shown as south of the reference mark, and beside the mark "To camp N 15 E."

Commentary on Journal Four
Establishing Cantonment
North Fork Canadian River

ON DECEMBER 30, 1878, THE OFFICIAL NAME OF Camp Supply was changed to Fort Supply, denoting its status as a permanent post.[1] The initial entry for 1879 in the register of letters received by the adjutant general's office at Washington, D.C., related to "Cantonment," the new post at a site to be selected by Dodge.[2] These details of official action mark the heightened attention that Army headquarters was directing to the western sections of Indian Territory bordering on Texas and Kansas. The renewed escape of Dull Knife and his people a few days afterward, this time from the guarded barracks at Fort Robinson, Nebraska, underlined the potentially severe consequences should the Northern Cheyennes still in Indian Territory also attempt flight. Dull Knife's sadly reduced band was no longer a military force to be reckoned with, except as an unwelcome precedent. Little Chief and his people at the agency must be pacified if possible, but in any case they must be kept under control.[3]

1. G.O. 9, December 30, 1878—MDM (AGO Register LR).
2. AAG MDM to AG, January 2, 1879 (AGO Register LR). In the period prior to its existence and for months thereafter, the new post in Indian Territory was designated in various ways: as "the new post," New Cantonment, Cantonment, Canadian River Cantonment, New Cantonement [sic] north fork Canadian River, New Post on the North Fork of the Canadian, and "New Post" on North Fork Canadian River, among other permutations. The term cantonment, ordinarily used as a generic term to designate any temporary post, became by implicit acclamation the proper name given the post established by Dodge. Though intended by General Pope to be granted permanent status, the post was marked by its name as permanently temporary. For the Army's use of *cantonment*, see Frazer, *Forts of the West*, p. xxi.
3. The political cartoonist Thomas Nast produced for *Harper's Weekly* a devastating full- page caricature of Carl Schurz, secretary of the interior. Under the rubric "No More Outbreaks," the secretary was portrayed as a cabinetmaker who had

From the time of his enrollment at the Cheyenne and Arapaho agency, Little Chief, an astute politician, professed his willingness to accept the decision of the United States government as to where he and his people would live. However, he also made known his unalterable desire to return north, as he and his people had been promised they might do if they wished. On several occasions Little Chief assured authorities that he would never seek to take matters into his own hands in the foolhardy way Dull Knife had done. But he was not taken at his word—not so much because he was thought to be lying as because, according to report, members of his band were responding badly to the constraints and privations of reservation life. Second Lieutenant Heber W. Creel, the young officer who was living with the newly arrived Northern Cheyennes, reported to General Sheridan in early March that the Indians were extremely discontented and made grave accusations against Agent Miles, from whom they received little charity or sympathy.[4] Ben Clarke, the post interpreter at Fort Reno who had accompanied the Indians on their journey south from Sidney Barracks, reported similarly to Pope, as did Mizner.[5] Even Charles E. Campbell, Miles's assistant, admitted the difficulties. On March 5 he warned the Commissioner of Indian Affairs that unless decided measures were taken at once, Little Chief and his people would attempt to escape. According to Campbell, the modest Army garrison at Fort Reno would be unable to restrain the Indians. "Contemptible in numbers," he wrote, "they can yet repeat the effort of Dull Knife, Wild Hog & Co."[6] On March 22 the *Army and Navy Journal* published a letter from a "well-informed correspondent" who had recently visited the Cheyenne and Arapaho agency. This person assured the editor that "a more determined set of savages does not exist on the

---

awkwardly attempted to nail shut a rickety chest. However, the drawers of the chest kept flying open (January 25, 1879, p. 61).

4. Creel to AAG MDM, March 7, 1879 (AGO LR).

5. SW to SI [enclosing an affidavit by Clarke], January 4, 1879 (SW LS); Mizner to AAG DMO, April 12, 1879 (OIA LR, C&A). See also SW to SI, January 4, 1879, transmitting the text of a daunting speech to Mizner by Little Chief (SW LS).

6. Campbell to Ezra A. Hayt, March 5, 1879 (OIA LR, C&A).

North American continent than the Northern Cheyennes." The likelihood of their sudden departure must be recognized at once, "so that in the next outbreak, which is considered inevitable, it will be known where to place the responsibility."[7]

The force of such opinions led General Pope to move his reserve troops into Indian Territory with deliberate speed. Under command of Colonel Davis, the headquarters of the Twenty-third Infantry, with companies B, E, F, and H, began the march from Fort Dodge to Fort Supply on February 3, arriving there five days later. Davis assumed command of the post, and Fort Supply now housed a force of five companies, including one of cavalry.[8] Dodge remained at Fort Hays for several more days, until the wagon transportation for his battalion could return to Dodge City and be readied for further use. The work of preparing for the change of station left him no time for impatience. Before resigning command of Fort Hays, he completed an estimate of value for the public property to be left there. He arranged for a baggage car that would accompany his troops, carrying goods and supplies for immediate use, with the balance of supplies to be stored at the fort until it was brought to the cantonment later. He applied for delivery to the new post of ordnance stores from the depot at Jeffersonville Barracks, Missouri. He arranged with the departmental signal officer for issue of odometers and prismatic compasses. He requested an informational circular from the Medical Department. From the adjutant general's office in Washington, D.C., he requested a copy of the *Revised Statutes* and a variety of standard forms for office use. He ascertained that W. H. Keeling, his selection for post trader, had been confirmed in the position by the adjutant general. Sensing that the three thousand dollars earlier allocated for wood to build the cantonment was gone forever, he made the case for a steam-powered sawmill for cutting boards from wood found near the post site.[9]

7. *ANJ*, March 22, 1879, p. 587.

8. Twenty-third Infantry Regimental Return, February 1879; Fort Supply Post Return, February 1879.

9. Documentation of Dodge's duties, in the order given above, is as follows: RID to AAG DMO, February 10, 1879 (AGO Register LR); RID to W. B. Strong, February 17, 1879 (Fort Hays LS); Circular 1, January 27, 1879 (Fort Hays Orders and Circulars);

During days like these when a myriad of details required attention, the cooperation of Lieutenant Trout was most welcome, for as Dodge had once observed, his efficient quartermaster could cause a complex military operation to run "as smoothly as a Sewing machine."[10] He was especially grateful to Trout at this time, for he knew that the press of duty was causing his subaltern considerable physical pain. During his service under Dodge on the Black Hills expedition, Trout's leg and ankle had been badly broken by a falling tree. Although he had recovered sufficiently to perform the ordinary tasks of garrison life, he was unequal to some forms of duty that were expected of a company officer, such as participating in an extended march. Though still far from retirement age, Trout was ready to leave the Army. With regret, on February 9 Dodge forwarded Trout's name to the departmental adjutant, praising him as "an exceptionally valuable officer" but explaining his incapacity and designating him as a proper subject for action by a retiring board.[11] However, sensible of his commanding officer's support and good opinion, Trout had agreed not to end his Army career until the new cantonment was built and running smoothly.[12]

On February 18, 1879, Dodge left Fort Hays with Companies C and K, traveling by regular passenger car to Topeka, where they transferred to two chartered cars occupied by three units from Fort Leavenworth—Companies A, D, and G. Arriving at Dodge City the next day, the battalion remained in camp nearby until February 21, when it began its march, moving twelve miles to Mulberry Creek. The next day it continued to Bluff Creek, fourteen miles; the next, to Bear Creek, eighteen miles; the next, to Cimarron Creek, fourteen miles; the next,

---

Ordnance Office, War Department, to RID, February 17, 1879 (Fort Hays LR); AAG DMO to C.O. Fort Hays, February 10, 1879 (Fort Hays LR) and RID to AAG DMO, February 15, 1879 (Fort Hays LS); RID to Surgeon General, February 5, 1879 (Fort Hays LS); RID to Adjutant General, February 7, 1879 (Fort Hays LS); RID to AAG DMO, February 15, 1879 (Fort Hays LS); RID to Chief Quartermaster DMO, February 4, 1879 (Fort Hays LS).

10. *PREJ*, pp. 147–48.

11. RID to AAG DMO, February 9, 1879 (Fort Hays LS). For Trout's injury and Dodge's reaction to it, see *BHJ*, pp. 184–85.

12. Endorsement by RID, John F. Trout to AAG DMO, June 5, 1879 (CNFCR LS).

John F. Trout (Roger D. Hunt Collection, U.S. Army Military History Institute)

crossing into Indian Territory, at Buffalo Springs, seventeen and one-half miles; and the next, at Wolf Creek near Fort Supply, twenty miles. The command remained in camp at Fort Supply for one day before resuming its journey on February 28, keeping to the south side of the river. Amos Chapman served as guide and scout from this point.

On the first day out from Fort Supply the battalion marched eighteen miles and camped at Cedar Bluff, where it remained on March 1 owing to a snowstorm. The next day it moved eighteen and one-half miles further along the military road, to Persimmon Creek. On March 3 a delay occurred when an inexperienced wagonmaster attempted to move two wagons at the head of the train across Sheep Creek, which flowed between steep banks on either side. Using ropes held by troops, he ordered the loaded wagons to be eased down into the sandy creek bed, where they promptly became stuck. Dodge appeared on the scene just as the men were about to unload the stranded supplies so that they and the wagons could be dragged up the incline on the opposite side. Recognizing the necessity of a long wait should the contemplated plan be adopted, he sent to the rear for Trout's right-hand man, Sergeant Christian F. Sommer, Company C. When the quartermaster sergeant arrived, Dodge asked him whether he had any experience in situations like this one. Being answered in the negative, Dodge informed Sommer that it was about time for him to acquire some. After considering the problem, Sergeant Sommer directed twenty men with picks and shovels to begin cutting down the side of the opposite bank. Within an hour a wagon road had been hewn out, steep and narrow but capable of passing a government wagon. With some energetic encouragement of the pack teams, the creek was soon forded and the command was back on the march.[13] It camped that night at Muddy Creek after a march of thirteen miles. The next day it moved eighteen miles, to White Horse Creek, where it remained in camp one more day. On March 6, after a short march of four and one-half miles, the command went into camp at the site Dodge had selected

13. Christian F. Sommer, "Cantonment North Fork of the Canadian River" (Thoburn Papers, Oklahoma Historical Society).

for Cantonment North Fork Canadian River.[14] As he had anticipated, the final determination was a simple matter once the terrain lay open to view. Two days later he reported his choice of location to departmental headquarters, characterizing it as "one of the best I have ever seen. It is high, well drained and should be perfectly healthy."[15] Already looking to the future, he added that as soon as he received a sawmill he could begin building a permanent post. The midwinter movement of 180 soldiers, with teamsters and wagons, over 161 miles of sometimes broken country had been a solid success.

In the days that followed Dodge and his men played the role of Robinson Crusoe, imposing human order and arrangement on a wilderness. In such situations, as soldiers of the era often complained, enlisted men became in effect day laborers. Dodge assigned details to cut down trees, build storehouses, construct a charcoal pit, burn lime, construct bridges, seek out building stone, begin a post garden, and plant peach trees around the perimeter of the future parade ground. As supplies continued to arrive from Wichita, he sketched plans for buildings and debated about their best locations. Writing and receiving letters by the dozen, he dispatched them by courier first to Fort Supply, but later, after several experiences of irregular delivery, to and from Fort Reno. The pressure—and if the tone of his journal entries is an accurate indicator, the pleased excitement—of these early days kept him from exploring the vicinity and so discovering just how near he had established the post to his campsite of January 9 and 10, on the north side of the river.

Between March 16 and April 14, the period covered by Journal Four, the entire population of the cantonment, numbering more than 250 men including civilians, lived in tents or in makeshift shelters under

14. Twenty-third Infantry Regimental Returns, February and March, 1879; Fort Supply Post Return, February 1879; CNFCR Post Return, March 1879.

15. RID to AAG DMO, March 8–10, 1879 (CNFCR LS). Three months afterward Dodge specified the geographical position of the post as on the "south or right bank of the North Fork of the Canadian River, in Section 13, Range 19 latitude about 36'6" longitude about 98'38," and approximately three miles due south of the point noted as Barrel Springs on First Lieutenant Ernest H. Ruffner's 1875 map of Indian Territory (RID to AAG DMO, June 9, 1879—CNFCR LS).

paulins. Conditions were primitive, and when buffeted by dirt-laden wind or attempting to move over rain-sodden ground, officers and men alike must have recalled with nostalgia the comfortable normalcy of Forts Hays and Leavenworth. However, work went forward, and with it a measure of daily amusement. Whist, cribbage, conversation, and letter-writing diversified the evenings and Sundays, as did libations of whisky for those few persons with a private supply. The post trader had opened his store shortly after arrival, but the sale of liquor was illegal in Indian Territory, and Keeling had not yet been granted the special dispensation he sought.[16] For Dodge, hunting and fishing were natural accompaniments to his tours of the near vicinity in search of resources that could be put to use. He gave such zestful accounts of these amusements in his journal entries that an uninformed reader could scarcely be aware of the potentially explosive state of affairs at the Indian agency only sixty miles away. The name of Little Chief goes unmentioned in the journal, as if Dodge were unaware of his existence. Emphases and omissions like these were his means of amusing but not alarming his parents, whom he knew to be at once proud of his military position yet fearful for his safety. Though fully occupied by endeavors that interested him much from a military point of view, he was glad to provide family members with selective transcripts of his daily life that recounted other adventures afield with a lively interest all their own.

In the initial weeks at Cantonment, Dodge was virtually powerless to provide material assistance to the Army forces at Fort Reno should violence erupt at the agency or should the Northern Cheyennes break away. Only one of the six companies under his command, Captain George M. Randall's Company I, had been designated as mounted infantry and so could pursue a foe rapidly. However, Randall's unit had not been part of the battalion that had marched from Fort Dodge, and until he arrived at the post from another mission, Dodge could do nothing in case of need except send some

16. Dodge had requested the exception on behalf of his men while still at Fort Hays (RID to AAG DMO, February 15, 1879—Fort Hays LS).

of his men to Fort Reno to swell the numbers there. Meanwhile, other frustrations tested his mettle as commander of a post that had not yet established its identity within the region. The presence of Colonel Davis and regimental headquarters at Fort Supply implied precedence of that post over Cantonment, even though the latter had been assigned a greater number of troops and was located closer to the focus of military concern. Davis, a stickler for detail and an officer not above appropriating certain perquisites for himself and his men, created small inconveniences and interruptions that must either be ignored as beyond remedy or else somehow discouraged without disrupting the command structure. Dodge addressed himself to these irritations decisively and with success, thanks to support from General Pope. At Cantonment he found himself an object of curiosity, naturally enough, to the Indians who resided in the vicinity. Many of these sought interviews, sometimes for no particular reason but on other occasions on matters evidently of real importance to them. These visits were frustrating on both sides, for communication was limited to rudimentary sign language. A related source of embarrassment was that the Indians begged for food that a post commander had no authority to dispense to them.

Despite a variety of such difficulties and small disappointments, Dodge's journal conveys clearly that he was pursuing his work at Cantonment with zest and confidence. Expeditions in search of building materials yielded pleasant surprises—lime, building stone, and stands of white oak, all within practicable distance. The labor of creating a substantial post from resources ready at hand moved ahead so rapidly that the stately leather-bound folio volumes that were to serve as repositories of the post records no longer seemed so presumptuous as symbols of an established military order. The sites of the temporary cantonment and the prospective permanent post were contiguous, the latter on a level space above the slight inclination southeast toward the river along which the former was situated, so that work on the two could go forward simultaneously. Once the storehouses were erected, Dodge could begin seeing to the construction of barracks, officers' quarters, and his own commander's residence. Whatever might develop at the Cheyenne and Arapaho agency, the establishment of Cantonment was proceeding well.

By mid-April 1879, Cantonment North Fork Canadian River had become a credible new presence in Indian Territory. Nevertheless, several important questions remained unanswered for its commander. Would the sawmill arrive, making possible the transmutation of timber into boards for building? Would Amos Chapman or some near-equal be made available to him as scout and interpreter? Would the garrison be made a more effective force in the field by the designation of a second company as mounted infantry?[17] Would Cantonment be declared a permanent post, as Pope anticipated? As Dodge awaited answers to these questions, he saw potential for other problems that had not yet assumed definite shape. Colonel Davis was absent from Fort Supply on duty in New York, but his successor as post commander, Major Alexander H. Dallas, was probably smarting from a defeat by Dodge in an official skirmish. The same was true of First Lieutenant William F. Rice, the regimental adjutant, who had suffered an embarrassing comeuppance. Further, at Fort Reno, Major Mizner had already betrayed an inclination to call upon Dodge for troops that were needed to continue constructing Cantonment. At the Cheyenne and Arapaho agency, Little Chief was an imponderable, but Agent Miles threatened to be an enemy hardly less dangerous. The influence of Miles had already made itself felt at Cantonment, and as a result, as Dodge reported to Pope, a fresh set of problems seemed likely to develop.[18]

Facing unanswered questions and sensing the potential for new troubles, Dodge pursued his ambitious plans for the new post as energetically as circumstances permitted. Cantonment was isolated, being seventy miles from Fort Supply and sixty miles from Fort Reno and having as yet no military road that connected it directly to a railroad depot to the north. Forts Supply and Reno each had its own

17. On March 29, 1879, General Pope requested permission of the adjutant general to designate Company A, Twenty-third Infantry, as a mounted unit (AGO LR). On April 21 he was informed that he had been authorized to do so when he judged it necessary (SW LS). However, Pope never took this action.

18. RID to AAG DMO, April 4, 1879 (CNFCR LS).

connection, and for efficiency and economy Cantonment must have one too. Other duties had kept Dodge from fulfilling his promise to Pope to lay out such a road, but by mid-April he was ready to direct the survey of a route northeast to Skeleton Ranch, along the Wichita–Fort Reno road not far south of the Kansas state line. With that new lifeline established, Cantonment would be on approximately equal footing with the older posts that flanked it along the river to the east and west.

Journal Four
March 16–
April 14, 1879

Cantonment
North Fork Canadian
Indian Territory[1]

Sunday, March 16, 1879

Finished my diary book No 5[2] last night & sent it by this a.m. mail to Father – in lieu of a letter.   Miserable day   Cold, windy & generally disagreeable.   Had all arranged for a hunting fishing & exploring party, & all had to be abandoned.   Did'nt get through writing letters until nearly 12 last night.   The late hours or the whiskey or some equally potent cause operated <b>very badly on my digestive organs, & I have been thumping at the heart & swimming at the head all day. I can never get well, until I get some teeth.[3]   Not being able to do

---

1. This manuscript journal consists of sixty unnumbered pages; it is identical in style and dimensions to Journals One, Two, and Three except that a sheet of unlined, laid paper serves as a flyleaf within the front and back covers. A few of the inside sheets have come loose from the notebook along their serrated tear lines. On the front cover Dodge wrote an identification in black ink: "No 6 [/] [*flourish*] [/] March 16, 79 [/] April 14, 79." The journal text is otherwise entirely in pencil. The flyleaves, pages [1] and [60], are blank except that a brief notation is written on p. [60V] with the notebook in reversed position. At the top of p. [2R] the text begins with this heading.

2. Diary Books 4 and 5, presumably covering the period February 1–March 15, have not been located.

3. Digestive troubles, which Dodge denominates *dyspepsia, dysentery*, and *diarrhea* more or less interchangeably, were his chief medical complaint, to be supplanted in future years by rheumatism. For an incident concerning a lost set of false teeth, see the journal entry for November 9, 1879 (Journal Six).

anything outdoors I have spent the day writing letters & gassing with the Officers.   Took a short walk about & above camp.   No work today, except that Lockwood kept up his survey –[4]   Some of the Civilian employees went out & killed two Turkeys very poor, not fit to eat.

Monday, March 17, 1879

"St Patrick's day in the Morning"—a great day in N.Y. but Pat has small chance of showing his blood out in the wilderness.

Very cold last night – & by no means mild during the day.   Had a pretty hard time with my dyspepsia yesterday but am better today. Took a party of my Hd Quarter guard[5] & went up to set the stakes for the trees in the new post.   Worked from 9 to 4 with intermission for the men's dinner, & got every stake set in the Officers part of the Parade.   Sent Sergt Leonard & his party out after the trees[6]   He got back just after dinner.   After which they went to work digging holes, & by the time I came away he had about 30 trees set, & very well done too.   I am afraid they will not do very well   The soil is very sandy & porous, & will not I fear hold moisture enough for them.   I'll make them grow or ["]*bust*" my water wagon.

Great numbers of geese flying north today.   They are principally a small variety, of which I know but little.   White on back & generally white all over the body.   The breast is sprinkled with slightly reddish – looking as if the bird had fallen in the mud.   The head is <a pale ye> spotted with pale red.   The beak is pointed & strong.   The ^quill^ feathers of the outer joint of the wing are perfectly black.   The wing

---

4. Second Lieutenant James B. Lockwood had been ordered to survey the military reservation that surrounded the cantonment, four miles square with the site of the future permanent post at the center.

5. The headquarters guard, under Corporal Martin Joste (sometimes spelled Yost, Yoste, or Youst), Company A, consisted of Joste and seven privates, one from Company C and two each from Companies A, D, and G (S.O. 1, February 19, 1879— CNFCR).

6. Sergeant Patrick Leonard, Company A, was on duty in the quartermaster's department with six privates of his company (S.O. 2, March 6, 1879—CNFCR).

coverts are mouse color.   Its wings stretch over 3 feet, tho' it is a much smaller bird than the Brant Goose.[7]

A flock, maybe a hundred in it, passed over me while I was at work, one of the birds being almost black.   I must investigate these fellows. I know little about them.

Had a huge appetite for dinner – but dared only soup.   It was delicious.   7 or 8 of the Goose described killed today & some few ducks.   I propose attending to them tomorro.

Have written several letters & got my correspondence pretty well up.   Trout is going on splendidly with the store houses.   Will have roof on one tomorro if it dont blow too hard.   Weather has moderated greatly –   Cribbage with Trout – & to bed, before 10 pm.   Our hens average 24 eggs per day[8]

Tuesday, March 18, 1879

Extra Session of Congress meets today – but dont care a snap for Congress.[9]   Had a regular field day.   The weather being good, though cool, I started out at 9 am with Trout, & a couple of orderlies to do the Country.   I had not yet been on the other bank of the river, <or>nor fixed the localities visited by me, last winter when looking for this site.

Very greatly to my surprise (for I thought it much further) I found my Camp from which I had hunted the country & selected the slopes

7. This was the white-fronted goose, or speckle-belly (*Anser albifrons*), a regular but scarce migrant across the region. See Sutton, *Oklahoma Birds*, pp. 56–57. Dodge included a passage on the Brant goose in *PNA*, referring to it there as the largest of plains birds (p. 225).

8. Like other post commanders, Dodge maintained a brood of chickens as a source of food. In May 1870, while in command of Fort Lyon, Colorado, he had 175 chickens and hoped for 400 later that spring (RID to Julia R. P. Dodge, May 27, 1870—Dodge Papers, Yale Collection).

9. The Army appropriation bill for the coming fiscal year had not been passed at the regular session of Congress, and a special session was convened on this day to consider it. According to the *Army and Navy Journal*, the main point at issue was that the Democrats, who controlled both houses, would support no bill that did not contain a clause forbidding the use of troops at the polls (March 8, 1879, p. 548). As approved on June 23, 1879, the bill did include such a provision; see *Statutes at Large*, 21:30–35.

adjoining the one we are on.[10]   I continued up the river, came to
Naked Bend, which is less than a mile outside of the Reservation – (4
miles square – the Post being the center)   <We>This was my camping
ground on the night of my return from Eagle Chiefs Creek.   Went on
up river, & in 3 or 4 miles, came to one of my Camp[s] with Remington.[11]   I must have a good bump of locality for I recognized every
spot, & could go direct to each pond & thicket.   On the route up,
both Trout & I got a goose each –

The ponds at the lower end of Sheridans Roost were full of ducks
& geese – but they are so large, & the approaches so open that it is
difficult to kill anything.   A flock of geese flew over me.   <&>I fired
two shots, the first No 6 shot bringing down the largest Brant goose
I ever saw. –   The second barrel with No 2 shot was fired full into
the posterior of another fellow, with no other apparent effect than to
make him go off faster.   Trout got 3 butter ducks, from a flock which
flew over him.

We then turned about, for home by another route – each taking a
course for himself – but keeping within sight.   On rising a little knoll,
I saw a turkey flying up, & another on the ground.   The latter I could
see indistinctly but he was acting queerly.   I tumbled off my horse &
made for <him>this fellow, which was now perfectly quiet.   When
I had got within 40 yards another turkey flew up before me.   I settled
him at once, & looking to the first, which I expected would get up at
the report of the gun, I saw a large wild cat, leap from the spot into a
ravine.   Taking in the situation, I rushed to the place & as I expected
found a fine turkey yet in his death agonies.   I bagged him, & then
picked up my own.   The cat had just caught the Turkey, & his spring
on it had caused the flight of the one I saw first.   I did not see the
spring, but I caught him in the act, & took his turkey.   I've no doubt
that cat thinks I did a mean thing.   I got 2 turkeys, & shot at but one.

Some distance further on we saw a large flock of geese in the river,
& making a wide detour came upon them, <as>I hoped at short range.

10. See the journal entries for January 9 and 10, 1879 (Journal 3).
11. On the night of November 27, 1878.

To my great disgust they were too far off.   Trout who was with me at this moment spied a few above & very near.   He made a dash for them.   Each of us fired 2 shots.   I wounded my birds but did'nt get one.   Trout bagged one with each barrel.   If I had seen the ones he went after, we could have gotten 4 as easy as not.   We came on well satisfied.   Crossed the river just where Reynolds is cutting the wood for the Post,[12] & got home at 4.30 pm – after about 20 miles of as delightful a jaunt as I've had in many a day.   5 geese, 2 Turkeys & 3 ducks.   Came in by the Post site.   The trees are going in rapidly – at least 70 being set out.   A train of stores in today.   Randall will probably arrive tomorro.[13]   Everybody out hunting today.   Clark[14] got 4 Turkeys & 2 Ducks.   Havnt heard from the others.   Will stop Turkey hunting in a few days, as they are beginning to nest.   Saw 3 deer but got no shot.

Wednesday, March 19, 1879

An awfully mean day – a perfect gale blowing from early morn, till bed time howling through the trees as I lie here in bed & write up this diary 10 p.m.

We are camped in one of the cosiest, most sheltered little nooks ever seen, & I have experienced no inconvenience except when I tried to go out.   With the wind fairly howling through the trees near

12. A crew employed by George E. Reynolds, the contractor, was cutting firewood.

13. On February 15 Captain Randall had transferred to a representative of the State of Kansas the seven Northern Cheyenne prisoners who were to be tried for crimes committed during the outbreak the previous September and October (Randall to AAG DMO, February 15, 1879—AGO LR). On March 6 Randall, then at Fort Leavenworth, received orders to take post with his company at the new cantonment. Acting as escort to fourteen additional Northern Cheyenne prisoners, he was to proceed by rail to Wichita, Kansas, and march from there to the point where "the road to the new post" diverged from the one to Fort Reno. At that point Randall was to send a detachment under a trusty non-commissioned officer to Fort Reno with the Indians. He was to proceed with the remainder of his company to the new post, the detachment following him once they had completed their errand (S.O. 43, March 6, 1879—DMO).

14. First Lieutenant William L. Clarke, whose surname Dodge usually misspells, was ordinarily attached to Company G, Twenty-third Infantry, but since December 17 he had been on special duty with Company A.

me, my tent barely shakes – scarcely moves.   On the hill the wind was so bad, that we had to send the men away from their work so I have lost a day –   Have devoted the day to letter writing, & send off tomorro a small package of ten (10)

About 1 pm the mail came in.[15]   Postal card from Dad – Letter from Genl Pope in answer to a long personal one from me.   Most satisfactory permanent post & we can work with a will –[16]   One from Fry enthusiastially commending the boy.   He says Fred "is a prodigy.   I was perfectly amazed.   It is wonderful how well he did," &c &c.[17] All of which is very pleasant to me.   Letter from Cath & several from outsiders on various matters.   Not a Herald, or Journal – only a few miserable 11 Worth Times   All have evidently gone to Standing Rock Agency.[18]

There is a rumor that this is to be Fort Pelouse.[19]

18th Infy ordered up on the Northern line – Milk River[.]   Cletz 10th goes to Lakes – 22d Stanley to Texas.[20]

15. From Fort Supply. In Circular 2, March 14, Dodge announced that mail would leave Cantonment on March 16, 20, 23, 27, and 30. At this time the mail wagon drove all the way to Fort Supply under escort by two enlisted men. Shortly afterward, an arrangement was devised whereby wagons departed from each post and met halfway to make exchange.

16. Pope's assurance that the post would become permanent was based only on his sense of its likelihood. Construction of a permanent post required recommendation by the General of the Army, approval by the secretary of war, and appropriation of funds by Congress (*Revised Army Regulations*, p. 143). In the case of Cantonment, none of these had yet occurred.

17. Dodge's old friend Colonel James B. Fry, a West Point graduate in the class of 1847 and formerly provost marshal general, was assistant adjutant general for the Department of the East. Fry was stationed at Governor's Island, New York, a posting that made it possible for him to witness stage performances in New York City by Dodge's son, Frederick.

18. The Standing Rock agency lay on the Missouri River in Dakota Territory, hundreds of miles away. Dodge refers to the *New York Herald*, the *Army and Navy Journal*, and the *Leavenworth Times*.

19. After the late Brevet Brigadier General Louis H. Pelouze (1831–1878), a Civil War hero who had served afterward in the office of the Adjutant General. A summary of his military career is in *ANJ*, June 15, 1878, p. 721.

20. The Eighteenth Infantry, which Generals Sheridan and Sherman had discussed as possibly serving a stint in Indian Territory, was to change station about April 1 from Atlanta, Georgia, to Yankton, Dakota Territory. The Tenth Infantry, commanded by

Wrote until nearly 10 pm got tired & went to bed to write up this diary.

<Sent>Ordered Chapman back to Supply, at request of Jeff.[21] Indians visited me today for first time –

Thursday, March 20, 1879

Mail left this am –   The south storm of yesterday changed suddenly in the night to a Norther, & it was very cold.   I made the order for an Offr. & 20 men to go out to cut logs for building – & sent for Pratt & gave him instructions.[22]   About 11 am it having moderated a little I determined to take P out & show him where to camp, & what to do. Before the horses were ready Yellow Bear & one of his wives came in.[23] I sat with them until the horses came, tho' we could'nt talk Chapman having gone.   He is an Arrapahoe of some note & an inveterate old beggar.   He told me that he was very hungry (by signs)   I gave him an order for a very scant supply of sugar coffee & flour.   He went off to the Comy, expecting no doubt to load the squaw, with his presents. In the meantime I rode off with Trout & Pratt.   George, my servant tells me this evening that he soon returned very much disgusted.   "The Big Chief gave him no bread["] –

I was delighted with my trip.   I found a splendid bunch of oak that I missed when last out, & it <was>being better than any I had found,

Colonel Henry B. Clitz and headquartered at Fort McKavett, Texas, was being transferred to Fort Wayne, Michigan. The Twenty-second Infantry, headquartered at Fort Porter, New York, under Colonel David S. Stanley, was en route to Fort McKavett (*ANJ*, April 5, 1879, p. 616).

21. Amos Chapman was still employed as scout and interpreter at Fort Supply, where he received a salary of one hundred dollars per month.

22. S.O. 7, CNFCR, dated March 20, directed First Lieutenant Edward R. Pratt with two non-commissioned officers and eighteen privates to go to a point designated by the commanding officer and begin sawing logs to build the new post. The detachment was to be rationed through March 31. "Company commanders will see that none but old soldiers are put on this and similar details."

23. Yellow Bear was one of thirty-two Indians of this region who were imprisoned for "education" between 1875 and 1878 at Fort Marion, Florida. He and his family now lived part of the year on a plot of land not far from Cantonment. Photographs of Yellow Bear are in Hoig, *The Peace Chiefs*, pp. 40, 41, 79.

Yellow Bear, Arapaho (Western History Collections, University of Oklahoma Libraries)

I told Pratt to camp near it, & cut till it was all down.[24]   Saw lots of Turkeys, but we made so much noise that they were already alarmed. Killed a grouse.   Saw an abundance of fish, & will go for them tomorro. Got back 4 pm, well satisfied.   Cribbage with Trout at night

Friday, March 21, 1879

Started Pratt & party out after Saw logs.   Went out soon after taking my fishing tackle, hoping to get some fish.   Made almost a dead failure. The wind was easterly & they would'nt bite.   In pools where yesterday I[25] saw & could have caught 50 to 100 fish, <I>not one was to be seen & very few caught.   I got 8 or 10 perch & cats

Pratt got to work at 1 pm & when I visited him at 2 he had about 15 trees down & fine ones at that.   Got back to Camp about 3 pm. Trout has got the roof on one storehouse & it will soon be finished. Went up to look at my trees.   Sergt Leonard is nearly through, only about 50 trees to set.   As soon as he finishes, I will go to work to plant out the lower part of post.   Wrote a letter to Fry tonight in answer to his congratulating me on Fred's success.   Have been making plans of houses at all intervals today.   Have got a right good draughtsman –[26]

Saturday, March 22, 1879

Soon after Office hours, I went up with some of my Hd Qr Guard to the Post site.   Worked until after 4 p.m. with intermission for the men's dinner   Got all the lower part of the post laid out, & set stakes for all the trees on the parade ground.   My surveying has been done entirely with the eye, that is every stake has been located on a line once established, by lining it on other stakes.   Yet my measurements come out so accurately that I will have no need for architects to locate

24. On March 20 Dodge endorsed as follows a requisition then being forwarded to the departmental quartermaster for a sawmill: "I find the timber here is principally oak and other hard lumber. I have therefore directed the Quartermaster to make the requisition for a more powerful engine than that asked for previously" (CNFCR LS). On March 30 he received notice that the revised requisition had been approved (CNFCR Post Return, March 1879).

25. Dodge wrote an ampersand, evidently anticipating the one that follows.

26. Corporal William Arnold, Company A.

the positions of houses   All this has been done, & done accurately enough for any garrison – within an inch or two every time.

Randall arrived while I was at work.   He has been taking it very leisurely – only about 15 miles a day – taking care of his horses.[27]   He tells me that Genl Pope spoke of my leave as a fact[28] – so I guess I'll get it.   Wrote to Father & Mother –   To Fry & a long letter to Fred. Randall brought me an extra good criticism on his performances, giving him credit for more knowledge of Shakespeare than all the commentators.   Crib with Trout & to bed at 11 –

Sunday, March 23, 1879

A miserable blustery day.   Fortunately there was no work to do outside

∧   , & I spend the morning drawing plans of buildings for the new post.   I have the Officers Quarters completed – & will soon have the men's, & the other buildings.

Transferred Dodge & Heyl back to their Comp[anie]s much to the disgust of Randall.[29]   I would like to do as he wishes, but I must be just tho' the Heavens fall.   Sent off part of my Hd Qr Guard, & an extra detail of 4 men to cut pickets for my house – my Cantonment house, not my Post Qrs. which will scarcely be ready for occupancy before next winter.   Detailed a party to cut wood & <build>burn a

27. Randall and his company had arrived at Wichita on March 12 and eight days later separated from the ten-man detachment that escorted the Indian prisoners the rest of the way to Fort Reno. The detachment reached Cantonment on March 29 (Twenty-third Infantry Regimental Return, March 1879).

28. On March 10 Dodge had applied for one month's leave of absence, with permission to apply for an extension of two months (RID to AAG DMO—CNFCR LS). This was granted him on April 18, but owing to fears that he might be required to command troops in the field, he did not avail himself of it at that time (ANJ, April 26, 1879, p. 672).

29. First Lieutenant Frederick R. Dodge, of Randall's Company I, had been on temporary duty with Company G since February 14. On March 18 he formally requested to resume duty with his proper company (CNFCR Unregistered LR). Second Lieutenant Charles H. Heyl had been on temporary duty with Randall's company since February 24, when he reported at Fort Leavenworth after completing his survey of the road from Wichita to Barrel Springs (ANJ, March 8, 1879, p. 548). His proper unit was Captain Wheaton's Company G. Dodge returned the two officers to their regular units (S.O. 8, March 23—CNFCR).

coal pit.[30]   About 2 pm the mail arrived.   I recd a long & very affectionate letter from Julia, giving me the history of Fred's successes –

The Old Lady is very proud & happy.   She has cause to be for whatever of success the boy has in life, will <be>come not more from his own Genius, than from the devotion of his Mother –   He is a good & tractable boy, & she will I hope be well repaid for all the anxiety & worry she has had on his account.[31]

Started some letters this evening, but was too lazy to finish any one. A letter from Laura –   She is heart broken & very lonely.   She will be worse when she finds I am not to come for them until near the 1st July.

Crib with Trout in evening & got badly whipped.   Nothing specially new

Monday, March 24, 1879

Started out with Trout & Hugh Patton, my scout[32] to examine the stone said to be on divide between here & the Cimarron.   Made my orderly Robinson[33] lead our horses, while he & I took to the 2 horse wagon.   The road is abominable.   Just on the divide I espied a flock of Turkeys.   They had not discovered us & were feeding away from our sight.   A huge old Gobbler brought up the rear, & he

30. On March 20 Trout had requested a detail of ten men to build a corral and to burn charcoal pits "about five miles from the post or wherever suitable Timber can be found" (CNFCR Unregistered LR). The party designated by Dodge consisted of Corporal John Vail, Company D, with ten privates (S.O. 8, March 23—CNFCR).

31. Dodge and his wife had lived apart during most of their twenty-one-year marriage, the conditions at remote frontier posts being too spartan for her tastes and health. The task of rearing their only child, Fred, had been primarily hers. Fred had been a sickly child, subject to seizures as late as 1870, but in the years since then he had strengthened markedly. He accompanied his father in the Black Hills expedition of 1875 and enjoyed himself immensely, though it was clear by then that he would never become a rugged outdoorsman. Success in amateur theatricals at Omaha Barracks and Fort Leavenworth during these years confirmed his inclination toward the stage. In 1877 Fred and his mother toured Europe together, and after their return to the United States they continued to share a residence.

32. Formerly a civilian employee at Fort Hays, Hugh Patton had accompanied the command to the new post as a teamster, willing to take whatever work he could. Dodge describes him more fully in the journal entry for September 3, 1880.

33. Private William Robinson, Company A.

seemed to have made up his mind not to go over the little ridge which hid the other.   Strange to say that though we were in plain sight, & scarcely 200 yds away, not one of them discovered us.   As soon as all were out of sight I dismounted, took my gun & ran forward   I had some difficult creeping & cant see why they failed to discover me.   I finally got a good position.   Two hens were quite near me together & I could have got both at a shot, but my heart was set on the gobbler.   Just as I raised my gun he saw me, & stuck up his head until he looked 4 feet high.   In another instant he was dead.   Could then have bagged a hen, but fired at another gobbler on the wing at a long distance, but failed to bag him.   My prize is the biggest bird yet brought in, weighing at least 20 pounds tho not very fat.

The Stone turned out poorly.   Taking a drink & mounting our horses, we sent the wagon back by my orderly, & struck across country south by east searching for stone.   We found immense quantities of Gypsum in great boulders & layers - & some fairly good stone, though not in very great abundance   We did not find enough to suit us and were disappointed   <O>We struck out on an entirely new route coming back covering a distance of 16 to 20 miles.   No suitable stone rewarded our labor, but such a forest of white oak as we found, would soften a heart of Adamant.   Enough & to spare to build our whole post, with what we already have -   Have another trip on hand for tomorro, on this side of the river.   We must have stone —

I did not get back until nearly 5 p.m. & have had no opportunity of seeing what has been done today.   Sergt Leonard reported 393 trees already planted.

Almost everybody at my tent tonight, & we had a high old gas. Randall set them all out[34] staying until nearly 10 p.m.

Before going out this am I finished the plans of the Officers Quarters, & have nearly completed those of the mens Quarters.

---

34. That is, he outsat them—stayed longer.

Tuesday, March 25, 1879

Have had a very hard but most satisfactory day.   Had an early breakfast, & taking Trout, Hugh Patton, Robinson (my mounted orderly) &
Boone my ambulance driver,[35] I started for a field day in search of
stone.   Our destination was rock hill, a mountain like eminence to
the south of us.   I sent Hugh there a week ago & he reported stone
abundant, but he had also reported an abundance on the ground we
went over yesterday & which turned out to be only masses of gypsum
—   He took us a round-a-bout way 12 or 15 miles, & got us to the
foot, but with a deep & impassable ravine between us & it.   In hunting
a road to the hill, I came upon a small flock of Turkeys, & after 20
minutes of most scientific maneuvering I got within about 70 yards,
when they discovered me & were about to fly when I fired.   I had in
my gun a wire cartridge of heavy shot in one barrel, & an ordinary
charge of No 4 in the other.   Habitually when I load with different
sized shot, I put the heaviest in the left barrel.   These Turkeys were
so far off, that I dared not trust No 4, & fired my left barrel.   One fell
dead another fluttered off a short distance – another flew up & lit
within 40 yards, & I snapped at him with the right.   On taking out
my cartridges I found that I had killed with No 4 – at that immense
distance – the heavy wire cartridge failing to explode.   I got 2 fine
gobblers.   Soon after we got to the Hill, & dismounting went prospecting.   The hill is probably 80 feet above the level of the high plain
in the vicinity.   A rise of 30 feet brought us to a bench.   A horizontal
layer of stone extends across the whole, & crops out all around.   It
will average 6 feet in thickness.   The stone is a white & red sand
& lime
    ∧   stone & is so stratified that it can be got out without blasting.
50 feet above is another layer, not so thick.   There is excellent stone
enough to build this Post of that Material alone & to spare.   Trout
insists that one layer of it is lime stone & will put a party to trying a
kiln on Monday next –

35. This was Boon Tomlinson, another former employee at Fort Hays.

When, in prospecting we got on the top of the mound, we found a flat surface of probably 100 yards in diameter.   On the top was a cairn of stones & at i[t]s foot lay an Indian, who was evidently as much surprised at our appearance as we at his   He hardly noticed our salutation & from his surroundings, I saw that he was "Making Medicine." These people are very religious – more so than any Christians.   This was a young man.   I would not let any of my party come near him, & we continued our prospect making a clear Circuit about him.   This was terribly bad medicine for him, & he came to the edge of the precipice & motioned us to leave.   We paid no attention to him & after getting through with our work went back to the ambulance, had it driven to a sheltered spot, got out our lunch basket, & sat down to enjoy ourselves.   Human nature could not stand that, & <th>soon the Indian came stalking down & sat down near us.

We talked to him by signs.   He told us that he is the son of Yellow Bear an Arrapahoe Chief, (who is now at Reno.)   He had come up to this medicine mountain on foot from the agency, to make Medicine – that is to go into what a Catholic would call "retreat" –   He was entirely naked, except a blanket wrapped about him.   He had with him no food or drink – no weapon, no mockasins even – only the blanket.   He said he had been 3 days on the Mountain without food or water, (& he looked wretchedly enough to warrant us in believing him) & had to remain 3 days longer when he would return to his home.   He had with him an Indian Clarionet, the most perfect one I ever saw, & it had a very sweet tone, & the notes seemed perfect. We tried to get him to play, but he said he could only play when the sun went down – (part of his Medicine –)   He however ran over the

scales in a way to satisfy me that his _∧ knowledge of music is far
superior to that of any Indian I ever saw.[36]

natural

36. Dodge describes in *OWI* an Indian "pipe or flute, ingeniously constructed," that conforms to the "Clarionet" referred to in this entry. "The only music on them is the repetition again and again of a few chords, low, slow, and sometimes very sweet and weird" (pp. 349–50).

I cut a huge chunk out of a can of Corned Beef & putting it between two biscuits gave it to him.   It was too much for his vow of fasting. He took it, & swallowed it in a very few minutes finishing with equal celerity a canteen of cold coffee that Patton gave him.   He said he would come into the post in 3 days & see me – when I will have to feed him again

What a wonderful power Religion has over the ordinary human mind.   Here is a poor devil, inflicting tortures on himself because he thinks it will appease the Bad God – who will then let the Good God aid him in some project he has on hand.[37]   Superstition is strong in almost all of us –

When we left the Mountain I started in the proper direction. Hugh said "Col[onel] you cant possibly get through that way with wagons.   I've been over the ground & know its badly broken"—— I said, "Hugh, I may not be able to get through, but I am going to try the shortest line back.   If we make it, all right, if we fail we will then hunt a better & longer road.   I claim to be a thorough woodsman & tho' I have never been here, I believe I can make a straight road to the Post, & cross but one creek.   I am going to give you a lesson in Plains craft"

He laughed & thought it a good joke, & we went on

Trout had a pet idea of how, to get a road to the hill from the post, & wanted to go another way.   When we had come on the proper directions about 2 miles & had got onto the divide, I could see far in advance, over ground over which I had travelled & what was better could see the very angle where I wanted to cross the Creek.   I didn't say much, for I was sure I was all right & wanted to surprise them Trout growled all the way, said I was too far to the west, & that I would not come within 2 miles of the logging Camp.   I told him I would cross the creek 1/2 mile from that camp.   We got to the creek, the very spot I wanted.   I found a place where the ambulance could

---

37. In *PNA*, Dodge describes the Cheyenne Indian as believing in two gods, "equals in wisdom and power," one of which supports him in all undertakings, the other of which is always his enemy. These are, respectively, the Good God and the Bad God (pp. 247–50).

cross, & pushing over came spang[38] on a camp & riding up found Pratt.   The logs had given out below, & he had moved up half a mile. Trouts face brightened up.   I didn't say a word to any of them, but Hugh <sa>thinks I am the best guide to be found, & Trout says he will bridge the creek at that spot.   All gave it up –   After a drink with Pratt, I went down the creek, & caught 14 cat & perch, & got home 4.30 after 25 or 30 miles of travel, & a day of hard work.   Am very tired & went to bed earlier than usual after beating Trout at Cribbage

Wednesday, March 26, 1879

Soon after breakfast I went up to the Post site to finish up the work. Was stopped by recall & <g>being short of pins.   Two hours work will finish it now – & I am very proud of it.

Sergt Leonard has finished planting the trees in the upper or ornamental section of the Garrison – & has today completed the fence around the useful or Soldiers end.

Great quantities of Stores arrived today –

Randall tried a foolish experiment with his horses today – turning them loose.   Result, he returned at 11.30 pm with all the horses but having ridden from 9 am at least 70 miles.

The mail brought nothing of importance.   No news of my leave. Wrote long letter to Father & Mother – one to Genl Pope, & one to Joe & Laura.   This matter of the leave is very unsatisfactory   I wish Pope would say yes or no.   Delightful day   Comy Building completed[39]

Thursday, March 27, 1879

After Office hours I went up & completed the work on the hill. Every stake is driven, & my part of the work – the laying out – is done. Had all finished by 11. am.   Sergt Leonard's party is working well. They have dug nearly half the holes[40]   for planting the trees in the lower half of the Parade.   A lot of Indians called on me today.   I

---

38. *Spang*: "An expletive signifying fullness or completeness of action, like the occasional use of the word 'full'" (Thornton, *An American Glossary*, 2:835).

39. A storehouse for commissary supplies.

40. Dodge wrote "poles."

could not talk to them, but that made no difference to them, & they stayed with me until dinner –   I gave some of them to eat.   They all understand that.   It has been a terribly hot day.   Thermometer about 90°.   Sent out 5 wagons & drew in the first lot of stone for my Post. They went & came over the route I laid out on 25th & all pronounce it almost perfect.   Trout went out & built a bridge over the creek at Pratt's camp.

A heavy wind storm at night with a little rain & some hail.   This has cooled the atmosphere & it is now very pleasant   All going on well –

Friday, March 28, 1879

It rained quite heavily during the night, & towards morning, not so much as I wanted, but enough to make this day a most comfortable one.

I went out in the morning & laid out the Cantonment.   Have got a good position.   In the afternoon I selected the site for my own house & had several loads of logs dropped there.   No stone wagons went out today as having no hay, we are obliged to let the animals graze at least every other day.   Tomorro I send out 5 wagons for stone

Went up to the post site.   Sergt Leonard is doing finely & will entirely finish his work tomorro.   When I came back to Dinner Trout was perfectly wild over the catching of 13 black bass by one of the soldiers. After dinner we all started out – that is Clark Trout & myself.   Clark got a good bass 1 1/4 lbs.   I got 2 perch & a cat.   Trout 2 cats & a perch. I'll do better next time I think.

Wrote a long letter to Julia which I did'nt close.

Saturday, March 29, 1879

Started out with Clarke for a jamborée.   Heard there was good fishing in the Creek beyond Rock Hill.   Went out in my ambulance. The stone wagons beat us out there & we found the men busy getting the stone down the hill.   The day turned out oppressively warm, & though we found many nice holes, the fish would not bite.   We tried them with live bait, grasshoppers & liver to no effect. Clarke didn't get one[,] I did, but that was all. After lunch we started back very leisurely, & it was very pleasant in the ambulance. Arrived at Prattes camp & told him I would send for his party tomorro. Then went down the creek to try the fish again – I never took more care or fished more faithfully – & I got one perch. C. got 2, so we are even. Got back 5.30 pm. Made a tour of inspection of the work. The tree planting is done. A large lot of logs for my house. All right every way

Sunday, March 30, 1879

After breakfast I had a field day in the office – overlooked all the estimates & cut them down very considerably, to the disgust of some of the Captains. Then took a stroll around my domain & enjoyed the progress of the work.

I am delighted with the way everything is going on – as smooth as possible – no hitch no jar – & everybody working Sent out in afternoon to bring in Pratts party of wood choppers Corpl Youst of my Hd Qr Guard reported. He has got all the logs in his vecinity. His party will come in tomorro. Organized a party to burn lime & load stone. To be out a month – a Sergt, & 9 men.[41]

The mail arrived at 12.30 p.m. Not an item about my leave. I dont care particularly. Of course I want to see all I love – & am trying my best to accomplish it. I will not however be very greatly disappointed if I dont get it. I am very busy & very much interested in my work – & if I dont get leave now, I'll take 4 months next winter – A nice letter from Father & Mother The Latter threatened with malaria again. I hope they will go to Sis Annies soon.[42] Another

41. S.O. 13 (March 30, CNFCR) ordered Sergeant James A. Corbett, Company K, with five privates on duty to burn lime. By this order they were to be rationed for ten days. However, see the journal entry for March 31.

42. One of Dodge's sisters, Ann Sarah Glenn (b. 1831), was the widow of Captain Chalmers Glenn, of the Thirteenth North Carolina Regiment, who died at the battle of South Mountain in 1862. She lived in Leaksville, Rockingham County, North Carolina, a few miles east of her parents' home in Surry County.

copy of a letter to Mizner from Hd Qrs, giving he & I all the authority we want.[43]

No news of the action of Congress, except a rumor that the Senate has confirmed all the recent nominations.   Coppinger is Major of 10th, & Stillé takes his place here.[44]

Nothing important –

Monday, March 31, 1879

Had no monthly inspection this morning.   The Cos'[45] had their regular Sunday Inspection yesterday, & I could not afford to lose a day. Sent out Sergt Corbett & 9 men to burn a lime kiln, & load the stone wagons.   Made detail of 1 Off., <&>2 N.C. Offs & 20 men to cut saw logs.[46]   They have been grinding axes all day & will go out tomorro. Very miserable day – blowing and threatening – the air full of dust – & everything betokening a fierce storm.   It was just the morning for fishing for game & timid fish & I was hankering for them.   I sent Robinson to get some bait, but by the time he got back it had cleared & was hot as —— an oven –   So I sent him away, & devoted myself to letter writing.   <Sent>Wrote letters to Father & Mother, to Julia, to Joe & Laura & several other person[s].

Sent check for $100 to First National Bank Leavenworth, directing Cashier to send N.Y. check to Father – J R Dodge Salem, North Carolina This is to anticipate any possible shortness of the old folks – for Catlin on whom they have to rely just now is "mighty oncertain" –   It is for

43. On March 28, 1879, General Pope informed General Sheridan that he had directed Major Mizner to watch the Indians near his post closely "and at the first indication of a purpose to leave, to use his whole force promptly to capture and hold them prisoners whether called on by the agent or not" (OIA LR, C&A). Freedom to act independently of the Indian agent's request was the authority Dodge had in mind.

44. The rumor about promotions was accurate. Captain John J. Coppinger, currently on sick leave from duty with Company A, Twenty-third Infantry, was promoted to major, Tenth Infantry. First Lieutenant Louis R. Stillé, Company E, was promoted to Coppinger's former rank and position (ANJ, March 29, 1879, p. 609; June 21, 1879, p. 823; July 12, 1879, p. 885).

45. Companies.

46. Second Lieutenant J. Rozier Clagett, Company C, with two non-commissioned officers and eighteen privates, was to begin work on April 1 at a place to be designated by Dodge (S.O. 14, March 31—CNFCR).

the 28 May payment for Sis Molly –[47]   Also gave Trout a check on 11 Worth for, 81.45 for which he gave me the money.   Paid all my bills.   Settled all accounts.   Made out my Mess bill, & received all money due on them   At this instant I dont owe a cent – (except note to Joe) nor does any body owe me (except on notes).   Commissary Butcher <4>and <al>servants all paid.   About 4 pm the prospect of a Storm became almost a certainty & I sent for the Dr. for dinner thinking we had better get through with it.[48]   The Storm came, a most diabolical looking cloud, but expended itself in wind.   The Officers in <l>Camp below me are swearing blue streaks on account of the dust.   I get very little.   Pollock said tonight, "I think you have the first requisite for a Comdg Officer.   You know how to take care of yourself."   Having the bait & feeling certain the fish would bite I went out about 5 pm & got back after dark.   I took 2 magnificent black bass, (one of 2 1/4 – the other 1 1/4 –) 3 very large perch & 3 fine cats, before it became too dark to see the float.   My big bass created a sensation in Camp & he is a real beauty.   I used only live bait – Everything taking it –   Had about 2 hours of splendid fishing. There are great number of fish in this little brook but they are hard to get hold of.   Finished up all my official work after I came back.   Played Cribbage with Trout, & beat him as usual, then wrote a long letter to Saxton another to Gilman and one to Amos Chapman.[49]   It is blowing a gale now – but I scarcely feel it –

47. The $100 was provision for Mary Helen Dodge (b. 1835), Dodge's youngest sister, who was blind. See *BHJ*, p. 111n.

48. Dodge sent for his messmate, one of the two physicians on duty at Cantonment— Assistant Surgeon Victor Biart and Acting Assistant Surgeon C. H. Shriner, Jr.

49. The contents of these unrecorded letters must remain conjectural, but they may be tentatively inferred. On April 14, Lieutenant Colonel Rufus Saxton wrote to the post quartermaster, directing him to invoice the Dougherty wagon that had been brought to Cantonment from Fort Leavenworth by Captain Randall (CNFCR Unregistered LR). On April 10, Captain Jeremiah H. Gilman informed Dodge that fourteen thousand pounds of potatoes would be loaded the next day for shipment. Bricks for bake ovens had been invoiced on March 31, but onions could not be found (CNFCR LR). On March 30 Dodge, painfully aware of his inability to communicate with Indians unless through an intermediary like Amos Chapman, requested authority from the departmental adjutant to employ an interpreter and also one Pawnee Indian as a scout (CNFCR LS).

Tuesday, April 1, 1879

Cold raw day.   Issued an order prohibiting the killing of Turkeys grouse or quail – until further orders[50]   Soon after ordered my horse & with Trout & my orderly started out to see how the Log cutters are getting on.

They had just completed pitching camp, & were all well pleased. The game seemed to know of my order.   I have seen today at the very least a thousand Turkeys – & could have killed a great number.   Some of the old Gobblers tried me most severely, by getting up almost under my feet.   We have seen about 20 deer, & many grouse.   I was proof against it all for I could not violate my own order.   After an examination of the Camp & timber, I went east intending to take a cursory look at the Country & return to Camp.   One view led me to want another & I finally found myself at the foot of the great divide, & within 7 or 8 miles of the Cimarron.   I have found & located a route which I am sure will be far better than the road we have.   Unfortunately it is too far to go to Cimarron & return in a day, & it [is] impossible to say what difficulties are beyond where I went.   If I dont get my leave I will be out there in a week or so, for I think I can make a road to Skeleton Ranche within 45 miles – better than the present road 52 miles[51]

Returning to Camp I very carefully went over the ground & timed my horse.   It is about 4 miles to my logging camp, & some 5 or 6 from that to the foot of the Cimarron hills.   Got back tired & worn out.   Made a ride of 25 or 30 miles, & the wind was high   I am tanned & burned so that my cheeks feel like blisters –   I had on my overcoat & fur cap.

<Tro>Clark came in to tell me that he had taken 7 fine bass in the holes on other side of the river.   All the work going on well.   Cribbage & to bed.

50. This was Circular 6, April 1, 1879 (CNFCR General Orders).

51. According to the measurement made by Lieutenant Heyl, Barrel Springs was 155.94 miles from the railroad depot at Wichita, Kansas, by the road he staked out in February 1879; Skeleton Ranch was 103.09 miles from the depot (Heyl to AAG DMO, February 24, 1879—AGO LR).

Wednesday, April 2, 1879

Soon after Guard Mounting I went out to reconstruct the canton-ment, which did not suit me.   I was to go out fishing with Clarke, but did not get off until after 2 pm – & when I got to the fishing ground I found that they had already taken at least 20 fine bass, & that the fish had quit biting.   I waited patiently however, & got (7) seven one a beauty of 3 1/4 lbs. the others from 1 to 2 lbs.   <Trout> Clarke & his 2 men both good fishermen made one of the finest strings I have seen in many a day taking 35 fish that would weigh at least 70 lbs, tho' mine was the biggest caught.   Goodale, poor fisherman as he is, got 8, but he was at it all day.   All these bass over 50, were taken in a few hours from one pond in the Sand Hills, without inlet or outlet, but clear beautiful water.   I think all the sloughs in the vecinity have bass, & if so, the fishing here will be superb.

Cribbage & to bed early

Thursday, April 3, 1879

Nothing of special importance.   A cold disagreeable day –   They are getting on very well with my house, the outside walls being nearly completed.   Went out fishing about 1 pm but had bad luck – getting but two bass.   Robinson got 2 with my other line.   Clarke got 3 little ones.   Found Dr Loring & Lt Bolton here on my return.   Dr is a witness on the Court Martial.[52]   Letter from Dr OBrien.

Friday, April 4, 1879

Directly after office hours I started out to give Dr Loring a chance at the bass.   Fished faithfully for 4 hours.   The Dr. got one good one, 3 3/4 lbs, a little larger than my best, & the <s>largest yet caught *that has been weighed*

52. Assistant Surgeon Leonard Y. Loring was post physician at Fort Supply. Second Lieutenant Edwin B. Bolton, also from Fort Supply, was preparing an odometric measurement of the road between that post and Cantonment. The general court-martial referred to by Dodge, ordered to meet on April 1, was to consider the cases of enlisted men referred to it from posts in the area (S.O. 51—DMO). Members of the court were all officers stationed at Cantonment; the judge-advocate was Lieutenant Clarke.

It was his only bite.   I got 2 bites & 2 fish small – the largest 1 1/4 lbs.   Clark hooked a little chap but lost him.   We got tired of it by 1 pm & came back.

The mail got in about 2 pm, bringing me lots of papers.   No letters of importance – none from Julia Fred or the Old Folks.   A long letter from Rice trying to explain his taking the ambulance.   Wrote an answer sitting down on him very hard, but very kindly.   Giving him official fits, in the kindest possible way.[53]   Letter from Chapman, says he will be down in a few days.   Took Loring up to post site.   He is delighted   Got him to Doctor my chickens which are afflicted with a terrible disease of the eyes & throat.

Am authorized to employ 5 Indian scouts, but there is no money for the employment of an Interpreter.   Letter from Haskell.   He seems to be enjoying himself.[54]   He & Madam went to see Fred, and

53. The issue here was a Dougherty spring wagon in use at Cantonment. On being driven to Fort Supply, it was kept there, another wagon being substituted for the return trip. First Lieutenant William F. Rice, the regimental and post quartermaster, wrote to Trout on March 25 that he had made the exchange by direction of Colonel Davis and that the wagon kept at Fort Supply was one from Fort Leavenworth for which he was himself responsible (CNFCR Unregistered LR). Upon being informed of Rice's action, Dodge at once forwarded his note to departmental headquarters with an endorsement calling into question the purported history of the wagon, explaining its present location, and protesting the action taken by Rice: "If the Quartermaster at this post had public property for which Lieutenant Rice was accountable there was a proper way of obtaining possession of it. He claims that his action was only by order of the Post Commander. That does not better the matter. The taking a wagon which I had sent to perform a special and important service was bad enough in itself, [but] the replacing it by another old and barely serviceable was an act properly to be reprehended only by a Court Martial. If the Quartermaster or Post Commander of another Post can appropriate the wagons belonging to this Post he can also appropriate any mule or other public property to which he may take a fancy. I will not dare to send a party off on any occasion lest some of the public property belonging to this Post be taken away and other property substituted. I protest against this appropriation of the wagon and respectfully request the Department Commander to order its return" (CNFCR LS). Colonel Davis, who on March 28 transferred command at Fort Supply to Major Dallas, appears to have played no further part in this official quarrel. The matter was now in the hands of General Pope. Dodge describes its resolution in the journal entry for April 13.

54. Captain Joseph T. Haskell of Dodge's regiment was still on recruiting duty at David's Island, New York Harbor.

pronounce him a great success – & predict a bright future.   Plenty of worry in Congress.   They don't worry me any ——
    My back Heralds and Journals came by mail today

Saturday, April 5, 1879
    Soon after Guard Mounting Dr. Loring left us.   He is a most admirable gentleman.   I wish I had him here in Biarts place.[55]   He would gladly come but that he has his family with him & there are no quarters here.
    The day has been utterly abominable.   A heavy gale has been blowing from the South all day – bringing clouds of dust loosening the tents & flies & making everything uncomfortable.   With it was a hot sun.   You could'nt stay inside the tent for the heat, or outside for the wind & dust.   However the day wore away as all days do.   Wrote a letter to Rice & gave him fits.   Another to Chapman telling him to send down the Pawnee boy.[56]   Wrote to Father & Mother.
    Went over everything in the cool of the evening.   The work is going on nicely in spite of wind.
    Crib with Trout – a good bath & to bed 10 p.m.

Sunday, April 6, 1879
    Started out with Trout soon after Guard Mounting on a "general service" expedition.   First we went to the stone quarry – located & planned a lime kiln.   Found the men there in a great state of excitement.   They had just completed a rifle pit around their camp.   To my enquiry as to the cause of the war like preparations, they said there had been a great deal of yelling around Camp last night.   The Sergeant had gone out to see if he could find any tracks.   They are

55. Assistant Surgeon Victor Biart was relieved from duty at Cantonment on May 13, 1879, on a surgeon's certificate of disability. He did not return to Cantonment, being replaced on June 2 by Assistant Surgeon Louis A. La Garde.
    56. Apparently this was the Pawnee Indian whom Dodge had earlier requested authorization to employ as a scout (RID to AAG DMO, March 30, 1879—CNFCR LS).

evidently scared at my Panther, who having been run out of the saw log creek has taken refuge in the Quarry creek.   I found some beautiful specimens of stone – very like marble.

We then went off on an exploring expedition down the creek. Although it is Sunday, we somehow found our fishing tackle along with us.   We tried in several beautiful holes & got a few perch.   A huge bass made off with my cork – but I could'nt induce him to touch the hook end of the line.

It has been a day simply terrible.   The wind has been blowing a stiff gale all day, the tents are down, & those that withstand the shock are full of dust.   One can't open eye or mouth without getting it filled with *Dust*.   I think that my whole Comd Offs. & men would desert on the smallest provocation, and I dont blame them.   To be blown about forever is one of Dante's most terrible punishments, & we have it here with all the most disagreeable accessories.   Every mouthful one eats is half dirt – & there is no remedy except houses.

Several Officers up tonight all wo-begone & miserable   All saying bad words of this climate & country.

It is a horrible country for wind & dust & there is no going back on that fact.   I think the news that Congress had disbanded the Regt. would be received with delight.   One month here this day –

Monday, April 7, 1879

A lovely day & everybody happy as "big sunflowers."

About 1 pm mounted my horse & taking Robinson, my orderly, & my fishing tackle I started out to explore the Sand Hills.

Tried in the old place but could get no bite though a soldier, with an eight foot stick for rod, no float, with dead minnows put on like a worm, caught 4 near me in half an hour.   I became disgusted with fish of so little taste & went off.   Found a new pond long & wide but I fear not very deep.   There are many fish in it – but they are principally small cats   I got 8 or 10, & could have got a quantity but I was hunting holes – & only stopped a short time.   Got back late.   After dinner went the rounds, all have worked well.   The news tonight is that Dunn, the Inspector will be here in a week or less.[57]   Lot of stores arrived.   Perfectly lovely night —

Tuesday, April 8, 1879
    After making my usual morning tour of the post I went to the Trader's store & ordered a thousand feet of lumber, to fix my house up in good shape.   The wind has been blowing a gale all day, & when Clark proposed that we should go fishing, I jumped at the idea – more to get out of camp, than with any expectation of fish.   We started in the ambulance about 1 pm – & crossing the river went down about 3 miles to a pond Clarke had found in some of his hunts. We had beautiful sport in spite of the wind which blew so hard that we could hardly manage our lines.   After a hard contest, we quit exactly even – 5 bass & 1 cat each.   My biggest bass beat his biggest by 1/4 lb   Not a bass was taken under 2 1/4 – the largest weighed 2 3/4 –   This is no guess work, I had my fishing scales along & weighed each fish as it was caught.   I never saw a prettier or more uniform lot of bass in my life.   Got home before dark.   One of the Officers got a letter from his wife last mail, saying that she had heard my leave would not be granted.   Genl P. did not think he ought to spare me at a time of so much importance –[58]   Building & possible Indian troubles –   Will likely know tomorro –
    Crib at night.

Wednesday, April 9, 1879
    Trout went out to the lime kiln this am   Returned 1 pm reports everything doing well.   I prowled around all morning looking at the work.   My main house is nearly done, & both will be ready for

57. Pope's senior aide-de-camp, Captain William McKee Dunn, Jr., was also acting assistant inspector general for the department.
58. Pope anticipated a breakout by the Northern Cheyennes any day, as he reported to Sheridan on March 25: "Every indication, not only in acts but in statements of the Indians themselves, make[s] it certain that they are only waiting a good time and opportunity to get away" (OIA LR, C&A).

occupancy by Saturday night I think.   I am going to line it with common sheeting – & that may take a day or two longer.

Mail arrived 2 1/2 pm   Letters from Father & Mother Cath, Fry & others –   Got check for my April interest 4 pr ct bonds $15.[59]   Father & Mother go to Annies in a few days.   Had evidently not got my check for $100.   Letter from Laura.   Wrote to Father & Mother, to Joe, to Hay, Platte & Saxton – Also to Dallas   Wrote official letters to Genl Pope about Interpreter –[60] another about cutting loose from Supply & sending to Reno for our mail.[61]

Assumed Comd. of Regiment & reported fact to Dep Hd Qrs[62]

59. A notation on p. [57V] of Journal Three may refer to this investment, apparently in 4 percent registered United States bonds issued in January 1879.

60. Having been informed on March 28 that "absolutely" no funds were available to pay an interpreter, then told on April 4 that he might employ five Indian scouts but not an interpreter, Dodge renewed his request in strong terms. He asserted that "it is simply impossible for me to do my duty here satisfactorily, even to myself, unless I have means of communicating with the Indians." He emphasized the strategic necessity at his post for information about Indian activity in the area: "At a time when trouble with Indians may be anticipated daily, it is of the utmost importance that the Commander of this Post have means of Communication with Indians who are coming in all the time. This Post from its situation on the line of any outbreak is one of the most important in the Department, and if an Interpreter cannot be sent here from some less important Post, it would be better to discharge some of the Teamsters or others . . . to pay an Interpreter" (CNFCR Post Returns, March, April, 1879; RID to AAG DMO, April 8, 1879—CNFCR LS). This statement of the case proved effective. On April 28 Pope directed that Amos Chapman be transferred from Fort Supply to Cantonment, where he would remain on duty (CNFCR Unregistered LR).

61. On April 4 the departmental adjutant informed Dodge that General Pope thought Cantonment should receive its mail via Fort Reno, where a daily service was established, rather than via Fort Supply, where mail came thrice weekly (CNFCR Unregistered LR). Dodge's letter of April 9 informed the adjutant that beginning on May 1 the mail party from his post would proceed to Fort Reno. He proposed an amendment to the Wichita–Fort Reno–Fort Sill mail route that would cause Cantonment to become a regular stop (CNFCR LS).

62. In full, Dodge's report to the departmental adjutant was this: "Sir: I have the honor to report that having official knowledge of the absence of Colonel Jefferson C. Davis 23 Infantry, I have this day assumed Command of the Regiment and ordered all orders, papers &c. requiring the action of the Regimental Commander to be sent to me at this post for action" (CNFCR LS). The unilateral assumption of command by Dodge sparked controversy and continuing discussion. See the journal entry for April 13.

Smith applied for a months leave, which I forwarded approved. He is a good Officer but has been so full of whiskey lately that I am glad to let him go.[63]

Wrote to Joe & Laura to get ready to come to me, about the end of this month.   Got a splendid letter from Fry.   He is a most admirable man – as clear headed & upright as there is in the Army.[64]

When I went out fishing three days ago, I was bothered with a little

&
gnat not bigger than the point of a needle.   They settled in <the> ∧ behind my ears & the only intimation I had of them was a bite.   I paid little attention to them at the time, but they left their cards. My ears are swollen yet, & itch frequently.   No fishing today.   It blew a gale this a.m. but has been very pleasant this p.m.   Wrote letters & played Cribbage with Trout.   He got away with me tonight.

To bed late.

Thursday, April 10, 1879

After getting through the office work this a.m. I started in the ambulance, with Clarke to see if we could not find some new fishing holes.   Went up the river on the other side, through the sand hills for near ten miles.   Found plenty of ponds, but all so shallow, that

63. On April 14, Captain Thomas M. K. Smith was granted one month's leave of absence (S.O. 72—DMO). The *Leavenworth Times* of May 4 reported an incident on Smith's journey from the post to Wichita. His ambulance met a group of emigrants en route to Leadville, Colorado, one of whose members had just died and was to be buried. The dead man's wife, an Episcopalian, wished the burial rites of the church to be read over him. "The Colonel [Smith], true to his natural instincts, acquiesced in this, and though he had no book . . . he repeated such of the ceremony as he could from memory, his impressive delivery adding much to the solemnity of the occasion." The man was buried, Smith's hand was clasped, and the parties went their separate ways (quoted in *ANJ*, May 17, 1879, p. 731).

64. Dodge's regard for Colonel James B. Fry stemmed not only from long acquaintance but also from shared literary interests. Like Dodge, Fry was a soldier-author. His *Army Sacrifices; or, Briefs from Official Pigeon-Holes. Sketches Based on Official Reports—Grouped Together for the Purpose of Illustrating the Services and Experiences of the Regular Army of the United States on the Indian Frontier* had just appeared (*ANJ*, February 22, 1879, p. 519; March 1, 1879, p. 542).

they had no fish – or the deep water was so far from shore that we could not get at it –   On the way up we saw three immense cranes – perfectly white, except the first joint of wing which is black. Clarke took his shot gun & I my rifle & we crept up to within about 100 yds   There was no chance to get nearer, so I leveled on one & fired, making a center shot.   I brought him in.   He measured nearly 6 feet in height, & 8 feet 3 in[ches] from tip to tip of wing.   We found a good many ducks – they were wild but I got <3>4 Shovel bill & 3 teal.   Clarke got 2 teal, 1 rabbit & a coot.   We searched faithfully but found no decent fishing place.   Came back & tried at the post ponds but got no bite, & came home.

The work has been going on nicely today.   My main house will be done tomorro – & the other will be ready by Saturday night   I will move in next week.

Plan –

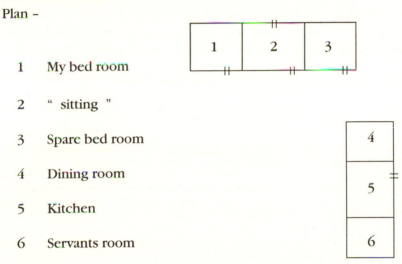

1   My bed room

2   " sitting "

3   Spare bed room

4   Dining room

5   Kitchen

6   Servants room

The houses are built of logs stuck in the ground, chinked & daubed, covered with poles also chinked, & a coat of mud 3 ins. thick over all. Over that comes a paulin of heavy Canvass to keep out rain.   The logs are not hewed & have the bark on.   The house is a rough one but will be very comfortable

Cribbage with Trout in evening beat him mildly.

Very windy all day.

Friday, April 11, 1879

A little touch of dysentery made me fly out in the middle of the night & I've been doing the same nearly all day.

Got on the hill however soon after G[uar]d Mounting & set the stakes for the 100 peach trees that are to be here in a few days.   It was no easy job to locate them properly in the yards when neither houses or yards had been located but I finally got it all right I think

I have been bothered with Indians ever since noon.   They are a terrible nuisance   They want everything (particularly soap & water). They beg for meals for Comy. stores, for corn.   They complain of my cutting their timber.   Our Communication is of the most meagre.   I can understand some of their ideas - expressed in the sign language - but cannot convey ideas in turn except positive yes or no.   An old man complained that my men were cutting timber on the creek below, that it all belonged to him, & he desired me to issue an order stopping cutting.   I told him *No*, but I could'nt tell him *why*, & he went off mad as a Hessian.[65]   It has been a delightful day - a little hot

---

65. However unsatisfactory for lack of a means of precise communication, this interview was yet more troublesome for the evidence of governmental bad faith it gave to the Indian who claimed ownership of the land he occupied. On April 4 Dodge had informed his departmental adjutant of "a new cause of difficulty with the Indians [that] seems likely to manifest itself." The agent at the Cheyenne and Arapaho agency had earlier authorized chiefs or heads of families under his charge to claim sites for their occupancy along the North Fork of the Canadian River. The Indians had situated themselves in well timbered areas, and when Dodge's men or else contractors supplying firewood for the post began cutting down trees, the "owners" objected. Yellow Bear, for example, had demanded bacon to pay for wood cut on land he considered his own. However, Dodge pointed out in his letter that the Indian agent had no legal power to grant title to the occupied sites. Accordingly, as post commander he was paying no attention to the supposed claims, authorizing timber to be cut wherever found and not reimbursing Indians like Yellow Bear. Nevertheless, he warned, the extralegal arrangement of the Indian agent could have serious consequences: "There are already sufficient causes of trouble between the War and Interior Departments, and if the action of the Agent is continued and rendered authoritative, the Indians will soon claim all the timbered land in the vicinity of posts, and the army be forced to pay for every pole or log for building and every cord of fire-wood" (CNFCR LS). However fanciful Dodge's apprehension of trouble might seem, it proved accurate. The right of the military to cut and use wood on an Indian reservation without payment to the Indians was not definitely affirmed by the secretary of war until years later, and then amidst controversy. See *ANJ*, July 10, 1886, p. 102.

in the sun, tho' the ther[mome]ter in the shade was never over 75. No wind, & everybody happy   My house getting on splendidly roof on the small building.   Will get in I think by middle of next week – a great number of logs in today

Saturday, April 12, 1879

Soon after G[uar]d Mounting I started with Clarke to hunt up some fishing holes that he claimed to have seen one day when he was hunting turkeys   After a long search we found them, but they did'nt have much fish.   We then went to the hole where we got 5 each a few days ago.   Fished faithfully – but were utterly outdone by the Gars.   Last time we had no gar bites   This time we had nothing else & they were incessant   I must have lost 50 minnows, & minnows are a scarce & important article down here.   I caught 4 of the beasts but they are good for nothing.   I got one small bass, Clarke got hold of a good one but lost him.   After exhausting patience & using up our full stock of bad words we gave this place up & went to ponds that I knew of.   Here we fished faithfully with not a single bite   We had no boat of course, & could not get our lines into deep water.   I bagged 6 ducks, (3 spoon bills, 1 widgeon & 2 Tontos or <b>Butter ducks).   Old Bunk[66] behaved beautifully.   Heyl got a deer today.

Issued orders in regard to Post Gardens.   Put Goodale in charge.[67] House getting on well.   Hope to get in it next week.   Had a hard but delightful day.

Sunday, April 13, 1879

Was quite busy this am over office work.   Wanted to go up the river to look for a place for garden but finally let Goodale & some of the Captains go.

66. Bunkie, one of Dodge's hunting dogs. See *BHJ*, p. 192, and the journal entry for September 9, 1880 (Journal Eight).

67. Captain Goodale's detachment planted the post garden almost completely in little more than two weeks. On April 28 Goodale informed the post quartermaster that he would require approximately thirteen hundred pounds of seed potatoes (CNFCR LR).

About 10 am a man named Tramp came with a letter from Miles the Indian Agent at Reno   He has with him 29 Cheyenne Bucks who come to cut wood on the Contract of Lee & Reynolds   They have their families with them.[68]   In all 138 redskins —   I put them on the other side of the river about 3 miles from the Post, & told the man in charge to keep them away from the Post.   Stone Calf, a Cheyenne Chief, & his outfit came up to settle down for the summer on his claim about 4 miles north west of this Post.[69]   The country is getting thickly populated.

A man came to see me about mail matters.   He represents the mail route from Caldwell – (Wichita) & Ft Reno, & proposes if we will sign petition to give us a daily connection from Skeleton Ranche.   It is just what we want & he shall have his petition numerously signed.

The mail came in about 1 pm – & soon after came a party from Supply bringing the wagon Rice took from my party some weeks ago. The mail brought an order from Dep Hd Qrs directing the Comdr of Fort Supply to send that wagon back to me, & receive back the one they <took> sent me[70]   In other words, I gained a complete triumph over Davis & Rice.   I had investigated the case, & satisfied myself that the wagon was one used at Ft 11 Worth as Hd Qr wagon.   Rice wanted it at Supply & turned it over to Hoyt for transportation.   He invoiced it with others to Leiffe at Ft Dodge.   He not knowing or not caring for the special predilection of Supply people, turned it over to Trout, who receipted for it, & brought it here.[71]   Sending it up some time after

68. Dodge concluded this statement with a comma.

69. Stone Calf was one of the first Southern Cheyenne leaders to accompany Brinton Darlington to the new Cheyenne and Arapaho agency in 1870. In later years he played a prominent role in the efforts of his tribesmen to live at peace on their reservation while preserving something of their earlier ways of life. A photograph of him and his wife is in Hoig, *The Peace Chiefs*, p. 153.

70. As Dodge indicates, a letter of April 7 from General Pope's adjutant directed the commanding officer at Fort Supply to return the appropriated Dougherty wagon to Cantonment and exchange for it the one earlier substituted. "After this has been done the Department Commander will be prepared to consider the question of, to which post the wagon belongs" (CNFCR Unregistered LR).

71. The officers referred to were Captain Charles H. Hoyt, depot quartermaster at Fort Leavenworth, and First Lieutenant John G. Leefe, Nineteenth Infantry, post quartermaster at Fort Dodge. Dodge had pieced together the chain of events through documentation supplied him by Trout.

with the mail party to Supply, Rice bagged it, & I made the row.   I had no special need of that particular wagon, but I was not going to have my property bagged in that arbitrary way.   Having gained all I sought in the fight I magnanimously ordered the Corporal to take that same wagon back & have accompanied it with a letter telling them that I give it to them as an act of Courtesy.   I am heaping those coals of fire on their heads.[72]   Another fight I had on the arbitrary transfer of some men, resulted equally in my favor –   So I am well content.

Dallas wrote me a long letter about my assumption of the Comd. of the Regt.   He yields of course, but thinks I am wrong.   I have replied in a kind personal letter, in which I propose to fight that fight out to the end, should Genl Pope fail to sustain me.   I am acting against precedent, but I am right, & I am going to change the precedent, even if I have to carry it to the Secy of War.[73]

72. The greater part of Dodge's letter to the commanding officer at Fort Supply constituted a review of established facts, which placed Lieutenant Rice and Colonel Davis both in an unfavorable light. He concluded by stating the rationale for his objection: "I made the fight to test the right of one Post Commander or Quartermaster arbitrarily to seize upon public property belonging to another Post, and having settled that point to my satisfaction, I send you the wagon as an act of courtesy" (CNFCR LS).

73. "Precedent," as embodied in the *Revised Army Regulations*, Article IX, provided that "An officer not on duty with or belonging to any of the companies, battalions, regiments or Corps composing a command cannot assume the command or put himself on duty therewith without orders from competent authority" (p. 11). By this rule, Dodge could not take command of the regiment, not being present at regimental headquarters. Presumably his position was that, as the ranking officer of the regiment available for duty after the departure of Colonel Davis, he ought to assume command and cause the regimental headquarters to be brought to him. For Major Dallas, the issue was complicated by his being both acting regimental commander and post commander at Fort Supply. If an officer in Dodge's position assumed command of a regiment, did he also assume the right to issue orders to the regimental officer whom he displaced, that officer being a post commander? Second, if ordered by the new regimental commander to perform a duty that involved setting aside, even for a short time, his position as post commander, should the displaced officer comply? To Dodge and Dallas alike these were not unimportant questions of military law and discipline.

General Pope made no objection to the action Dodge had taken, even though in a letter of April 13 Dallas stated his concerns and asked whether the present arrangement met Pope's approval. Not receiving a reply from Pope, on May 10 Dallas addressed to the Adjutant General of the Army through departmental headquarters a detailed discussion of the above two questions, requesting answers to them. On May 28 General Sherman returned to Pope a legal opinion prepared for him by one

A good fight is a splendid sharpener of the intellect, & keeps a man from rusting out.   I recd. a nice letter from Father & Mother   One from Joe & Laura begging to come back.   I will send for them in a short time –   I also got a letter from Mrs Adair, in Ireland begging me to use my influence to protect their Cattle Ranche on the Palo Duro in the Texas Pan Handle.[74]   She & her husband have been through this country, but they fail to realize its extent   I am more than 100 miles from their ranche.   Letter from Chapman.   He can't get to me.   I think however I'll get him yet.   Letter from Gus Bibby in California. She is a dear old girl, & has a hard life of it.   They have failed to realize the bright future they hoped was in store for them.[75]

I learn that Dunn did not go to Fort Reno, & I need not therefore look for him here.   I think I will start in a day or two on my road making expedition to Skeleton Ranche.   Genl Pope expects it, & I

---

of his aides-de-camp, Colonel John E. Tourtelotte, noting however that Tourtelotte's view "is entitled to consideration, but is not conclusive."

Tourtelotte placed the responsibility for ensuring a smooth succession of command within a regiment on the departmental commander: "When a Colonel is detached, the Lieut. Colonel cannot surrender his post, and proceed to the post just vacated by the Colonel, to take command of the regiment, without an order of his Department Commander, nor can he command the regiment technically when detached by superior authority from the post named in superior orders as the Regimental Headquarters.

My decision, therefore, is that when the Colonel is ordered away, as Colonel Davis was, the Department Commander should order the Lieut.-Colonel to proceed to, and take post at the Regimental Headquarters, or modify previous orders so as not to deprive the Lieut.-Colonel of his right of succession to command."

Dallas's letter of May 10, with the responses of General Sherman and Colonel Tourtelotte, appeared in *ANJ* for August 16, 1879, under the heading "The Command of a Regiment" (p. 29).

74. Mr. and Mrs. John G. Adair, owners of the JA Ranch in northern Texas, had met Dodge in October 1874, when he accompanied them and their mutual friend William Blackmore on a ten-day hunt along the South Platte River (Blackmore Papers, Museum of New Mexico).

75. The nature of Dodge's earlier acquaintance with Gus Bibby and, presumably, her husband is not known. On August 29, 1883, then in San Francisco, he sought her out and, as he wrote in his journal entry for that day, "was really touched by the demonstration of affection of herself & Mamie. They quite 'set me up' – I have not had so much kissing in many a day" (Dodge Papers, Graff Collection). *Langley's San Francisco Directory for 1881*, p. 151, lists a Mrs. Alfred Bibby, widow, as residing at 418 Post Street (*City Directories of the United States*).

have promised.[76]   Febiger[77] came in today from the logging camp – Reports about 200 logs a day.

Beat Trout at Crib.

Monday, April 14, 1879

Have had a busy day.   There was a good deal of work in the office getting off estimates of clothing for the Companies.   The heavy rough work is very hard on the clothing of the men & they wear out more than twice as much as they would in Barracks.   Trout was in a fine piece of temper because he thought the estimates too large, & made himself absurd by the nature of his comments until I finally told him to clear out & consolidate the estimates as I had signed them that 'twas none of his business.

He is by far the best Qr Mr I have ever seen but he requires as much management as a balky horse.   In his duty, he is like some people in their religion – not content to do the best he can for himself but continually & forever worrying over the short comings of others – He tries my patience terribly some times, but I put up with a good many peculiarities on account of his many extraordinarily good qualities.

I have been pestered to death with Indians all day.   Since 10 am they have besieged me continually, begging & loafing around.   I have no interpreter.   As soon as I get one I shall put a stop to their non-sense at once.   But when I can't explain to them, & can indeed com-municate only the most curt ideas, it seems even to me cruel to drive them away.   They are full of curiosity.   One old fellow told me that he had come from the Agency – "Three Sleeps" that is he had taken 3 days to come, just to see & have a talk with me.   He had no business whatever, but was actuated simply by curiosity.   Most of those here

76. In transmitting to departmental headquarters an itinerary of the "extremely crooked" route from Cantonment to Skeleton Ranch, on April 9 Dodge wrote that, while a straight road was "almost impossible," he had found a "much better and shorter route to Cimmaron" and hoped to reduce the distance to the ranch by six or eight miles (CNFCR LS).

77. Second Lieutenant Lea Febiger, Company A.

today are Cheyennes – <of whom> the Tribe which I made my type in my Book.[78]

They are a fine looking body of men, the most nearly aboriginal of any Indians now to be found.   These a[re] Southern Cheyennes & have been living peacably on their reservation for some years.   A good many have selected claims & cultivate small farms.   One woman had a child about a year old very pretty & bright.   It took the greatest fancy to me & wanted to stay on my knee all the time.   I wrote to Father & Mother directing the letter to Leakesville – to Cath, & to several outsiders.

I had a long interview with a mail agent in reference to getting a daily stage, to connect us with the regular Reno Stage at Skeleton Ranche.   We got up a petition & I hope it will get through all right.

Corpl Arnold completed the copy to scale of my plan of the post. It looks tip-top.   All the distances & measurements are marked & it is a complete working map.   I am now ready to commence work – if I only had my saw mill.   My house is completed my dining room also   The kitchen & servants rooms will be done in a day or two – the kitchen tomorro I think.   My hen house & other outhouses will be done in a day or two.

I have given all orders in regard to my start tomorrow.   I take Heyl with me to <m>take the courses & distances, & he will make a map on our return.   I take Hugh Patton as scout, an Ambulance wagon, & my Hd Qrs Guard, a Corpl & 6 men.   I dont expect to do much but survey out a route.   If I succeed in finding one, I will send a party to make the road.

I shall be gone about 6 days I think.[79]

78. See *PNA*, pp. 238–39 n.

79. The party was away from Cantonment from April 16 to April 22. Second Lieutenant Heyl surveyed the route but on his return to the post was taken ill and granted a seven-day leave of absence. The map and itinerary showing the new route were prepared by Second Lieutenant James B. Lockwood, the engineer officer of the post. The new route reduced the distance to Wichita by seven and one-half miles. It passed west of Skeleton Ranch, joining the Wichita–Fort Reno road seventeen miles north of it. Pond Creek Ranch was approximately six miles north of the junction. The itinerary map by Lockwood is in Envelope 277, AGO Miscellaneous File, Record Group 94, National Archives and Records Administration.

I have nothing more to add of interest   I will start another book tomorro & send it to you when it is full.   If you can make them out, I know they interest you more than letters – as they give you my daily life.

With love & kisses – your affec

Boy Baby[80]

80. Pages [59V]–[60R], which follow, are blank. The final page, p. [60V], includes only the notation "153," written at a diagonal with the notebook reversed.

Commentary on Journal Five
The New Post: Multiple Missions

THE DECISION TO ESTABLISH CANTONMENT WAS made in response to events elsewhere in Indian Territory, at the Cheyenne and Arapaho agency. As General Pope conceived of the post, its value lay in the strategic position it occupied should the Northern Cheyennes again bolt from their reservation. General Sherman also considered the proposed new post in terms of antici- pated needs at some distance from its immediate locale. Authorizing an increased military presence within the territory where troubles were likely to occur seemed to him more propitious than attempting to patrol the state borders that Indians might try to cross. Some practical consequences for Cantonment of the two generals' ideas became evident as events unfolded in the spring of 1879. While still at work constructing the new post, Dodge and his men became caught up in the Army's need to deal with emergencies elsewhere. Although stationed sixty miles from Fort Reno and almost seventy miles south of the Kansas state line, troops at the post were called into service at both locations. Increased military activity was proving necessary, not only to secure the reservation tribes inside Indian Territory but also to keep prospective settlers out. Called upon to fulfill multiple missions, the six-company garrison of Cantonment was soon reduced to three.

On his return in late April from the road surveying expedition, Dodge found projects at the post moving ahead at a steady pace. The strain of travel and frontier duty had told on Lieutenant Trout, but he was in his element amidst the activity and continued to work with a

will.[1] The sawmill was expected soon, and in the meantime fatigue
details were erecting picket huts for temporary use—rows of raw logs
stood on end in trenches forming rectangles, with roofs also of wood,
covered by paulins and daubed with a layer of dirt.[2] If only sufficient
wagons were at hand to transport the excellent stone that had been
found eight miles away, work could begin on a really splendid permanent post. At any rate, the sawmill would make possible the erection
of frame buildings.

A stream of civilian laborers and artisans began flowing into Cantonment, looking for work. If hired, they were issued passes by the
post provost marshal permitting them to remain on the military reservation and their names, occupations, "peculiarities," and other data
were recorded in a "Pass Book" kept at headquarters. Most of these
employees were between twenty and forty years of age, and almost
all were Americans and without specialized skills. Except for Samuel
Coleman, a forty-one-year-old man from Pennsylvania employed as
engineer, and a few others, skilled laborers were of foreign extraction.
F. Schlegel, thirty-eight years of age and "heavy set," was Prussian; John
Berry, thirty, and T. H. Davis, thirty-one, were masons from England;
George M. Young, thirty-five, a butcher, was from Germany; William

1. On April 23 Trout renewed his application to appear before a retiring board,
enclosing a statement of his incapacity signed by the post physician, Victor Biart
(Trout to AAG DMO, April 23, 1879—CNFCR LR).

2. Sergeant Sommer, who with Lieutenant Trout was responsible for supervising
their construction, described the company quarters more fully: "The barracks were
to be of equal size, 100 feet long by 20 feet wide, built of pickets placed on end in
trenches 3 feet deep,—and covered by paulins, 24 by 30 feet. The ends of the pickets
were to be sawed off and held together by 2 x 4 or 2 x 6 scantling; ridge poles, 20
feet long to be placed on the tops of the pickets lengthwise to provide and give
elevation to the paulins, which were to [be] fastened to the side of the buildings and
openings were to be manufactured from lumber estimated for, glazed windows to
be also supplied by requisition to be made. All open spaces between the pickets were
to be chinked, the mortar to be made from clay and hay intermixed" ("Cantonment
North Fork of the Canadian River"—Thoburn Papers, Oklahoma Historical Society).
For further description of picket huts see Pierce, *The Most Promising Young
Officer*, p. 82. A photograph showing picket construction at Tongue River Cantonment, Montana Territory, in 1876–1877 is in Greene, *Yellowstone Command*,
p. 116.

Hershey, twenty-nine, a clerk in the post trader's store, was Canadian. Occupations listed in the Pass Book included farmer, harness maker, woodchopper, herder, laborer, wagonmaster, servant, carpenter, cook, and others. "Peculiarities" were recorded for only a small number of the men. John Gallagher, a teamster, had "left leg short"; James Coleman, employed by Company C, was an "Irishman"; James M. Mallory, a carpenter, had "left arm crippled"; John Robinson, thirty-one, a laborer from Pennsylvania, was identified as "N." for Negro—the only man so signified.[3] Within the first year of the post's existence more than 160 civilian employees were granted passes, some for only a few days but most for an unlimited period.[4]

Families and furniture began to make their way to Cantonment as the inhabitants of the post made themselves less uncomfortable. Early in June the sprightly wife of Lieutenant Clarke professed herself "agreeably disappointed"[5] at what she saw. Captain Gilman at Fort Leavenworth forwarded fifteen pounds of Old Judge smoking tobacco, his whole stock on hand. The post trader, H. C. Keeling, was doing a brisk business in miscellaneous articles, though he still lacked permission to sell alcoholic beverages. In March the officers and men had submitted a petition on his behalf, which was denied after some delay. They appealed, and this time Dodge provided them a vigorous statement of support. In a letter to the adjutant general, he warned that if liquor were to be officially prohibited at the post, the word would spread and illegal sources would multiply: "Cut off the supply entirely and the old Adam is yet so strong in human nature, that even the habitually sober men will get beastly drunk from these contraband supplies, and my command will be debauched not only by the quantity but by the quality of the stuff sold to them by these Kansas pirates." On the other hand, Dodge argued, moderate use of liquor could easily be ensured if its distribution could be controlled

3. Entries for Dodge's domestic servants Joe and Laura do not appear in the Pass Book, nor does one for George, the Negro man he had hired in November 1878 as a personal servant.

4. CNFCR Pass Book.

5. See the journal entry for June 7, 1879.

at the post.[6] Given additional force by favorable endorsements from Pope and Sheridan, these considerations prevailed. On May 24 notification reached Cantonment that henceforward Keeling could sell wines and liquors in accordance with policies to be established by Dodge.[7]

In fact, the most serious challenge to Dodge's success in administering the post during the first months of its existence came not from drunken soldiers but from more serious delinquents, deserters. By the end of May approximately one-eighth of the enlisted men had absconded, and without sufficient manpower the cantonment could not be built. Some men were captured, but the greater number made good their attempts to flee, often carrying with them the clothes and supplies they had been issued. Given the poor living conditions and sometimes heavy labor imposed on them for low pay at frontier posts like Cantonment, their inclination to take up lives elsewhere is not surprising. Dodge had given thought to the issue in terms of general Army policy, for the problem of desertion badly troubled the service at this period. As a practical matter, early in June he decided to discourage further desertions by displaying publicly the ignominious result of a soldier's being captured.

The man placed on display was Private George D. Myers of Captain Pollock's Company C. On the march from Dodge City to the new post, Myers had disobeyed positive orders from Pollock and the attending surgeon to remain with his company. Instead he had stayed behind at Fort Supply, whence he was later transported to Cantonment, charged with desertion. A few days before his trial by court-martial, Myers wrote to Greenbury L. Fort, a congressman from Illinois, appealing for assistance in securing a discharge from the Army. Since their arrival at Cantonment, he wrote, he and other men had been given hard work and treated like dogs, even as his own health had deteriorated.[8] Fort forwarded Myers's letter to the secretary of war, who passed it

6. AAG MDM to AG, March 27, 1879, forwarding the petition (AGO Register LR); RID to AG, April 30, 1879 (CNFCR LS).

7. AG to C.O. CNFCR, May 14, 1879, cited in CNFCR Post Return, May 1879.

8. CNFCR Register LR.

along through military channels for comment. Meanwhile, in proceedings that began on April 1, Myers was found guilty of desertion and placed in the guardhouse.

Upon receiving a request for comment on Myers's plea of ill health, Pollock responded that the soldier had reported at sick call almost constantly since December 1878. He had been examined by Drs. Loring, Comfort, Biart, and Shriner, but none of them could find anything wrong with him. They judged, and Pollock agreed, that Myers was a chronic malingerer who was attempting to deceive them in order to gain a discharge in grounds of incapacity.[9] On May 25, when Pollock wrote his endorsement, Myers was still in the guardhouse awaiting promulgation from department headquarters of his sentence—likely to be incarceration in the military prison at Fort Leavenworth for a period of years. On the night of June 5 he escaped, and upon learning of his flight, Dodge acted at once. He alerted Amos Chapman, who quickly organized a posse of Indians to scour the vicinity in search of the fugitive. Myers's flight to freedom lasted only about twenty-four hours. At guard mounting on the morning of June 7, his capture and one part of its consequences were made public: in view of the assembled troops he was placed in irons.[10] Whether as a result of this sobering sight or from other causes, the problem of desertion at Cantonment was much less serious thereafter.

In spite of aggravations from isolated soldiers, in general Dodge was well satisfied with his command, both officers and men.[11] As in the Myers incident, his effort to maintain order was made easier by assistance from small bands of Indians who were encamped along creeks near Cantonment. Beginning in May, five Cheyenne scouts were regularly employed at the post; and within ten miles in either direction

9. Endorsement, May 25, 1879 (CNFCR Register LR).

10. See the journal entry for June 7. General courts-martial were convened twice more to consider charges against Private George D. Myers. On August 27, 1879, he was sentenced to two years in confinement and dishonorably discharged from the Army (Office of the Judge Advocate General, Registers of General Courts-Martial; CNFCR Post Return, August 1879; *ANJ*, November 1, 1879, p. 237).

11. R. B. Marcy to W. T. Sherman, November 25, 1879, enclosing an extract from an inspection report on Cantonment by Major John J. Coppinger (AGO LR).

were twenty lodges of Cheyennes under Stone Calf, ten under Coho, thirteen under Big Back, and five under Minimick. Arapahos residing within the same distance included fifteen lodges under Little Raven, four under Yellow Bear, and two under Lame Deer. These Indians were all peaceable and well disposed.[12] Chapman's appointment as post interpreter as of May 1 had deprived Fort Supply of a valuable employee, but he was even more useful in his new posting, for he related well to Indians, citizens, and soldiers alike. With assistance from him, Dodge was able to learn his neighbors' impressions of conditions at the Cheyenne and Arapaho agency and gain insight into the mode of existence they chose to adopt along the river in preference to residing nearer the agency. Out of sympathy for their poverty and respect for their efforts to eke out a semi-independent existence, he devised a plan to promote the gainful labor of a group under Minimick as woodchoppers outside the military reservation.[13]

Reports received by mail and by courier kept Dodge generally apprised of developments in the region, but his post existed in semi-isolation, away from the areas of most intense military concern. Rumors that the Northern Cheyennes were quietly accumulating horses and keeping them hidden in the blackjack timber for unspecified purposes reached the post in mid-May, but without Chapman, who was then absent, Dodge could not be certain what to make of the news and so was "much in the dark about Indian affairs."[14] Even if definite information about an emergency had reached him, he lacked the resources to respond to it effectively. He "earnestly" urged Pope to consider assigning another company of mounted infantry to

12. This enumeration, based on the inspection report cited in the preceding note, describes the Indian population around Cantonment in early November 1879, after crops had been harvested. According to Coppinger, most of the Indians ordinarily in the vicinity had by that time already returned to the agency for the winter.

13. RID to AAG DMO, January 9, 1880 (CNFCR LS). For further discussion of the arrangement devised by Dodge, see below, pp. 227–28, 326.

14. RID to C.O. Fort Reno, May 16, 1879 (CNFCR LS). Dodge was writing in response to a request of the day before by Mizner for fifty mounted men to reinforce his garrison.

Cantonment,[15] but none was forthcoming. Fuel for cynicism was here, had he chosen to view his responsibilities in that light. He was expected to pursue fleeing Indians without horsemen, and as he wrote in his journal, "to build a $50,000 post without money."[16] However, as an Army officer of long experience, Dodge was inured to just such impossibilities as these. What concerned him most was that levies on his command for service elsewhere were interfering with the construction of the post.

Military authorities in Washington, D.C., snapped to attention on April 26, 1879, when President Hayes issued a proclamation warning prospective settlers in Indian Territory that their effort would be illegal and that trespassers would be expelled, by force if necessary.[17] A widely copied article in the *Chicago Times* of February 15 had alerted readers to the existence of some 14 million acres of unoccupied lands in the territory. To persons like Charles C. Carpenter, who in 1875 had organized a peaceable invasion of the Black Hills by citizens who ultimately established a right to remain there, these federal lands offered another opportunity to promote settlement. Railroad companies that served towns along the borders of Kansas, Missouri, and Arkansas stood to gain handsomely should new communities grow up in Indian Territory, and they helped fan the enthusiasm. Advertisements in Kansas towns including Wichita, Caldwell, Coffeyville, Independence, Chetopa, and Baxter Springs encouraged homesteaders to enter the territory and set up claims. In April Carpenter, who called himself "Colonel" in respect of his Civil War service, set up an agency in Independence, Kansas, to enroll settlers who would accompany him into the unoccupied lands and help found a "colony" there.[18]

15. Dodge reported that he had been unable to comply with a call for mounted troops from Mizner since those he had were already committed elsewhere. As a result, "the present condition of this garrison is such that I can hope to do nothing whatever in case of an outbreak. . . . The Country being impracticable for vigorous pursuit by Infantry in wagons" (RID to AAG DMO, May 16, 1879—CNFCR LS).

16. See the journal entry for June 3, 1879.

17. *Statutes at Large*, 21:797.

18. Rister, *Land Hunger*, pp. 36–49.

Though not ceded to particular tribes, the lands Carpenter and others had in view were part of Indian Territory as defined by Section 2147 of the *Revised Statutes* and were not available for general settlement. President Hayes considered that the good faith of the United States government was being threatened by the effort to occupy this region, which had been set aside for eventual use by Indians. On the basis of other provisions in the *Revised Statutes*, he directed that the War Department, in consultation with the Indian Bureau, should repel any attempt to contravene the law.[19] Acting on directions from the secretary of war, on May 2 General Sherman ordered General Sheridan to send detachments of troops to towns along the southern border of Kansas, with orders to warn emigrants that if they entered Indian Territory they would be ejected. "Some judicious officer, say Col. C. H. Smith 19th Infty, or Lieut. Col. R. I. Dodge of the 23rd," with a few young officers, should patrol the border cautioning emigrants in the same manner.[20] In the Department of the Missouri, Sherman's orders were quickly complied with by the adjutant, General Pope then being absent in New York at a court-martial.[21] Colonel Smith, who was currently posted at Fort Leavenworth, left for Coffeyville and other points on May 4, and companies from Forts Supply, Dodge, Reno, Lyon, and Gibson were soon in the field. On May 7 Sherman, with the president

19. Section 2149 of the *Revised Statutes* authorized the Commissioner of Indian Affairs, with approval of the secretary of the interior, to remove by force from a tribal reservation any person there without legal authority or judged detrimental to the peace and welfare of the Indians. Section 2150 authorized military forces to be employed in Indian Territory, as directed by the president, to apprehend intruders, seize property, repel persons attempting entry, and destroy distilleries (p. 374). For a map showing the "Unassigned Lands," see No. 33, "Indian Territory, 1866–1889," in Morris et al., *Historical Atlas of Oklahoma*.

20. Sherman to Sheridan, May 2, 1879 (MDM Settlers in I.T. Special File).

21. The trial, an outgrowth of a long controversy between Colonel William B. Hazen, Sixth Infantry, and Colonel David S. Stanley, Twenty-second Infantry, took place at Governor's Island, New York, at intervals in April through June. The proceedings attracted much attention, and their results were made public on June 17. Colonel Stanley was found guilty of conduct to the prejudice of good order and military discipline for threatening Hazen and other inappropriate acts. He was sentenced to be admonished in General Orders by the General of the Army (*ANJ*, April 12, 1879, pp. 654–56; April 26, pp. 674–75; May 3, pp. 693–94; May 10, pp. 710–12; June 21, p. 331).

and the secretary of war standing in his office, telegraphed Sheridan to send out yet more troops, using whatever cavalry units could be spared from Forts Supply and Elliott. He added that Army officers were free to act without consulting representatives of the Indian Bureau, and free also to use force if necessary.[22]

Reports from the field suggested that, upon recognizing the government's determination to resist their effort, would-be settlers had abandoned the idea at once. On May 4 an inspector for the Indian Bureau, John McNeil, came upon Colonel Carpenter in Coffeyville and found him "the same bragging, lying nuisance" he had known during the war. At Independence, a few miles north, Carpenter had arranged to be paid by local merchants upon his delivery there of a certain number of potential homesteaders, but he had not been able to keep his side of the bargain.[23] An Army officer at Vinita, in the northeast corner of Indian Territory, reported that an Indian agent had noticed many marked-off claims, with the claimant's names carved on tree trunks, but the settlers themselves were not to be found.[24] Near Wichita, on the western edge of the span of territory where an invasion of settlers seemed likely, emigrants had either homesteaded north of the state line or else gone home.[25] On May 11 General Pope, who had returned to his headquarters to direct operations, pronounced the supposed invasion "not only greatly exaggerated but practically a humbug." He suggested it had been a test case to ascertain the strength of the government's will to enforce the law.[26]

The prompt work of the military—even if against an unarmed and mainly invisible foe—won praise in Washington, D.C. The president and the secretary of war were much pleased with the result, especially since it had been achieved without violence to any emigrant. However, turning back new settlers had corrected only part of what General

22. Sherman to Sheridan, May 7, 1879 (MDM Settlers in I.T. Special File).
23. John McNeil to E. A. Hayt, May 4, 1879 (MDM Settlers in I.T. Special File).
24. Captain John A. Wilcox to AAG DMO, May 26, 1879 (MDM Settlers in I.T. Special File).
25. C. H. Smith to AAG DMO, May 15, 1879 (MDM Settlers in I.T. Special File).
26. Pope to Sheridan, May 11, 1879 (MDM Settlers in I.T. Special File).

Pope believed could be a continuing problem—namely, settlers already established in Indian Territory who had been overlooked by the troops passing along its northern border. He ordered military units already away from their posts to scour the areas where they were then located, ejecting any unauthorized citizens they might come upon. For a similar purpose, he also ordered Major Mizner to send a mounted detachment scouting east toward the Sac and Fox reservation, since the prospective capital of the emigrant movement was said to be located somewhere in the area. To round out the investigation, on May 12 Pope ordered Captain Randall's company of mounted infantry to move northward from Cantonment to the Kansas state line in search of settlers, then east to the Wichita–Fort Reno road.[27] Randall and his men, with Amos Chapman as guide, left the post four days later.

Dodge had known little if anything of the "mythical invasion,"[28] as Pope termed it, until May 9, when telegraphic instructions from General Sherman to post commanders in the region reached him. He had instead been expecting a call for assistance from Fort Reno, where tensions had heightened.[29] The band under Little Chief had dwindled slightly, to about 175 persons, but its influence was disproportionate to its number. Most of the other five thousand Cheyennes and Arapahos attached to the agency were reconciled in varying degrees to their enforced new mode of life, but the unruly Northern Cheyennes stirred up sympathetic sentiments in some of their neighbors. In recent weeks a new grievance had been added to the angry band's list of resentments. In accordance with the Indian Bureau's policy to educate its charges, Agent Miles was making a determined effort to enroll their children in the agency school. Little Chief in particular objected strongly to this initiative, claiming that General Sheridan had promised that no such requirement would ever be made of him. Some of his

27. Pope to Sheridan, May 14, 1879 (MDM Settlers in I.T. Special File).

28. Pope to AG, June 3, 1879 (AGO LR).

29. On April 2 Dodge had pledged to Mizner his assistance "to the extent of the whole available force at my command" in the event of Indian trouble near Fort Reno. "I have only one (1) mounted company but have sufficient wagons to transport 50 to 100 Infantry at short notice" (CNFCR LS).

children had already died in the Indian Territory, he said, and he would not give up his only remaining school-age child to do manual labor and be made a slave at the school.[30] Miles could make no headway on this point. He considered withdrawing rations to compel compliance, and he even thought of calling in the military. Prudently, however, for the time being he decided not to attempt compulsion.

What was to be done with these troublesome Indians, whose recalcitrance threatened to set back the Indian Bureau's civilizing mission at the agency? Agent Miles and his assistant Charles E. Campbell agreed that, if the band was to be kept in Indian Territory, the use of force would be necessary. On March 10 Miles inquired of the Commissioner of Indian Affairs what long-term policy the Bureau intended to adopt with regard to Little Chief. A few days later Campbell posed the same question in a different way. The chieftain wished to know whether his wish to depart from Indian Territory would be granted by the authorities in Washington, D.C. Why not permit him to journey there and learn his fate "from the fountain head"?[31] Eventually this proposal was judged a good one, and the confrontation over school enrollment was set aside. Preparing for the journey as Little Chief's escort, Agent Miles reminded Hayt that the policy to be made known to the visitors was still not known even to him. The Indians with him knew, he added, that Dull Knife's comrade Little Wolf had recently been permitted to remain in the north, and they could see no reason why that rebellious segment of the tribe should possess any stronger claim to consideration than they.[32]

Agent Miles arrived in Washington, D.C., with Little Chief and five other head men on May 14 and remained there a fortnight. Several conferences with Secretary Schurz, whom the Indians named Big Eyes for his thick glasses, proved unsatisfactory, especially to the secretary.

30. Campbell to E. A. Hayt, March 14, 1879; Miles to Hayt, April 24, 1879 (OIA LR, C&A); Senate, *Report . . . on the Removal of the Northern Cheyennes*, pp. 52, 87, 188.
31. Campbell to Hayt, March 4, 1879; Miles to Hayt, March 10, 1879; Campbell to Hayt, March 14, 1879 (OIA LR, C&A).
32. Miles to Hayt, April 24, 1879 (OIA LR, C&A).

Little Chief, Northern Cheyenne (Western History Collections, University of Oklahoma Libraries)

Schurz was unable to answer their chief question until he had conferred with the president; and when he had done so, he found it impossible to make them comprehend the federal statutes that applied to
their case.[33] At last he turned them over to Commissioner Hayt,
admitting that "I can do nothing more with them." By his own account,
Hayt read to them the treaties and the law and told them "it was their
duty to obey the law and go South." After a long conversation, Hayt
later testified, they agreed to stay in the South and be "'good Indians.'"
The question of school attendance was not resolved to everyone's satisfaction in this interview, but Little Chief was granted an exception for
his school-aged child. Hayt promised each visitor fifty dollars, a suit of
clothes, and for Little Chief's band an extra supply of wagons and
cattle that had been requested. On the whole, the visit to Washington,
D.C., appears to have been mutually satisfactory, even though the
Northern Cheyennes had not been granted their wish. Before their
return to Indian Territory, Hayt and Miles took them to New York City,
where from their hotel window they watched a great parade, with
several thousand former soldiers in uniform, moving down a city street
on Decoration Day. The scene impressed the Indians greatly, Hayt
reported, revealing to them "the power of the government."[34]

The policy of the Indian Bureau was now known to Miles and the
Indian leaders, but the Army had not yet been informed. Pope was
certain that, should Little Chief be denied his wish, he would resort
to violence at the first opportunity, possibly with devastating results.
It was essential to know what course Secretary Schurz had decided
upon. Pope made this point in a telegram to Sheridan on May 14 and
more urgently in another to the adjutant general two weeks later.[35] At
last, on June 2, Schurz informed the secretary of war that the Indians

33. *New York Times*, May 16, 1879, p. 5; May 20, 1879, p. 1; Senate, *Report . . .
on the Removal of the Northern Cheyennes*, pp. 86, 146–47, 188. According to the
Army and Navy Journal, Little Chief told Schurz that he would rather die than
conform to the white man's ways (May 24, 1879, p. 745).

34. Senate, *Report . . . on the Removal of the Northern Cheyennes*, pp. 87, 186,
188–89.

35. Pope to Sheridan, May 14, 1879 (MDM Settlers in I.T. Special File); Pope to
AG, May 27, 1879 (AGO LR).

would remain on their reservation in Indian Territory.[36] The next day, with the Indian delegation already en route to Wichita, Pope took action. Leaving infantry troops stationed along the Kansas border to discourage any further efforts at invasion, he directed all cavalry units that had been brought to the state line to return to Fort Reno. In addition, he explained to the adjutant general that "our only course is to keep the Indian and some of his principal men in some mild custody" for the present, at the same time disarming and dismounting the rest of the band. Adopting this course would set aside the Army's mandate not to interfere with Indians unless requested by a representative of the Indian Bureau, and Pope therefore asked authorization from the General of the Army. "These measures may be necessary only for a short time," he urged, "but surely such precaution is better than the undoubted risk, especially after last year's experience."[37]

Under these tense circumstances, on June 3 Dodge received from Mizner a call for two companies from Cantonment to further reinforce the garrison at Fort Reno.[38] Little Chief's tribespeople had by now learned of the government's decision in their case. They remained quiet, expecting to learn more on the arrival of their leaders, but Mizner wished to be fully prepared in case of emergency. Dodge was chagrined to lose this many more of his troops, not because he underestimated the seriousness of the situation, but because he judged that Mizner was unlikely to use an augmented military force. Of course, the departure of two companies from Cantonment would effectively put an end to construction work there. Begun so auspiciously, the effort had soon been impeded, first by the effort to repel the settler invaders and now by the need, in Mizner's phrase, to "overawe opposition" from Little Chief.[39] However, as Dodge remarked in his journal entry for June 6, "sich is life." Within a few days he hoped to depart from Cantonment himself, on a long delayed leave of absence.

36. Carl Schurz to SW, June 2, 1879 (AGO LR).
37. Pope to AG, June 3, 1879 (AGO LR).
38. CNFCR Post Return, June 1879; S.O. 47, June 6, 1879, CNFCR.
39. Mizner to AAG DMO, June 4, 1879 (AGO LR).

The journal that follows, with entries written between May 23 and June 18, 1879, conveys Dodge's confident satisfaction that he had done all he could while at Cantonment thus far, and that he had indeed accomplished a great deal. If the post was not yet what he wished, the circumstances that had held back its construction were beyond his control. He would return, and perhaps at that time his grand vision for the permanent structures would be realized. Before leaving Cantonment he wrote out instructions, offered some good advice to his successor Captain Randall, and paid a call on all the resident ladies, just as he would at a long-established post. He was pleased at the camaraderie that had developed between himself and the younger officers, whom he called his "boys."

Dodge's most recent leave of absence had been in December 1877, eighteen months previous,[40] and he had not seen his wife and family since. Absence from Cantonment would permit him to resume that other life in some measure, and he looked forward to it with eager anticipation. Traveling with his escort along the road past Skeleton Ranch, he saw for the first time Caldwell, Kansas, a colorful frontier town on the verge of a boom in speculation on land, railroad development, and other enterprises both legal and otherwise.[41] Along the road to Wichita he caught sight of Little Chief and his party, riding in the opposite direction. He wrote afterward that the Indians "created a sensation" among lookers-on: "A brawny buck with white shirt, elaborate necktie and felt hat, had buckskin leggings, and moccasins, and held over his head a lady's parasol. Another buttoned to the chin in a thick coat, had his nether extremities covered in the same way, was without a hat, but fanned himself incessantly with a huge gaudily painted Chinese fan. Not one had a full suit of civilized clothing, and if each had studied his 'getup,' for a month, he could not have fitted himself out more ridiculously."[42] At that moment the Northern Cheyennes

40. Twenty-third Infantry Regimental Returns, November and December, 1877; RID Personnel File—AGO.
41. For a contemporary account of Caldwell during this yeasty period in its history, see Freeman, *Midnight and Noonday*, passim.
42. *OWI*, p. 300.

were objects more of amusement than concern to Dodge as they completed their journey toward the "mild custody" Pope and Mizner had in store for them. From Wichita, his journal records a journey at railroad speed across the continent, breaking off with him in upstate New York on the night before he was to surprise his wife Julia by his return.

Journal Five
May 23–June 18, 1879

Friday, May 23, 1879[1]

All going on as usual.   Hot as blazes.   Have some men mowing the parade ground.   The saw mill ready for work by noon tomorro.

Walls of Drs house & Compy Kitchen nearly up.   Got to work on my cellar & wash house – doing well.   Wrote to Genl Pope private – about going on leave.   Wrote to Coppinger asking him to come & take Comd. during my absence.[2]

Caught up with the trees

Saturday, May 24, 1879

A busy day.   Before I went to the office, I laid out the foundation for my temporary hospital[3]   Attended to office work, looked at the saw mill & made my rounds as usual.   More desertions last night – making 21 in all - & reducing my strength tremendously   Only about four fatigue men today in all this Garrison – but theres lots of extra &

1. The manuscript journal, which consists of sixty unnumbered pages, is identical in style and dimensions to Journals One, Two, and Three. Like Journal Four, it includes a sheet of unlined laid paper that serves as a flyleaf within the front and back covers. On the front cover Dodge has written an identification in dark ink: "<Ute Campaign> [/] Cantonment [/] 1879." The remainder of the journal text is in pencil. At the bottom of the front cover, in the handwriting of a person other than Dodge, is the notation "May 23/ 79 to [/] June 18/ 79." Pages [1] and [38V]–[60] are blank. The text begins on p. [2R].

2. Major John J. Coppinger had relinquished the small remaining portion of a sick leave and reported for duty at Fort Leavenworth on May 14.

3. Subsequently enlarged to accommodate twenty-six beds, the temporary hospital consisted of a series of large tents issued especially for use by the Medical Department (R. B. Marcy to W. T. Sherman, November 25, 1879—AGO LR).

daily duty men.[4]   About noon the mail arrived.   No private letters. Dr. Comfort is coming in Biarts place.[5]   I am pleased with the change – for he is a good Dr. & sensible man.   Wrote to Genl Pope, to Coppinger, Misses V. V – Cousin Cath, Genl Saxton   Mailed my diary to Father.[6]   Later in the evening a Sergt & party came in from Randall, with provision returns but not a line or scratch of a pen about any thing.   I sat down & wrote him a scorcher – for not sending Chapman back & not letting me know something of his work.[7]   I also wrote to Chapman telling him that if he did'nt come back in 3 days, I would discharge him, & get another Interpreter –

Coppinger is appointed Asst Inspr Genl of the Dept. – so my eloquence was wasted on him.[8]

Wrote a short note to Father & Mother at night.   Wanted to write more but was prevented by Clarke who stayed an unconscionable time.   Made the rounds again this p.m.   Everything lovely.   For the first time in the history of the World, the Whistle of the engine resounded in the valley of the North Fork.   The Engineer got up steam & sawed one log, just to show, & he did it splendidly

Wh - o - o - o - o - p

4. Fatigue duty was labor at digging, cleaning, road building, and similar projects. Extra duty was work requiring special skills, such as that performed by masons, wheelwrights, and tailors; soldiers assigned to it received thirty-five cents per day in addition to their regular pay. Daily duty was employment on a continuing basis in a particular department, such as the adjutant's or quartermaster's office. See *Revised Army Regulations*, p. 151; Rickey, *Forty Miles a Day on Beans and Hay*, pp. 91-98.

5. On May 11 Assistant Surgeon Biart, then on sick leave, had been transported to Atchison, Kansas, for treatment (*ANJ*, May 17, 1879, p. 727; S.O. 34, May 11—CNFCR). Acting Assistant Surgeon Aaron I. Comfort was being transferred to Cantonment from duty at Fort Hays (S.O. 96, May 16—DMO).

6. Probably this was Dodge's journal, now lost, covering the period April 14 through May 22.

7. Randall and his company were moving toward the Kansas state line in search of settlers. His orders were to send to Wichita regular reports that would be forwarded to departmental headquarters, but Dodge expected to be kept informed as well (S.O. 38, May 15—CNFCR).

8. Coppinger was named acting inspector general for the Department of the Missouri on May 20 (*ANJ*, May 31, 1879, p. 765).

Sunday, May 25, 1879

All quiet & lovely this bright morning.   Nothing to do, & I did it. Took a short walk after office hours, & then sat down to read my papers, & anything that came to hand.   Very hot but got through the day comfortably.   Walked in afternoon looked after my trees. Everything needs rain & if I had any influence with the Clerk of the Weather, I'd exert it.

Monday, May 26, 1879

Work all going on well.   Started Sergt Reese & his party back to Randall[9]   Went out with Trout to visit the lime kiln & rock quarry, & was delighted with every thing.   The openings made show me that I have stone enough[10] to build two or half dozen posts, & on careful examination I find that I didn't know half the value of the limestone. There is a thousand times more than I supposed & that under cover is almost pure marble –   I am most agreeably surprised both by quantity & quality.   I would greatly prefer to build the Post of stone. The only drawback is the lack of wagons.   I have written for more & if I get them I will build the whole Post of stone & the Comdg. Offrs Quarters shall be of Marble.[11]

If I can rig a stone saw to the engine, I will cut Mantel pieces, & other fancy things for every set of quarters at the post –   The lime kiln is in full blast, & the Sergt promises 400 bushels of better lime than we have heretofore had.

Then we went fishing on the creek near the Quarry.   I got forty, cats perch & bass – all were small fish though some of the perch were large of their kind.   It was quite warm but I had a very delightful day.

---

9. These men were Sergeant Charles Reis, Private Charles A. Whren, Lafayette Van Ordan, and Thomas Steward, all of Company I (S.O. 42, May 23, 1879— CNFCR).

10. Dodge wrote "enought."

11. While in command of Fort Lyon in 1869-1871 and Fort Dodge in 1872-1873, Dodge had supervised the construction of several stone buildings, some of which remain in use today. Army regulations specified that any post that housed two or more companies must include a separate residence for the commanding officer. The latter residences tended to become showplaces.

Trout & Boon (the ambulance driver[)] got about 15 each.   We had a fine string.   To bed early

Tuesday, May 27, 1879

A pleasant day.   The Saw Mill has been going all day, & has done beautifully.   Chapman got in about 1 p.m.   He did'nt meet Sergt Reese, & did'nt get my letter.   Randall kept him.

Work going on well.   A little hitch today from scarcity of roofing poles.[12]   Will try to rectify it.   Estimates for Hospital go in by next mail –

Wednesday, May 28, 1879

The mail party got in about 1 pm. with 20 water barrels, some iron & steel & a small box of ice – all from Ft Reno.   Mail brought many letters but only two private – one from Father & Mother, the other from Sis Annie thanking me for letting the estate off some interest[13] A semi- official letter from Pardee, tells me that Coppinger is A. I. G. of the Dept.   Pardee got his delay.   He says that Genl Pope entirely approved my assumption of the Comd of the Regt. & made an endorsement to that effect on Dallas' paper.[14]

Wrote a letter to the latter about his geography   Very official & dignified but will gall him to the quick.   He tried to make me send out to bury a dead soldier, when the remains are 35 miles from him & over 75 miles from me.[15]

12. Poles extending from the top of the outside walls to the peak of the roof.

13. As the next day's journal entry makes more clear, Dodge was making provision for his sightless sister, Mary Helen Dodge ("Sis Molly"), by not requiring the payment of interest on funds he had loaned to family members.

14. First Lieutenant Julius H. Pardee, the post adjutant, had accompanied Dr. Biart to Atchison, Kansas, and was now on one month's leave of absence, the inception of which had been delayed at his request (S.O. 34, May 11—CNFCR; S.O. 93, May 12—DMO). By "Dallas' paper" Dodge refers to the letter of May 10 in which Major Alexander H. Dallas had raised questions about the propriety of Dodge's unilaterally assuming command of the regiment. See the journal entries for April 9 and 13, 1879.

15. Dodge's letter, in response to one of May 12 from Dallas, concerned the exposed remains of Private George Sand of Captain Sebastian Gunther's Company H, Fourth Cavalry. Sand had been killed the previous September 13 at Turkey Springs (CNFCR LS). See Wright, "The Pursuit of Dull Knife," pp. 147–48.

I wrote a report to Genl Pope, about the removal of the settlers, & took occasion (presumptuously perhaps) to recommend a certain line of action to the President –[16]   Wrote to Father & Mother also to Julia – Wrote to Platt about Smiths coming back to this post – & urged that he be put on some duty which will keep him away until I get back.[17]

Played Crib with Pollock at night & got beat.   Work going on admirably   Made the rounds, & spent an hour in my Orchard

Thursday, May 29, 1879

Nothing of importance to record.   Made the rounds morning & evening – found everything going on well.

Had to pitch into the men who are mowing the parade ground, for laziness.   Wrote to Sis Annie, & proposed to transfer to her the notes she gave me   ∧   as executrix   for money loaned the estate – for the $1000 which would be hers after death of Father & Mother.   If she agrees it will all go to Sis Molly.

Fridy 30, 1879

Nasty day, with a high & hot south wind –   Wanted to go fishing, but put it off.   Was too much like work.   Work going on well, but not so rapidly as in cooler weather.

16. Writing on the basis of a report from Randall with further information from its bearer, Amos Chapman, Dodge expressed his belief that settlers expelled from Indian Territory would return to their places of residence or occupation there as soon as troops left the vicinity. He proposed a draconian solution: "This case can be entirely prevented and these border troubles settled for all time by directing the Comdg officers of Posts within or near the Territory to send out from time to time scouting parties with directions to destroy all improvements made by settlers within the Territory and to capture all cattle and stock therein found and turn it over to the Agent for the benefit of the Indians. An order from the President to this effect will effectually put a stop to all further attempts to invade the Indian Territory" (RID to AAG DMO, May 28, 1879— MDM Settlers in I.T. Special File). The recommendation was not acted upon.

17. Captain Thomas M. K. Smith's leave of absence had already been extended one month (S.O. 55, May 22—DMO). His effectiveness as a company commander had been compromised by his drinking habit, but Dodge felt himself capable of exerting a good influence on him. See R. B. Marcy to W. T. Sherman, November 25, 1879 (AGO LR).

Made my rounds & worked at my trees.   392 are growing well, of 774 put out.   Looked like rain, but it wont come, though we need it greatly.   Crib at night with Pollock & beat him badly.

Saturday, May 31, 1879

Ordered the saw log choppers in.   Have made up my mind to build the post of stone.   The timber is quite abundant, but of poor quality, & I don't dare trust to it alone.   I can get all the joists rafters, & sheathing I need   The stone is ample for all our wants, but we need more wagons –

After Office hours, I ordered the ambulance & went down the river fishing   The river is a mere brook – a broad sand bed with a narrow shallow thread of water.   Where it strikes the banks it cuts out holes in which the fish keep hid.   I fished faithfully & covered a great deal of ground but got only about 20 – only one of decent size – 1 pound.

Saw an Indian ∧ woman cutting steaks off a horse drowned in the quick sands.   The Arrapahoes are almost starved.[18]   The Agent has cut off their supplies for some reason.[19]   The poor creatures have a hard time, & those who ought to be their friends treat them worst

Sunday, June 1, 1879

Blew up quite cold last night & this the first day of summer is the coolest & pleasantest day for six weeks.   I was quite tired after my

18. Dodge records this scene as an instance of near starvation among the Indians, echoing Amos Chapman's controversial statement of the previous September that Cheyenne Indians had been driven by hunger to eat the flesh of horses dead from disease or natural causes. The notion of the Indians' eating carrion had then become a focal point for controversy between those who attacked or defended the Indian Bureau's administration of the Cheyenne and Arapaho agency; see above, pp. 55-57.

19. Dodge soon learned the reason. On learning that Indians in his charge were cutting cordwood in an arrangement devised by Dodge for their benefit, Agent Miles or his assistant had ordered them to stop work and return at once to the agency. When they refused, they were deprived of their rations and, Dodge later wrote, "came near starving" (RID to AAG DMO, March 4, 1880—CNFCR LS). See the journal entry for June 1.

fishing yesterday – & after dinner I laid down on my bed went to sleep, & slept 4 hours, then waked enough to get up & undress, & put in another 8 hours without a struggle.　The mail got in early.　No private letters.　Smith has an extension of a month – Pardee authorized to delay another 10 days, & Heyl ordered to report to Supdt Rec[ruitin]g service to bring out recruits.[20]　Moral – dont let an Officer go – as you can never tell when he will come back –

Clarke started yesterday to Dodge City after his wife – should be back in a week.

Wrote to Bickford the contractor about the wood – Indians have 420 cords.[21]　Wrote long letter to Father & Mother – about proposal

20. Second Lieutenant Charles H. Heyl had been ordered by the War Department to report to the General Recruiting Service in order to conduct recruits to the Department of the Missouri (*ANJ*, May 31, 1879, p. 765).

21. Dodge's letter to L. H. Bickford, firewood contractor for the post, has not survived, but its background and contents are evident from a report on another matter, dated March 4, 1880. Early in April Minimick (also spelled Mah-ni-mick, Minimic, Mehnimick, and in other ways), a Southern Cheyenne, arrived in the vicinity of the post with his band of about 150 persons under an agreement to cut wood for the current contractor, Lee and Reynolds. However, Dodge subsequently learned that the wood being cut was not intended solely for present use at Cantonment. Instead, following a practice Lee and Reynolds had adopted at Forts Reno and Supply, the Indians had orders to cut and rack all the available wood within easy reach of the post on behalf of their employers, who would claim it as their own. When a new contract was to be let, they would sell the unused wood at a greatly increased price, having made competition all but impossible. On April 25 Dodge informed J. E. McAllister, agent for Lee and Reynolds, the contractors, that this procedure would not be tolerated. The Indians were to stop cutting as soon as the present contract was filled, and no right of property in any additional firewood would be recognized.

The Indians stopped work at once, but a few days afterward Dodge received a letter from Charles E. Campbell, Agent Miles's assistant. Campbell explained that Minimick and his people had expected to support themselves by cutting cordwood for Lee and Reynolds as an alternative to farming. Without that employment they would soon suffer, since the agency lacked the means to support them throughout the summer. Dodge, on friendly terms with some of the Indians and wishing to support their effort to help themselves, worked out a scheme that he thought would satisfy all parties. He gave the Indians permission to cut and rack cordwood, with the understanding that the wood would remain unsold for the time being but would be made available to the next contractor at the rate of $1.25 per cord. The Indians gladly agreed, and by the time the next contract was let—to Bickford—the wood was ready. The letter to Bickford referred to in this day's journal entry concerned the amount he was to pay the Indians, which he did (RID to AAG DMO, March 4, 1880—CNFCR LS).

I make to Sis Annie   Wrote out instructions to Post Comdr. in my absence.   Paid my bills & went to bed happy

Monday, June 2, 1879

Work going on better today, there being all the men who came in from the wood party.

Dr. Le Garde[22] & wife arrived about 2 p.m.   She is the first Lady at the new post.   It has been a fine bracing day, & everything has gone on well.   Arranged to increase size of hospital.   Dr.s house in fair way to completion   Crib at night with Pollock beat him –

Tuesday, June 3, 1879

A beautiful day, tho' warm.   After getting through my mornings work, I was in the act of changing my dress to go fishing, when a courier arrived from Ft Reno, bringing a letter from Mizner, making a demand on me for 2 Companies – 60 men –   I knew this would be the case when Pope gave him authority to call on me.   He is a fuss & feathers kind of man – always wanting more troops & swelling about his Command.   There is no <s>possible use for Infantry at Reno at present, & he knows it as well as I do.[23]   When Little Chief gets back, there may be a reason for calling on me –

22. Assistant Surgeon Louis A. La Garde, previously on duty in the Department of the East, was transferred to the Department of the Missouri on May 14 and assigned to Cantonment as his first posting. Taking up his duties as post surgeon on June 2, he served in that capacity until June 1882 (G. O. 14, June 2—CNFCR; CNFCR Post Returns).

23. Mizner did prefer cavalry to infantry as reinforcements for his post. Early in May he had visited Cantonment and discussed with Dodge the troops he might draw upon, but Randall's company of mounted infantry was not available owing to its commitment elsewhere. Wishing to assist Mizner, Pope proposed to Sheridan that four or five companies of the Fifth Cavalry be sent to Fort Reno for duty through the late fall (Mizner to AAG DMO, May 11, 1879, with endorsements—MDM Settlers in I.T. Special File). These reinforcements were not forthcoming, so on June 2 Pope ordered to Fort Reno two companies then at Vinita, Indian Territory, under Captain J. A. Wilcox, Fourth Cavalry (ANJ, June 14, 1879, p. 804). Combined with the units under Wilcox and the regular garrison at Fort Reno, the two infantry companies from Cantonment made eight companies that would be under Mizner's command when Little Chief and his companions arrived at the agency after their trip to Washington, D.C.

which I will gladly respond to – but I dont gladly respond to this. It breaks into all my arrangements, & almost entirely stops work on the post.   The "powers" expect me to build a fifty thousand dollar post without money, & now it is proposed I shall do it without workmen.   The result is that I shall run away on my leave early in next week.[24]

I went out fishing in spite of my disgust, & got about 30 cats & perch.   They were small, & not much sport, but I have the satisfaction of knowing that no other man at this post could have taken half as many.   Killed a 3 1/2 lb buffalo fish[25] with rifle – the only one I have seen in this vecinity.   Killed also one or two gars, which bothered my hook – one I caught fairly, and bagged him – the other I shot to get rid of.   The river is so low that it seems incredible that any fish should be in it.   The wide sand bed has the merest thread of water.   The fish are in shallow holes under the banks.

Whist at Pollocks after Taps – until 12 pm   We came out even in spite of Pollocks bad play –   He was my partner

Wednesday, June 4, 1879

After office hours I went to call on Mrs La Garde.   Found her a very pleasant woman, not pretty nor stylish – but with a very sweet & good expression & manner.

About 5 pm Randall reported with his Compy   He had recd. a telegram from Genl Pope ordering him to return to the Cantonment with all speed[26]   He had not finished his work of clearing out the settlers, but of course came at once on the order.

---

24. A one-month leave of absence, with permission to apply for an extension of two months, had been granted Dodge on April 18 (S.O. 76—DMO), but he had not yet been able to avail himself of it. A subsequent order on June 5 brought his time off duty a step closer. He was "to proceed from his post to Fort Leavenworth, superintending en route the construction and repair of the road to Wichita" (S.O. 110—DMO). After he had transacted business at Fort Leavenworth, his leave of absence would begin.

25. A fish of the genus *Ictiobus*, having a humped back.

26. The intent of the order, officially confirmed by S.O. 107, June 2, DMO, was to place Randall and his company nearer Fort Reno in the event of trouble.

John K. Mizner (Massachusetts Commandery, M.O.L.L.U.S., U.S. Army Military History Institute)

Soon after his arrival I went up with the head Carpenter and laid off the foundation of the first set of Company Qrs.[27]   My old lines run by the eye, are almost absolutely correct.

Beautiful night, & Randall and I sat far into it, gassing on all sorts of topics –   Dr La Garde being in Randalls house the latter stops with me –

Thursday, June 5, 1879

Made the rounds as usual & found all the working parties doing well.   Got my wash house nearly completed today & will go away leaving Joe & Laura well fixed –   Mail arrived about noon bringing a letter from Father & Mother – very satisfactory.   Nothing from Mizner, who calls for men, but dont tell what he wants with them. Trout put in an application for sick leave today, having a very full & careful certificate from the Dr.[28]   Letter from Smith asking how he is to get back.   Wrote to him that I didn't know.   Wrote a personal & also an official letter to Mizner.   Wrote to Father & Mother telling them of my determination to start on Tuesday 10 –   They will hop! – The men have done a fine days work today, & if Mizner had let me alone for ten days I'd have had my cantonment completed.   He wont hurt me much however —

Friday, June 6, 1879

Just 3 months today since we took up our residence at this spot – then a wild country without a habitation within 60 miles.   Now we

27. Only two civilian carpenters were employed at Cantonment during June 1879. One, who worked at the rate of seventy-five dollars per month, was Charles Zann, thirty-five years of age. He returned his pass to the provost marshal on June 5, having worked only five days during the month. The other, who worked at thirty dollars per month, was W. H. Collard, thirty-nine years of age, who worked twenty-two days (CNFCR Pass Book; CNFCR Post Return, June 1879).

28. Trout was requesting a six-month leave of absence. Endorsing his application, Dodge wrote: "Lieut Trout suffers considerably and is getting worse daily. His services are almost invaluable, but he has consented to remain here and discharge his duties until I return from leave of absence, after which he should be granted leave or retired" (CNFCR LS).

have comfortable houses for the Officers, good store houses a saw mill, & most of the evidences of civilization

Issued orders this am for K & D Cos, under Goodale to report to Maj Mizner at Reno.   It will hurt me greatly in my work, but "sich is life" –   I would not mind it at all if I thought Mizner would do anything with these troops, but he wont.   They will be kept near his post to swell his importance all summer unless the Indians break out. An Employee of the Indian Dept came up today.   He says Mizner is on a war footing everything ready, but that all the troops are at the Fort, while the refractory Indians are from 15 to 20 miles away –[29]   I have told him that I would send him every man I can spare if he wants to "round up" the Indians, but I dont propose to send Troops there to sit around & do nothing all summer when I need them here.   Ordered Dr Shriner to go with Goodale & return immediately   Clarke & his wife got in tonight about 9 pm –   Madam is said to have stood the trip well.   I have not seen her.   Lots of orders & letters to get off today –   Very little work done by the men since 1 p.m.

Saturday, June 7, 1879

On the night of the 5th a prisoner escaped from the guard house. He was an utterly worthless fellow but I wanted to stop this deserting business.   Sent to Chapman at once & by daylight on 6th there were about 50 Indians scattered all over the country looking for him.   This morning about 2 Ock, Chapman came & knocked at my door.   I went out & there were about a dozen Indians & my deserter in their midst.   He was taken down & turned over to the Guard, securely tied & this morning at Guard Mounting I had him ironed.[30]   This will pretty effectually stop the deserting business.

29. It was not uncommon for Indians to encamp some miles away from the agency, nor was it surprising at this time, given the unusual number of troops stationed near there. However, Mizner was convinced that his show of military strength was a deterrent to trouble (Mizner to AAG DMO, June 18, 1879—OIA LR, C&A).

30. This was Private George D. Myers. See above, pp. 209-10.

Goodale & his Command got off about 8 am.   He came to me before I was up, to get more wagons – but I told him he could'nt have any, & that if he could not take his property on the Wagon, he must leave it.   He went off, & I learned soon after that he had taken everything.   Dr. Comfort arrived today.   <They>He went into O Connors Qrs, until his house can be fixed up.   The saw mill is nearly completed.   The roof will be done in one more good days work.   Called on Mrs. Clarke[31]   She is very jolly & happy & "agreeably disappointed" –   Letter from Dallas about transpn.   Pardee will be here on 12th.[32]   A hot & lazy day.   Men worked well, & a lot of stores came from Wichita

Sunday, June 8, 1879

Having been out of sorts for a day or two from lack of exercise, I made this a day of healthful work.   After office hours I took the ambulance & putting in Joe and Laura the Baby, & Boon the driver, & Robinson my factotum on bait &c, I started out – first to make a final inspection of my stone quarry & lime kiln, next to have a good fish. Am more than delighted with the Quarries –   I would be glad to give my Venerable Uncle Sam all the money, bonds & notes, I possess for it.   It is a fortune.   There is an immense supply of stone.   Of the lime stone I can only conjecture, the 3 kilns already burned, taking only surface stone & so little that it can scarcely be missed.   I believe there is a million bushels at the very least –

After Inspecting all the works thoroughly, I went down to the Creek, & put in a line   Of course it was not my fault, dear Mammy, that the fish were hungry on Sunday – but they were, & I have never at this post have had such a days fishing.   I fished for 4 hours & took over 80 fish – or an average of 3 a minute –   I got 7 Bass – 2 good ones the

31. While her husband was posted at Fort Leavenworth, Mrs. Clarke and he had appeared in amateur theatricals there. In "an amusing farce" entitled *Who is Who? Or, All in a Fog* she performed on February 28, 1877, as Cicely, "Mr. Brambleton's daughter, with a will of her own." Lieutenant Clarke played Mr. Simonides Swanhopper, a "model young bachelor" (Ovenshine Papers, USAMHI).

32. On his return to the post, First Lieutenant Pardee would resume his duty as post adjutant. First Lieutenant Edward B. Pratt was substituting in his absence.

others small – the others were perch and cats   Had a nice lunch along & made the whole thing a pic-nic.   I enjoyed every moment, & feel a great deal better tonight   Got back at dark –   Shortly after the bell rang & Laura had a supper of fish and other things.   Randall was visiting me & accepted my invitation to come in & see what was to be had – & enjoyed it greatly.

Randalls men have been behaving badly for a day or two & quite a lot were in the Guard house – expecting to sober up & have an easy time until Monday.   I put them all to work this a.m. cutting the grass on Parade Ground & policing generally.   They have worked well, but are a terribly demoralized lot & I dont believe next Saturday will see a repetition of the frolic

Visitors at night, but got to bed by 11 pm

Monday, June 9, 1879

I was so beset by the rapscallions of boys last night that I had no opportunity to write my diary until near 1 am & then I was so overcome by sleep & the various potations I had to take that I left this duty for another day.   It is pleasurable to have all <go as> ones subordinates fond of him.   My boys are good boys.   I treat them well, place confidence in them, & they repay me by an affection of which I am very proud.   I can say from long & ample experience that comparatively few Comdg. Officers have the affection of their subordinates <Hd Qrd &c>if they do their duty   I have a way of "setting down" on my boys which is very telling, & never makes them mad or causes one to forfeit his self respect.[33]

33. Although perhaps written with the approval of his parents as a consideration, Dodge's statement seems genuine. Nine years before, when less accustomed to the role of post commander, he had discussed the same topic in a letter to his wife from Fort Lyon. It was a pleasure, he wrote, "to know that while I am doing what I think is right, I should also secure the approbation and good will of my subordinates. . . . I do deserve commendation for my conduct in com[man]d of this post, more than I ever have before. I have controlled with more dignity, impartiality & success than ever before, & the result is that I *command*. I have no trouble, & my will is law to everyone about me, not as that of a Tyrant, but as that of a Brother Officer, who has the interests of all at heart, but who will permit no question or cavil" (RID to Julia R. P. Dodge, January 16, 1870—Dodge Papers, Yale Collection).

Had a good deal of work in the office this a.m. Before I got through the mail arrived. There was no private mail for me except a letter from Mizner, in answer to mine by last mail on the Indian question. He has an overwhelming force but he dont know what to do with it, & will lose those Indians sure – I have the vanity to believe that were I in his place I would settle this whole matter in two weeks. He will play the Grand Seigneur & lose them in the end – & run a big risk of losing his Commission at the same time –

The saw mill was finished today. I gave Trout a permanent detail of 6 men to finish up the few houses of cantonment yet to be erected. All ought to be done in a week or ten days at furthest. I am afraid that Randall & Trout will have trouble. The latter is the very best Quarter Master I have ever seen – but he has a bad temper & an infinity of little meannesses, which rankle in a temperament like Randalls. I manage him perfectly, by severity sometimes – but oftenest by flanking him – & I am so imbued with an appreciation of his real value that I put up with many things that I would not tolerate from a less valuable man. I had a long talk with Randall, urging him to be careful & lenient – but I dont believe they will get along. Randall is quick tempered, fussy in some things, & perfectly honest frank & straight. Trout is quick tempered vindictive & not truthful – & its the latter traits that Randall is so down on. Well, they must "paddle their own canoes" ——[34]

Left detailed instructions for whoever comds the post in my absence – & also for Trout. Have cleaned the whole matters up, & established a rule of action for all, which if all will act up to it, will save all trouble, & I go away feeling that I have done all possible for the post & the service

34. On June 27, hardly more than two weeks after Dodge's departure, at his own request Trout was relieved from duty as post quartermaster and commissary of subsistence (S.O. 61—CNFCR). On July 22 he appeared before a retiring board, which found him incapacitated for active service. Soon afterward Trout was granted leave of absence until further orders on account of disability. He retired from the Army on March 15, 1883, but his career was far from over. In later years he became chief inspector and commissary for the Pullman Palace Car Company, traveling extensively in the United States and Canada from an office in Chicago (*ANJ*, September 5, 1885, p. 99; December 22, 1888, p. 323).

Visited and bade good by to the Ladies - & after tattoo all the officers came up, & we had a pleasant evening.   Some did not go away until after 1 am, & I lost my nice hot bath & my diary ——

The evening presented all the appearances of a tremendous rain storm but though we needed it badly, it went around   Detailed party to go with me tomorro & got all ready for an early start

Tuesday, June 10, 1879

Laura waked me up at dawn.   I bounced up - had breakfast & was all ready to start before reveille.   The wagons did not however get up until after that call - & I got off at 6.30   Have an ambulance & escort wagon - Corpl Yost[35] & 4 men.   The North Fork is not running - water standing in holes.   Arrived at Cimaron at 11 am   It is nothing but a sand bed   Stopped at 11.30 on Game Creek to noon.   Had lunch & then took in about 50 small perch - stayed there until 2.30, then came on.   Would have camped on Elm Creek but there was no water except some stagnant pools.   Came on to Turkey Ck.   Very hot today & the road is abominable - but we made 37 miles - more I think.   My road is infinitely better than this[36]

Wednesday, June 11, 1879

Broke Camp 5.46 am   Arrived at Skeleton Ranch 8.30.   Fired several times at an antelope.   Think I hit him, but he went off.   A great many prairie chickens plover & curlew.   The plover are very tame each old lady having one or two young - some of them nearly grown.   Arrived at Pond Creek 12.30 - making a good march, it being a very hot day   Distance 34 miles.

Yesterday's journey knocked me up.   I think twas the water in Game Ck which tasted sedgy.   Any how my latter end went back on

35. Corporal Martin Joste, Company A, occasionally received special assignments from Dodge, who regarded him as "a good soldier, and a man of irreproachable character" (Entry of January 10, 1880, Endorsements—CNFCR).

36. Dodge designates as "my road" the as yet uncompleted one from Cantonment directly to Pond Creek, as distinguished from the longer and more southerly one he was traveling, which passed Skeleton Ranch before reaching Pond Creek and meeting the Wichita-Fort Reno road.

me, & I have been dilapidated all day – eating nothing until sundown tonight when I got away with 4 soft boiled eggs, & a bottle of beer.

Met Lt Budd on the road returning from leave   He is joining his co[mpany] Hempills at Reno[37]   He had no news & was terribly down in the mouth because his leave was not longer –   Had a long talk with the Stage Agent at Pond Creek about Roads &c –[38]   He tells me that the Stage ride from Caldwell to Wichita is horrible & I have consequently determined to take my Comd. to Wichita.   I'll gain time & comfort. They lose two days which every rascal of them thinks is clear gain from the work of the Post.   The roads are not good – there has been rain here, & with a good deal of freighting the roads become bad   Pond Ck is up, or I would have had some fish tonight, peaked as I feel.

Thursday, June 12, 1879

Got off at 5.50 a.m.   Slept better last night & was not nauseated or restless, but Shob feeds me on nothing but bacon & though I like it better than any other meat, it is greatly conducive to thirst & I had to get up 3 or 4 times in the night to rinse out my "innards"

I feel a great deal better today than yesterday.   Arrived at Caldwell at 11 am   It is a town of some 50 houses – possibly 300 inhabitants & every mothers son or daughter (true to the western instinct) believes himself or herself to be a proud resident of the Great Future Emporium of the Western Country.[39]   It is in fact well situated too

37. First Lieutenant Otho W. Budd, of Captain William Hemphill's Company I, Fourth Cavalry, was stationed at Fort Supply. His unit was on temporary duty at Fort Reno after patrolling the Kansas border in search of illegal settlers. Budd had been on leave since April 8 (Fort Supply Post Return, April–June, 1879).

38. This was William E. Malaley (also spelled Melily, Mellily, Mullaly), owner and proprietor of Pond Creek ranch, postmaster, cattle rancher, contractor, and dealer in real estate. A photograph of Malaley is in Freeman, *Midnight and Noonday*, p. 154.

39. Dodge's parody of the language of boosterism was appropriate to Caldwell. In its issue for October 9, 1879, the *Caldwell Post* characterized the town's recent metamorphosis: "Three months ago it was only Caldwell, and unknown beyond the narrow confines of its own county. Now it is spoken of with many tongues, and at numerous places. . . . It is fast rising into prominence as a town of business and future promise. It presents a scene of life and bustle that leads you to almost believe that the wand of the magician has not been waved in vain. The cause of all this prosperity is the near approach of the railroad and the future promise of the town as a shipping

near the State line for purely legitimate business but just near enough to get a large & profitable contraband trade.   By contraband I do not mean violation of the Revenue Laws – but a trade outside the Law. For instance the Law prohibits any citizen from occupying the Indian Territory.   Numbers of Cattle men occupy it – on the edges, ready to run when danger comes – & these hold Hd Qrs at Caldwell.   The Law prohibits Citizens cutting timber on public lands or reservations without special authority.   Caldwell people cut all they want, and haul it through the streets with impunity —[40]

The R R extension from Wichita, is expected to reach Caldwell this year & the town is full of speculators.[41]   Quite 2 square miles – or enough for a city of 20,000 people has been laid off in town lots which are selling rapidly   If I have any money when I come back in Sepr. I'll buy some as an experiment.   It is a wonderfully busy place – specially now that it is the post[42] as one may call it of two Military posts.   Met Keeling, Bickford, and Ingersoll the lumber man of 11 Worth.   Spent several hours with them.   Took dinner at Pacific Hotel.   Think I'll go to the other next time.[43]   Bought some i<s>ce, beer, butter eggs – also some hay.   The ice is a Godsend.   Two of the mules of my escort wagon were sick when we got in – but got over it.   At 3 pm I pulled out & struck towards Wichita   Went 14 miles & camped at the farm

---

point" ("Caldwell as a City," p. 2). Even John D. Miles was later quoted in the *Kansas City Times* as considering Caldwell "the 'Future great' of Southern Kansas" ("The Oklahoma Movement," n.d. [*circa* February 1880]—OIA LR, C&A). See also Freeman, *Midnight and Noonday*, pp. 182, 185.

40. On May 19, 1879, Captain William H. Clapp, Sixteenth Infantry, reported that on a recent trip over the road to Fort Reno he had seen many teams hauling timber to Caldwell from the vicinity of Pond Creek. He judged that the activity was well established and warned that if permitted to continue it would "quite strip the country of timber" (Clapp to Post Adjutant, Fort Reno, May 19, 1879—OIA LR, C&A).

41. The extension from Wichita to Wellington, twenty-six miles north of Caldwell, was operational by the end of 1879, but the railroad did not reach the latter town until the summer of 1880 (Freeman, *Midnight and Noonday*, p. 192).

42. Dodge may have meant "host," referring to Caldwell as a depot for supplies bound to Cantonment and Fort Reno.

43. The Grand Pacific Hotel was advertised in the *Caldwell Post* for February 19, 1880, as "thoroughly rennovated [*sic*]" and "a first-class house" (p. 1). The other hotel, Caldwell's first, was the City Hotel, erected in 1872. It was destroyed in 1885 amidst a rash of arson and mysterious fires (Freeman, *Midnight and Noonday*, p. 183 n).

House of a man named Wells near Shoo Fly Creek who gave us wood & grain and was very clever generally.   He has a fine farm & the best looking peach orchard I have seen in Kansas, but he says he was swindled & all are seedlings.[44]

Friday, June 13, 1879

Woke up this am to find one of the best of the ambulance mules sick with colic.   It changed all my plans.   I ordered the Corpl & party to stay where they are, & hitching up a mule of the escort team in my ambulance I put out for Wichita

Reached Wellington in good shape in 2 hours said to be 12 miles I think about ten.   Went on - intending to go some 15 miles further & noon it, but it was a showery day, & I kept on.   About 12 m. when I felt that I had exacted all that I could in humanity from my mules I stopped at a creek 8 miles from Wichita & turned out -   <Th>As there was a stream on hand I couldn't resist fishing & went at it with vim catching 17 nice perch and throwing them back when caught -

The showers & cool day kept the mules to their work & about 2.30 I hitched up and came to this *City* - & a very wonderful town I find it, with more business than ten Cities of equal inhabitants in the tame east —[45]

Put up at the Occidental Hotel.   Not much of a hotel but the best to be had.[46]   Hunted up Hermaker the Qr. Mr. Agent[47] & had my

44. Fruit orchards were a prominent part of the southern Kansas economy at this period. In 1876 Sedgwick County, in which Wichita was located, had 224,000 peach trees and smaller numbers of apple, plum, cherry, and pear trees (Miner, *West of Wichita*, p. 87).

45. A bird's eye view of Wichita in 1878, reproduced in Miner, *West of Wichita* (p. 50), confirms this impression. According to Miner, at the time of Dodge's visit the city was moving away from its original economic bases—hunting, government contracting, trading, and cattle—and toward those of a metropolitan center—industry, land speculation, construction, and agricultural processing. Wichita was on the verge of a real estate boom (p. 167).

46. Boasting seventy-six rooms in the hotel proper and five stores on its ground floor, the Occidental building, at Second and Main, was the object of local pride. See Miner, *West of Wichita*, pp. 98–99.

47. Dodge misspells the name of the quartermaster's agent, William Heimke (*Official Register of the United States* [1879], 1:232).

ambulance team & people taken care of.   Met the Offrs of 16th Infy stationed here.   Had a very fair dinner.   Could'nt get a bath.   They dont wash in this country, so took it out in a basin.   Took a look at the Town before dinner, & after I naturally fell into a billiard room, where in spite of my lack of practice I beat all who tackled me, and

those three ∧³ said I could beat any man in Wichita.   Got to bed at last – about 1 am ——

Saturday, June 14, 1879

Was called at 5 am   Jumped up, sponged off took a cup of coffee & soon after was speeding along in the fresh morning air, through one of the loveliest vallies on earth.   Hooked on to the regular train at Newton got breakfast 9 am at Florence – Dinner at Topeka, & reached Kansas City shortly after 3 pm –[48]   The new Union Depot has been completed.   It is very large – a regular Caravansery – but it was Crammed with people.   The R R war is at its height –   Passengers go to St Louis for a dollar, & to Chicago for fifty cents.   Everybody is taking advantage of the occasion & I never saw such crowds of traveling people except on 4th July in N.Y. or at the Centennial.[49]   It took me nearly an hour to get a ticket to Ft Leavenworth, & then the train started without my trunk.   I was about to utter some sentiments when the Conductor signalled to stop & a moment after a barrow of trunks was rapidly bundled up by a Darkie – among which was mine.

I telegraphed to Coppinger from Topeka – & on my arrival I was met by Volkmar who drove me up to Illsleys house.[50]

He & Copp live together but neither are at home.   So I have the whole house to myself   Volkmar came down & took a cup of tea with

48. Dodge rode the Atchison, Topeka and Santa Fe to Newton, where he caught the Kansas Pacific to Kansas City.

49. The exposition at Philadelphia in 1876, commemorating the United States' one hundred years of existence.

50. First Lieutenant W. J. Volkmar, Fifth Cavalry, was an aide-de-camp to General Pope and chief signal officer of the department. First Lieutenant Charles S. Ilsley, Seventh Cavalry, was also an aide-de-camp.

me – after which, (after 9 pm) I called on Mrs Davis[51]   When I left her it was too late to make other calls so I came back & found Dodge, who remained until about 12 –[52]

Sunday, June 15, 1879

Breakfasted at 9 am with Volkmar & wife.   Went to Hd Qrs, & tried to do something but I find that nothing can be done in the absence of the Comdr.   Had a great deal of talk, amounting to just nothing –

Called on Genl Smith[53] then on the Ladies of 23d.   Dinner at 2.30 - nap after.   Intended to have gone east today but Old Coppinger appeared on the scene arriving here about 11 am.   He insisted on my staying & I finally yielded especially, as I am yet very tired.

We called together at Dr. Perins, & Platts & on Mrs Ives – The latter out – at Church[54]   Rucker - paymaster called at night, & we had quite a gas on hunting &c —[55]

To bed at 12 –

Wednesday, June 18, 1879

Not much chance to write diary.   On evening of June 16 I started.   Old Cop went to Depot to see me off.   Got ticket from

51. The wife of Colonel Jefferson C. Davis had not accompanied him to Fort Supply. At this time he was absent in New York as a member of the Hazen-Stanley general court-martial.
52. On May 14 First Lieutenant Frederick L. Dodge had been detached from duty with Randall's company and assigned as quartermaster and commissary of subsistence to the military prison at Fort Leavenworth (S.O. 95—DMO).
53. Colonel and Brevet Major General Charles H. Smith, Nineteenth Infantry, was post commander at Fort Leavenworth.
54. Dodge and Coppinger paid calls on Lieutenant Colonel Glover Perin, medical director of the department, Major E. R. Platt, General Pope's adjutant, and— apparently—the mother of Second Lieutenant Edward B. Ives, Nineteenth Infantry, who was now stationed at Fort Leavenworth. After meeting Mrs. Ives at Camp Supply the previous December 5, Dodge had set her down as "a rank Catholic."
55. Though stationed at Fort Leavenworth, Major William A. Rucker had ample opportunity for hunting on his regular journeys to pay troops at remote posts.

11Worth to N.Y. for $21 – twenty-one dollars thanks to the R R war.[56] Sleeper 8 – making $29 – the cheapest trip I have made – except the Centennial Year & then I was sent all over creation by all the by-roads of the land.

The weather has been exceptionally delightful   Rains have cooled the air & laid the dust.   I came from St. Louis without change of car – on a Palace Hotel car – & very nice and comfortable it is – but they do gouge on eating awfully.   Fifty cents for one thin slice of beef – about 2 ounces – 25 cents for 2 eggs.   As I did not want my bills to make me appear a gourmand[57]   I came through at about $4 per day, but in a half starved condition   Arrived all right & well in N.Y.   Took the Elevated R R to go up to Rossmore – & was heartily sick of it.   I am dizzy and billious from my long journey – & the Elevated fixed me.   I had'nt gone 6 blocks before I felt as if I were about to turn inside out, & my head ached badly – for almost the first time in my life.   I resolutely stuck it out   Got to Rossmore about 11 p.m. – find that the Old Lady is a mile & a half away at the Westmoreland flats – so I have taken up my abode for the night here at Rossmore.[58]   Took a big drink as soon as I arrived & filled my stomach, with pates, salads & croquettes from a free lunch I found in the bar room – & now I feel all right so long as I dont look out of a window.   I have elegant accommodations – parlor bed & bath-room.   Have slung my things all over the elegant suite of rooms, & really almost feel at home —   "Shall I not take mine ease in mine Inn"?[59] –

56. A rate war between railroads leading east from St. Louis and Chicago had begun in May ("The Western Railroad War," *New York Times*, May 23, 1879, p. 1).

57. Following "gourmand," Dodge wrote "& <I>I," neglecting to cancel the ampersand.

58. On arrival in New York City, Dodge took the Elevated Metropolitan Railway—fare, ten cents—to the Grand Central depot, where at 11:00 a.m. he caught the New York Central's express train to Albany. There he boarded a westbound connecting train which he rode to a few miles past Utica, in a region favored by summer cottagers and vacationers. He stopped at the Rossmore Hotel, apparently expecting to find his wife a guest there. Westmoreland was a village a short distance south of the railroad.

59. Falstaff's line in *King Henry IV, Part One* III.iii.91.

The Hotel has changed hands since I was here, & there is no one in it that I know —

The old Lady will be astonished when I walk in on her tomorro a.m. Have only spent fifty four dollars since I left my post, which I regard as the cheapest thing on record — specially as I gave several dollars to my escort —[60]

60. The pages that follow, pp. [38V]-[60V], are blank.

Commentary on Journal Six
The Indian Bureau and the Army: Organizations at Odds

THE MISSION OF AGENT MILES

John De Bras Miles, the Indian Bureau's chief representative at the Cheyenne and Arapaho agency, was in the opinion of most observers an able and industrious administrator who performed a difficult task about as well as anyone could. Before assuming his position as agent in 1872, Miles had acquired a varied fund of experience that prepared him well for his duties. He had taught school, attended a business college, worked in the manufacturing trade, and even performed a diplomatic errand to the Republic of Mexico.[1] Assisted by his wife and brother on a modest annual salary of twenty-four hundred dollars, Miles directed the activity of fourteen agency employees and superintended the procedures to obtain and distribute food and supplies to more than fifty-five hundred Indians, some of whom were acknowledged to be the most dangerous of any on the continent and the least disposed to tolerate "civilizing" efforts. The greater number of his Indian wards were reasonably well satisfied with the programs for gradual amalgamation to American culture that he administered. They recognized that their former nomadic mode of life was no longer viable, and they were growing accustomed to supporting themselves by farming, raising cattle, or earning money by employment provided through the agency.

John H. Seger, a practical man of affairs, conducted the agency school at Caddo Springs with conspicuous success despite his own

---

1. Collins, "Ben Williams, Frontier Peace Officer," pp. 521-22 n; Le Van, "The Quaker Agents at Darlington," pp. 94-98.

limited education. Seger's good results resulted in large part from the personal relationships he had formed with some of the Indians, based on his respect for their ways.[2] Miles, a Quaker, never grew so close as Seger to the Indians under his charge, though two of his five children did teach at the agency school. He devoted himself energetically to the task of ensuring the Indians' survival and fostering their progress toward what he understood as a higher state of civilization. A tall, spare man, forty-seven years of age in 1879, Miles drove himself, and his gaze shone with a quiet intensity.[3]

When the defeated Northern Cheyennes, numbering 937, arrived at the agency in August 1877, the officer in charge of their military escort, First Lieutenant Henry W. Lawton, described to Miles an almost successful plot by some of the Indians against his own life during the journey south. Lawton warned the agent that his recent enrollees were not to be trusted,[4] and Miles soon came to feel uneasy apprehension, not only for his own welfare but lest the newcomers should infect the already resident Indian population with their treachery. He made known his security concerns to Major Mizner, who at once began petitioning General Pope for additional troops. However, at the time of the Dull Knife outbreak in September 1878, no reinforcements had yet been provided. Three months later, when the band under Little Chief arrived at the agency, the garrison at Fort Reno still consisted of only four companies, two of cavalry and two of infantry.

During the spring of 1879 the threat of violence from the Northern Cheyennes under Little Chief was only one of several serious problems faced daily by Miles as he sought to perform his duties. For the great majority of the Indians in his care, Miles's most intense effort was necessarily to provide for their basic physical wants. As an agent he

2. Seger, *Early Days Among the Cheyenne and Arapahoe Indians*, pp. xii–xiii, 25, 88, 131.

3. In addition to the photograph reproduced in this volume, see Peery, "The Indians' Friend: John H. Seger," opposite p. 576; Berthrong, *The Cheyenne and Arapaho Ordeal*, p. 160.

4. Miles to editor, *Kansas City Star*, February 27, 1908; quoted in Peery, "The Indians' Friend, John H. Seger," pp. 968–69.

John D. Miles (Courtesy Archives Division, Olkahoma Historical Society)

had no authority to purchase food, clothing, farm implements, or medical supplies. He could only draw up detailed estimates, submit requisitions, and store and distribute the provisions authorized for delivery by the Indian Bureau in Washington, D.C. In order to encourage Indians to take responsibility for their own livelihood through pursuits like farming, the Indian Bureau made provision for food rations that were insufficient by themselves to sustain life. To complicate matters, Bureau officials exercised little effort to ensure that supplies were delivered on time. Given the inadequate and sometimes tardy ration supplies, Agent Miles was forced into a vigilant search for ways to enable the Indians to feed themselves. In the early years of his tenure, a fall buffalo hunt west and south of the agency was a recourse. It brought the Indians into perilous proximity to ranches and cattle herds along the Texas frontier, but it yielded an abundance of the food they preferred and enabled them to feel that some part of their traditional mode of support was being preserved. However, with the depletion of the buffalo herds through predation, the annual hunts began to prove unavailing. Miles arranged for the employment of some Indians by contractors who served the agency. He obtained wagons and teams to provide Indians with work as teamsters, encouraged them to settle in fertile bottoms along the North Fork of the Canadian River, and permitted them to sell cured hides and trinkets to the authorized Indian trader in return for credit at the agency store.

In Miles's view some of the Indians' social customs, such as polygamy and the bartering that occurred between a prospective husband and the father of an intended wife, were reprehensible in themselves and required correction as soon as possible.[5] The latter custom seemed to him demeaning to the woman, a sort of prostitution, and when practiced on the reservation it had other grave consequences. For example, an American citizen might decide to purchase at a modest price some comely girl for his pleasure, but then at his convenience simply abandon her. Behavior like this interfered seriously with Miles's mission as

5. Miles to E. A. Hayt, January 5, 1878 (OIA LR, C&A); House, *Report of the Commissioner of Indian Affairs* (1879), p. 77.

steward to the moral and physical welfare of the Indians under his charge. Moreover, the men who "intermarry (so called)" with Indians could then claim membership in the tribe and use their status as warrant to avail themselves of privileges intended by the federal government for reservation Indians alone. They could raise cattle in Indian Territory, trade with Indians, claim rations and treaty goods, and in short retain their privileges as United States citizens while also enjoying other privileges as Indians.[6]

Early in 1878 Miles proposed to the Commissioner of Indian Affairs a regulation that would deny Indian status to citizens who took Indian wives. The result, he assured Commissioner Hayt, would be "a much better class of white men" choosing to cohabit with Indian women than the unsavory squaw men that infested the agency.[7] One year later he returned to the subject, observing testily that inaction on the matter would not only further corrupt the Indians through contact with unscrupulous persons but would "foist a number of halfbreed bastards on the government." Miles urged that the Indian Bureau issue a circular to assist agents in combating the "barefaced prostitution" of Indian women,[8] but none was forthcoming. At last, early in 1880 he took it upon himself to expel sixty unworthy husbands from Indian Territory.[9] However, he soon discovered that his powers as agent were subject to legal and political challenge. Senator Preston B. Plumb of Kansas inquired of Secretary of the Interior Schurz whether Miles's action was in accordance with Indian Bureau policy.[10] One determined citizen, Peter Keffer, refused to remain outside Indian Territory, returning repeatedly to his wife and family at the agency. Miles had Keffer arrested, but in order to place him in the hands of the United States commissioner at Fort Smith, Arkansas, he had to arrange for the accused man's transportation to a point almost two hundred miles

6. Miles to Hayt, September 18, 1879 (OIA LR, C&A).
7. Miles to Hayt, January 5, 1878 (OIA LR, C&A).
8. Miles to Hayt, January 22, 1879 (OIA LR, C&A).
9. Miles to Commissioner of Indian Affairs, February 24, 1880 (OIA LR, C&A). On the other hand, in this letter Miles also detailed the cases of eleven squaw men who he believed should be permitted to remain in Indian Territory.
10. Preston B. Plumb to Carl Schurz, January 19, 1880 (OIA LR, C&A).

away.[11] Owing to the absence of support from his superiors and the difficulty of access to legal authorities, Miles found that his aim of protecting his Indian charges from victimization was all but impossible to achieve.

Technically, Agent Miles did possess authority to enforce federal law as it applied both to the inhabitants of the Cheyenne and Arapaho reservation and also to the lands themselves. However, with only a small contingent of Indian police, he could not cope effectively with a range of abuses that beset the region. American citizens were not permitted to conduct business in Indian Territory without authorization, but taking advantage of long distances and feeble enforcement, they did so anyway. Outlaws from Kansas used the Indian Territory as a place for tactical retreat or else raided within it for horses and cattle. Cattlemen from Texas drove herds over reservation lands without permission, sometimes causing damage. They grazed their herds in places they had no right to occupy, trespassing for weeks at a time in order to fatten their animals for market. Dealers in timber poached wood and carried it north across the Kansas border. Settlers built shelters and stables in remote locations, effectively establishing permanent residence. Miles understood the provisions of the *Revised Statutes* that governed all this behavior, but he had little power to combat it. Other than to waylay the occasional whisky peddler and destroy his wares,[12] he could accomplish little except to maintain at his agency an oasis of administrative order in a desert of lawlessness.

Though formidable in themselves, the challenges faced by Agent Miles in the performance of his duty were in his view made more onerous by the active efforts of others to interfere with his work. Like many employees of the Indian Bureau since implementation of President Grant's Peace Policy in 1869, he believed the United States Army

11. Peter Keffer to Carl Schurz, February 23, 1880; Miles to Commissioner of Indian Affairs, March 12, 1880; Miles to Commissioner of Indian Affairs, October 23, 1880; Miles to Stephen Wheeler, U.S. Commissioner, Fort Smith, Arkansas, November 3, 1880; Miles to W. H. Clayton, U.S. District Attorney, Fort Smith, Arkansas, November 27, 1880; Miles to Commissioner of Indian Affairs, December 10, 1880 (OIA LR, C&A).

12. Seger, *Early Days Among the Cheyenne and Arapahoe Indians*, p. 27.

was inimical to his effort and sought to undermine it. Congressional hearings to consider the possibility of turning over to the Army the conduct of Indian affairs were held almost annually, and the arguments in support of such a change were well known. Army proponents held that entrusting the care of savage peoples to representatives of various religious denominations was folly, since without a present potential for the use of force against them, Indians would never conform to policies they did not like. In the Army view, efforts to civilize Indians through moral example and gentle persuasion alone were a waste of time. Moreover, Indian agents supposedly qualified for office by their approved piety were administrative innocents, vulnerable to the chicanery and fraud of contractors and others with which the Indian Bureau was said to be afflicted.

Awareness of contemptuous attitudes like these caused Miles to insist, sometimes truculently, that he not be interfered with by Army officers. More than once he emphasized that he, not they, possessed authority as the primary representative of the federal government in his section of Indian Territory. Miles expected adherence to General Order 28, issued by General Pope to troops in the Department of the Missouri on September 26, 1870, as the framework for proper working relations between Army officers and Indian agents like himself. This order specified that Indian agents held sole jurisdiction over all matters of conduct and the protection of rights on reservations, and that military forces were placed there solely to assist the agents in preserving order. Except under specific directions from departmental headquarters or higher authority, Army officers were to assume no jurisdiction and exercise no control over Indians or their agents. When troops were required, agents would state their wishes in writing, explaining the reasons for their request and the objects to be accomplished through military intervention.[13]

Beginning with the establishment of Fort Reno in 1874, Agent Miles maintained a reasonably smooth relationship with representatives of the Army, especially with Major Mizner, who commanded there

---

13. The text of General Order 28 (DMO, 1870) is reprinted in Appendix B.

beginning in April 1876. The arrival of the Northern Cheyennes in the following year produced some deterioration in the cooperative effort, for the reports by Lieutenant Lawton and others placed Miles and the Bureau he represented in a negative light—as allegedly incompetent, inhumane, and even dishonest. With the outbreak of September 1878, relations took a decided turn for the worse. Miles and Mizner were both drawn into the campaign of recrimination and countercharge that followed, their vitriol aimed not at each other but at detractors of the organizations they served.

In early June 1879 Miles's latent antagonism toward the Army flamed out in response to events about to occur at Fort Reno, as Little Chief and his five companions approached the agency after their visit to Washington, D.C. In accordance with instructions from General Pope, on June 8 Mizner ordered Ben Clarke, who was accompanying the Indians as interpreter, to bring Little Chief and the other five men to him at once upon their return—by force if necessary. None of the Indians was to return to his people until he had first complied with this requirement.[14] Mizner hoped to obviate difficulty with Little Chief through the interview, which would not necessarily lead to the "mild custody" Pope had envisioned; however, the effect of his order was to stir up trouble with Agent Miles. On June 12, having just returned to the agency, Miles informed Mizner that his instructions to Clarke could not be complied with. The compulsion of such an order would destroy whatever good effects the visit to Washington, D.C., had worked on the Indians, "and I must emphatically decline to allow, except under the strongest protest and only with the Consent of my superiors, the Execution of the line of action proposed by you." Reminding Mizner of the provisions in General Order 28, Miles directed him not to intervene in matters that concerned the Indians until asked.[15]

On June 19 Commissioner Hayt informed Secretary Schurz of the incident, emphasizing the importance of keeping faith with the Northern Cheyennes and recommending that Mizner be officially

14. Mizner to Ben Clarke, June 8, 1879 (OIA LR, C&A).
15. Miles to Mizner, June 12, 1879 (OIA LR, C&A).

forbidden to meddle any further. Schurz obliged with a letter to the secretary of war in which he deplored Mizner's "unnecessary interference" in areas not properly his concern.[16] Meanwhile, even as the assertion of Indian Bureau primacy re-echoed from official to official, Mizner managed to obtain an interview with Little Chief in his post commander's office. Contrary to military expectation, the old chieftain was clearly peaceable, even though still hoping to return north at some time. Mizner informed Pope that danger seemed past for the present, but in view of the constant risk posed by the Northern Cheyennes, he wished to reduce the enlarged garrison of Fort Reno only gradually during the summer.[17] For his part, Agent Miles was satisfied that the Indians' stay in Washington had resulted in "great good."[18]

During the summer and fall of 1879 Agent Miles's chief military adversary, placed among the Indians within his jurisdiction by military authority and permitted to remain there against his wish, was Second Lieutenant Heber W. Creel, Seventh Cavalry. This officer was performing a double duty, as linguistic-anthropological student of the Northern Cheyennes and also as a confidential observer for General Sheridan of their behavior and disposition. He enjoyed the confidence of the band—living in their camp, setting about building himself a residence there, and even entering into negotiations for a Cheyenne wife. His summary reports, beginning in March, sometimes included criticism of Agent Miles. For example, the initial assessment included claims that Miles showed no good feeling toward his recent arrivals and conducted agency business in a manner that seemed suspicious.[19] A month later Creel reported more favorably, granting that Miles was zealous in his labors but criticizing as unwise his insistence that children in the band of Little Chief should be sent to school.[20] On June 15, immediately after the return of Little Chief, Creel reported to an

16. Hayt to SI, June 19, 1879; Schurz to SW, June 19, 1879 (AGO LR).
17. Mizner to AAG DMO, June 15, 1879; Mizner to AAG DMO, June 18, 1879 (AGO LR).
18. Miles to Hayt, June 25, 1879 (AGO LR).
19. Creel to AAG MDM, March 7, 1879 (AGO Register LR).
20. Creel to AAG MDM, April 22, 1879 (OIA LR, C&A).

officer at Fort Reno that the angry Indians would surely make a break for the north soon. In view of his own close association with the band, he suggested that he be permitted to run the agency school.[21]

Miles had little direct contact with Lieutenant Creel, but the agent was aware of the officer's activities and heartily resented them. Beginning in September 1879 Miles wrote a series of letters complaining of Creel as "an acknowledged enemy" and protesting against his unsettling influence on the Indians.[22] Miles accused Creel of attempting to prostitute the women he lived among and of conducting a campaign of insinuations and outright efforts to belittle and malign both himself and the Indian Bureau.[23] The terms of General Order 28 had been tacitly set aside, and Miles was powerless to reassert their force except through vigorous appeal to his superior. By whose authority, he demanded of Commissioner Hayt, had Creel ever been granted the right to live among these Indians? Miles wished him expelled from Indian Territory before any further damage was done. On November 1 he wrote that he could "not submit to be harassed by the insidious attacks of this man. . . . I do not ask the assistance of Lt Creel or any other military officer, in the management of the Indians, but I must insist that he shall not be allowed to hinder me in carrying out the orders and policy of the Indian office."[24]

Frustrations like these led Miles to refer in his published annual report for 1879 to "enemies of the department" who had intensified the discontent of the Northern Cheyennes by assuring them that they had been denied their just dues.[25] Fortunately for his equanimity, an opportunity to present the facts of his recent work in a public forum occurred in August of that year, when a special Senate committee to examine the original removal of the Northern Cheyennes from the Sioux reservation to Indian Territory arrived at Fort Reno. Composed

21. Creel to Major Barbar [the brevet rank of First Lieutenant Merritt Barber, Sixteenth Infantry, who was stationed at Fort Reno], June 15, 1879 (OIA LR, C&A).
22. Miles to Mizner, September 10, 1879 (OIA LR, C&A).
23. Miles to E. A. Hayt, September 16, 1879. On September 19 Miles wrote again to Hayt, protesting Creel's baneful influence (OIA LR, C&A).
24. Miles to Hayt, November 1, 1879 (OIA LR, C&A).
25. House, *Report of the Commissioner of Indian Affairs* (1879), p. 164.

of Senators Samuel J. Kirkwood, John T. Morgan, Henry L. Dawes, and Preston B. Plumb, the committee took testimony at the Cheyenne and Arapaho agency between August 19 and 21. Witnesses included Little Chief and five other Indians, Miles and three other agency employees, Mizner and two other Army officers, and Ben Clarke. The committee's inquiries were thorough and wide ranging, but they centered upon a few general subjects: the treatment of the Northern Cheyennes—both the Dull Knife and the Little Chief bands—in Indian Territory; the administration of the Cheyenne and Arapaho agency by the Indian Bureau; the unsuccessful effort by the military to waylay and capture Dull Knife and his people; and the policy of forcing a northern Indian tribe like the Cheyennes to take up permanent residence in Indian Territory. Agent Miles appeared before the committee almost the entire day on August 20 and was recalled for further testimony on August 21.

Two committee members, Senators Kirkwood and Dawes, were well acquainted with the Indian Bureau and its practices, and the committee as a whole gave Miles a sympathetic hearing. In its report, published months afterward following further testimony from Mizner, General Crook, Colonel Nelson A. Miles, and Colonel Ranald S. Mackenzie of the Army and Ezra Hayt and Carl Schurz of the Department of the Interior, the select committee found little fault with Agent Miles. It praised him for having "done his duty faithfully and bravely in almost every particular, [with] a most difficult task to perform." Mizner too was recognized for providing "the most enlightened and dutiful support" to measures intended to ensure the peace and welfare of the Indians.[26] In the committee's view the blame for the Dull Knife outbreak, the devastations that followed, and in part the continuing dissatisfaction of Little Chief and others rested in general on the federal government for not complying with its treaty obligations. More particularly, the committee concluded that the "neglect and indifference" of the Indian Bureau to requisitions and warnings from its own employees

26. Senate, *Report . . . on the Removal of the Northern Cheyennes*, p. xxv.

in the field had helped bring matters to a crisis.[27] Among its recommendations was that agents like Miles be made more independent of control by the Indian Bureau, whose derelictions they often felt obliged to conceal by shifting blame to the Indians.

Even though the report of the Senate committee would not be issued for some time, its official visit to the agency afforded an opportunity for all witnesses to air their views before a thoughtful audience. The proceedings were almost entirely free of recrimination between the Army and the Indian Bureau, and Little Chief conducted himself with dignity and quiet eloquence.[28] He enumerated instances in which the government had broken faith with him and his people, but he did so in a diplomatic manner, professing once more his resolution not to leave the reservation without government approval. Nevertheless, when the committee ended its hearings and left the agency, Little Chief's future was still in doubt.

As fall approached, the agency returned to the conditions that had prevailed before the brief interlude of official attention. Agent Miles had no doubt received expressions of support from the senators, but

27. The committee also recorded its judgment that the annual reports and testimony of Agent Miles refuted statements by Commissioner Hayt that the Northern Cheyennes had no real cause for dissatisfaction (Senate, *Report . . . on the Removal of the Northern Cheyennes*, p. xv).

28. In response to a question whether women of his tribe were bearing children in Indian Territory and whether the tribe was increasing or diminishing, Little Chief answered: "A great many children have been born. I do not know whether more have been born than died or not. A great many have been sick; some have died, and some have got well. I have been sick a great deal of the time since I have been down here— homesick and heartsick, and sick in every way. I have been thinking of my native country and the good home I had up there, where I never was hungry, but when I wanted anything to eat could go out and hunt the buffalo. It makes me feel sick when I think about that, and I cannot help thinking about that. I like the white people up there better than I do the white people down here, too. I can get along with the white people up there; they appear more sensible people than the people down here. Everybody knows us up there, and everybody treats us like brothers. I served with the soldiers up there, and they all knew me and treated me well. I can get along there much more pleasantly than here. For my part, I was never raised to be dependent on an agency at all; I was used to living by hunting all the time. It does not make me feel good to hang about an agency and have to ask a white man for something to eat when I get hungry" (Senate, *Report . . . on the Removal of the Northern Cheyennes*, pp. 52–53).

he now had to deal with the same difficulties he had before their arrival. One of these, Cantonment and its large garrison, had gone unmentioned in testimony before the Senate committee.[29] Existing at a considerable remove from the agency, and having been established in response to events whose causes the committee was considering, the new post was ancillary to its concerns. To Agent Miles, however, Cantonment loomed in August 1879 as one more obstacle to progress in his mission. For example, in April Dodge had written a letter concerning lands occupied by Indians along the North Fork near Cantonment. This letter set in motion a process of official review and consultation that threatened to interfere seriously with arrangements already made by Miles. On May 27, then in Washington, D.C., with the Little Chief delegation, Miles had explained to Hayt his motives for encouraging the Indians to support themselves by improving lands near the river. He tacitly granted Dodge's point that the Indians possessed no valid title,[30] but he expressed hope that legislation could be enacted that would permit them to possess those properties in severalty. Subsequent investigation confirmed the accuracy of Dodge's views. Through a complicated series of revisions, practical accommodations, and unratified adjustments since adoption of a treaty in 1867, the legal boundaries of the reservation remained in doubt and confusion.[31] As Commissioner Hayt informed Miles on July 31, the Cheyennes and Arapahos could claim no legal right to the lands they had occupied and improved.

29. On August 13 Senator Plumb had requested that Amos Chapman appear before the committee. Three days later Second Lieutenant W. C. McFarland, Sixteenth Infantry, informed the commanding officer at Cantonment of the request, and Chapman was at once ordered to report to Fort Reno (CNFCR Unregistered LR; S.O. 89, August 16, 1879—CNFCR). However, statements by Chapman did not form part of the extensive testimony appended to the committee's *Report*.

30. Miles to Hayt, May 27, 1879 (OIA LR, C&A).

31. An undated "Brief history of Cheyenne & Arapahoe Reserve" documents the Indian Bureau's effort to ascertain which lands these Indian tribes were legally entitled to (OIA LR, C&A [1880]). The Senate committee observed in its report that "no part of [the land then occupied by the Cheyennes and Arapahos] is included in either of the treaties with these tribes, and it has never been conferred to them by act of Congress" (Senate, *Report . . . on the Removal of the Northern Cheyennes*, p. ii).

Agent Miles's irritated response to that ruling was the first of several indirect attacks he made on Dodge, whom he evidently viewed as an official enemy. While not disputing Dodge's position, he nevertheless claimed his own right to grant occupancy on the lands concerned, by virtue of an Executive Order of the President dated August 10, 1869.[32] He noted that progressive Indians like Yellow Bear and Little Raven had occupied lands on Dodge's military reservation long before Cantonment ever existed. By right of occupancy, he added, they had good reason "to object to the wholesale destruction of every stick of valuable timber adjacent to their farms." After all, Dodge had seen fit to "rob the best disposed of our Indians of the principal inducement that led them to locate and undertake farming." Miles wondered whether the Department of the Interior had ever sanctioned the establishment of Cantonment and expressed doubt as to the necessity of such a post. "I have the honor," he concluded, "to ask whether a military officer has any right to exercise any such interference over peaceable and industrious Indians."[33]

In raising the issue of land ownership, Dodge had sought to draw attention to a potential cause of discontent among Indians who resided near Cantonment, not primarily to call into question the arrangements made by Agent Miles. Nevertheless, by his "interference" he had created a new set of problems for Miles, and like Major Mizner and Lieutenant Creel he had aroused the agent's ire. Miles was sensitive to criticism, aggressive in asserting his primacy as a representative of the United States government, and inclined to portray his detractors as morally deficient. Dodge sympathized with the sufferings of the Indians he saw and regarded the Indian Bureau and its employees as incompetent if not dishonest. Both men were convinced of their own rectitude, expressed themselves with skill, and were not shy of official controversy. Ironically, both wished the Indians well. Open conflict had not yet broken out between them, but given their ideas and the adversarial relationship of the two organizations they represented, a clash seemed inevitable.

32. This order was reprinted as an appendix to *Report . . . on the Removal of the Northern Cheyennes*, pp. 229–32; see also pp. 307–12.
33. Miles to Hayt, August 14, 1879 (OIA LR, C&A).

TROOPS IN CANTONMENT

Under the leadership of Captain George M. Randall, construction work at Cantonment moved ahead at a brisk pace during the summer of 1879. By the end of June the two companies on temporary duty at Fort Reno had returned, and in the three months that followed the garrison remained at full strength.[34] Of perhaps forty civilian employees at the post the largest number were teamsters, who earned thirty dollars per month ferrying supplies and personal belongings, chiefly from the Wichita{n}Fort Reno road. Accompanying wagons drawn by four- or six-mule teams, they brought freight including bricks for a bake oven and windows, doors, and casings for use in the picket huts until they could be re-installed in permanent structures.[35] Three stone buildings were being erected, an undertaking almost without precedent for a post not yet designated permanent.

The most highly paid civilian employee was the engineer and sawyer, who supervised operation of the sawmill and a shingle machine at the rate of four dollars per day.[36] Only one civilian mason was employed during this period, at a monthly wage of seventy-five dollars.[37] Hoping to complete by winter all the permanent buildings that Colonel Dodge had planned, Lieutenant Trout's successor, First Lieutenant William L. Clarke, requested in July that nine additional masons be hired. However, he was informed a month later that no funds were yet authorized for the work he had in view. The three hundred thousand shingles already produced were therefore placed over the mud roofs of the temporary huts.[38] In September 1879 Lieutenant Clarke spent

34. Companies D and K, Twenty-third Infantry, returned to the post on June 24 (Randall to AG, June 24, 1879—CNFCR LS). On September 14 Company K was transferred to Fort Supply, leaving Cantonment with a garrison of five companies (S.O. 106, September 14—CNFCR).

35. Thoburn, "The Story of Cantonment," pp. 70–71.

36. According to Sergeant Sommer, the shingle machine was donated by the post trader ("Cantonment North Fork of the Canadian River"—Thoburn Papers, Oklahoma Historical Society).

37. This was Leigh Smedley, forty-nine years of age, from England (CNFCR Pass Book). Sommer thought him "a very efficient mason" ("Cantonment North Fork of the Canadian River"—Thoburn Papers, Oklahoma Historical Society).

38. AAG DMO to C.O., July 30, 1879; AAG DMO to C.O. [date not shown; received August 27, 1879] (CNFCR LR); Thoburn, "The Story of Cantonment," p. 71.

$1,827 in salaries for employees of the quartermaster department, one-half more than for any of the previous three months, but thereafter the figure dropped to its former level or below.[39]

Randall's search for unauthorized settlers during May had been fruitful, yielding more than eighty ranchers, not all of whom submitted graciously to his order that they leave Indian Territory. A few insisted that they did possess a right to remain there, having purchased it from someone they termed "the Agent."[40] Shortly afterward, Senator Plumb of Kansas informed General Sherman that many citizens who had been expelled by the Army had indeed paid duly authorized agents of the Cherokee nation for the privilege of grazing their cattle on Cherokee lands. Sherman promptly directed officers still on patrol not to interfere with individuals who could produce licenses or receipts from the Cherokees.[41] In his report to General Pope of May 28, Dodge also mentioned ranchers discovered by Randall who claimed to have purchased a right to occupancy. Eventually this information reached the Department of the Interior and resulted in a call for further inquiry. Apparently interpreting "the Agent" to mean a representative of the Indian Bureau, Secretary Schurz requested the name of the offending person, who had acted without authorization.[42] Accordingly, on July 31 Randall ordered Second Lieutenant Stephen O'Connor to make copies of all permits possessed by William E. Malaley, a stock raiser at Pond Creek Station, and to estimate the number of horses and horned stock Malaley kept on the Pond Creek

39. CNFCR Post Returns, June–December, 1879.
40. This term is Dodge's, in his letter of May 28, 1879, to AAG DMO (MDM Settlers in I.T. Special File; CNFCR LS). Randall's report of May 24 had been delivered to Dodge by Amos Chapman, who gave him additional information at that time. When Randall wrote his report, he was only about forty miles from Cantonment and expected to require three or four more weeks to complete his errand (Randall to C.O. CNFCR—MDM Settlers in I.T. Special File).
41. Sherman to Sheridan, June 9, 1879 (AGO LS).
42. Schurz to SW, July 3, 1879 (CNFCR LR). This letter did not reach Cantonment until August 17. Schurz's interpretation of the report was reasonable. Referring to William Malaley [Mellily], Dodge had written: "Some of these men—notably one Wm Mellily station keeper of the stage station at Pond Creek (Reno road) have the permission in writing of the Agent to keep cattle in the Territory and this in Mellily's case is backed by the written permission of some of the Indian Chiefs."

range.[43] O'Connor's report named L. B. Bell, an agent for the treasurer of the Cherokee nation, as signing a receipt for tax on grazing eighteen hundred cattle "on Cherokee lands west of the Arkansas and North of the Canadian River" through August 1, 1880; the amount was not specified but was understood to be calculated at the rate of fifty cents per head. Malaley also informed O'Connor that he possessed a written receipt, signed by Cheyenne and Arapaho chiefs and countersigned and approved by Agent Miles, granting him their permission to hold cattle in Indian Territory. The latter document, he told O'Connor, was the only one of its kind he had possessed for the past two or three years, but unfortunately he had lost it and could not produce it to be copied. He claimed sole ownership of the cattle in his possession, but stockmen in the vicinity thought Agent Miles the real owner.[44]

By the time this new information reached the Department of the Interior, on September 16, the legitimacy of Bell as a representative of the Cherokee nation had been established.[45] Malaley and others who had paid the tax were free to graze their animals within the Cherokee Strip, a range of more than 6 million acres extending fifty-seven miles south of the Kansas state line and west to the one hundredth degree of longitude.[46] What action, if any, the Department of the Interior took in regard to the unsubstantiated evidence of Agent Miles's written permission to Malaley and secret ownership of a herd of cattle is unknown. Certainly the report by O'Connor deepened his fellow officers' distrust for Miles.

As the above summary of reports, referrals, and queries within a four-month period attests, communication of routine matter between Cantonment and Washington, D.C., was slow. The Army's cumbersome

---

43. S.O. 82, July 31, 1879—CNFCR.

44. S. O'Connor to Post Adjutant, August 17, 1879 (CNFCR LR). O'Connor characterized Malaley, a former employee of the Cheyenne and Arapaho agency, as a " protegé of the Miles family."

45. A half-blood Cherokee Indian, Bell had earlier been expelled from Indian Territory as an illegal settler. See AG to Pope, June 18, 1879 (AGO LS); SW to Attorney General, July 17, 1879 (SW LS).

46. See Morris et al., *Historical Atlas of Oklahoma*, No. 33, where this section of land is designated the "Cherokee Outlet."

system of forwarding documents from office to office was one part of the problem, but another was that messages went to and from Cantonment either by courier or by an erratic postal service.[47] The nearest telegraph station was at Wichita, 155 miles away and two long days distant by horseback. To remedy this deficiency and enhance cooperation within the region, in May 1879 plans were set in motion to install a 376-mile telegraph line that would link Fort Sill, Fort Reno, Cantonment, Fort Supply, and Fort Dodge. Poles were to be cut and set in place, twenty per mile, by detachments from the several posts, and the work of stringing the line was to proceed under supervision of Second Lieutenant James A. Swift of the Signal Corps, beginning at Fort Sill.[48] At Cantonment, parties of twenty-four men first under the command of Second Lieutenant Charles H. Heyl and later under Second Lieutenant Lea Febiger, set about the task.[49] The work was difficult and dangerous; in September, two soldiers were seriously injured in collapses of graded banks and later died in the post hospital.[50] However, telegraph communication was achieved from Fort Reno on September 1; from Cantonment on September 20; and from Fort Supply on September 29.[51]

Meanwhile, Dodge's one-month leave of absence was twice extended, enabling him to spend the entire summer in the eastern states. After a visit with his wife in upstate New York, he worked his way south-

47. The poor mail service had been a source of aggravation to Dodge almost since his arrival at Cantonment. On October 4, 1879, he complained to the departmental adjutant that, after several adjustments and assurances from the postmaster general, the service was no better than it had been in May (CNFCR LS). On October 24 the postmaster general informed the secretary of war that improvement on present arrangements for Cantonment would not be possible until a further appropriation was received from Congress (CNFCR Unregistered LR).

48. Pope to AAG MDM, May 24, 1879 (AGO Register LR); James A. Swift to C.O., August 13, 1879 (CNFCR LR).

49. S.O. 81, July 28, 1879—CNFCR; S.O. 100, September 2—CNFCR; Julius R. Pardee to Second Lieutenant Lea Febiger, September 4, 1879 (CNFCR LS).

50. G.O. 21, September 27, 1879—CNFCR, announced the death on September 26 of Private Archie Gray, Company D; G.O. 22, September 29, announced the death on September 28 of Private John McKeever, Company G.

51. CNFCR Post Return, September 1879. Telegraph communication between Fort Sill and posts in Texas had been established in 1874. Fort Dodge, located near a major railroad, had also had access to a telegraph station for several years.

ward toward the home of his parents in North Carolina. During the week of July 19 he was a guest at the St. Nicholas hotel in New York City[52] and probably visited his son Fred, who was making arrangements for a tour as lead actor in a "traveling combination" that fall. His repertory company would present performances in the opera houses, lyceums, and theaters of towns and cities connected by railroads across the east. While in England Fred had studied the work of Henry Irving, a distant relation and a Shakespearian actor of note.[53] Having observed both Irving and the American tragedian Edwin Booth in roles that had won them fame, he had developed his own fresh interpretation of the characters. Ambitiously for a man only twenty years of age, Dodge's son was to be billed under the stage name Frederick Paulding as "The New Hamlet."

During the week of July 26 Dodge registered at the Ebbitt House and at the War Department in Washington, D.C.[54] In all probability he made progress while in the capital on a creative effort of his own. Following the example of his friend Colonel James Fry and other Army officers, he searched the files of the adjutant general's office for documents that might find a place in a future book.[55] After some quiet

52. *ANJ*, July 12, 1879, p. 885; July 19, p. 909; July 26, p. 930; CNFCR Post Returns, June and July, 1879.

53. "Lyceum Theatre," *New York Times*, February 26, 1879, p. 5.

54. *ANJ*, July 31, 1879, p. 93.

55. In a published letter to officers and former officers of the Army, on February 8, 1878, Dodge had expressed his interest in writing a volume describing incidents of Army life on the western frontier, especially before the end of the Civil War. He called upon his colleagues for reminiscences that might be used in such a work, "anything which will illustrate the characteristics and mode of life" of Army men, frontiersmen, and Indians (*ANJ*, February 23, 1878, p. 459). Probably his studies in Washington were in connection with this project.

Surviving evidence of Dodge's activity includes the copied proceedings of a military commission, convened at Denver, Colorado, on February 9, 1865, to investigate the conduct of Colonel J. M. Chivington in his campaign of the previous year against Cheyenne Indians. Written on legal-size sheets that bear the decorative device of "Blanchard and Monda, Washington, D.C.," the document details among much other information Chivington's unprovoked attack on a large Cheyenne village at Sand Creek, Colorado, wherein two-thirds of the Indian casualties were women and children. It refers to "fiendish atrocities" and "atrocious barbarities" by the force under Chivington (Dodge Papers, Graff Collection).

summer days at his childhood home, he reported at Fort Leavenworth in early September and was assigned the task of superintending further construction and repair of the military road as he returned to Cantonment. Fortuitously, he reached his post on September 22, two days after the initiation of telegraph communication there.[56]

These were critical days, for dissatisfaction among Indians—not only at the Cheyenne and Arapaho agency but also around Cantonment—was approaching another crisis. Earlier in the month Agent Miles had received directions from Indian Bureau headquarters to reduce the rations he issued so as to make the budgeted supplies last through the current fiscal year. That meant cutting the weekly ration of beef from three pounds per person to two, a reduction that Miles believed would cause great suffering, especially after the poor growing season just past. Before acting on the instructions he had received, on September 15 he telegraphed Commissioner Hayt, warning that the change of policy would create a serious disturbance and could result in collisions with citizens away from the reservation. Four days later he addressed a letter to Hayt explaining in greater detail the causes of his concern. He pointed out that news of the mandated reduction had already gone abroad and that the Indians were clamorous, asking many times daily whether the directive from Washington, D.C., had been withdrawn. Miles appealed for some provision to make possible the delivery of additional food,[57] but he received no satisfactory reply. Supplies of foodstuffs such as flour were already low, and in the present week he had authorized the issue of additional beef to compensate. In the week that followed, having no authorization to the contrary, he was obliged to reduce the beef ration to a level below the normal amount.

Ben Clarke, who served as informal intermediary between the Indians, the agency, and Fort Reno, sensed the gravity of the situation and on October 1 reported to Major Mizner the views of several Indian leaders. Little Chief said he had not come south to beg and so would

56. S.O. 177, September 11, 1879—DMO; CNFCR Post Return, September 1879.
57. Miles to Hayt, September 19, 1879 (OIA LR, C&A).

not make trouble even if he starved. Still, it was hard to see his children hungry. Whirlwind, another Northern Cheyenne, said it had been difficult enough to live on the rations before; he did not see how one could survive on them now. According to Clarke, all the Indians felt cheated. Some proposed to scratch along quietly in hope that the government would relent, while others urged breaking away for a hunt. Stone Calf said they should die on the prairie rather than remain at the agency and starve.[58]

These desperate sentiments had quickly spread to the Indians around Cantonment. Interviews with some of their leaders, including Stone Calf, Minimick, White Horse, Raven, and others, convinced Dodge that immediate action was necessary. On October 4 he telegraphed an urgent message to departmental headquarters, the latter portion of which appears below:

> They say they cannot live on the rations furnished by the Agent. Chapman informs me that the general talk among them is becoming reckless, that they say they had better be killed than starved to death. He anticipates serious and widespread trouble unless something be done immediately. There are no buffalo. If the Indians are permitted to go west to hunt they will kill cattle and cause trouble in the Pan Handle.
>
> If possible please prevent Chapman going to Lawrence as he is needed here daily.[59]
>
> Can I be authorized to issue a small quantity of subsistence stores to prominent Indians?
>
> This may prevent serious complications.[60]

Dodge's message reached Washington, D.C., on October 7, accompanied by a recommendation by General Sheridan that instructions

---

58. Clarke to J. K. Mizner, October 1, 1879 (OIA LR, C&A).

59. Earlier in the summer Amos Chapman had been sent to Dodge City to assist as interpreter for the Northern Cheyennes who were to be tried for crimes during the first Dull Knife outbreak (S.O. 55, July 7, 1879—CNFCR). He had now been subpoenaed to appear as a witness at the Indians' trial, being conducted at Lawrence, Kansas. On October 14 the departmental adjutant informed Dodge that persons summoned as witnesses need not appear, as the case had been closed (CNFCR Unregistered LR).

60. RID to AAG DMO, October 4, 1879 (CNFCR LS).

be issued for distribution of emergency rations. However, before being acted upon the communication was referred to the Department of the Interior, and the next day Secretary Schurz informed the adjutant general that steps had been taken to relieve the necessities of the Indians.[61] Rations at the Cheyenne and Arapaho agency returned at once to their normal level, and the excitement soon dissipated. Dodge's intervention had helped correct a serious problem, but however well intended, it had brought him to the brink of "interference" with Agent Miles and the Indian Bureau. Among the Indians near Cantonment he was winning reputation as a friend, however little he could do to provide them substantial assistance. To Agent Miles he was becoming a known critic and, by his association with agency Indians, potentially a disruptive influence on them.

Shortly after returning to Cantonment, Dodge resumed his earlier responsibility as acting commander of the Twenty-third Regiment of Infantry. Colonel Davis, who had been absent from Fort Supply since March, was in poor health and on July 31 was granted a six-month leave of absence.[62] Beginning in July, Major Dallas was also away from regimental headquarters on a surgeon's certificate of disability.[63] Unlike the incident in April when Dodge had elected to assume command of the regiment by his own action, on October 1 an order from the Department of the Missouri directed the unit's headquarters and staff to be removed to Cantonment, where Dodge would serve as both post and regimental commander. The adjutant, First Lieutenant Patrick Brodrick, with his clerks and the regimental band, arrived at their new station on October 11.[64]

Within a week after Dodge had sent the message on behalf of the Indians near his post, Agent Miles's chief subordinate, Charles E. Campbell, made official complaint against alleged illegal trading with

61. SW to SI, October 7, 1879 (SW LS); Schurz to AG, October 8, 1879 (AGO Register LR).
62. S.O. 177, July 31, 1879—AGO; Twenty-third Infantry Regimental Return, August 1879.
63. *ANJ*, July 26, 1879, p. 930; Fort Supply Post Returns, July and August, 1879.
64. AAG DMO to C.O., October 1, 1879 (CNFCR Unregistered LR); CNFCR Post Return, October 1879.

Indians conducted at Cantonment by H. C. Keeling, the post trader. Acting on information provided him by George E. Reynolds, the authorized Indian trader at the Cheyenne and Arapaho agency, Campbell reported that the five Cheyenne scouts employed at the post regularly purchased from Keeling articles that were not for their own use.[65] This practice exposed the authorized Indian trader to competition from a concern that could claim no such warrant from the Indian Bureau. Campbell therefore asked the Commissioner Hayt whether the five scouts were in future to be regarded as in effect soldiers rather than Indians who were permitted to trade only at their agency. Two days later he wrote again, alleging on information just received that Keeling had dispensed with the cover of selling only to the five scouts. He was now conducting business "openly and above board" with any Indian who wished to purchase items from him. For example, he kept in stock "stranding beads, paints &c" that were clearly intended for the Indian trade but were of no particular interest to the five scouts.[66]

Petty accusations like these might seem frivolous at a time when the Indians' very survival had just been threatened, but they involved two issues of serious concern to representatives of the Indian Bureau: protecting the rights of its authorized traders, and ensuring that the Army and persons associated with it, such as Keeling, did not interfere with its activities and policies. The information from Campbell was taken seriously in Washington, D.C., with the eventual result that on November 19 Dodge received instructions from General Pope to make a thorough investigation of the charges and submit a report of his findings.[67] Accordingly, on the next day Dodge informed Keeling of the accusations and requested a response to them in writing before he investigated further. Keeling answered at once that his store had sold goods to the scouts "for their own use," had indeed kept in stock a few beads at the request not only of the Indians but of officers of

65. Campbell to E. A. Hayt, October 9, 1879 (OIA LR, C&A).
66. Campbell to Hayt, October 11, 1879 (OIA LR, C&A).
67. RID to AAG DMO, January 9, 1880 (OIA LR, C&A).

the garrison, and knew of no goods being sold but in a legitimate manner.[68]

On November 28 Dodge informed Assistant Agent Campbell of Keeling's denial and asked for documentary evidence and the names of witnesses "by whose evidence you expect to make good these charges."[69] On the same day he also responded to Miles, who had recently asked him to inform Indians in the vicinity of Cantonment that they must at once move closer to the agency. The agent's expressed rationale was that in future the Indians would be issued their rations weekly rather than monthly as heretofore. Whatever Miles's motives, Dodge replied to him with pointed politeness, expressing his willingness to pass on the message to the Indians but tacitly holding the agent to the terms of General Order 28 and making clear that he took no direct orders from officials of the Indian Bureau. He wrote: "I shall not however feel warranted in the use of force to carry out your wishes, until you shall have communicated with General Pope, and he with me. I shall be very greatly relieved if you succeed in getting these Indians away. They are a source of constant annoyance and trouble. Stone Calf says he cannot move, as the white thieves have stolen all of his ponies. I recommend that you send a few wagons from the agency for him; this will have a good effect I think on the other Indians."[70] Sending "a few wagons" more than sixty miles over a primitive road was, of course, no small matter.

By the fall of 1879 Cantonment had become a fully functioning military post, a regimental headquarters housing five companies of troops, connected by telegraph to other posts in the region, and their full peer in every regard except its still temporary status. True, Dodge's ambitious plan to have in place permanent stone buildings by winter had not been fully realized. The mud-and-shingle roofs of the picket huts, buffeted by wind and made porous by dry heat, had already begun to leak. The stone officer's quarters afforded little privacy and

68. Keeling and Co. to RID, November 20, 1879 (CNFCR LR).
69. RID to Campbell, November 28, 1879 (CNFCR LS).
70. RID to John D. Miles, November 28, 1879 (CNFCR LS).

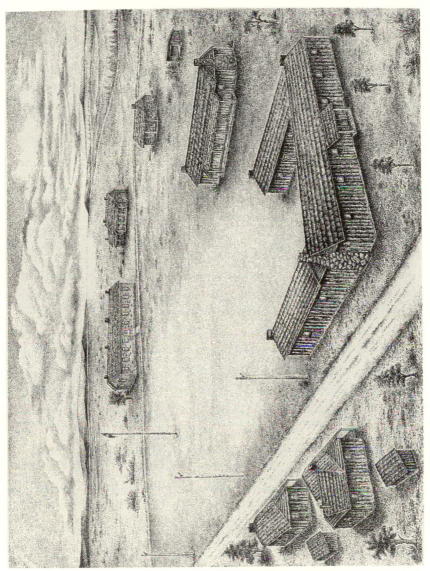

Cantonment North Fork Canadian River (Artist's conception based on contemporary descriptions, early photographs, and a sketch in the Oklahoma City *Daily Oklahoman*, September 4, 1949)

small space for its occupants, prompting some complaint.[71] An inspection report in November noted that some of the troops were still being sheltered in canvas tents.[72]

Despite its imperfections, Cantonment was not without comforts and amenities. The wives of several officers and the post physician had arrived, and they comprised a small social circle. Some enlisted men had been joined by their wives and families, including twenty-four children. No post school was yet in session, but for adults the reading room adjacent to the adjutant's office afforded a goodly selection of newspapers and magazines.[73] On October 15 a citizen, R. H. Cosand, was issued a sixty-day pass as post photographer. Two canteens and billiard rooms were in operation—one for enlisted men, which closed at 8 p.m., the other for officers, which remained open until midnight. The post trader's store was authorized to sell liquor by the drink only, but it was open for business until 8:30 p.m.[74] Several officers and even some enlisted men employed domestic servants, as did Amos Chapman and a few other civilian employees. Authorized laundresses, the wives of non-commissioned officers, were on duty for each of the companies, and two hospital matrons assisted Dr. La Garde.[75]

General Pope made particular mention of Cantonment in his published annual report for 1879. Describing the circumstances that had

71. Second Lieutenant James B. Lockwood, an unmarried officer whose rank placed him at the bottom of the pecking order for allocation of living space in the officers' quarters, complained that the one room he occupied was "small and wholly inadequate," without room "even for a stone [stove?]" (Lockwood to Post Adjutant, October 22, 1879—CNFCR Unregistered LR).

72. R. B. Marcy to W. T. Sherman, November 25, 1879 (AGO LR).

73. The newspapers received included, from New York, the Herald and the Times; from Chicago, the *Times* and the *Inter-Ocean*; from St. Louis, the *Globe-Democrat*; and from Toledo, Ohio, the *Blade*. Magazines included the *Army and Navy Journal, Catholic World, Harper's New Monthly Magazine, Harper's Weekly, Irish World, The Nation, Scientific American, Scribner's Monthly*, and *Spirit of the Times* ("Monthly Report of Schools in Operation," CNFCR, December 1879; "List of Children of Enlisted Men at the Post," n.d.—CNFCR Unregistered LR). In March 1880 a post school was under construction.

74. CNFCR Pass Book; G.O. 25, October 20, 1879—CNFCR; G.O. 1, January 1, 1880—CNFCR.

75. L. A. La Garde to Post Adjutant, August 1, 1879 (CNFCR Unregistered LR); CNFCR Pass Book.

dictated its establishment, he predicted that despite its still uncompleted state the troops hutted there would be able to pass the coming winter without suffering. Still, in future years the post would prove increasingly vital, "as well for the protection of Indian Territory against white invasion as for the security of the Kansas frontier against Indians." He therefore asked an appropriation from Congress of fifty thousand dollars to build a permanent fort.[76] On November 16, little more than one month after submitting his report, Pope returned to the subject of Cantonment in a letter to the adjutant general. Here he dwelt more forcibly on the healthfulness and strategic value of its location, noting that instances of extreme unrest among the agency Indians during the summer had shown the wisdom of maintaining a military presence at that site. The large quantity of canvas thus far used at the post as makeshift was expensive, required frequent replacement, and afforded only partial protection. Pope now recommended that sixty thousand dollars be requested at the coming session of Congress to make possible the construction of an appropriately substantial permanent post.[77]

Dodge was no doubt aware of these initiatives by his commanding officer, for they addressed the focus of his intense professional activity for almost the whole year past. Nevertheless, in the journal that follows, with entries dated from November 6 to December 10, 1879, he made no mention of Cantonment's official status nor of the need of further construction funds. In both subject matter and tone, this journal is different from those he had compiled in the spring. The excitement of creating a new post, and potentially a handsome one, out of the wilderness; the satisfaction of watching picked men perform their tasks promptly and well; the sense of significant events transpiring just out of view: all these are absent from his description of later events—which, however, embodies merits of a different variety. Cantonment was now past the initial stage of its existence, and Dodge's purpose in writing his journal entries had also evolved.

76. House, *Report of the Secretary of War* (1879), p. 84.
77. Pope to AAG MDM, November 16, 1879 (AGO LR).

Since November 1878 he had been addressing himself to a select audience, his parents and close family members, as a means of sharing with them something of his "daily life." He was now writing less than before about his official duties and more about his personal concerns. In the present journal he emphasizes two main themes that he knew would interest his family: a road-building excursion to Pond Creek Station that afforded a good opportunity for hunting, and a hurried journey from Cantonment to Leavenworth, Kansas, for a reunion with his wife and son.

The final preparations for Frederick Paulding's dramatic tour of 1879–1880 were made in August, when his agent Aaron Appleton placed an advertisement in the New York *Dramatic Mirror* inviting theater managers having open dates for Paulding and "a first-class combination" to contact the agency office on Broadway.[78] The company's cast included Paulding as leading man and as leading lady, Gussie De Forest, a well-known actress, with three additional women and five men. The stage manager was E. T. Taylor, and the repertory for the season included *The Bar Sinister* and *The Fool's Revenge*, two works by the popular English playwright Tom Taylor; Edward Bulwer-Lytton's *The Lady of Lyons;* an adaptation of a tale by W. M. Thackeray entitled *Lovell's Wife's Secret;* and two traditional favorites, *Hamlet* and *Macbeth*.[79] Following its debut performance at Troy, New York, on September 27, the company moved north into Canada, with dates in Toronto, Hamilton, London, and St. Catherine's, Ontario. It returned to the United States for a booking at Erie, Pennsylvania, on October 18, followed by three weeks on "the Ohio circuit."[80] The routine of a nightly performance in a strange theater, often followed the next day by a railroad journey and performance that night in a new town, was taxing work. Nevertheless, Frederick Paulding won considerable praise for his efforts. Although attendance was sometimes disappointing,

78. New York *Dramatic Mirror*, August 23, 1879, p. 7. The same advertisement ran in the following week's issue. Appleton was manager of the Lyceum Theatre in New York City.
79. New York *Dramatic Mirror*, September 20, 1879, p. 4.
80. New York *Dramatic Mirror*, October 11, 1879, p. 4; October 25, p. 4.

Mrs. Dodge, who accompanied the players, helped make up for losses by financial contributions of her own.[81] Being short of funds during the summer, she had prevailed upon her husband for a loan of fifty-four hundred dollars.[82]

Dodge had entertained some hope of witnessing his son's success onstage during the fall, but he had abandoned it when, on November 28, he received a telegram informing him that Fred and the company would appear at Leavenworth three days hence. The result, memorably recounted in his journal, was a journey with all possible speed, followed by a moment of recognition at the Leavenworth Opera House on December 1 as the night's entertainment neared its close. In the days that followed, he was a faithful if uncritical observer of his son's performances in leading roles as the company moved from town to small town. Writing to his parents, he confided the grateful wonder he felt as he watched young Fred's metamorphosis into The New Hamlet and his delight that, after an estrangement, his wife had "'kinder' fallen in love with me again." Dodge's journal entries were now the medium through which, with Cantonment left behind him for a time, he recorded these few happy days as a father and husband.

81. *Atchison (Kansas) Globe*, April 6, 1880, p. 4. See also the journal entry for December 10, 1879.

82. RID to Frederick Paulding Dodge, July 17, 1884 (Dodge Papers, Graff Collection).

Journal Six
November 6–
December 10, 1879

November 6, 1879. Gypsum Creek[1]

I had previously made preparations for a trip to complete my road to Pond Creek, but the day was so dark & lowering, that I concluded to put off my start until the weather looked more favorable. About 10 a.m. it had so far improved that I decided to attempt it any how, & ordered my party to load the wagons. It was a slow job, but we finally got off at 11:15 am

The party consists of Myself, Lt Lockwood (my engineer & map maker) a Corporal & 6 Infantry, & one mounted man – Chapman (the Interpreter) and 3 teamsters & Joe Laura & the baby. I have a 6 mule team a 4 mule team & an ambulance. I have my horse – Lockwood one & Chapman & the orderly each one. My Comd has rations until 20th & forage until 16th. I have my rifle, shot gun,

---

1. This manuscript journal is identical in style and dimensions to Journals One, Two, Three, and Five. It includes fifty-seven unnumbered pages, followed at the end by the stub of one additional sheet that has been torn away. On the front cover Dodge has written in dark ink an identification: "Road Making [/] from [/] Cantonment I.T. [/] to [/] Caldwell KS." At the bottom of the front cover, in the handwriting of a person other than Dodge, is the penciled notation "Nov 6/ 79 to [/] Dec 1/79." (In fact, the entries continue through December 10.) The remainder of the text is in ink; it begins on p. [1R].

According to an itinerary later prepared by Second Lieutenant James B. Lockwood, the junction of Gypsum Creek with the Cantonment–Pond Creek road was approximately eleven miles northwest of the post, two miles past an intervening stand of blackjack timber on a range of sand hills (AGO Miscellaneous File).

lots of ammunition & my dog.[2]   In all respects I am well fixed & if we dont have a good time, it will not be from lack of preparation

Some time ago I sent Chapman out to locate a better road through the black Jack timber & Sand hills, north of the post.   He succeeded very well.   We came over the route today.   It is much better than the other road & at least 1 1/2 miles nearer.

At 3. 1/2 we camped in a very beautiful spot on Gypsum Creek.   A large sand bed, with but little water now, & that unfit for use, tho' the animals like it.   We brought along enough for supper & breakfast. The day turned out well, & we had a pleasant march   Kept on road – did not hunt at all & saw no game.   To bed very early.

Distance 11 miles –

November 7, 1879. Walnut Creek

Took it easy this morning, & started at 8.30 am –   While the wagons were being packed I found a covey of true western Quail. I got them up three times, bagged 3 birds, & wounded two more which I did'nt get, but I could not get the covey scattered.   They rose as one bird & were off like shot every time   Put up stakes at the point where my road<s> leaves the old one, & planted occasional stakes all along, though I dont think they are needed as the trail is pretty well marked.   Any ordinarily good plainsman can follow it.   Had quite a little spirt of excitement, as we came towards the Cimmaron Divide.   Tried a shot with my rifle at an owl about 80 yds off, & plugged him through & through Center   Long shot 400 yds at a running wolf – another at same 500 yds –   Covered him with dust each time.   Scraped the top of another running rascale at 200 yds.   Bagged 2 enormous rattlesnakes

2. The soldiers not named by Dodge included Corporal Martin Joste and Privates William O'Brien and Isaac Tol, Company A; Privates John Bernhart and Leander Swan, Company D; Private William Slimm, Company C; Private Patrick Birmingham, Company G; Private William T. McKean, Company I. The mounted man was Dodge's orderly, Private George Routzahn, Company I (S.O. 133, November 5, 1879—CNFCR). One of the teamsters was Boon Tomlinson; in the entry for November 10 Dodge identifies his hunting dog as Fanny, a pointer bitch.

Camped on Walnut Ck 3 pm.[3]   Nice camp – plenty of Turkeys.   All hands turned out at dark – but the night is too dark, the leaves yet too thick.   I bagged only 2 – tho' I killed 4.   Lockwood killed 3, bagged 1. Boon killed 4, bagged 2.   The soldiers did well as they had rifles & bagged 7 or 8 – tho they shot lots of times.   The firing was like a small battle.   What with the dense thicket & the unusual exercise, I broke down early, & came back covered with perspiration in 3/4 of an hour.

We remain here tomorro   A party goes back to work the road passed over today –   I shall look for a good bridge crossing of this creek.   If I cant find it, I will cross on my old trail.

I hope to bag a deer tomorro.

Weather perfect –

It is blowing a gale now, 10 pm, but is not cold.   It did the same last night so I hope for a good day tomorro.

Distance 15 miles.   Game all told 1<2>3 Turkeys – 3 quail – 1 owl & 2 rattlesnakes

November 8, 1879

There was last night some talk of a hunt this am by moonlight – that luminary only getting up about 2 am – but during the night it commenced raining & kept at it until about 7 am   I laid snug & cozy in my bed & when finally I was forced to get up by the importunities of Laura, that breakfast would be spoiled – I could not find Lockwood

Just as I finished my meal L. made his appearance, draggled miserable, but happy.   "What did you get[?]" I asked.   "I have only one here," he replied, "but I have 15 more cached up at the Roost, & I wish you would let me take a wagon & go for them, before the wolves get at them" –

I made him get his breakfast, & then sent out the ambulance & we soon had all his 16 drawn & hung up. –

I sent Chapman with the Corpl & 5 men to work the bad places on the road we came over yesterday – & about 9 am I started to kill a deer if possible.   Went up the creek, Lockwood Joe & my orderly with

3. According to the Lockwood itinerary, Walnut Crossing was 12.88 miles past the Cimarron River on the road north.

me.   Looked in vain for a deer or even a deer track.   The Indians have cleaned them out effectually.   There were plenty when I came over the route before   Finding the deer "no go" & coming on a covey of quail, I went at them.   Killed 7 – one single & 3 right & lefts, which did me more good than 6 turkeys.   Found several flocks of turkeys, & had a dozen shots, & knocked over at least a dozen birds – but I bagged but four.   I have been shooting by preference No. 4 shot, & am now disgusted with them.   I have not killed – that is bagged a single turkey with No 4.   The turkeys are not yet fat, & they have a great deal of vitality –   Twice today I knocked over 2 at a shot, only to see them get up & go off.   I finally got mad, & commenced putting No 2 Elys wire cartridges into them & all the birds I bagged are due to them. Lockwood got one & Joe none.

It turned very cold while we were out & I came home early.   Examined the creek & fixed upon the point where the road is to cross. Cant make a bridge as I wished as the drift wood indicates water higher than I can make a bridge with my force.

Chapman & the party got back about 3 pm & report the road all good.   Have determined to send Boon in tomorro with Turkeys.   I have 26 hanging in front of my tent & if we do well tomorro, I hope to send in at least 40   Have written to Clarke for a lot of things especially more ammunition

Just at dusk Lockwood Joe & I went out again to try the roost of last night.   Joe found one solitary bird & bagged it.   The others evidently think this an unhealthy neighborhood   Weather still cloudy but clearing, & has moderated much.   Game today 25 Turkeys 7 quail. The men got tonight 2.   Total Turkeys 38.

November 9, 1879. Walnut Creek

Punctually at 4 Oclk the sentinel called me.   I was already wide awake, for I am getting into the bad habit of old men, of anticipating the hour.   I was anxious to send a big lot of Turkeys to the Post – & was a little excited & nervous.   In a short time horses were ready & we started – & then commenced a series of misfortunes   As the Indian would say, "my Medicine has been very bad today."   First of all, one of Boons (Boon is the driver of my ambulance a character & very useful man) mules had got loose in the night, & when we started it insisted on following.   We had got out several hundred yards when we found it out.   I wanted Boon to go into the post today, and didn't want to risk losing the mule in the Black Jack (where it would become perfectly wild in a week)   So all turned back driving the mule.   About 300 yards from camp a terrible accident happened.   I sneezed suddenly & violently, & my teeth flew out on the prairie –   Imagine the situation.   A frantic man groping for his teeth at 4 in the morning of a dark night & in the midst of a grass covered prairie, refusing all assistance, for the careless tread of a heavy foot would either demolish or send them out of sight in the soft sand.

At last I had to give it up & tying my handkerchief to a small bush very near the scene of the catastrophy, I went back stirred up Boon, had the mule caught, & went on with the hunt.

But the stiffening had been taken out of me.   My loss worried me, to be reduced to "gumming it" after enjoying the luxury of teeth.[4] Visions of Dyspepsia assailed me.   Finally we arrived at the Turkey roost, & entered the dark thicket.   All was silent, not a Turkey to be seen or heard.   I at once suspected that those rascally soldiers had been in here last night.   I had told them to go lower down –

Up and Up the creek we went.   Day was breaking & not a Turkey was to be seen – but now I could see the tracks of those d—— soldiers. Excuse me I was mad – for everything went wrong.   More than a million of twigs stuck in my eyes –   I was hung by Bamboo briers several hundred times & pitched down banks on numberless occasions by roots & vines.

At last I came upon a little rise that overlooked a semi-circular little bottom – & every tree that fringed the stream was ornamented with Turkeys, until it appeared like the old pear tree in Grandfathers Yard.[5]

4. In his journal for March 16, 1879, Dodge had written: "I can never get well, until I get some teeth."

5. Probably this at the home of Dodge's maternal grandfather, a member of the prominent Williams family of western North Carolina. His paternal grandfather, Richard Dodge (1762–1832) lived in Johnstown, New York, a climate not favorable to pear trees.

But that is all the good it did.   It was already so light that they were beginning to leave the roost, & the air was resonant with the piping of those on the ground, calling on their lazy companions to get up – or down.   I got into the creek and tried to wade up under cover of the banks, but each tree was vacated by the time I came within shot.

In utter desperation I sent a wire Cartridge after one or two of the latest goers.   They then went rapidly enough & the only consolation I have is, that by this time one or more are food for wolves (& I dont seem to derive much consolation from that either)   Coming back, I caught one fellow asleep & bagged him, & we got one other.   Reached camp soon after sunrise & put Boon Chapman & an intelligent teamster to looking for my teeth.   The situation was an anxious one – an excellent breakfast was almost ready, my appetite was ferocious – but suppose they did'nt find those teeth.   Laura called out that breakfast was ready.   Instead of responding with my usual alacrity, I walked out to meet the searchers – coming with triumph in their faces. Boon had found them in good order, & as reward I immediately forgave him the scolding I intended to give him for letting his mule get loose in the night –   Ah, how I did enjoy the[6] quail on toast – the beefsteaks, the turkey hash the more than delicious batter cakes – the rich coffee &c &c.   Tis said that a man enjoys life more after having been in great danger of losing it.   I doubt the proposition but I can aver from my own experience that a man never enjoys a breakfast more, than when he has just escaped the terrible danger of losing his teeth –

After breakfast set the Corpl & party to making a crossing of this Creek – then went with Chapman out to the Black Jacks, to see if my original route through them can be improved.   Left him to look up the situation & went off on an earnest & faithful effort to get a deer. Hunted as well & faithfully as ever in my life, & did'nt even see a track. There were plenty here when I made the first route across.   The Osage Indians have been camped for 2 weeks on this creek & have

6. Dodge wrote "enjon."

completely cleaned out the deer.[7]   Not enough are left for seed.   On my return I went into the creek bottoms to try & get some quail for breakfast.   Found none, but did find 3 squirrels – which I bagged, 2 with shot gun, & one with rifle, from the top of a high cottonwood. Could see only a part of his head, but knocked that off.   Squirrel shooting with a good rifle, has more charms for me than any other sport,[8] & a squirrels head seems to have some peculiar attraction for a rifle ball.   I'd rather shoot at the head any time than at the body, & rarely fail to hit it.

Got home in time for a good dinner.   Then took a nap, for an hour. Joe wanted to go in to the Post with Boon so <I>they got off about 9 am, with 28 Turkeys

Just after dark one of my Indian scouts came in with a note from Broderick about the transfer of Routzahn.[9]   Brodrick has hunted on his own account today & got one small duck.[10]

Wrote an answer to be sent back tomorro.   Broderick & Chapman spent the evening with me – played solitaire then went at this –

Game – 2 Turkeys 3 squirrels – 1 duck –

Stopped the mens shooting as punishment for last night.

November 10, 1879

Slept the sleep of the Just – That is I waked up only periodically when Fanny, my pointer bitch, made a rush at the wolves to whom she will not be reconciled.   I have argued the point with her in words & remonstrated with a strap, but whenever the wolves commence

7. The Osage reservation lay between that of the Cherokees, in the northwestern section of Indian Territory, and the Cherokee Outlet in which Dodge's party was now hunting. Fall hunts in this region were customary as a means for tribes to supplement their rations from the Indian Bureau during the winter.

8. In a letter to Dodge of January 4, 1884, his nephew James D. Glenn regretted his absence from Leaksville, North Carolina, where the squirrel hunting was excellent just then. (Dodge Papers, Graff Collection).

9. Private Routzahn, Dodge's mounted orderly since October 16, had been a member of Company K, Twenty-third Infantry, then posted at Fort Supply. He was being transferred to Company I (S.O. 124, October 16, and S.O. 132, November 3, 1879—CNFCR; CNFCR and Fort Supply Post Returns, November 1879).

10. Lieutenant Brodrick, the regimental adjutant, was not a member of Dodge's roadmaking detail that left Cantonment on November 6.

their dulcet notes, she goes with a scramble, a rush & a howl of defiance to meet them.

Breakfasted late   Sent out my working party.   About 9 am Lockwood & I started down the creek – saw some ducks but got none Made a careful hunt after deer, & am fully satisfied there are none here. Ambulance came back from Cant[onmen]t about 4 pm.   Clarke also in his wagon to have a hunt.   We are to start 3:30 am tomorro – am not very sanguine.   Camp moves tomorro.   Men got 3 turkeys   Total 42 –

November 11, 1879. Walnut Creek

Started about 4 a.m., went up on other side of creek – as the best travelling – for about 4 miles – when we reached what I took to be my roost.   We dismounted & tied our horses & went in<to>   A very short examination showed me my mistake.   The roost was near 1/2 mile above.   Clarke came out of the thicket about same time I did. Day was just breaking.   There was no time to go back after horses – so we started on a "go-as-you-please"[11] for the roost

Twas a beautiful sight.   Hundreds & hundreds of Turkeys were in sight at once – but that was bad for our success in getting them.   It was too late.   At the first fire the large majority went away to the Black Jacks.   All of us worked hard, and by a little after sunrise, I yelled the boys together, having already sent my orderly back for the horses.   Our bag was light.   I had five, but the others only had one each.   We got back to Camp at 9 am.   The clouds looked very threatening & by the time we got through our breakfast, it began to rain. The tents were all down except the mess tent, so I had one or two pitched, to shelter things that might get damaged by the rain.   For two hours it came down in torrents & when it finally began to clear, I had the old camp re-pitched, as the prairie was too soft to travel over well.   In the afternoon we went out & got some quail.   The day turned out well, & we enjoyed it.

7 Turkeys, 9 quail.   Total Turkeys 49 –

11. An excursion unconfined by rules (Thornton, *An American Glossary*, 1:365).

Wednesday, November 12, 1879. Turkey Creek[12]

I was so tired last night that I did not do justice to my diary.   About dark an Indian arrived with our mail from the Post.   A letter from Father & Mother   One from Cath.   One from Mrs Lieut Dodge inviting me to stay at her house during my visit to Fort Leavenworth to meet Julia & Fred.[13]   One or two on business & some papers. Wrote a letter to Jordan who ought to be at Pond Creek today,[14] & another to the Station Agent at Pond Creek –

This morning the first thing I started the Indian on to Pond Creek with these letters.   Last night Clarke & Lockwood made up another hunt for this morning.   I plead exemption on account of age two midnight starts in succession being too much for me.   They started however at 3.30 am – while I rolled over & took another snooze. Got up about sunrise, & busied myself in various ways until they returned about 7.<8>30 am   They had one Turkey.   Not having my efficient guidance they arrived late at the roost & Lockwood in carelessly handling his gun, let it go off – when all the Turkeys followed suit & went off also.   Clarke got only two long shots at flying birds – but got none.   Camp was struck as soon as we got breakfast, & at 9.30 am we started.   Clarke pulled out at the same time for the Post.

I forgot also to mention in my yesterdays diary that I gave two men permission to go out hunting in the afternoon, after we all got back & they returned at dark with 3 turkeys.   This am before I was up a man discovered a Turkey in a tree near camp & bagged him.   I gave all the Turkeys we had to Clark to take in to the Post   There were only 7 all told – for I never take away any from the men.

12. According to the Lockwood itinerary, the military road crossed Turkey Creek 38.39 miles from Cantonment on the route to Pond Creek Ranch.

13. Although at this time Dodge anticipated a meeting at Leavenworth with his wife and son, he was to be disappointed for a time; see the entries for November 19 and 28. Dodge and First Lieutenant Frederick L. Dodge were not related.

14. This was Robert C. Jordan, who arrived at Cantonment on December 14 and remained there until January 15, 1880, evidently on a pleasure visit (CNFCR Pass Book). See the journal entries for December 1 and after.

When the Camp broke, I started up the Creek, well to the west in the Black Jacks, for I still have visions of deer.   Hunted carefully but did not see a single deer, & scarcely a fresh track.   I however came on to a couple of huge old gobblers & bagged one of them.   I also bagged 3 quail - regular wild fellows - born and bred in the <b>Black Jacks.   After swinging around a pretty wide circle, I came on to my road, & met my party & wagons just coming through the Black Jacks on east of Walnut Ck.   Joined & came on with them.   Arrived at Turkey Ck about 2 pm.   Joe rode down to water his mule & scared up 3 fine mallard   Soon after he dislodged a snipe, which after tearing around in the air for some time came near enough to give me a long & difficult shot -   But I bagged him all same.

As soon as camp was pitched I put the men to work making a crossing of this Creek.   They have not yet finished it, but it will be done by 8 am tomorro, & a good crossing it will be.   I have changed my road here from my preliminary line, making it straighter & saving two bad crossings -   Day perfect.   Game today, 3 Turkeys 3 quail, 1 snipe, 1 opossum, 3 rattlesnakes.   Total Turkeys 55, Quail 22.

November 13, 1879. Cold Water Creek[15]

I took it so leisurely about getting up that the crossing was done almost by the time I was up, & we did not get off until about 9 am. It was very cold, though clear when I got up, but by the time we were ready to start, it had every appearance of a furious storm. However I went on & by noon it was clear and warm.   It is now cloudy again, & looks like snow.   We have been very fortunate in weather & at this season can hardly hope to escape a storm before we get in.

Made a good crossing of another pretty bad creek.   While the men were at work I took my dog & went down the creek to look for quail. There were several small thickets of young willow & tall grass.   Joe

15. Dodge first wrote as his location "Wild Horse" Creek, then canceled it and wrote in "Cold Water" Creek. According to the Lockwood itinerary, the military road crossed Cold Water Creek 51.93 miles from Cantonment on the road to Pond Creek Ranch.

was on the bank behind me, & as I went into one thicket he yelled out in great excitement that a large panther was going off from the other side, not 30 yards off.   Slipping in a wire, buck shot cartridge, I ran after him, but the grass was too high – & he disappeared over a hill 300 yards away.   He was an enormous fellow.   I then returned to my quail hunting   <T>On the edge of a similar thicket a little further on my dog came to a stanch point.   As the little willows were almost too high to shoot <well> in well, I tried to make her flush the birds, but she would not, so I walked in barrels charged with No 7 shot, & all ready for snap shooting.   From just under my feet, not more than a yard from me, a huge panther bounded into the thicket. He startled me, but before he had gone 15 yards I filled his bottom with a whole load of No 7 shot – & such running as he did, I never saw before.   The little bitch was good pluck,[16] for she ran him for full 300 yards, he however going 5 feet to her one.   Had I had any suspicion of there being another panther there I might have got him with buck shot.

I am terribly sorry I did not get him, though I have been tickled ever since with the idea   After the terrible stories of panthers that I read in my juvenile days,[17] to find my pointer standing one like quail, & I putting a load of quail shot into him is too funny.   I put in proper loads & hunted all around, tho' as I know they generally go in couples, I hardly expected to find more.   I got no quail – nor game of any sort. Joe got one prairie chicken.

My Indian met me this afternoon, bringing a letter from the Mail Agent at Pond Creek.   Jordan has not been heard from, & I have about given him up.   I will know tomorro for sure.

This is a day of a new experience – for in all my frontier life & after killing numbers of panthers, I have never before had one pointed by a bird dog, nor shot at him with No 7 shot.   Its too funny, & have enjoyed it all day.

16. Perhaps Dodge meant "had" or "was of" good pluck.
17. Dodge had earlier made the same point in print. See his discussion of the panther in *PNA*, pp. 209–10, and with regard to popular notions about wolves, pp. 208, 374.

November 14, 1879. Pond Creek, I. T.

The sun rose clear & beautiful, but he had hardly pushed his rosy face above the horizon than the heretofore clear atmosphere was changed into mist, & the whole of our surroundings was at once enveloped in a dense fog.   I have never seen it come on so before but have formed a theory.   The night was pretty cold.   All the moisture in the atmosphere (& there was plenty of it) was frozen. The day broke clear – the sun rose clear, & it was clear.   But the sun's rays soon thawed out the frozen moisture.   There was heat enough to thaw – but not enough to evaporate.   Consequently a dense fog.

By 11 am it was clear & the afternoon was warm.   Taken all together it has been a delightful day –   No work en route, so we arrived at Pond Ck by 12.30 pm.   I am well satisfied with my new road   It is nearer and far better.   Had a long talk with Melily, (the owner of this station) about the country, Indians &c.[18]   He is very enthusiastic over the new road, & as we agree in our general ideas about things I think him a very intelligent man, especially as he gave me two beautiful female pigs.   Jordan is not here – nor has any one heard of him.   I dont know what to make of the matter & have about given him up –

Wrote to Father & Mother at night.   Caused Lockwood to make an itinerary of the route to be stuck up on Melilys door.   If the Grangers[19] don't take my road after that, they may suffer on the old.

Shot at an antelope at about 600 yds, but did'nt get him.   The only one seen on the trip.

Bagged 1 grouse – game more than scarce today.

18. William E. Malaley, whose authorization to graze cattle Second Lieutenant O'Connor had copied during the summer, had resided in the vicinity for several years. He was known as an excellent horseman.

19. Dodge uses this term in an unusual sense, apparently referring to travelers on foot or by wagon rather than to farmers or members of a grange.

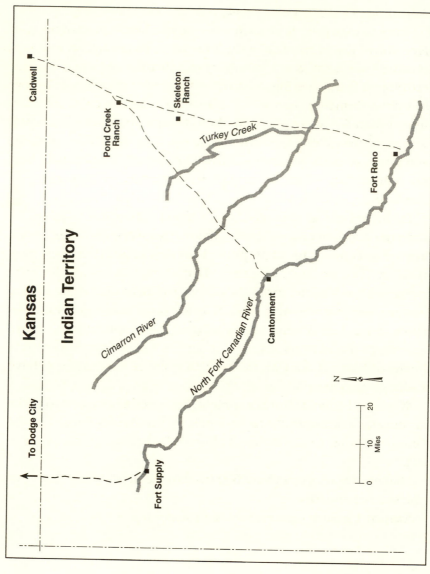

The vicinity of
Cantonment,
showing the
wagon roads
north

Saturday, November 15, 1879. Panther Creek

Paid Jarratt (the man who keeps the mail station)[20] for the chickens I got, & also for feeding my Indian and his <mule> pony.   Mellily was to have come out with me to this camp, but went out early & did not return.   A cattle man's life is more than slavery.   Boxed the pigs in the front end of a wagon & I hope they are comfortable.   Laura was sick in the night, & not able to cook breakfast, but we had a very good one nevertheless.   We got off at 8 am.   I left word for Jordan to come out, or send out, if he should come by today's stage, but I do not expect him –

Put up a notice about the new Road at the station, & put in a heavy sign post at forks of road —

There is a most "plentiful lack"[21] of game in this region.   Have seen today 1 antelope 2 grouse & about 8 quail –   Bagged 1 grouse & 3 quail.

Camped 19 miles from Pond Ck, on the creek where I encountered the panthers.   As soon as I got to the place, I loaded with wire Buck
thickets
Cartridges & scoured all the   ∧   but Mr & Mrs Panther had moved.   No sign of them since we were here   Found one small covey of quail & got 3 – ought to have had more, but for Lockwood – to whom I gave half the shooting, & who did not get anything. Laura all right tonight.   Day delightful.   The last two nights very cold

Sunday, November 16, 1879. Walnut Creek

Absolutely nothing to record except that I practically finished my road today, making several "cut-offs," & driving stakes to mark the proper route.   There is no game on this route – one might as well

20. According to Second Lieutenant O'Connor, Jarrett rented the house and outhouses and corrals of Pond Creek Ranch from Malaley, using them as "a place of entertainment for travelers and stage companies' employees" (O'Connor to Post Adjutant, August 17, 1879—CNFCR LR). Dodge describes the facility in his entry for November 29.

21. *Hamlet* II.ii.204.

travel through a desert.   The country is very pretty prairie plains, cut up by water courses & dry ravines on many of which there is timber.   Saw some antelope & 3 deer but they did not tempt me to break the Sabbath or rather the Sunday, (the days being different) I did however shoot a prairie dog, making five holes in & through him apparently in opposite directions with a single rifle bullet.   I brought him in & showed him to Chapman and Boon but none of us can pose him to correspond with the evident path of the bullet. 20 miles – lovely day, tho' windy.   Reduced to ham and bacon   No fresh meat, unless Lockwood brings in some tonight   He and Chapman went out at dark to get turkeys.   I hope they may succeed.   I would not go, because my horse's back is sore.   They are not likely to get much for we are camped only about 1 1/2 miles above our old camp on this Creek, & every portion here & for two or three miles above has been hunted over again & again   Boon tried hard to get a deer this afternoon but failed.   Looks like a storm tonight   If it comes I'll go in tomorro.   I would be ashamed of the record if this were a real hunt.   As the doings of a party engaged in the laborious work of opening a new road, it may do, but even the cook turns up her nose at sportsmen who cannot furnish fresh meat for daily consumption.   No deer, no antelope – quail all told, would be only a tolerable days hunt in N. C. while ducks & grouse are hardly enough to count.   Our Turkey record is all that redeems us ——

November 17, 1879. Cantonment

A real old fashioned norther struck us last night.   A terrific wind & very cold.   Made up my mind that the sooner I got home the better for all hands.   Started with ambulance before the wagons were packed – at 8 am.   Caught two coons out on the Cimarron bottom & bagged them.   Nasty murky, windy disagreeable day.   Rode my horse for about 8 miles then took to the ambulance   We made good time & reached home 2 pm (27 miles –)   Found all right.   Directed Lockwood & wagons to camp at Gypsum Ck.   Joe greatly used up by the cold today.

Rice & others from Ft Supply have been here went back this am.[22] Paymaster arrived at 3 p.m. found me all in a pucker.[23]   Randall invited us to dine with him & so it was arranged   After dinner we visited the Ladies, or some of them   & wound up at Hay's.   He is celebrating his Tin Wedding[24] tonight.   Gibson plead business & we got away in good season.

November 18. Cantonment

Gibson paid the Troops & we are having a high old drunk tonight. More than half the enlisted men of the Comd are under the influence of liquor, but they are very quiet.

November 19

Gibson left at daylight, for Supply.   Have given Randall & Dr. Comfort a leave for a week to go to Supply.   They start tomorro & go through in one day.   Wrote to Father & Mother – to Clitz & to Coppinger.   The papers say Freds Troupe is "busted" & gone back to N.Y.[25]   I have therefore written to Cop, that I dont want to go to Ft. 11 Worth.[26]

Men continuing their drunk & have had to put a number in the Gd. House.   This is unusual with me, for my men have behaved so well that I have had no guard – not a prisoner to look after[27]

---

22. First Lieutenant William F. Rice was post quartermaster at Fort Supply.

23. Major W. R. Gibson was on a tour to pay the troops for the two-month period ending October 31. His itinerary included Fort Dodge, Fort Supply, Fort Elliott, Cantonment, Fort Reno, Arkansas City, and Wichita (*ANJ*, November 8, p. 255). Apparently Dodge was "in a pucker" from exposure to wind and cold.

24. His tenth wedding anniversary.

25. In its "Dates Ahead" column for November 8 and 15, 1879, the New York *Dramatic Mirror* recorded a terse announcement for the Frederick Paulding company: "Earlier dates cancelled."

26. Major Coppinger had earlier played host to Dodge on his visits to Fort Leavenworth.

27. The "Monthly Statement of Persons in Arrest or Confinement" for Cantonment confirms Dodge's assessment, showing no prisoners in October and only one in November and December, 1879.

November 20

Randall & Comfort got off early this a.m.   Very cold for the season. Masons not doing much   Everything else going on well.   Brick Kiln burned & all O.K. *<one or two words unrecovered>*

November 21

Not a thing of consequence   My horse's back is sore (not my doing) & I cant get out.   Lovely day & I wanted an "outing" – but could'nt get it.   Am trying to buy a good Indian pony   Set Chapman at it —

November 21 - 22 - 23

Nothing of importance.   Wrote letters to Father & Mother – to Cath & several on business – to go off on mail tomorro.[28]

November 24

Clarke & I had fixed on a hunt for Thanksgiving   Took out 2 four mule teams, & 3 men to help & started at 11 am today.   Went up the river about 12 miles   I got 2 ducks 2 quail & one turkey.   Clarke was in bad luck & did'nt get anything – though he had good shots at both turkeys & quail.   I have'nt missed a shot today, & have done well for the game found

Camped where I expected to find a fine Turkey roost, & after dark hunted faithfully without finding a bird –   Weather perfect.   Lovely camp.   Sat out & enjoyed the moonlight until 9 pm. then went to bed.   Wrote this Epistle & now go to sleep ——

November 25, 1879

Passed a good night, & was up by sun up.   Clarke & I started about half an hour before the Wagons – going up the river, & about a mile from Camp had the mournful satisfaction[29] of seeing a fine flock of

28. Either Dodge meant "in" or "with" mail, or he omitted a word like "wagon" after *mail*.
29. Possibly an adaptation of "heavy satisfaction" in *All's Well That Ends Well* V.iii.100.

Turkeys coming out of a wood that we had not thought of hunting last night.   We went after them & by good strategy I managed to get a long shot which killed nothing but which scared them so badly that some of them squatted after their first flight.   I shot in poor luck knocking down four birds, & bagging but one.   Clarke also got one. We then came on.   Found three flocks of quail, & bagged altogether 8.   I killed 4 – Clarke 2 & Monahan 2.[30]   It is singular how completely this western quail can conceal himself.   Mark a covey down, go to the spot & the best dogs will get up only one or two birds.   Of the first covey properly marked, we got up but one bird which I bagged. Of the second I got one & Monahan 2.   The third <was>consisted of only 4 birds & Clarke & I got all of those.   We were striking for a suppositious Lake, & by the best luck we came through the Sand Hills directly upon it – & camped about 2 1/2 p.m.   After lunch, I told Clark that I would take my rod, stick it in the bank & enjoy the "dolce far niente" – Smoking dozing & fishing at the same time – for I really did not expect to catch anything more than a small Catfish – especially as the lake appears shallow.   After a while I got a bite and landed my fish which proved to be a Bass of 1 3/4 lbs.   My bait was beef & I have very rarely taken Bass on beef<f>   Went on with my work & in an hour took 5 Bass, weighing all together 7 3/4 lbs.   The largest 2 1/2 – smallest 3/4 – & wound up with a pound catfish –   So my labor was "dolce" but not "far niente"

After dark we started to hunt a splendidly appearing mass of timber for a Turkey Roost.   Hunted it all through.   Found only a fringe of timber & not a single Turkey   Came back to Camp disgusted by 7 pm. Let the men go out & they returned about 9 pm with nothing but having discovered a big camp of Pawnee Indians 2 miles below us,[31] & who have been hunting around here for a week & have driven or killed off the game.

The day has been lovely, & I have enjoyed it all, though we got so little game.   The Bass compensates.   I'd rather have them than 5

30. John Monahan, a teamster from Missouri twenty-three years of age (CNFCR Pass Book).

31. The Pawnee Indian reservation was approximately one hundred miles east.

Turkeys.   I shall try them again tomorro morning.   Clarke could not get a bite, but he promises to be even with me tomorro.

2 Turkeys, 8 quail, 5 bass, 1 catfish –   Total 3 Turkeys 10 quail &c

November 26, 1879

The fates are against us on the Turkey question & our Thanksgiving has to be without that noble bird.   This morning I expected to go to Osage Springs, above on the river & where I found a splendid Turkey roost last Novr.[32]   All our expert shots were out last night & not a single Turkey killed

Immediately after Breakfast, I went to fishing, with good success, although it was an abominable day so far as wind was concerned. Until 11 am it looked like rain & blew like blazes.   The fish were biting, slowly but they did bite, so I hated to leave them.   When I had about made up my mind to start my orderly told me that Corpl Beck[33] who had gone out Turkey hunting last night had not yet returned & was supposed to be lost.   I at once ordered Boon & Monahan to go out & look for him.   They came in about 11 am & reported seeing his track, but they could'nt find him.   I sent them out again with orders to find him if they could do so before dark, & gave them 2 good horses.   They came back with him about 3 pm

Of course we could not move.   The scouts report Indians all around us.   A big Camp of Choctaws 2 miles below[34] – another of Pawnees 2 miles above.   No wonder we dont find any game   The Choctaws have killed 7 or 8 Bear, & over 100 deer just about here   Everything is run off & we have no chance.   But Clarke & I have taken<t> it all very quietly –   We are intent on Bass – & have fished all day.   I have taken 5 Bass & 23 Catfish Clarke 4 Bass & 6 Catfish, of which I landed 3 for him.   The Bass weighed about 1 lbs. average.   We each got one of near 2 lbs, but the others were smaller – not one however falling below 3/4 lb.   The cats run near of a size, & will average 1 lb.

32. See the journal entries for November 29 and 30, 1878.
33. Corporal Henry Beck, Company A.
34. Like the Pawnees, these Indians were far from their reservation, which was located in the southeastern corner of Indian Territory.

We tried fishing after dark – regular Nigger style – building a fire &c[35] – but had no success.   Clarke got 2 shell drake about dark, one of which contained a 1/4 lb. Bass.   How he swallowed the fish is a mystery.   Very windy today & bad for fishing but not cold.

9 Bass – 30 cats – 2 shell drake – 2 quail.

The Indians have so cleared the country of game, that I shall go in tomorro – & next time, I will keep away from the main streams.

I am delighted with the discovery of this Bass Pond or Lake.   Next time I come I'll have proper bait & make a record.   We will go in tomorro though I hope to get a Bass or two before I start.

Thanksgiving Day, November 27, 1879

The wind changed in the night, & by morning we had a Norther, not very cold, but gloomy & disagreeable.

Corpl Beck had been found the game was gone & our coffee & sugar were out, so nothing remained but to go in – specially as after hard trying the fish would'nt bite   Got 2 catfish during the night – having left my line in the water.   While getting ready to move a small covey of quail came to the Lake to drink.   We got all but one, Clarke potting 4 on the ground the first shot & I bagging 3 ^single birds^ on the wing.   Going home we found only 3 Grouse.   I got 2 Clarke 1. On small game I have shot unusually well on this trip – missing only one quail since Ive been out.   I had a shot at a magnificent Buck about 200 yds, standing head on facing me.   I thought I would surely get him – but I didn't.   I heard the bullet strike with a heavy thud and was sure I had hit him but when I came to examine his trail & found that he ran on all 4 legs, & that there was no sign of blood, I had to admit that I missed him

Got in about 3 pm & found everything all right.   Found letter from Father of 14th.

35. Having passed his childhood along the Yadkin River in North Carolina, Dodge was well acquainted with folk customs like the one referred to here.

Total of hunt
Turkeys 3
Grouse 3   Ducks 3
Quail 18   Bass 14
Catfish 33

November 28, 1879. Cantonment

Recd. a telegram from Lt Dodge early this am telling me that the newspaper reports were false, that Fred would play in Leavenworth

on 1st & 2d Decr. - Made up my mind I could ∧ get there in time,   ^{not}
& telegraphed to that effect.   Mail came in about 12 m, bringing a letter from Jordan telling me that the whole family would be in Leavenworth on 1st sending their love & begging me to meet them. Every ambulance & team I have is out, two of them sent away this am to accommodate other officers.   So I had to rush around to see what I could do.   Result that I start tomorro at 5 am or as soon after as possible for Pond Ck.   Clarke sends out a relay tonight & if all goes right we will reach Pond Ck tomorro night 67 m   This will get us in to 11 Worth on evening of 1st.

Have been flying round lively since 12 m.

November 29. Pond Creek

Had given orders for a very early start.   Laura called me at 4 a.m. - Keeling[36] who was to breakfast with me did not put in an appearance until nearly 5.   We got our breakfast, & found no wagon.   He being the younger went off after it, & in half an hour or so it came up.

Loaded up & got off at 6 am - it being still very dark - only a few faint streaks of daylight yet being visible - -   In the darkness and number of wood roads, we lost my new road, & got into the old one almost as soon as we had crossed the river.   There was no time to

---

36. This was H. C. Keeling, thirty-five years of age, who ran the post trader's store for his elder brother William. The younger Keeling's account of his years at Cantonment is found in "My Experience with the Cheyenne Indians," pp. 59-68.

lose in hunting nearer cuts & we went on –   About 9 am we felt able to eat a little, & went for our lunch baskets.   At 10.45 am, we came to my turkey camp on Walnut Ck,[37] where we found the team sent out last night.   It was a pair of little rats of mules – in excellent order – but after the big horses that had brought us so far, looked too small to pull us –

However we pulled out at 11.20 am, & at <6>7.05 we reached Pole Ck,[38] having made 41 1/2 miles in less than 8 hours with this same team of *rats* —   The whole distance 66 1/2 miles was made in 13 hours exactly.   The day has been very delightful – a little cool but the wind came from our rear – & did not annoy us.   Had we been riding against it we would have suffered.   Some rascally grangers or hunters set fire to the Black Jacks just ahead of us, & we had to run the Guantlet crossing the line of fire twice.   It looked a trifle squally for a few moments, but we got through all right.

Saw a great number of wolves & some antelope   I had my rifle along but my bullet pouch was mislaid & hid among our numerous wraps & bundles & I didn't get a shot.   Had plenty of lunch along & lots to drink – but was both hungry and thirsty on arrival at Pond Ck. We soon had supper, & by 9 pm went to bed   Fell asleep at once, only to wake up in half an hour.   Heard the clock strike 10, 11, 12, 1 & 2.

Pond Creek ranche consists of a log house 20 by 18 – 2 stories high.

room
6 people occupied the upper <story> ∧ – Keeling & I sleeping in one bed.   The Lower floor was occupied by the Ranchman & wife, five children & 2 dogs —   I being awake & consequently not snoring our room was quiet enough.   Down stairs was different   First the baby (4 months)[39] commenced yelling & was after toil & patience

37. According to the Lockwood itinerary this was 25.51 miles from Cantonment, but having missed the better road in the pre-dawn darkness, the party had come a few more miles.

38. An error, meaning Pond Creek. Dodge may have been thinking of "Polecat," the name of a deserted stage station north of Pond Creek Ranch.

39. Dodge wrote a hyphen instead of an end parenthesis.

quieted by its mother   Then the puppy (which must have burnt itself against the stove[)] set up a piercing & prolonged wail – a series of wails which were only terminated by Jarratt – (the Ranchman[)] catching & dropping him out of doors.   The noise waked the youngest boy 2 years – the owner of said pup – & hearing that pup yell, he set up a yell in sympathy   An awful & interminable howl it was – & finally to quiet the boy the unhappy ranchman had to get up & let the pup in again.   Six times at least did that Ranchman have to get up & do something   At 12 ock, there was a loud rap on the door, & a voice announced another belated wanderer –   Jarrat went out & put up the team – & the new comer was put to sleep on the floor among the puppys & babies –[40]   Soon after I went into the land of dreams, of pork & late suppers.[41]

November 30. Wellington

Up before the sun –   The newcomer of last night proved to be our team telegraphed for by Keeling when it was decided we were to go on this trip.   Hugh our driver,[42] so far, was ordered to return to the Post.   We were gentlemanly lazy about starting, getting off at 8 am. We had a very good light wagon, with curtains all around, which proved very comfortable as the wind was very cold, tho' in our backs. At 1 pm arrived at Caldwell, & got dinner.   Started again at 2 pm with a fresh team & arrived at Wellington 6 pm   51 miles today – in 9 hours Put up at the Hotel De Bernard, a shingle palace, where a whisper is heard all over.[43]   This is a busy & growing town.   Lots from $50 to

40. Mrs. D. B. Dyer wrote an evocative account of Pond Creek Station at the time she saw it in 1885. By then it offered more comforts than when Dodge visited, but it still provided "a most favorable opportunity to study the customs and manners of the crude phase of human nature" (*Fort Reno*, p. 25). As to the decor, "Hammocks were everywhere; in the hall, in the dining-room, and along the veranda . . . so that any number of unexpected guests could be strung up for the night without inconvenience" (p. 29).

41. This concluding phrase is an odd one. Perhaps Dodge meant "port."

42. Hugh Patton, a teamster whom Dodge employed in various capacities. See the journal entry for September 3, 1880.

43. W. H. Barned, the proprietor of the Hotel De Barnard, claimed to be "one of the first on Kansas soil, and one of the first in the county. His long experience in his business enables him to lead the trade" (*Caldwell Post*, February 19, 1880, p. 1).

$1500 – everything on a Boom.[44]   Dont think it will amount to much – & wont invest.   Keeling asleep long ago, & now I'll follow suit.   117 miles in 2 days

Monday, December 1, 1879

Slept like an Infant Angel until aroused by a knocking somewhere & a hoarse voice saying "2 Oclock" –   As we were not to be called till 3, <I>& as there was no other train or reason that I could see for getting up at that time, I imagined I had made a mistake in the call – that it must be 3 Oclk, & this worried me wide awake & I got up. Twas only 2 but I could sleep no more.   At 3 we left the Hotel, & were soon speeding over the prairie, at the rate of 30 miles an hour. Struck all our connections just right, & arrived at Leavenworth about 7 pm   Went to the Hotel.   Put on some clean clothes, got supper & then started out to look for the show people who were at another Hotel.   All gone to the Opera House.   There I found Jordan, who introduced me to Mr Lawlor[45] who is now managing the Compy. Josie Jordan was inside,[46] & Fred in his dressing room.   In a few moments the house began to fill.   I would not go behind scenes to see Fred as I wanted to surprise him.   No one knew that I was in town, & I was running all over the house to see friends, & being hand-shaken all to pieces

Soon the Curtain rose & in due time Fred came on, so hideously made up that I would not have known my boy.   I followed him closely & watched him narrowly with a most critical eye and brain.

---

44. A line of the Atchison, Topeka and Santa Fe Rail Road had recently reached Wellington, now its southern terminus. In 1880 Caldwell, twenty-five miles south, supplanted Wellington as the shipping point for goods bound to Indian Territory and cattle bound north (Bryant, *History of the Atchison, Topeka and Santa Fe Railway*, p. 55; Freeman, *Midnight and Noonday*, p. 232 n).

45. The troupe was now known as Frank Lawlor's Company, though in newspaper advertisements its performances continued to be announced under the name "Frederick Paulding" in boldface type.

46. Dodge's friend Robert C. Jordan, who resided in Grand Island, Nebraska, was traveling with his family. According to J. Sterling Morton, in 1850 he married Mary Elizabeth Clugsten, with whom he had two daughters—Maria, born in 1851, and Caroline, born in 1858 (*Illustrated History of Nebraska*, 3:370). Which of these three women, if any, was nicknamed Josie is uncertain, but Caroline seems the most likely.

In one of his falls in the last scene, he missed the table on which he was to fall, & he and table went to the floor together.   I supposed it intentional.   After the Curtain went down & the applause was over I went to Freds dressing room.   He met me with the warmest hugs & kisses, & every evidence of delight, & told me that as he turned to fall on the table, he caught sight of me, & was so surprised that he did not strike it properly

We all went up to the Fort.   I stayed with Coppinger.   Julia is to be here tomorro.   We had a grand time & finally all got to bed.

Tuesday, December 2

Lt Dodge went down for Julia, as I had to attend to business.   Mrs Lt D. had arranged a reception, & Julia got in in good time to dress for it.   The whole post turned out to do us honor, & we had a glorious time.   Freds play last night was the Fools Revenge.[47]   Tonight it is Hamlet.   I cannot realize that the loving boy at home is the great actor on the stage.   His Hamlet is simply grand – better than any I have ever seen.[48]   It has been a proud & happy day for me –

Wednesday, December 3

The Company went to Kansas City this am   Julia Fred & I remained until evening.   I have been overwhelmed with congratulations.   Genl Pope says Freds Hamlet is the best he has ever seen

---

47. He had played Bertuccio, a malignant man in motley. The *Leavenworth Times* was enthusiastic over Fred's performance: "He was all his friends had expected, and more; and he was applauded to the echo with a heartiness which showed the appreciation of the audience. Nor was there any lame support to mar his acting; everything was thoroughly artistic" ("Frederick Paulding," December 2, 1879, p. 3).

48. The *Leavenworth Times* was hardly less positive, entitling its review of the performance "He is a Wonder." The reviewer regarded Fred as "attaining a preeminence as a master tragedian that is as remarkable as it has been rapid. The frequent applause he won last night told how he was appreciated at his old home which he left so very recently to enter, literally alone and unaided, the dramatic world; where, asking no favors, but relying only on the fact that nature had created him for the sphere he was entering, he assumed a front rank in so short a time that it is hardly to be credited. Perhaps no actor has ever received so many and such enthusiastic encores as did Mr. Paulding last night" (December 3, 1879, p. 3).

Frederick Paulding Dodge (From *Annals of the New York Stage. Vol. 11,* by
George C. D. Odell. © 1939 Columbia University Press. Reprinted with the
permission of the publisher.)

& he has seen Macready Forest Booth, Barrett & all the other great Hamlets[49]   Have got acquainted with all the company & like them all.   Excelent Articles in all the papers on Freds Acting.   Fool's Revenge at night

Thursday, December 4

Happy day – Papers enthusiastic – Julia loving & happy.   Fred as boyishly affectionate as if he were not a Star.   Josie Jordan as sweet as pie – but we leave her here – much to our regret for she is a dear sweet girl.   Lawlor & the Compy have taken a great shine to me – & we are all a mutual admiration society, as proud & happy as possible. Hamlet at night to a most enthusiastic House.[50]

Friday, December 5

Left for St Jo.   Had the stiffening taken out of us by a thrice miserable Hotel, but the best in town.   Fool's Revenge to a small but most enthusiastic house – Rainy bad night

Saturday, December 6

Matiné Lady of Lyons.   Fred lovely as Claude Melnotte[51]   At night a fair house to see Hamlet.   Perfectly enthusiastic.   Called him out after every act.   Applauded every point, & seemed to want to take him off the boards –

49. Pope was being extremely generous, for his list included celebrated actors who had distinguished themselves in the part on both sides of the Atlantic: William C. Macready (1793-1873), Edwin Forrest (1806-1872), Edwin T. Booth (1833-1893), and Wilson Barrett (1846-1904).

50. The *Atchison Globe* of December 6 included this commentary on Fred's reception in St. Joseph, Missouri: "The St. Joe papers speak very highly of Frederick Paulding, the 'New Hamlet.' . . . Evidences are accumulating that Frederick Paulding . . . is really a wonderful fellow. We not only have newspaper evidence of this, but gentlemen who have seen him in neighboring cities were very much pleased with his superb acting" (p. 4).

51. In Bulwer-Lytton's play, Claude Melnotte is the accomplished yet humble lover of Pauline Deschapelles, proud daughter of a merchant of Lyons. In the final act the two are rapturously united.

Sunday, December 7

Hotel so bad we determined to decamp.   Took morning train to Atchison –

Monday, December 8

Hamlet to a full & appreciative house.[52]   St Joe papers wild over the boy – as were also the Kansas City papers   After performance had to cut & run to get the train for Omaha.   Got off at 12 1/2.

Tuesday, December 9

Arrived at Omaha about 8 am.   Excellent Hotel – Withnell House.[53]   Met many of my old Citizen friends   Jordan & I got the money matters arranged with the Bank.   My $3,000 has not yet been invested – the payor of the Mortgage having acted shabbily.[54] Note from Bob Williams, excusing himself & wife from coming down on a/c of sickness.[55]   "Fools Revenge" at night.   Fair house, but not an Officer.   No[56]

52. The *Atchison Globe* for December 9 reported that, when the curtain fell at the Corinthian Hall the night before "and the applause became deafening, the young actor's dear old mother grew almost frantic with joy, and applauded as heartily as the most enthusiastic of the auditors" (p. 7).

53. Although in his *History of Nebraska* (1880) Harrison Johnson characterized the hotel accommodations of Omaha as "entirely inadequate," he described the Withnell House, opened in 1878 at the corner of Harney and Fifteenth Streets, as "a new and first-class house" (pp. 300, 301).

54. Dodge's wife had inherited a substantial sum from her mother, who had died in 1876, but funds in the estate were not yet available to her. With Jordan's assistance, Dodge was helping her along by disposing at par, without dividends, three thousand dollars in government bonds and loaning her the proceeds (RID to A. B. Cruikshank, December 20, 1883; RID to Frederick Paulding Dodge, July 17, 1884; Julia R. P. Dodge to RID, July 23, 1888—Dodge Papers, Graff Collection).

55. Lieutenant Colonel Robert Williams, assistant adjutant general for the Department of the Platte, was employed at departmental headquarters in Omaha but lived at Fort Omaha, three miles north.

56. The intended content of this fragment may be set forth in the next day's entry.

Wednesday, December 10, 1879

Burt & Foot two of the Officers of 9th Infy who were with me in the Black Hills[57] called, and these were the only calls we had.   Those named Officers, Gentry[58] & one 2d Lt, went to the Matiné, "Lady of Lyons" done more beautifully than I have ever seen it.   Burt, who claims to be a literary & Artistic Cuss was very enthusiastic over the Boy – but not so enthusiastic as to come to see Hamlet at night.[59]

Hamlet well nigh perfect in evening & not a single Officer or Army Lady.   I was told by a Citizen that there was some jealousy & I suppose that is the reason – though I think the real secret was that each man & woman was so conscious of his or her own ignorance in such matters, that they were really afraid to go.   They would not have known when to applaud, or whether to applaud at all or not, & they saved committing themselves by staying away.[60] Some such reason must be at the bottom, for all the prominent Officers had Complimentary tickets which they did not use.   The Citizens gave us a full & most appreciative House – & the papers are most complimentary

This was to be my last night "with the show" so I determined to give the whole company a supper party after the play.   Eighteen of us sat down to a Champagne & Oyster Supper & had a most glorious time.

57. Captain Andrew S. Burt, Ninth Infantry, and First Lieutenant Morris Cooper Foote, adjutant of that regiment, were stationed at Fort Omaha. For Dodge's many experiences with them during the Black Hills expedition of 1875, see *BHJ*, index.

58. Major William T. Gentry, Nineteenth Infantry, was post commander at Fort Omaha.

59. In 1875, while in the Black Hills, Burt had served as correspondent for the *New York Tribune*. In 1882 he wrote *May Cody; or Lost and Won*, a four-act drama starring "Buffalo Bill" Cody (Mattes, *Indians, Infants, and Infantry*, pp. 242–44). In 1883 his comic opera in two acts, *Robin Hood and Rosalind*, was produced at Angel Island, California, where he was then posted (*ANJ*, May 26, 1883, p. 967; September 22, 1883, p. 147).

60. Dodge was perhaps not far wrong in his uncomplimentary estimate of brother officers and their ladies. A month afterward, the New York *Dramatic Mirror* quoted a Columbus, Ohio, newspaper describing a performance of *The Fool's Revenge*: "Some idiotic persons present to witness Paulding's Bertuccio, 8th, made themselves conspicuous by incessant laughter. Probably imagined it was a burlesque troupe" (January 17, 1880, p. 2).

Julia & Fred were specially delighted, & it was really a Godsend to the poorer players – for I had everybody – even to the baggage man —[61] We did not break up until near 3 am.   When I shook hands with and wished Good luck to all the men – kissed all the (pretty) women & went back to my Hotel.

I think my dear old wife has "kinder" fallen in love with me again, for she now insists that she will cut loose from the Boy for a few days & go back with me to Ft Leavenworth – & remain there with me until I have to start for my Post.

I can't even in parting do justice to my feelings & ideas with reference to the Boy.   He is little short of a miracle.   Only two years ago he was a backward boy, playing in preference with the smaller children.   Now he stands forth not only as a perfect marvel in Shakespearian knowl-edge, but as one of his very finest exemplars on the Stage.   I have loved & read Shakespeare all my life, yet the boy of 20 shows me beauties & meanings, I never before thought or heard of –   In truth he is the "New Hamlet" & his rendition suits my idea, better than that of any other player I have ever seen.   He has a most glorious future before him if he can only keep his health.

With love & kisses

The Boy Baby
Rich

61. On a later occasion Dodge's wife treated the entire troupe to free tickets at a performance of *M'liss*, a stage adaptation of a story by Bret Harte, starring Annie Pixley (New York *Dramatic Mirror*, January 17, 1880, p. 2).

Journal Seven
December 11, 1879–
May 26, 1880

THE SEGMENTS OF JOURNAL TEXT THAT FOLLOW were written at intervals over a period of more than six months. It was another unusually active time for Dodge—early in the new year he wrote that the days went by so fast he could hardly keep track of them. Perhaps this was one reason why he made no effort to set down a complete record of his experiences. When he did write journal entries, he ordinarily dealt with subjects that he knew would interest members of his family, but he said little about his work as an Army officer. Some information from outside the journal is thus necessary to describe his official activities during these months. There are four month-long hiatuses in the journal—between the entries dated December 19, 1879, and January 20, 1880, January 27 and February 18, February 24 and March 25, and April 5 and May 7—and here supplementary matter is introduced as editorial commentary. The journal entries and the interpolated material together offer varied glimpses of Dodge during a time when multiple facets of his character and official role were expressing themselves.

The initial journal entry recounts events in Omaha, Nebraska, on the day after the conclusion of Journal Six.

JOURNAL: DECEMBER 11–19, 1879

Thursday, December 11, 1879[1]
The company started on the early train for Council Bluffs, but Julia

Fred & I remained until the evening.   The dear old Lady wanted to
hire a carriage & go up to the post to call on some of our Friends (?),
but I did'nt see it & put my foot down.   So we had a pleasant day
together & in the afternoon started on our way.   At the Union Depot
near Council Bluffs we parted from Fred & Jordan.[2] I was loath to give
up the Boy.   He is so loving & affectionate – so much the tender boy,
with all his genius, that I find my heart very full of him.   It was a hard
struggle to give him up, & my eyes filled with tears when he repeatedly turned back to dance along the track on which he was walking
& yell & signal to us.   Very soon we were hitched onto by our Engine,
& were speeding towards Leavenworth.   The Agent at the Depot
assured me we could get across the river without difficulty.   The
conductor tells me that there has been no connection for a month.
So I paid our way to Kansas City – & we went to bed –[3]

Friday, December 12, 1879
    Was waked up at <4>5 am by the porter –   We had been in Kansas
City two or more hours.   We got up, & about 6 am had breakfast.

---

1. This manuscript journal, manufactured by Reynolds and Reynolds of Dayton,
Ohio, measures 3 5/8 by 6 11/16 inches. It consists of brown, flexible cardboard
covers at front and back, secured to the pages inside by a strip of tape at the top. Like
the first and last leaves of Journals Four and Five, the endpapers are of light blue
unlined paper. The inner leaves are of cheap cream-colored paper lined horizontally
in pink ink and with a perforated cut near their upper edge to permit easy ripping
away. The notebook includes sixty unnumbered pages. On the front cover Dodge
has written in black ink an identification: "Cantonment [/] 1879." Below, in the hand
of a person other than Dodge, is a notation in pencil: "Dec 11/ 79 to [/] May 25/ 80."
The remaining text of the journal is in pencil. Pages [1V], [28V], [56V], and [57R] are
blank. Pages [57V], [58], and [59] are written with the notebook in reversed position,
as are parts of pp. [1R], [56R], and [60V]. Page [1R] includes miscellaneous calcula-
tions, a crude map, and in reversed position, notations of "Pay" and "Dep" with the
number 294,45 written below each. The text begins on p. [2R].
    2. Fred was rejoining his company, which was scheduled to perform at Rock
Island, Illinois, on December 17 and 18 and at Peoria on December 19 and 20. Jordan
was en route to Cantonment for a visit.
    3. The train passed south from Council Bluffs, Missouri, on the east side of the
Missouri River. It was unable to cross the railroad bridge to Leavenworth, on the west
side, and so continued south to Kansas City.

About <9>7 we took the train for Leavenworth, where we arrived early & went to the Planters House.[4]   I went out & did a lot of work. Julia remained in her room resting until after 12 Oclk dinner when she went out shopping & to hunt up Minty.   About 3 pm Lt Dodge came with an ambulance & carried us both off to Ft 11Worth, to his house – where we were made as happy & comfortable as possible — Had another dinner & paid a lot of visits

Saturday, December 13, 1879

Went down town early first visiting Genl Pope   Spent the day there, & bought all I want for this trip.   Came back loaded with bundles, &c. Spent the evening receiving visits.

Sunday, December 14, 1879

Went to Pope's Sunday School[5]   Met all the Officers, & had a "Chin" ad lib - very pleasant morning.   Julia went to Church. Spent the evening visiting.   Returned all my calls & had a nice time.

Monday, December 15, 1879

Julia & I went down early to 11Worth, for I was to take the Cars, and start for my Post.   We arrived at Depot waited & waited.   The train by which I expected to catch the A. T. & S. F. R. R[6] was not even made up.   So wofully annoyed we made some few purchases & returned to the Fort.   We had made up our minds to go to Kansas City on the evening train, stay there over night & start from there tomorro.   We had a pleasant stay with the Dodges, who have been as kind & hospitable as any people could be, & at 4.15 pm started for Kansas City - where we arrived at <6>5,30.   Stopped at the R. R. House.   Had a good supper, excellent rooms, & every comfort.   Minty joined us at the Leavenworth City Depot.

4. Situated "only five minutes walk from the depot," the Planters House offered rooms at $2.00 and $2.50 per day (*Leavenworth Times*, March 31, 1880, p. 2).
5. What this weekly gathering entailed is not known.
6. At Topeka, Kansas.

We had a real old evening of comfort.   Tooty[7] scrubbed my head, & we were all very happy.   I have never seen Julia more happy & more loath to give me up.   She has evidently a new case

Tuesday, December 16, 1879

I got off at 10 am leaving Julia & Minty.   They will remain at the hotel, and go to Rock Island tonight.   It was hard to part with the dear "Old Lady," but I am tough.   Long tedious ride.   Dinner at Topeka. Supper at Florence.   Change cars at Newton & arrive at Wellington 12 at night.   Went to see about conveyance tomorro, but got little satisfaction   To bed at 1 am –

Wednesday, December 17

Up early & to see Hardenbrook about conveyance.   He had promised to take me through to Pond Creek, with a relay at Caldwell, in one day for $10.   He sent the relay down to Caldwell, but finding passengers there it came back same day.   After considerable trouble the conveyance came – with 2 mules hitched in front & 2 horses tied to the back.   The horses were to be my relay   Got off at 9 am, & got to Caldwell nicely by 1 pm.   Got dinner & the "rig" came for me with the horses hitched in.   It was very hard on them but "twas none of my funeral" – & I said nothing   At "Pole Cat" station, about half way, one of the horses showed symptoms of illness   Hard driving, alkali water & a feed of corn.   However it was so slight that the driver after

bleeding the horse ∧ started again.[8]   We went on nicely for some time, but the horse was evidently growing worse   On & on we went. The driver was frightened & wanted to stop.   I know all the tricks of alkali & assured him that his only chance of saving the horse was to keep him going   However the fellow at last pulled up in spite of me, & the horse almost immediately laid down.   We got him out of the

7. Dodge's wife, Julia. In his journal entries he had not referred to her by this affectionate nickname since December 1876; see *PREJ*, p. 130.
8. The intended sense is "that after the driver had bled the horse, we started again."

harness.   He got up, staggered around a moment & fell dead.   We made the other animal a pack horse, piling all the things on him & trudged into Pond Creek, where we arrived, at 7 oclk at night – having walked 4 miles in the dark

Found my party with ambulance &c, tent pitched, bed made, & after a good supper I turned in & slept all the better for the mishaps of the day.

Thursday, December 18

Got off at 9 am.   Paid my driver $12 for conveyance, & $1 for himself.   Wrote to Julia a short note & started off lighthearted with good teams & all right —   Camped on Walnut Creek.

Friday, December 19

Hoped to have got some Turkeys last night but was too tired.   It has been quite cold.   Had to make something more of a march than I intended, yesterday as we found the grass burned where I wanted to camp.   Got off 8.30 am, & arrived at Post without accident at 1 pm.   Found every thing going on well – Joe much better in health & all serene.   Am glad to get the comfort of home.[9]

COMMENTARY: DECEMBER 19, 1879–JANUARY 20, 1880

Cantonment Not Permanent

During Dodge's absence from Cantonment it had been decided not to designate the post as permanent nor to request of Congress the sixty thousand dollars proposed by General Pope. Rigid economy was necessary, since the appropriation to the War Department for the present fiscal year, approximately $40 million, was less than that for 1878–1879, and no change for the better was anticipated in the coming year. In 1879–1880 the Quartermaster's Department had available only $1 million for new construction, despite the admitted need for addi-

9. This day's entry ends on p. [8R] of the manuscript; the text that follows the editorial commentary begins on p. [8V].

tional posts at several points in the West.[10] The presence of Sitting Bull and his people in the British possessions mandated the establishment of Fort Assiniboine in Montana Territory. The recent violence of the Ute Indians in western Colorado clearly warranted at least one new post there. Conditions along the Texas-Mexico border, in Arizona Territory, and elsewhere all required sustained attention by the Army.[11] General Pope's rationale for expenditures at the site of Cantonment was perhaps reasonable, but the military situation in its region no longer seemed so explosive as it had a few months earlier. General Sheridan saw greater need for a post between Forts Concho and Elliott in Texas to help secure the western border of Indian Territory from incursion by cattle herds being driven north to the railroads. Unlike Fort Reno, which he agreed should be enlarged to accommodate an increased garrison, Cantonment was adjacent to no anticipated source of danger. "I do not think a permanent post at the site named a necessity," he wrote on December 5, "and an appropriation of sixty thousand dollars for that purpose would be a needless waste of public funds."[12] On December 10 General Sherman concurred, and on December 18, the Secretary of War. Pope's letter with its unfavorable endorsements was returned to the adjutant general's office on December 19,[13] the same day Dodge returned to "the comfort of home" at his post following his twenty-day leave of absence.

There is little likelihood that Dodge had learned this news while at Fort Leavenworth, for the adjutant general's office made no official comment on the matter until December 22.[14] Still, the decision was

10. For the 1878-79 Army appropriation bill, see Statutes at Large, 20:145-52; for the 1879-80 and 1880-81 bills, see *Statutes at Large*, 21:30-35, 110-14.

11. See House, *Report of the Secretary of War* (1880), p. 54.

12. Endorsement by Sheridan, Pope to AAG MDM, November 16, 1879—AGO LR. On the post in Texas, see the endorsement by Sheridan of Pope to Sheridan, December 16, 1879 (MDM Settlers in I.T. Special File) and Sheridan to AG, December 18, 1879 (AGO LR); House, *Report of the Secretary of War* (1880), p. 56. For the enlarged garrison at Fort Reno, see Sherman to AG, December 9, 1879 (AGO Register LR).

13. Pope to AAG MDM, November 16, 1879, with endorsements and inked stamp showing date of receipt (AGO LR).

14. AG to Sheridan, December 22, 1879 (AGO LS). A copy of this letter was sent to the quartermaster general.

probably not surprising to him. He was familiar with the reluctance of Congress to support the postwar Army,[15] and indications in recent months within the Department of the Missouri had not been encouraging. However, in months to come the military picture might change, directing renewed attention to the question of Cantonment's status. Meanwhile, as he later wrote, "the foundation stone of an army is obedience, its key-stone discipline."[16] As the officer charged with establishing the post, he had performed his task with interest and energy, but its incomplete fulfillment need not be a source of deep personal regret. "I get enthusiastic & ardent," he later wrote to his son, "work with all my might & main to attain my end, but if I fail there's an end to it. I never worry."[17]

The Keeling Investigation

An incitement to renewed effort in the present was a letter from Agent Miles that awaited Dodge on his return to Cantonment. This was in reply to his request for documentary evidence and the names of persons who could supply testimony to support the charges made in October against Keeling and Company. Miles sent no documentation, but he named several potential witnesses. They included four Indians— Little Raven, Big Back, Mahminick [Minimick], and George Bent, a mixed-blood interpreter at the agency, and four "white men"—George E. Reynolds, Jake Zallwager, William Frass, and Amos Chapman, the latter three all married to Cheyenne women.[18] The list from Miles made possible a further investigation of Keeling's alleged activity, and on December 20 Dodge assured the agent of his intention "to sift this

15. On December 26, 1877, Dodge had responded with terse impatience to an inquiry from the Senate Committee on Military Affairs seeking information that might make possible a further reduction in financial support of the Army. See House, *Report . . . Relating to the Reorganization of the Army*, pp. 147–48.

16. RID, "The Enlisted Soldier," p. 261.

17. RID to Frederick Paulding Dodge, July 17, 1884 (Dodge Papers, Graff Collection).

18. Miles to RID, December 2, 1879 (OIA LR, C&A). Although his assistant had provoked the inquiry by his complaints against Keeling, from this point Miles himself acted on behalf of the agency.

matter to the bottom." Informing Miles that he had requested three of the "white men" to come to Cantonment and give evidence (Amos Chapman being already at hand), he asked his assistance in causing the Indians to make the journey as soon as possible.[19] On December 30 Miles telegraphed that the Indians would report after New Year's Day.[20]

Thus far the Army officer and the Indian agent had cooperated in businesslike fashion in setting up the inquiry. However, the ten days that followed brought on a confrontation between them, caused in part by mere chance but intensified by their mutual suspicion and disrespect. On January 6 Dodge received from Amos Chapman a written deposition asserting that he had on many occasions purchased goods of the post trader on behalf of his wife, her near relations, and other members of her band. According to Chapman, "squaw men" regularly assisted their wives' extended families in this way. He reported that in August, when he had visited the agency in connection with the Senate committee's inquiry, Agent Miles had asked him to "do all he could to help the Indians along" back at Cantonment. In his opinion, the purchase of items like calico, flour, and bacon—either direct from Keeling or as surplus from company messes—was precisely the sort of help he had been called upon to give.[21] On January 7 three clerks at the trader's store submitted written statements to Dodge that they had sold goods to the five Indian scouts but not to other Indians.

At this point Dodge believed he comprehended the nature of Keeling's business contacts with Indians. Having just received from George E. Reynolds, the original complainant, a note excusing himself from providing testimony on account of illness in his family, on the morning of January 8 Dodge telegraphed Agent Miles that the additional witnesses from the agency need not make the journey to Cantonment; he had examined several witnesses and closed the case.[22] But later that same day the additional witnesses arrived at the post,

19. RID to Miles, December 20, 1879 (OIA LR, C&A).

20. Miles to RID, December 30, 1879 (OIA LR, C&A).

21. Amos Chapman to C.O. CNFCR, January 6, 1880 (OIA LR, C&A).

22. George E. Reynolds to RID, January 6, 1880 (OIA LR, C&A); RID to Miles, January 8, 1880 (CNFCR LS).

accompanied by Miles. Arrangements were hastily made to accommodate the unexpected arrivals and secure their testimony. If at this point Miles suspected he had almost been circumvented by Dodge, who perhaps had not wished to consider evidence from persons at the agency, his suspicion was heightened by the hearings that ensued. Dodge examined the new witnesses—Zallwager, Frass, and in the presence of two interpreters, Minimick and Big Back—but the examinations were held in private. (George Bent, one of the interpreters, did not give testimony, for reasons later made clear.) Miles was miffed at being excluded from a formal inquiry into alleged practices that set at nought his authority as agent to regulate the trading of Indians in his care.

Dodge's fifteen hundred–word report, dated January 9, 1880, was a model of due documentation, accompanied by twenty-two exhibits of his correspondence and the written and oral testimony he had received in the case. Drawing upon evidence that included what had been provided by Zallwager, Frass, and the two Indians, he related their statements to the deposition given him earlier by Chapman. He reported that Indians in the vicinity of Cantonment—scouts, farmers, wood contract workers, and the relatives of all these—had indeed purchased items from Keeling and Co., not directly, for the post trader was "too shrewd" to do anything for which he might be liable to disciplinary action, but through intermediaries. Keeling's indirect patrons had been glad to trade with him since they claimed to receive "four or five times as much for their money" as they did from Reynolds at the agency. "I have known of this all the time," Dodge wrote, "but have had no cause or right to interfere. There is no law prohibiting any white man from purchasing a hundred pounds of bacon, or one or more sacks of flour from the Post Trader—and if he then chooses to give it to the Indians I know of no law or power which can prevent him." Keeling's clerks may have trespassed occasionally on the injunction against doing business with Indians, but these lapses had been without authorization. No evidence indicated clearly that incidents of the kind had even occurred. Dodge concluded the report with a ringing statement of his frustration with laws that in effect prohibited assisting the Indians: "It is simply impossible to prevent this trade. An

Indian comes with a pitiful story of starvation and suffering of himself and family – somebody will be so charitably disposed as to help him. I and other officers of this post, have not infrequently bought small quantities of stores from the Post Trader for the benefit of Indians; and though the trader is thus really trading with, or for the benefit of Indians, the practice will continue just so long as the law of humanity is superior to the law of Congress."[23]

Sent to the adjutant of his department and forwarded through military channels to the Department of War, Dodge's report was not received by the Office of Indian Affairs until February 13.[24] Agent Miles was thus unaware of its precise contents, but he early suspected its drift.[25] Resentful of the treatment he had received at Cantonment, he was frustrated at his inability to restrain a military trader like Keeling and Co. from dealing with Indians. He had no recourse except to state his case in strong terms to the Commissioner of Indian Affairs and appeal for support. On January 19 Miles therefore addressed a heated letter to Commissioner Hayt in which he branded Dodge's official inquiry a whitewash, designed to "Completely Exonerate Keeling." He trained his rhetorical firepower on Dodge, suggesting by innuendo and slanted statements that not all was what it should be at Cantonment, not merely in regard to Dodge's inquiry but more generally. He mentioned that Amos Chapman, " a known representative of Keeling," had been permitted to attend the secret proceedings as interpreter while he—presumably more objective—had not been admitted. The accusations against the post trader were, he claimed, "evidently well founded and true in every particular."As proof of this statement Miles appended to his letter affidavits by four of the witnesses—Zallwager, Frass,

23. RID to AAG DMO, January 9, 1880 (OIA LR, C&A).

24. SW to SI, February 10, 1880, with inked stamp showing date of receipt (OIA LR, C&A).

25. In a letter to Commissioner Hayt of January 12, 1880, Miles expressed a need for more competition at the Cheyenne and Arapaho agency with Reynolds, the licensed Indian trader. He also asked for instructions from the Indian Bureau concerning four issues, all germane to the investigation of Keeling. For example, his third query was: "Can a white man, married to an Indian adopted by the tribe and considered a member thereof, trade with that tribe without a license[?]" (OIA LR, C&A).

Minimick, and Big Back—whose testimony before Dodge he had not heard. Ironically, these statements were virtually identical in content to the ones appended to Dodge's report. As the climax to his letter, Miles claimed that George Bent, an expected witness at the Cantonment proceedings, "was furnished with liquor" shortly after his arrival at the post and remained "intoxicated for five or six days."[26]

When Dodge's report reached the Office of Indian Affairs, it was filed without further action. However, Miles' statement of January 19 made its own way through official channels to the War Department and eventually back to Dodge for comment. On February 25, stung by Miles's claims but contemptuous as well, Dodge commented vigorously. Dispensing with the formal decorum of his official report, he responded in kind to Miles's accusations of favoritism and bias. He defended Amos Chapman as an honest man, "known for his gallantry and faithful service." He asserted that when at Cantonment, George Bent had first served as interpreter, then gotten himself drunk. Inquiry had revealed that the alcohol he consumed came from a bottle of Jamaica Ginger and another of red ink that he had induced a soldier to purchase for him. "As Bent is said to have drank the entire contents of both bottles within a few moments, his five or six days' 'intoxication' is easily accounted for."[27] As to Miles and his affidavits—which

26. Miles to Hayt, January 19, 1880 (OIA LR, C&A).

27. Miles had tried unsuccessfully for some time to deny George Bent access to alcohol. Among the reasons why he had wished his enemy Philip McCusker kept off the Cheyenne and Arapaho reservation was that man's allegedly furnishing Bent and other Indians with whisky. See A. C. Williams to Philip McCusker, May 26, 1878 (OIA LR, C&A). On October 2, 1878, Miles caused Jack Martin, a scout and interpreter at Fort Reno, to be confined in the post guardhouse for furnishing liquor to Bent. Major Mizner learned that Martin had not purchased "intoxicating liquor" from the post trader but only four bottles of Jamaica Ginger which had apparently made their way into Bent's hands. Since no violation of law had occurred, Mizner ordered Martin released. In an endorsement dated October 5, Miles wrote: "This is but one instance of many, where this same person [George Bent] has been furnished with liquor, by such parties as the one now released. Whatever may be the name or purpose for which the article given to Bent, was originally intended, the fact remains that Alcohol is its principal component and that it produces intoxication as effectually as Whiskey. If no action can be taken in cases where Jamaica Ginger is furnished to an Indian we can only look forward to the continuance of a nuisance which has at times been a source of great trouble, with this same party" (Miles to Mizner, October 2, 1878—OIA LR, C&A).

Dodge had not seen and did not know essentially duplicated those he had obtained—he directed against the agent the same slur about "squaw men" that had been used to malign Chapman. "I have no doubt," he wrote, "that Mr. Miles can furnish an unlimited number of affidavits towards the proof of anything he may assert. . . . The Agency is surrounded by a number of squaw-men, offscourings of humanity that will make affidavit on demand." Miles had impugned Dodge's honesty; Dodge returned the favor, representing Miles as being thought by some "the most heartless and cruel of swindlers."[28]

The war of words between these representatives of the Army and the Indian Bureau had rapidly become unseemly. Meanwhile, Keeling and Co. was permitted to continue operations at Cantonment on the same basis as before, but the controversy over the business it transacted was not over.

Dodge resumed writing in his journal on January 20, 1880. With the road to Pond Creek Ranch now complete and in regular use, he had recently ordered Second Lieutenant Lea Febiger, with a sergeant and eight privates, Amos Chapman, and an Indian scout, to survey and begin preparing for use another military wagon road. This would extend seventy miles almost due south from the post, connecting with an east-west stage road that already joined Fort Elliott and Fort Reno. Before setting out himself to superintend construction, Dodge organized a short hunt south and west of Cantonment.

His account of the hunt is preceded by a summary entry.

JOURNAL: JANUARY 20-27, 1880

Spent a month at home, with varying comforts & pleasures.   The days go by so fast, I can scarcely keep account of them.

Have put up ice made everybody comfortable – renovated and refitted my own house built me a stable, & now that the work is all done, I take a play day for a week preparatory to real military work,[29] which I commence 1st Feby.

28. RID to AAG DMO, February 25, 1880 (CNFCR LS).
29. Duty in the field, supervising work on the road to Fort Elliott.

January 21, 1880

Clarke & I started on a trip, to see if any game is left in the country. Left Post about 10 am with a nice escort & all comfortable.   Turned our heads south west towards the Canadian a country we have not before hunted in.   Travelled about 15 miles mostly across burnt ground, seeing nothing to shoot at.   Went into camp about 4 pm on a pretty little tributary of Canadian – unnamed on the maps – Excelent water, wood & grass.   The sandy bed of the creek, was marked in every direction with Turkey & deer tracks – but though Clarke & I went through beautiful woods looking for a roost, we found no sign of where any Turkey had roosted.   Came back & sent Boon up the creek on same errand.   He came back just at dark having found no sign of a roost.   This discouraged me, so I gave my gun to Boon.   Clarke is now out down the Creek & Boon up.   They have been gone an hour, & there has been no shot

Routzon, my striker[30] left my cartridges, so I sent an Indian back after them, & will wait tomorro until they arrive   I ought to get something tomorro morning – for there is plenty of sign of game.

January 22, 1880

Clarke came in about 11 last night with a magnificent Gobbler – 20 lbs at least   Only one he got a shot at.   Saw but 3 –   I started out about 8 this a.m. – worked hard found a large roost & came upon a drove of some 50 turkeys.   Got only 2 - though I am sure I mortally wounded several more.   Got back to camp about 12 m.   Clarke had gone down the Creek & saw nothing.   Told him about the roost & we planned a campaign.   Nap in afternoon.   We started out after dark, rode 4 miles to the roost & had the satisfaction of hearing a hundred turkeys go off the roost without our even getting a shot. Have never seen birds so wild.   My Cartridge came all right.   Shot

---

30. Private George Routzahn, Dodge's orderly, served also as his personal servant or *striker*. Although prohibited by law, the use of enlisted men as servants by Army officers was common practice. Soldiers could not be so designated without their consent, and their assignment did not exempt them from other military duties (Circular 4, August 4, 1878, Fort Hays General Orders).

a squirrels head off with rifle.   My bag 2 Turkeys 1 squirrel   Total 3
Turkeys, 1 squirrel

January 23, 1880

Broke camp at 8:30.   Took Febigers trail[31] hoping to come to some
good hunting ground.   Crossed Canadian near mouth of Creek, & on
south side found another beautiful Creek.   Plenty of water & well
timbered, but no game.   Soon discovered the reason in an abandoned Indian Camp – only ten days or 2 weeks old.   The very same
ruffians who spoiled our hunting on the other side of the river —

Followed Feb's trail for about 10 miles, when it turned up on the
high dry divide.   Left it, & pulled off to the North East.   Camped on
a small branch near river.   No sign of game of any kind.   Fanny my
setter Bitch distinguished herself today, finding several bunches of
grouse (prairie chickens)   They were however very wild, & it was
very difficult to get near them.   I managed to bag 2, one at nearly 80
yards off with a No 2 wire Cartridge.   Clarke was in specially bad luck
& got nothing   The water we are on is very alkali, & we have rather
a poor camp.   Tomorro I shall pull across the river, & try our luck on
that side.   There is nothing here.   In fact the country is denuded of
game by the Indians.   (We have been today through perfectly lovely
hunting grounds – & found nothing.[)]   Disposed to rain tonight.
Beat Clark badly at Cribbage.

Total bag – 3 Turkeys, 1 squirrel, 2 grouse.   Sent Turkeys to
Post.

January 24, 1880

Rainy during night & this a.m.   Did'nt like looks of clouds, & in
spite of rain moved camp across Canadian[32]   The bed is almost dry

now & <but> $\wedge$ ^{it} is easy to cross anywhere but a few inches of water

31. The trail made recently by the road surveying party.
32. Having already crossed the river going south, the party was now moving
northward toward favored hunting and fishing spots along the North Fork, between
Cantonment and Fort Supply.

changes it to one of the most difficult & dangerous of streams.[33] Came north & camped on a lovely little stream, far up in the hills. Clarke & I walked up to look for a Turkey roost.   We found a splendid one, but we found also the camp scarce a week old of that infernal batch of Indian[s] whose traces we seem destined not to escape from. We have passed 3 of their camps & they have cleared the country of game   They must have killed 50 deer in this camp, judging from the hair.   We got nothing of course - except 4 quail, from a small covey that came into camp in evening.   Clarke, Boon & Monahan went out after dark to try to find a roost on a creek further west - but came back empty.

Beat Clark again at Cribbage.   My bag today 3 quail   Total bag – 3 Turkeys 1 squirrel 2 grouse 4 quail –

January 25, 1880

Started about 9. am.   Clark went off to the west to hunt the creek he failed to find last night.   I had to remain with the wagons as we anticipated serious work getting through the Black Jacks   Boon & I differed as to the best chance for getting through, but though he had been well up on the route he proposed to take, I did'nt like it, & took my own way.   Result a perfect success - found a most excellent route & got through the Black Jack without cutting a branch.   I am certainly wonderfully successful in finding routes, & in taking wagons across country.   It is of course experience & knowledge to some extent - but if I were asked why I took the route I did today I could only answer that I thought it would prove the best.   I could give no reason beyond what might be a mere instinct.   Whatever the success comes from   – knowledge or mere luck - I am greatly blessed in having it.

I am now camped on the head of Deep Creek,[34] in country that Monahan said, two days ago - was utterly impassable for wagons.

33. Dodge describes the treacherous potential of plains streams for sudden flooding in *PNA*, pp. 114–18.

34. This stream entered the North Fork of the Canadian River from the south approximately thirty miles upstream from Cantonment.

Yet I came in today without the use of axe or spade, & shall go out tomorro just as easily.   I guess its knowledge – for luck would not always stick to me.   My teamsters almost believe I am a wizard for at the proper moment when the route in front seems absolutely imprac- ticable, I gallop ahead & in a few moments return to conduct the wagons through an easy gap, & all goes smooth again.

The dogs found a fine covey of grouse, but they were wild as hawks.   I got only one.   Saw a good many deer tracks in the Black- jacks, but all old.   After I got into Camp, I walked down the Creek for half a mile, found a covey of quail & got (5) five.   I also murdered a robin –

Our cook this morning told me he was out of fresh meat – so I was hunting for dinner & breakfast tomorro.   Clarke hunted all day but got nothing.   Boon went out after deer, but saw nothing, but a Bear track.   There is no game in the country   Cold disagreable south wind all day.   It is getting monotonous.   My bag, 1 grouse 5 quail Total, 3 Turkeys, 3 grouse, 9 quail, 1 squirrel 1 robin

January 26, 1880

Directed my party to go to our fish pond opposite the mouth of Deep Creek[35] & go into camp.   Clarke & I went off across country & crossed river about 2 miles above mouth of creek & went downward. When we got to the place where we ought to have found our pond it was not there.   Clarke insisted that it was below, & I thought so also – but before deciding I mounted a sand Hill & looked all about. At last I discovered what I believed to be Cottonwood Grove – which ought to be 5 miles below us but which was above.   I recognized the situation at once.   We had not camped on the head of Deep Creek but on a more easterly stream   Crossed the river, struck the road, & the trail of our wagons & arrived again at the river to find the 6 mule team stuck in quick sand.   Worked at them a little while & got them out.   Had a few good chances at grouse.   Bagged one early in the day – a very long shot.   My bitch came to a dead point on the trail above

35. See the journal entry for November 26, 1879.

Deep Creek.   I got down & walked towards her.   At about 60 yds off two grouse got up & went off leisurely.   I waited till they got together & brought them both down with a single shot.   Soon after we found a covey of 5 birds, which got up a long way off, but I took it coolly being loaded with wire cartridges –   When the two left birds got together I fired & both fell.

To my great surprise Clarke claimed them.   I am sure he could'nt have bagged them at his distance, for they were further from him than the others were & he was on my right.   I am very sure I bagged both but I allowed him one by Courtesy –   After we got in camp tried fishing, but got no bite.   A good many ducks came around, but were very wild & we got no shot –   Played Crib at night.   Clarke beat me 3 games in 30.

My bag 5 grouse –   1 quail
                                ∧   I claim –   Total bag 3 turkeys – 8 grouse 10 quail, 1 squirrel 1 robin.

Tuesday, January 27, 1880

Our luck has been so poor that I determined to go to the post today. Directed Boon to wait for me at my duck pond near Sheridans roost. Clarke & I went through the Sand Hills.   Found 2 coveys of quail   I bagged 9, & he 4.   I am now satisfied that I can beat him shooting 2 to 1.   Bitch came to a point, but the place was so unfavorable for quail that I rode up to her, & accused her of lying, when a Turkey got up before her, and then another.   If I had been properly loaded & prepared I could have got both.   *D — ing ——*

Found ambulance.   Put dogs in – got in ourselves & reached Post about 4 pm.   Letter from Sis Annie.   Mother & Father safe in Rockingham.[36]   Splendid notices of Fred.[37]

36. At the home of Dodge's sister, Annie P. Glenn.
37. On January 5 and 6 Frederick Paulding performed at Comstock's Grand Theatre in Columbus, Ohio. An unidentified newspaper account of his performance as Bertuccio in *The Fool's Revenge* included the judgment that, though "Mr. Paulding has been on the stage only a year and a half . . . [he] is rapidly rising to prominence" (quoted in New York *Dramatic Mirror*, January 17, 1880, p. 2). Frank Lawlor's Company performed in Raleigh, North Carolina, on January 19, in Norfolk, Virginia, on January 20–22, and in Lynchburg, Virginia, on January 23–24.

My bag of trip – 2 Turkeys 8 grouse – 18 quail – 1 squirrel 1 robin. Clarke 1 Turkey, 5 quail   Total 3 Turkeys – 8 grouse – 23 quail 1 squirrel 1 robin[38]

COMMENTARY: JANUARY 27–FEBRUARY 18, 1880

A Change in Command

Dodge's regimental commander, Colonel Jefferson C. Davis, never returned to Fort Supply. During the fall of 1879 he appeared at some public ceremonies, presiding at meetings of the Society of the Army of the Cumberland and attending an observance in memory of General George H. Thomas, his commander during a period of the Civil War, but he was in failing health. His last military duty was in Chicago, where he served as member of a military board to determine certain disputed facts about the battle of Chickamauga, in Georgia and Tennessee, in which General Thomas and he had played honorable parts.[39] Davis was already much weakened when a bad cold developed into pneumonia and carried him off on November 30, 1879. His death was marked by demonstrations of respect in several places, for despite the one incident of violence that permanently stained his reputation, he had served his country well. General Sherman eulogized him in statesmanlike fashion, as one whose "fame and history belong to the whole army."[40] Officers of the Twenty-third Regiment of Infantry wore badges of mourning for thirty days.[41]

38. This day's journal entry concludes on p. [19R] of the manuscript. The text that follows the editorial commentary begins on p. [19V].

39. *ANJ*, October 11, 1879, p. 179; December 6, 1879, p. 341.

40. S.O. 104, December 1, Headquarters of the Army; reprinted in *ANJ*, December 6, 1879, p. 341. Although Davis's killing his commanding officer was not mentioned by Sherman, anecdotes of the incident appeared in print elsewhere at the time of his death and in years afterward. See the article reprinted from the *Detroit Press* in *ANJ*, December 27, 1879, p. 404; Fry, *Military Miscellanies*, p. 501.

41. G.O. 23, December 2, 1879—DMO. See also G.O. 18, Headquarters Twenty-third Infantry, December 5, 1879, reprinted in *ANJ*, December 27, 1879, p. 401. An obituary tribute to Davis in the *Chicago Times* was reprinted in the *Leavenworth Times*, December 3, 1879, p. 3.

Even amidst these observances, the attention of a promotion-starved officer corps naturally turned to identifying Davis's successor. Promotions through the rank of colonel were made on the basis of seniority in the lower ranks—a system that denied some recognition for distinguished service but at least appeared evenhanded. According to lineal rank, the officer eligible to become colonel of the Twenty-third Infantry was Lieutenant Colonel Elwell S. Otis, Twenty-second Infantry. The *Army and Navy Journal* announced at once that "in ordinary course" Otis would succeed Davis.[42] However, a few days afterward another officer, Colonel Granville O. Haller, was named to the position. Haller had been restored to the Army a few months earlier, following official review of the action by which he had been summarily dismissed in 1863.[43] In an Army career that extended back to 1839, Haller had spent many years in the far West and Northwest. In October 1879 it was announced that he would assume command of Fort Townsend, a small post on Puget Sound that he had established in 1856.[44] However, the death of Davis opened another assignment to him, and the candidacy of Lieutenant Colonel Otis was set aside.

The appointment of Haller to command a regiment overslaughed some career officers, effectively setting aside both their lineal rank and their contributions during the sixteen years in which he had been absent from the Army. Appeals were made in regard to the precedent this action seemed to establish, but after some delay the appointment was confirmed.[45] On February 2, 1880, Colonel Haller received orders from General Pope to take command of the regiment at Fort Supply, and he did so at once, assuming the position he held until his retire-

42. *ANJ*, December 6, 1879, p. 341. Otis had been promoted to lieutenant colonel on July 28, 1866.

43. For a summary of the circumstances surrounding Haller's dismissal see L. R. Hamersley, *Records of Living Officers*, pp. 389–90; for a more detailed account, see *ANJ*, March 30, 1878, p. 537. The joint resolution of Congress authorizing a court of inquiry to examine the matter is in *Statutes at Large*, 21:489–90. For the bill restoring him to the Army, see *ANJ*, March 8, 1879, pp. 548–49.

44. *ANJ*, October 4, 1879, p. 157; Frazer, *Forts of the West*, p. 175.

45. S.O., December 11, 1879—War Department (*ANJ*, December 20, 1879, p. 381). According to the *Army and Navy Journal*, the officers passed over by the action sought a review by the attorney general (p. 383).

ment in 1882. On February 11 the regimental adjutant, with the sergeant major, clerks, books, papers, and band, were relieved from duty at Cantonment and directed to report to their new commanding officer.[46] Dodge's four-month tenure as acting commander of the regiment had ended. The question of succession to the colonelcy had been of obvious interest to him, but he had no prospect of appointment to the position and made no public comment on the appropriateness of Haller's selection. He and Haller soon struck up a friendly relationship based on shared tastes and associations, and they worked together thereafter without a hint of discord.

The Ute Woman

Later in February Dodge was called upon a second time to make report on a sequence of events alleged by Agent Miles to have occurred at Cantonment. On January 20, the day after he had accused Dodge of dishonestly attempting to exonerate Keeling and Company of illegal trading with Indians, Miles took the offensive on a new front. Wishing, he wrote Commissioner Hayt, "to check, if not altogether to stop, the practice now so common, the prostitution of Indian women by U.S. soldiers," he enclosed an affidavit describing "the fatal result of excessive sexual intercourse" by men at Cantonment with a Ute woman.[47] The affidavit, made the previous December 16 by Minimick, concerned the death of this woman in November, a few days after she had visited Cantonment to earn money as a prostitute. Miles's reason for not informing his superiors of this distressing incident at the time he learned of it can only be guessed at, but his motives for sending it when he did were evident. He wished to portray Cantonment as a sink of sexual license, probably both for the embarrassment his accusation would cause and to the end that Indians would be discouraged or prohibited from going there.

Miles' letter quickly received attention in Washington, D.C. On January 30 Secretary Schurz forwarded it to the secretary of war with

46. Twenty-third Infantry Regimental Returns, January and February, 1880; RID to Haller, February 7, 1880 (CNFCR LS); S.O. 20, February 11, 1880, CNFCR.

47. Miles to E. A. Hayt, January 20, 1880 (OIA LR, C&A).

the request that in future all post commanders be instructed to keep Indians "without proper passes from their Agents, outside the lines" of military installations.[48] If the claims of Miles were true, as Schurz and Hayt appeared to take for granted, they constituted a mortifying reflection on Army discipline. Presently the matter came before General Sherman, who reacted with cautious concern. It was easy for Indian agents to accuse soldiers of wrongdoing on the basis of "mere rumor," he wrote in his endorsement. He did not credit the charges, but they embarrassed the Army as a whole, and "now that a direct charge is made in some detail I want the case investigated." On February 7 an order for a full investigation and report went out from Army headquarters,[49] and after some delay the responsibility for the inquiry devolved upon Dodge.

The evidence Dodge subsequently obtained through depositions from local Indians, Amos Chapman, and the post physician yielded a sordid but clear picture. The Ute woman had been captured when a girl by the Arapahos and kept by them, as was common custom, as a servant. Eventually they began selling her services as a prostitute, either directly or through Indians who took her to camps elsewhere for a few days at a time. Later she had been purchased from the Arapahos by Scabby, a Cheyenne, and on his death she became the property of his widow, Yellow Woman. Known as "Hobbled Woman" because of her slave status, she was a fixture at the Cheyenne and Arapaho agency, where she had done a steady trade for years. Witnesses agreed that the Ute woman did not resent her place there. She was permitted to keep half of her earnings, and she seemed to like her work.

Stone Calf and Coho, Dodge's Indian witnesses, told a story of the few weeks preceding the woman's death that agreed in essentials with the testimony of Amos Chapman. Early in November, Yellow Woman came to Coho's camp and hired out Hobbled Woman to Indians who took her near the post at night and sold her to men there. Once in the

48. C. Schurz to SW, January 30, 1880 (AGO LR).
49. Disposition sheet with endorsements by Sherman and others, RID to AAG DMO, March 4, 1880 (AGO LR).

daytime she had come to Chapman's house begging. About three days before her death Chapman visited Coho's camp and found her there, so ill that the occupants of the lodge had set her outside to die. Examining her, Chapman found that she was suffering "a most horrible case of Syphilis." He obtained medicine from Dr. Comfort at the post and sent it to her, but she died soon afterward.[50]

The part played by soldiers at Cantonment in the activities and final sufferings of this woman Dodge attempted to ascertain from Dr. La Garde, the chief physician at the post. According to hospital records, between November 6, 1879, and March 4, 1880, one soldier had received treatment for constitutional syphilis, one for gonorrheal orchitis, and one for gonorrheal cystitis. All three cases had been contracted long before. However, Dr. La Garde also mentioned in his report two civilians whose cases of gonorrhea he had treated in December. These, he emphasized, were "*doubtless contracted in the vicinity of this post.*"The physician was unable to specify the source of the infection,[51] but his clinical observations were strong if not conclusive evidence that, while some men at Cantonment may have engaged in sexual intercourse with the deceased woman, soldiers had not.

Dodge's inquiry had not been difficult, but the charges were grave and taken seriously at Army headquarters, so he drafted his report with particular care. Itemizing first the facts supported by direct evidence and second those by presumptive evidence, he next summarized the report of Dr. La Garde and the affidavits of Stone Calf, "a chief of standing, and one of the most reliable Indians of my

50. Depositions by Stone Calf, Coho, and Chapman, all dated March 3, 1880, enclosed with RID to AAG DMO, March 4, 1880 (AGO LR). Stone Calf and Coho both deposed that Agent Miles had long known that the Ute woman was a prostitute. According to Coho, Miles's informant Minimick had twice pimped for the woman during her stay near Cantonment. This alleged fact had gone unmentioned by Minimick in his deposition for Miles and by Miles himself in his letter of January 20 to Commissioner Hayt. However, Miles did explain in the letter that pimping by male Indians was customary.

51. Louis La Garde to C.O. CNFCR, March 4, 1880, enclosed with the Dodge report (AGO LR). At the outset of his report, Dodge remarked that by their very nature the alleged sexual acts of soldiers were "almost impossible of direct proof or rebutment."

acquaintance," Coho, "to whose band the owner of the Ute slave belonged," and finally Amos Chapman. Observing that further affidavits would be "simply cumulative," he proceeded to his conclusion: "The charges made by Mr. Miles are utterly unfounded."

Dodge did not give prominence to Agent Miles in his report, except as the source of the statements he was investigating. However, at a few points he did refer ironically to Miles and his activities, suggesting that they might also warrant inquiry. For example, citing evidence that the agent had known for years of the Ute woman's prostitution at the agency and yet had done nothing to relieve her suffering during her lifetime, he observed that his "new born zeal is scarcely to be accounted for." In regard to Secretary Schurz's request that Indians be kept outside the "lines" of military posts, he mentioned that in the previous spring Miles had actually encouraged the presence of reservation Indians near Cantonment. He had allowed Indians to continue cutting and racking wood after their contract to supply firewood to the post had been filled—had in fact appealed to Dodge not to interfere with them. However, on that occasion his solicitude on behalf of the Indians lasted only until he learned that their labors would no longer benefit Lee and Reynolds, when he directed them peremptorily to return to the agency. "To an unprejudiced observer," Dodge slyly suggested, "there would seem to be some connection between Lee and Reynolds and the authorities at the Agency."

He pointed out that as a cantonment his post was without fortifications and, being situated along a public road, could not possibly be made secure against intrusion. However, he enclosed documents that demonstrated a sustained effort to discourage Indians from entering the military reservation except during stated hours and on business. He granted that in spite of the efforts of provost officers and guards, every day Indian women did come to the post begging for food or for work to enable them to purchase food. They behaved themselves well, he wrote, and never entered the men's quarters. The danger of sexual contact, if any existed, was not on the post or near it—Secretary Schurz's "line"—but away from it, in bushes and ravines where detection of clandestine activities was impossible.

Dodge's report on the death of the Ute woman was detailed, tightly controlled, definitive. In concluding it, he permitted himself a rhetorical flourish: "I do not believe that any Indian woman has been debauched by any soldier at this post. The Indian prostitutes brought to the vicinity at night by Indian pimps may have been used, and will probably continue to be used, as long as human nature is as it is. The social evil is an institution of savage as well as of civilized life, and if it cannot be stopped in the enlightened capital of this great country, it is hardly fair to expect post commanders to stop it among the savage tribes of the frontier."[52]

The report laid to rest the most recent set of accusations by Agent Miles. Forwarded to the secretary of the interior by the secretary of war, it elicited no further comment.

On February 18, "Per verbal instructions of the post commander,"[53] Dodge and his friend Captain Randall set out together on a week's hunt in the vicinity of Cantonment. Knowing that anecdotes from afield were always acceptable to his father, he resumed his journal entries.

JOURNAL: FEBRUARY 18-24, 1880

February 18, 1880

This time I took Randall with me.   Got off about 9 am –   Kept to ambulance until near Sheridans Roost, then took to our horses.   At a favorite duck pond 4 Mallards got up.   They were so far that I had no hope but I let fly.   To my delight one fell – so I let off the other barrel & got another.   It was too far for Jake[54] & his gun.

---

52. RID to AAG DMO, March 4, 1880 (AGO LR). The correspondence in this case is a consolidated file, AGO 768 1880. Copies of Dodge's report with its enclosures may also be found in OIA LR, C&A, and CNFCR LS.

53. This formula phrase was used in post records to document instances of the commanding officer's availing himself of his right to be absent without leave from higher authority for periods of up to seven days.

54. Randall's nickname. Local Indians and also the Sioux knew him as Black Beard. According to Knight, in earlier years the Apaches had named him Big Chief Jake (*Life and Manners in the Frontier Army*, p. 204).

Bagged 2 birds of a kind new to me, a species of Jay I think   Camped at Cottonwood Grove.   Plenty of water, & good camp   Bag – 2 Mallards.

Thursday, February 19, 1880

Very cold last night – the ponds froze & the ducks that were in had to seek other quarters.   Randal & I got on our horses about 7. am. & took to the sand hills.   Nothing rewarded our labors until we got near my favorite fish pond, when we discovered a small flock of Turkeys. I put after them as fast as old Buster[55] could go through the sand. Soon one got up before me, & I bagged him neatly.   After some hunting I flushed another & broke his wing.   My orderly, (Carter)[56] & I had a lively chase, & I had to shoot him again.   Randall got a couple of good shots, but his horse bothered him.   We then went to my pond.   A fine flock of ducks got up at long range, & I got 2, right & left.   One Long Tail, & one Widgeon.   Found several nice ponds but it is rather too early for the Ducks.   One had a fine flock of shell drakes.   I knocked down two, & set Randall to killing them.   They were wounded so they could not fly, but they could dive & swim to perfection.   I laughed till my ribs were sore at Jake.   He is not much of a shot & requires deliberation.   A duck would pop up, Jake take deliberate aim, & by the time his shot got to the duck, he was safe under water again.   He must have fired a dozen times before he suc-ceeded in killing them.   Just before we got to camp we came on a splendid drove of Turkeys, at least fifty.   They were not very wild & would not fly, but they managed themselves so well that I could not get a shot.   I might have done so by dashing up on old Buster, but the chance of bagging was so small that I preferred <try> waiting for tonight.   Camped at Osage Springs.   Excellent camping place.   Sent Boon out to hunt a roost – but he came back at dark without having found one.

Today has been very delightful, bracing, almost cold, & tho' we did'nt kill much we had fine fun   –

---

55. Dodge's horse.
56. Private Lafayette Carter, Company I.

Bag today – 2 Turkeys – 1 Long tail duck 1 Widgeon – 2 shell drake I shot remarkably well, & my gun outdid itself.

Friday, February 20

Bad Medicine today –   None of the hunters found a roost last night, so nothing is added to the bag.   The morning was wretched raw & very windy.   Hunted everywhere, but could not find Ewer's old trail Had to strike out on my own hook.   Struck head of main branch of Ewer's Creek,[57] crossed its dry bed & then took the divide between that & a Creek to the west, hoping to get down between them   The divide is high, & the branches on each side interlace, in Canons fifty to 100 feet deep & perpendicular   We got through two or three bad places by the skin of our teeth, but finally came to one, where the Cañons overlapped & ran together so as to make one Canon 100 feet deep – so we had to turn back.   To our right as we came I noticed an apparently good lateral divide.   Went back to it, & got along very well, knowing of course that we were getting into difficulty from which we would have to extricate ourselves tomorro.

Camped on main branch of Ewer's Creek – just where the water begins.   All this Country is Gypsum formation & the water horrible – we brought ours from Osage Sp.   Plenty of deer, but though I walked myself almost to death, I saw nothing but tracks.   Bears & panthers also plenty.   No signs of Turkey.   I fired no shot today – several shots were had at deer by the men   Not a thing bagged

Saturday, February 21, 1880

<My>One of my Indian scouts, Buffalo,[58] joined us last night – to my delight for I am tired of playing guide when I want to hunt.   This

57. Both trail and creek were named after Captain Ezra P. Ewers, Fifth Infantry, who had commanded precautionary patrols in the vicinity while stationed at Fort Supply in recent years. See Carriker, Fort Supply, p. 79. Ewers Creek flowed east and then north, joining the Cimarron River at a point about thirty-five miles from Cantonment.

58. Lieutenant Clarke had recently identified the five Cheyenne Indian scouts employed at the post as Stone, White Crow, Man That Walks High, Strong Wolf, and Running Buffaloes (Annotation of John D. Miles to RID, December 2, 1879—CNFCR Register LR). Dodge refers to the last.

morning I started him out with the wagons while I went down the creek hunting.   The gorge was so narrow & the thicket so dense that we had great difficulty in getting through, & made so much noise that all the game was scared off, before we could see it –   I saw plenty of fresh tracks of deer, but the animals themselves kept well away.   After a while the Canon became so bad, that I feared my Indian might get the wagons into serious difficulty –   So I went to them just in time. Got them over a terribly bad place.   Its an awfully broken country – almost as bad as the Black Hills,[59] & worse because it fools you all the time.   To stand on a high divide & look even an experienced plains- man would say "I can go so & so" but when he tries it he cant.   Like all other countries it is cut & scored in every direction by water ways. These being flush with the general level do not show but when you get to them they are nasty ditches 50 to 200 feet wide, & as many deep – with banks straight up & down.   Many of them cannot be crossed even on horseback, & wagons have to head them.   We have[60] made today not over 8 miles in a straight line – but we have travelled more than 15   It took us 6 mortal hours & only about 20 minutes of that in work —

I got after a small covey of quail, which were in a canon 100 feet deep, & not so wide.   I killed 3 birds in 3 shots but could not find one.   I was well satisfied to get 2, for I had no dog, & even had he been along he could have done nothing.   I got in with difficulty & had to climb a tree to get out.   Buffalo & Boon each got a Jack Rabbit

Near the mouth of Ewer's Creek, came to a cattle ranche.   They say that hundreds of hunters have been in the country & almost all the game is killed or run out.   Buffalo brought us across the Cimarron to a Turkey Roost he knew of, but on examination we find that Turkeys have all been run off.   So no game today –   A splendid day & I have enjoyed every moment.   Camped north of Cimarron

59. Dodge means the "bad lands" south and east of the Black Hills. See BHJ, pp. 232– 34.

60. Dodge wrote these two words at the end of a line and then repeated them as he began the line below.

Sunday, February 22, 1880

Had the only good shot at a deer, that I have had since the Winter Campaign of 1876-7[61]   Plastered him all over with buck shot, so that it only ran a few hundred yards & laid down.   This it kept doing, my luck being always to be a long way off, when it got up & none of the others could hit it.   Followed it over two miles through the sand hills by tracks & blood fired at it five times hit it every time, & yet it got away.   It was covered with blood & is undoubtedly dead now, but I didnt bag it.   Killed one rabbitt one grouse, & 2 ducks   Had a long hard journey 25 miles of sand.   Camped on Eagle Chief.[62]   Buffalo says he will show me some Turkeys tomorro.

Tried fishing but got no bite.   Lovely day but, a bit too warm.

Monday, February 23, 1880

Another lovely day.   Got a long shot, about 100 yds, at ducks & killed 3 - Wire cartridges

Got safely across the Cimarron.   I always have a certain uneasy feeling when I am on the wrong side of that abominable bed of sand & a corresponding feeling of relief when on the right side   Found two small coveys of grouse of which I bagged 4, Randall 1.   Buffalo got a Jack Rabbit, almost as big as a calf -   I think the largest I ever saw -

Went into camp on the edge of the Black Jacks about 2 pm   Buffalo found & fired at a flock of Turkeys.   I ordered all shooting stopped til night.   I went out on foot to examine this great roost, & very soon satisfied myself that it is not a regular roost, & that if Buffalo found them here very plenty it was because they had been driven from better roosts.   The timber is too small, & much scattered & the ravines in which they are, are almost impassible in daylight

I took a turn of about a mile, satisfied myself that I had no use for any such hunting -   Shot at & wounded a solitary old gobbler, which

61. On December 7, 1876. See PREJ, pp. 112-13.
62. A stream flowing east toward Medicine Wood Creek, which after their junction at a point approximately forty miles from Cantonment continued flowing southeastward toward the Cimarron River.

however got away [-] & came back to camp disgusted.   Let all the
would be hunters go out at night, lending one my gun   All came back
in an hour or two played out & disgusted.   Turkeys are here, but so
well protected by the nature of the ground, that even Buffalo came
back without one –

We are within 10 or 12 miles of the post.   We try one grand effort
tomorro –

Tuesday, February 24, 1880
Nothing – got in about 10 a.m.

————

Dear Father died –[63]

COMMENTARY: FEBRUARY 24–MARCH 25, 1880

Father and Son

Dodge and his father had shared much in common, both through
family associations and in tastes and traits of character. James Richard
Dodge was himself the son of a military man, Brigadier General
Richard Dodge, who had commanded United States forces at Sackett's
Harbor, New York, during the War of 1812[64] and whose given name
became his grandson's. James was born and reared in rural New York,
forming there the love of outdoors life that his own son later came to
share. A first cousin of Washington Irving, whose surname became his
son's middle name, James was one of the few members of his large
family who emigrated to the southern states.[65] Like his son, he was an
avid reader and an able writer.[66] At the outbreak of the Civil War, father

63. The bottom seven lines of p. [28R], on which this entry appears, are blank, as
is p. [28V]. The journal text that follows the editorial commentary begins on p. [29R].
64. Wheeler, *Reminiscences and Memoirs of North Carolina*, pp. 393–94.
65. Aderman, *A Genealogy of the Irvings of New York*, p. 7.
66. According to John W. Moore, James R. Dodge was "favorably known as a
humorist and lawyer" in his region of North Carolina. His "Epitaph on Hillman, Dews,
and Swain," Moore predicted, would be remembered long after his best known law
cases were forgotten (*History of North Carolina*, 2:135).

and son both remained loyal to the Union cause even though they could not gainsay their regard for colleagues and neighbors in North Carolina whom they had come to know well. After the war, James Dodge—seventy years of age in 1865—was employed for a few years in the New York custom house. His son doubted that he would ever be willing to return to his former home, where he and his wife had met.[67] However, the younger Dodge underestimated his father's adaptability and genial good nature, for he did return, and happily. His reputation as a man of solid trust in legal matters and a lively wit had not been forgotten, and his last years were serene. He died peacefully on February 24, 1880, at the home of his daughter Annie S. Glenn.[68]

Miles vs. Townsend

An eventful month had passed before Dodge felt moved to resume writing in his journal, which he had come to associate with his father. During that period Agent Miles had returned to the fray, this time as part of an effort to rid the Cheyenne and Arapaho reservation of "undesirable whites . . . ostensibly engaged in work for the military."[69] He sought the expulsion, among other persons, of Robert L. Townsend, an employee at Cantonment whom he described to Commissioner Hayt as a "worthless character" whose presence was "interfering with the effort to advance these Indians in civilization."[70] Townsend, a former soldier who had worked as a saddler while stationed at Fort Reno, had followed his trade at the fort for some time after his discharge. Miles had refused to legalize Townsend's marriage to a squaw whom he purchased, but the couple remained together and by 1879 had one small child. Recommended in September of that year for employment in the quartermaster's department at Cantonment, Townsend had moved there with his small family and begun work at sixty dollars per month.[71]

67. RID to Julia R. P. Dodge, July 24, 1870 (Dodge Papers, Yale Collection).
68. Wheeler, *Reminiscences and Memoirs of North Carolina*, p. 393.
69. Miles to Commissioner of Indian Affairs, February 24, 1880 (OIA LR, C&A).
70. Miles to Commissioner of Indian Affairs, March 8, 1880 (OIA LR, C&A).
71. Endorsement, William L. Clarke, n.d. [March 1880] (CNFCR Register LR).

On March 8 Agent Miles informed Commissioner Hayt that Townsend had recently been brought to him by the Indian police, partially intoxicated. According to Miles the police reported that he had entered an Indian lodge, "seized hold of an Arapahoe woman and evidently would have violated her person had he not been too drunk."[72] Townsend was sent to the guardhouse, and two days later he was brought before Miles for an interview. The agent's notes of this session included the information that Townsend's wife and child were enrolled at the agency and received rations there, but that the husband "[p]refers to have his wife live at the Military post where he is employed." Miles also recorded that Townsend habitually became intoxicated, buying his liquor at the "Military trading Establishment."[73] After five more days of detention Townsend was released and permitted to return to Cantonment, but Miles wished to take further action. He asked Commissioner Hayt whether any means were available to rid Indian Territory of such persons as this.

During the period when Townsend resided near the Cheyenne and Arapaho agency, he had not claimed the privileges due an Indian, as many other squaw men did. His only misdeeds noted by Miles were those that had led to his recent arrest. Certainly the alleged drunkenness and brutal behavior were serious matters, if true. The Townsend case was referred to the secretary of war and eventually returned to Cantonment for investigation and report, this time not by Dodge but by the post provost marshal, First Lieutenant William L. Clarke. Not surprisingly, upon Townsend's returning to work after more than a week's unexplained absence, Clarke had already made inquiries. At that time he was unable to obtain any evidence beyond a positive denial by Townsend that he had attempted to debauch the Arapaho squaw. Through renewed investigation Clarke succeeded at least in establishing the background of Townsend's journey to the agency. His wife had earlier gone there but wished to return to Cantonment, and he had requested permission to go and bring her back. Permission

72. Miles to Commissioner of Indian Affairs, March 8, 1880 (OIA LR, C&A).
73. Miles, Notes on an interview with Robert L. Townsend, March 1, 1880 (OIA LR, C&A).

being granted, he left the post in a sober state and without liquor, arriving at the agency three days later, approximately when his alleged drunken misbehavior had occurred. Clarke could obtain no further information about that incident, and in his report he therefore confined himself to a summary assessment of Townsend's reputation and customary behavior. At Cantonment "he has performed his work faithfully, does not drink to any excess, is in no sense of the word a worthless character, works for his living, and so long as his wife remained here supported her decently."[74] Clarke's comments were sufficient to end the matter. On June 7 the secretary of war informed the secretary of the interior that Townsend was "not regarded in any sense of the word as a worthless character" and so had not been removed from his position.[75]

Keeling and the Indian Bureau

Dodge played no direct part in the investigation of the post saddler, but in a matter of more wide-ranging importance he was an active participant. A small but substantial fraction of the fifty-five hundred Indians enrolled at the agency lived for the greater part of the year within a few miles of Cantonment.[76] Concerned for their welfare at that considerable distance from their authorized source of purchased food and supplies, and convinced also that they were being systematically bilked by the trader at the agency, Dodge encouraged H. C. Keeling to apply for permission to sell goods directly to Indians at his Cantonment store. Accordingly, through an attorney in Washington, D.C., Keeling requested of Secretary Schurz that he be allowed to trade with Indians "subject to the regulations prescribed for traders with the Indians generally." Senator Plumb, a valuable ally in such a petition, assured Schurz that Keeling was an able businessman and a

74. Endorsement, William L. Clarke, n.d. [March 1880] (CNFCR Register LR).
75. SW to SI, June 7, 1880 (SW LS).
76. In February 1880, rations and annuity goods were distributed to 5,543 persons in 1,143 families at the Cheyenne and Arapaho agency (S. Gunther to AAG DMO, February 24, 1880—OIA LR, C&A). The number of Indians enrolled at the agency who resided within a definite number of miles from Cantonment cannot be specified exactly.

person of good character.[77] Nevertheless, this direct appeal by a military trader to the department that administered the Indian Bureau was quickly denied. Late in March Keeling renewed his request, this time writing on his own behalf and intending for his letter to reach Schurz freighted with favorable endorsements from senior Army officers. Dodge was the first to express support for Keeling's proposal, and in his endorsement he did so in the strongest terms he could:

> Respectfully forwarded (through military channels). It is very greatly to the interests of the Indian that this request be granted. At present there is practically but one firm of Traders on the Cheyenne & Arapahoe reservation. The Indian has to buy at highest and sell at lowest prices. Many come to this post who have no food, but have means to buy. I cannot permit them to buy of the Subsistence Department, and as Keeling and Co. cannot sell to them, they sometimes suffer greatly.
>
> In the interest of humanity, I approve and recommend a favorable consideration of this request.[78]

Unfortunately, Dodge's appeal flew in the face of political reality. General Pope had supported him on many occasions before, but in this instance he declined. Recently Pope had written to the secretary of war that, so long as the present system of managing Indian affairs existed, he could not approve of post traders selling to Indians. "It would only introduce a fresh element of dissension between the Post Commanders and Indian Agents and between the War and Interior Departments," he wrote. What was more, disputes would occur between the traders authorized by the Army to sell to Indians and those authorized by the Indian Bureau.[79] Through his adjutant, Pope informed Dodge that he had not changed his opinion and could

77. J. H. Gillpatrick to Carl Schurz, February 4, 1880, with endorsement by Plumb (OIA LR, C&A).

78. Keeling and Co. to Commissioner of Indian Affairs, March 25, 1880, with endorsement by RID (Dodge Papers, Yale Collection; Dodge's endorsement is also recorded in CNFCR Register LR).

79. E. R. Platt, endorsement [after April 6, 1880], Keeling and Co. to Commissioner of Indian Affairs, March 25, 1880 (Dodge Papers, Yale Collection).

forward Keeling's request only with a negative endorsement. On April 20 Dodge therefore returned Pope's comments to Keeling, and there the matter ended, at least for some time.[80] The appeal to principles that transcended practical and political considerations had been a worthy one, but it seemed hopeless.

David Payne

General Pope's expectation in December 1879 that in the coming spring Colonel Carpenter and perhaps others would renew their effort to establish settlements in Indian Territory proved accurate. David Payne, who had arrived in Wichita in August 1879 and helped organize a group known as the Oklahoma Town Company, was now backed by a corps of devoted followers. He seemed determined to challenge the federal government to employ force against citizens who sought to take possession of the unassigned lands.[81] Alerted to this prospect, on February 12 President Hayes issued a new proclamation warning "evil-disposed persons" that all necessary measures, including military force, would be taken to repel any such attempt.[82] Two weeks later, troops from Cantonment were once again called upon to participate in the effort to quell the threatened invasion. Companies C, D, and I received orders to encamp near Caldwell, Kansas, and patrol the area.[83] Meanwhile, General Pope sought to obtain instructions from the secretary of war as to whether his men should expel persons who had already established themselves in Indian Territory and were flaunting the law. However, these were not forthcoming. General Sherman was as frustrated as Pope by the government's unclear policy—which he was expected to enforce

80. RID, endorsement, April 20, 1880, of Keeling to Commisioner of Indian Affairs, March 25, 1880 (Dodge Papers, Yale Collection).

81. Pope to AAG MDM, December 16, 1879 (MDM Settlers in I.T. Special File); Rister, *Land Hunger*, pp. 50–53.

82. *Statutes at Large*, 21:798–99; the proclamation was reprinted in *ANJ*, March 13, 1880, p. 641.

83. CNFCR Post Return, March 1880; *ANJ*, March 26, 1880, p. 621.

rigorously.[84] On April 15 Sherman was able to inform Pope that definite arrangements were then being completed with the Cherokees to permit cattlemen to graze herds on Cherokee lands. The two generals agreed that such a policy would deny the Army any way confidently to identify illegal settlers, since anyone who carried what appeared to be a tax receipt could move about in Indian Territory with impunity. However, Sherman wrote, "the result must be with the Secretary of the Interior, whose office it is to guard the interests of the Indians."[85] The Army could now focus its attention on the efforts of would-be permanent residents like Payne and his followers.

Thus in the spring of 1880 the garrison at Cantonment was again seriously depleted, as General Pope used troops stationed there to help deal with potentially troublesome conditions elsewhere. On March 19 Captain Randall, who commanded the detachment at Caldwell, was assigned to be post commander at Fort Reno, and shortly afterward his company was also transferred to his new post.[86] By the end of March Cantonment housed only two companies, and the two on detached service seemed likely to remain encamped near Caldwell for some time to come.

A Rising Young Tragedian

This spring the period of quiet at the post was propitious to Dodge, for it enabled him to take advantage of an opportunity to visit his wife and son for a second time within four months. The place of meeting was to be Leavenworth, where Fred expected to perform on April 1. In recent months Fred's company had enjoyed encouraging success. Newspaper critics were less disposed to comment archly on his youth and instead drew attention to his sensitive interpretation of the roles he played and his effective stage bearing. As one reporter put it, "Paulding is no doubt a rising young

---

84. Sherman to SW, March 6, 1880; Sherman to Pope, March 6, 1880; AG to Pope, March 11, 1880 (AGO LS).

85. Sherman to Sheridan, April 15, 1880 (AGO LS).

86. S.O. 51, March 6, DMO; S.O. 62, March 19, DMO. Major Mizner was transferred to Fort Sill.

tragedian."[87] During the early months of the year the traveling company had moved through the southern states. It played in Greenville, South Carolina, on January 29, in Atlanta, Georgia, on January 30–31, at Augusta on February 2–3, at Columbus on February 4–5, and at Charlotte, North Carolina, on February 6–7. By mid-March, when Dodge learned of Fred's plans to be in Leavenworth, the troupe was moving northward from New Orleans and had reached Tennessee.[88]

The prospect of witnessing his son's development as an actor and of seeing his wife again led Dodge to take up his journal on March 25.

JOURNAL: MARCH 25–APRIL 15, 1880

Thursday, March 25, 1880

My diary has lost its interest in a great measure, since dear Fathers' death – since much that I wrote about – particularly hunting & fishing was for his enjoyment.

Last mail I received a letter from Fred telling me that he & his Mother would be in Leavenworth on 1st April.   I telegraphed Genl Pope for leave got 20 days,[89] & started this morning, after getting everything at the post in excellent order.   At Walnut Ck found Randall in camp, & camped with him, tho I wanted to go further.[90]   He is on his way to take Comd. of Ft Reno.   His Compy has been detached

87. Unidentified newspaper article reprinted in New York *Dramatic Mirror*, April 10, 1880, p. 5. In some places Fred's relationship to Dodge received comment. On January 10, 1880, the *Army and Navy Journal* noted that the young man's success had "attracted considerable notice in Army circles at Washington," where he was to appear in a few days (p. 452).

88. New York *Dramatic Mirror*, January 31, 1880, p. 4; February 7, 1880, p. 4; March 13, 1880, p. 4.

89. On March 17 Dodge had received a telegraphic message that his twenty-day leave of absence would commence on March 25 (CNFCR Post Return, March 1880).

90. According to the Lockwood itinerary, Walnut Crossing was 25.51 miles from Cantonment on the road to Pond Creek Ranch.

from my Post entirely   He gives me good hope of my getting an expedition this summer.[91]

We gassed till 10 pm then went to bed.   Got 1 duck – redhead   24 miles

Friday, March 26

Up about 4 am   Roused Randall.   Had breakfast by Candlelight. Randall & I parted at sunrise   Road pretty good.   Boon an excellent driver.

Thousands of brown plover on the prairies – & some Curlew. Bagged 1 curlew & 8 plover.   Arrived at Pond Ck 2.50 pm   42 miles in 8 hours 20 m.   Escort wagon got in about 5 pm.   Hail & rain storm – tired went to bed early.

Saturday, March 27, 1880

A furious wind storm all night with occasional rain.   Soon after I went to bed I had to call the sentinel & have my tent secured.   He told me that a tree had just been blown down across one of the tents of the men.   He had heard it cracking & got them out in time.

I dont think I was ever in a more furious wind storm, but I finally went to bed & to sleep.   This morning when I came out I was not a little surprised to find a large branch of a tree lying on the tent cords of one side of my tent.   Ten feet more to the west would have saved

                              in this diary
any more writing   ∧   & given promotion to somebody.   I did not even hear it fall, the general commotion outside & inside preventing my noticing any special sound –   Very cold & blustery this am   Got off at 8 am, & arrived at Pardees camp[92] at 1 pm, tired cold & disgusted.   Found all right in camp.   The men have settled

91. Probably Randall was recounting rumors he had heard at Fort Leavenworth, where he had been called for consultation earlier in the month (S.O. 59, March 6—DMO). At the time he encountered Dodge, Randall was en route to Cantonment to prepare his personal effects for the move to Fort Reno.

92. Though ordinarily attached to Company D, First Lieutenant Julius H. Pardee had been assigned to Randall's company when First Lieutenant Frederick L. Dodge was transferred to duty elsewhere (S.O. 120, October 12, 1879—CNFCR).

down after their grand spree with 4 mos pay to spend & all seems to be in good shape[93]   After dinner I went up to Caldwell, to see if I could find some Onion sets &c.[94]   Nothing to be had.   Spent a quiet evening with the boys.   The prairie today was covered as I never before saw it with wild fowl.   Thousands of brown plover – some few field plover – Curlew, Killdeer[,] ducks, prairie chickens.   Had it been a decent day I could have bagged a load but twas so cold & windy that I did not hunt.   Shot two or three times at antelope at long distances & running.

Sunday, March 28

Left my baggage wagon at Pardees camp, & with Boon & ambulance went for Wellington, making the distance 24 miles in 3 hours 10 minutes.   Soon found Heimké, & got everything ready, for taking back – (seeds I mean).   Stopped at [blank] Hotel –   all the hotels poor –   Spent the evening with Heimké & wife.

Monday, March 29

Took Train 3.40 am, & arrived at Kansas City without delay or accident, 6 in afternoon   Found the Company at the Otis House, but to my great disgust the clerk told me as I registered that "Mrs Dodge is not with them" –   Went up to Fred's room found him with a bad cold, but otherwise well, sitting in a cold room writing – (found out afterwards that he is essaying a novel)[95]   He was delighted to see me – for he was by no means sure I could come to meet them.   Julia was left behind sick having been overcome with heat in New Orleans.

93. The paymaster, Major Frank Bridgman, reached these troops at the end of a tour that included Fort Reno, Cantonment, Fort Supply, Fort Elliott, and Fort Dodge. The payment was for service in the four-month period ending February 29, 1880 (S.O. 37, February 18—DMO).

94. On p. [59V] of the journal Dodge wrote "5 Bush. Onion Sets" in a short list that also included "Sweet Potatoes" and "Ch[ief] Com[missar]y - Sub[sistence] Potatoes for seed"— evidently identifying provisions and supplies to be purchased.

95. This work was not published. However, later in his career Frederick Paulding wrote several plays that were produced on the New York stage, including *Cousin Louisa* (1906) and *The Great Question* (1908).

He played Hamlet delightfully in the evening.   He has very greatly improved

Tuesday, March 30

Spent the day pleasantly with Fred, loafing about, shopping &c   At night he played Shylock.   It was only his second appearance in the part, but his acting was most marvellous.

Wednesday, March 31

All went up to Leavenworth   Fred and I went out to post & installed ourselves with the Dodge's - both of whom were delighted to see us.   Went to see the General & had a good time with my friends.   Lady of Lyons at night.[96]   A large party at the post but nearly all our friends went to City & saw Fred play before going to it. Fred & Mrs Dodge went & had a good time[97]   I went to bed.

Thursday, April 1

Telegram from Julia yesterday.   She will be here tomorro.   Had a good time all around, visited city & did some shopping.   Shylock at night

Friday, April 2

All the post wild over Fred's Shylock.   The company went to Topeka this a.m.[98]   I remained behind.   Fred had not been gone an

96. The *Leavenworth Times* reported on April 1 that, while Frederick Paulding was several times called before the curtain for his portrayal of Claude Melnotte, his "many friends are of the opinion that he will be much better this evening in the 'Merchant of Venice' as his style is better adapted to that class of acting"—namely, in "heavier plays" (p. 5). The next day the same newspaper was more candid: "Paulding is good as Hamlet, and splendid in The Fool's Revenge, but he should for the present erase The Lady of Lyons from his list of plays" (p. 4).

97. Mrs. Dodge's companion was her husband, First Lieutenant Frederick L. Dodge, not Dodge's son, Fred.

98. The company had earlier been booked at St. Joseph, Missouri, for April 2 and 3, to be followed by a one-night stand at Atchison, Kansas, on April 5 (New York *Dramatic Mirror*, April 3, 1880, p. 1). The writer for the Topeka *Capital* was unimpressed by Frederick Paulding's Hamlet, which he was said to regard as his best character (quoted in Atchison *Globe*, April 5, 1880, p. 4).

hour before Julia arrived.   She had been sick, with rush of blood to the head, in New Orleans & went to Macon, Georgia to recuperate.[99] While there an old sweetheart, Monroe Ogden found her out, & made her time very agreeable.   He is married & living there.   She had a series of adventures & wound up by losing her most valuable trunk. She is very well now, & happy to get back to cool weather.   A delightful evening – visitors keeping aloof.   Left Minty in town with her mother

Saturday, April 3

Went down town with Julia on a trunk hunting expedition.   Drew my pay for March & made many purchases.   We got back just before dinner.   Lots of visitors in evening.

Sunday, April 4

Julia & Mrs D. went to Church & I went to Popes Sunday School, where I met nearly all the higher Offs of the Post.   Fred arrived about noon.   All of us went to Mrs Dunn's to Tea,[100] & had a delightful evening.   Fred had poor houses in Topeka.

Monday, April 5

Left at 10.45 am – all hands of us, and "jined the show" again. Went to Atchison.   Miserable hotel[101] – poor house at night Lady of Lyons.[102]

---

99. Fred's company had played at Macon on March 17.

100. Probably this was the wife of Captain William McKee Dunn, Jr. Dunn's father was Judge-Advocate General of the Army.

101. The Otis Hotel in Atchison, owned by B. H. Alexander, was advertised in the local newspaper as "Strictly First Class" (*Atchison Globe*, November 21, 1879, p. 1).

102. The editorial writer for the *Atchison Globe* commented bitterly on this night's turnout and on the performance as well: "The entire receipts of the Paulding entertainment . . . were not sufficient to pay bill posting and hall rent. This is but a specimen of his success during the present season. The people are determined that Paulding is not an actor, but Paulding's mother is determined that he is, and is spending large sums of money in keeping the company on the road" (April 6, p. 4).

Tuesday, April 6

Went to Lincoln – good hotel   <Took Julia out riding in a buggy – Beautiful country> Hamlet at night to a poor house.

Wednesday, April 7

Took Julia out buggy riding.   Beautiful country & lovely day. Enjoyed ourselves   Fools Revenge – to a not very good house.   Telegraphed <Thursd>[103] to Genl Pope asking him to extend my leave five days –

Thursday, April 8

Reached Omaha 6 pm.   Found telegram extending my leave.[104] Several friends called, Mrs Crook among them.[105]   Shylock at night to a good House.[106]

Friday, April 9

Had to start at 5 a.m.   Hard work getting up, but Julia has gotten so she can "make an effort" when necessary.   No breakfast.   Miserable abortion of an eating house at Spoon Lake, & all accommodations abominable.   All of us glad to get to Des Moines at 1 pm.   Got dinner at once.   Went to Kirkwood House, a very fair hotel.[107] Played Romeo, to Miss Eldridges Juliet.   I forgot to say in the proper place that Miss Gussie De Forest has left the Compy & Miss Eldridge taken her place.   The latter joined us at Atchison.   She is very pretty

103. This cancellation, the first word at the top of p. [35V], was likely intended to begin a new dateline, not as a part of the day's entry.

104. By S.O. 78, April 8—DMO, Dodge's leave was extended five days.

105. The wife of General George Crook was a gregarious lady whom Dodge had seen often during his service in the Department of the Platte between 1874 and 1876. See *PREJ*, p. 169.

106. The *Omaha Herald* of April 8 ran an advertisement for "The Brilliant Young Tragedian" Frederick Paulding, supported by "Miss Lillie Eldridge and a powerful company," who would appear for one night only at the Academy of Music in "Shylock the Jew" (p. 1). The newspaper published no review of the performance.

107. "The Kirkwood," formerly the Savery House, was prominently advertised in the *Iowa State Register* of Des Moines as "in perfect appointment, and conceded to be the most eligibly situated Hotel in the city" (April 10, 1880, p. 1).

but too large for Fred, & not to my thinking as good an actress as Gussie.[108]   Freds Romeo is beautiful.[109]

Saturday, April 10

Blustery day.   Matiné – Claude Melnotte, Evening, Shylock, to good houses.[110]   Fred is well received in Des Moines, & is urged to play in Hamlet tomorro night.   He played two Sundays in New Orleans, but this is the first northern city where he has been asked to play on that day.   Being a good Catholic he has no scruples about it, & old man Loveday[111] announced his performance for tomorro, between the acts tonight.   Supper at night with Julia & Fred at a nice Restaurant

108. Louisa ("Lillie") Eldridge and Frederick Paulding had appeared together in a New York production of *The Lady of Lyons* more than a year before (New York *Herald*, March 2, 1879, p. 14). In recent months Eldridge had played a minor part in Edwin Booth's production of *Macbeth* and in an adaptation of *Richard III* (Odell, *Annals of the New York Stage*, 11:28–29). Fred's small stature in comparison to that of his leading ladies sometimes received comment. The *Leavenworth Times* remarked of his performance as Claude Melnotte that "in order to embrace Pauline, who was twice his size, he had to stand on his toes" (April 3, p. 4).

109. The *Iowa State Register* gave full and appreciative coverage to the company's performances. Of Fred's Romeo, its critic wrote that "with certain slight exceptions Mr. Paulding gives us the ideal lover that *Romeo* was meant to be. His acting is delicately shaded in giving the rapid transitions from happiness to misery, and from hope to despair. He plays with enthusiasm and a whole-hearted abandon, in those lighter scenes of the play where the course of true love promises to run smooth, and as the drama deepens to its fatal close, he rises to the full height of its tragedy" (April 10, p. 3).

110. The *Iowa State Register* praised several members of the cast for their performances on this day, but Frederick Paulding received chief mention as exciting wonder for his versatility. "Some think that while this young man's voice has hardly developed sufficiently to use to full advantage the grand orotund utterances so necessary to the expression of the strong passions of the more youthful characters assumed by him, it, however, seems well adapted to more aged parts, and there seems a peculiar fitness for it in Bertuccio in 'The Fool's Revenge' and '*Shylock*'" (April 11, 1880, p. 3).

111. A reporter in Columbus, Ohio, identified Charles Loveday as "an excellent old gentleman" who had formerly toured with Furbish and Shaughram (quoted in New York *Dramatic Mirror*, January 17, 1880, p. 2). In *Romeo and Juliet* he played the Friar; in *The Merchant of Venice* he was Gratiano, "and although probably a little too large and not 'made-up' young enough for Gratiano, was very acceptable in the character" (*Iowa State Register*, April 11, p. 3).

Sunday, April 11

Lovely day.   Took a long walk.   Julia went to Church   Fred played at night to a good house.

Monday, April 12

Went to Rock Island.   Fred well received.   Shylock.

April 13

Compy went on.   Julia & I remained.   Intended to go to Arsenale,[112] but was so windy that we staid at home.   I left her in the afternoon for Kansas City

April 14

Arrived Kansas City late   Ran into a car on side track, woke everybody up but me.   Delayed us 2 hours.   The A. T. & S. F. Train had waited for us - so nothing was lost.   Arrived Wellington midnight.

April 15

Ambulance & escort waiting.[113]   Started 8.30.   Arrived Pardees Camp 12.30 - lunched got my own teams - & arrived Pond Ck in good time.   16th Camped on Walnut.   17th got home - & thus ended a glorious trip without a flaw or accident —[114]

112. On Rock Island, located in the Mississippi River opposite Davenport, Iowa, and Moline, Illinois, was located a United States arsenal and armory, established in 1862. The facility attracted many sightseers. A chief object of interest was its clock tower, 107 feet high, that enclosed a clock with hands twelve feet long. The Rock Island Arsenal is thoroughly described in Tillinghast, *Three Cities*, pp. 12–20.

113. A notation on p. [59V] is that "Pardee is to have ambulance in Wellington on 11th without fail." However, having been granted five days' extra leave of absence since meeting Pardee on March 27 and 28, Dodge must have sent new directions.

114. This day's entry ends at the bottom of p. [37V] in the manuscript. The journal text that follows the editorial interpolation begins on p. [38R].

COMMENTARY: APRIL 5-MAY 7, 1880

Agitations in Spring

In the spring of 1880 troops at Cantonment were called upon to help solve several of the same problems they had responded to a year before. Little Chief was no less determined to win government approval of his desire to leave Indian Territory. The threat of the territory's being invaded by land-hungry citizens was even more immediate than in 1879. As the Atchison, Topeka and Santa Fe railhead neared Caldwell, the cattlemen of Texas seemed more determined than ever to blaze new trails across the Cheyenne and Arapaho reservation.[115] However, these issues received less attention from the Army than they had earlier, for its focus of crisis planning had moved far westward. Political and military considerations alike dictated that troops be sent to occupy remote positions in the mountains of Colorado, where they would protect settlers from further attack by Ute Indians and guard against reprisals, depredations, and attempts at illegal settlement in Ute country by miners and other United States citizens. Within days of his return to Cantonment, Dodge received notification that "before long" he and three companies under his command would leave the post to join the Fort Garland Column in southern Colorado.[116]

During the 1870s the advent of prospectors, mining companies, railroads, and towns to the mountains of Colorado had steadily increased the irritation felt by loosely confederated bands of Utes, to whom the mountain country was a birthright and an ancestral hunting range. In recent years Ouray, the respected chief of the Uncompahgre Utes, had sought to moderate the resentment of his tribesmen and achieve through diplomacy some mutually satisfactory arrangement

115. Responding to complaints from Indians living nearby, on April 27 Dodge telegraphed the commanding officer at Fort Elliott, Texas, requesting him to post a warning to cattlemen that if they persisted in driving their herds near Cantonment "they will likely lose their stock, as I will have it stampeded" (CNFCR LS). The warning was posted, but with little effect (Edward Hatch to C.O., May 3, 1880—CNFCR LR).

116. AAG DMO to C.O., April 13, 1880 (CNFCR Unregistered LR).

for coexistence between the tribe and the federal and state governments. However, not all bands were inclined to compromise. In September 1879 violence broke out at the White River Ute agency in northern Colorado. The agent, Nathan Meeker, and other agency employees were murdered, buildings were pillaged and destroyed, and Meeker's wife and daughter were taken captive. Troops from the Departments of the Platte and the Missouri were marching toward the scene at the time these events occurred, but one of the commands itself suffered severe casualties at the hands of the Utes. On September 29 a force under Major Thomas T. Thornburgh, Fourth Infantry, was waylaid and attacked from impregnable positions by the Indians when within a few miles of the agency. Thornburgh was killed, and his men were besieged until October 5, when they were rescued by a large body of troops under Colonel Wesley Merritt, Fifth Cavalry. Merritt pursued the retreating Indians southward through the mountains, but his advance was halted on orders from Washington, D.C. To prevent further bloodshed, the Department of the Interior wished to open negotiations with the Ute bands at once.[117]

The Meeker massacre and the threatened annihilation of the force under Thornburgh excited intense alarm within the region and gained nationwide attention. General Sheridan quickly concentrated a large contingent force at Fort Garland, Colorado, under Colonel Ranald S. Mackenzie, Fourth Cavalry, an energetic troubleshooter who had been operating in Texas along the border with Mexico.[118] By November 1879 two large bodies of troops occupied positions in the southern part of the state: the Fort Garland Column under Mackenzie, com-

117. House, *Report of the Secretary of War* (1880), pp. 79–81, 83–85; Sprague, *Massacre*, pp. 179–288 *passim.*

118. As expected, the transfer of Mackenzie from Texas produced strong objection from citizens there. However, Sherman reminded Senator S. B. Maxey of that state that, unless controlled, the Ute conflict might easily spread south to include the Navahos and Apaches of New Mexico and Arizona Territories. "The same old cause exists here for troops," he wrote; "viz: the pressure of settlement." He regretted that "Mackenzie cannot be everywhere" but assured Maxey that "overwhelming necessity" had compelled Sheridan to direct his transfer (Sherman to Maxey, October 17, 1879—AGO LS).

prised of six cavalry and seven infantry companies, and the Animas River Column, 120 miles west, under Lieutenant Colonel John P. Hatch, Fourth Cavalry, comprised of three cavalry and nine infantry companies.[119] Winter conditions in the region where these forces were stationed made active operations all but impossible, but General Sherman intended to take no "halfway measures" against the Utes and instructed Mackenzie to move toward Hatch at the first sign of an emergency.[120] If the Department of the Interior still wished the Army to delay preparations for battle, so be it. But should the necessity arise, he had determined on ordering General George Crook to command three columns of troops that would hem in the rebellious Utes in classic fashion, operating concentrically.[121] Citizen leaders were already applying incessant pressure to hurry troops into the fastnesses of the Colorado mountains. Early in January Sherman informed Pope that he would probably be called upon to supply perhaps one thousand men to strengthen Mackenzie's command, even if he had to strip the Kansas border to do it.[122]

Meanwhile, attempts to achieve an accommodation between representatives of the Ute bands and the federal government moved slowly ahead. On March 6 Ouray and other Ute headmen submitted to the Department of the Interior a proposal to sell to the United States the rights and title to the large Ute reservation in return for certain payments and a grant of other lands.[123] In order to be acted upon, this document would require ratification both by Congress and by three-quarters of adult male Ute Indians. The work of securing the

119. DMO, *Roster*, November 1879, pp. 14–15.

120. Sherman to AAG MDM, December 29, 1879 (AGO LS).

121. A force under Colonel Merritt would push the White River Utes southward, and the two units under Mackenzie and Hatch's successor, Colonel George Buell, Fifteenth Infantry, would press the southern bands by moving northwest and northeast respectively.

122. Sherman to Pope, January 6, 1880 (AGO LS). Sherman expected no useful results from the negotiations then under way, but he planned to defer any "systematic campaign" against the Utes until the Department of the Interior had confessed its inability to deal with them.

123. Sprague, *Massacre*, p. 307. For the act approved by Congress on the basis of this proposal, see *Statutes at Large*, 21:199–205.

necessary approvals would take time, and the criminal acts at the White River agency were yet to be dealt with. Still, a provisional basis for peaceful resolution of the crisis appeared to have been established. To the military, the prospect of peace remained only that, a possibility. On March 24 Sherman telegraphed to Sheridan that the continuing potential for violence between citizens and Utes necessitated occupying "with considerable force" two as yet ungarrisoned locations in Colorado. These were the Ute agency on the Uncompahgre River and some other point north of it, near the junction of the Gunnison and Grand Rivers.[124] The general and lieutenant general spent the next weekend at Chicago discussing specific possibilities, and the result was a letter of April 3 to the secretary of war in which Sherman outlined his military plans and his requirements of financial support for operations in Colorado.

The three columns that Sherman had deployed in December remained in their positions, but the one under Mackenzie was the strongest and most mobile since it could be supplied and reinforced by rail with relative ease. Sherman proposed to send Mackenzie to the Uncompahgre agency as soon as conditions in the mountains made wagon travel possible. From there, he would reconnoitre northward in search of the site for a new post whose presence should go far toward ensuring peace in the region. Because troops could not live in that high country without adequate shelter, Sherman asked an appropriation of one hundred thousand dollars from Congress at the earliest date possible, so as to have buildings constructed and supplied for winter by September. By that means, he assured the secretary, "the whole of western Colorado, a country supposed to be rich in gold and silver, can be explored and utilized, paying back the cost of these forts a hundred fold."[125]

124. Sherman to Sheridan, March 24, 1880 (AGO LS).

125. Sherman to A. Ramsay, April 3, 1880 (AGO LR). This letter was published in *ANJ* as "The Plan for the Ute Campaign," May 15, 1880, p. 844. Sherman also intended to build a new post on the Animas or San Juan River, in southwestern Colorado, using forty thousand dollars of already appropriated funds.

A Call to Colorado

The United States was neither at peace nor at war with the Ute Indians, but in the foreseeable future a military presence in their homeland was imperative. As the senior officer of the Fort Garland Column, Mackenzie would act under Pope, in whose department the operations would take place, rather than under Crook. An abler administrator than Crook, Pope had been engaged for several months in the preparations for Mackenzie's march into remote country. As spring approached and the movement overland of supplies began to seem practicable, he took steps to provide Mackenzie additional troops and designated for him a second-in-command, his former colleague in the Powder River Expedition under General Crook, Lieutenant Colonel Richard Irving Dodge, Twenty-third Infantry. While Mackenzie and his cavalry troops moved freely about the Uncompahgre region, searching for a suitable post site and by their presence discouraging mischief by Indians and citizens alike, Dodge would do journeyman work at the headquarters of the column, supervising transportation of supplies, construction of sheds and other buildings, and survey and construction of wagon roads. Of course, Dodge's activity in the past year at Cantonment had prepared him well for an assignment such as this. If it lacked something in military glory, the role would yet be an important one and would constitute field service, an opportunity Dodge always welcomed. Sentiment for peace among the Ute bands was not unanimous, and exactly what military duty the summer might bring remained doubtful. Whatever the result, Dodge would at least see southern Colorado, whose wonders he had often heard described.[126]

As Dodge awaited his orders to proceed to Fort Garland, events in the vicinity of Cantonment followed a pattern that had become familiar to many frontier post commanders: it was spring, and the

---

126. In 1870, when he has post commander at Fort Lyon, Colorado, Dodge hoped to make an excursion to the South Park of Colorado "and see the wonderful scenery, which tourists say is destined some day to interfere with the pleasure travel to Europe" (RID to Julia R. P. Dodge, July 17, 1870—Dodge Papers, Yale Collection). However, ten years later he had not yet done so.

Indians were agitated.[127] On April 20 Agent Miles received from the Indian Bureau a directive to enroll all school-age Indian children in the agency school, and on being informed of this plan Little Chief was moved almost to violence.[128] Captain Randall telegraphed Pope that his company of mounted infantry had better be ordered back from Caldwell in case Miles asked him to make a roundup of the Indians, for he believed Little Chief would resist. Pope agreed that the order given Miles would surely create serious trouble, "if not an open outbreak."[129] Dodge, who had gone to Fort Reno on a flyer, received there on April 21 a request from Pope's adjutant to use all his influence to dissuade Miles from attempting to put the order into effect.[130] But Miles had grown impatient of Little Chief's "almost open defiance," and if the chief and his followers were to remain at the agency he favored taking steps to "compel obedience."[131] However, other views prevailed on this occasion, and the Indian Bureau directed Miles to defer the attempt to implement its educational policy until he received further instructions.[132]

On April 27 Dodge received confirmation that he would shortly take the field, and with it a set of general instructions.[133] He was to march to Wellington, Kansas, with two companies of his choice and a designated third company, Captain T. M. K. Smith's Company D, proceeding thence to Fort Garland, a railroad journey of almost six hundred miles. Dodge selected Companies A and C to accompany him and named Captain Charles Wheaton as serve as post commander in his absence.

---

127. This observation was Sheridan's; see *ANJ*, April 24, 1880, p. 773.

128. Miles to R. E. Trowbridge, Commissioner of Indian Affairs, April 20, 1880 (OIA LR, C&A).

129. Randall to Pope, April 20, 1880, with endorsement (OIA LR, C&A). This letter was published in *ANJ*, April 24, 1880, p. 773.

130. C.O. to RID, April 21, 1880 (CNFCR LS). Between April 21 and 25 Dodge was away from the post on his own authority (CNFCR Post Return, April 1880).

131. Miles to R. E. Trowbridge, April 20, 1880 (OIA LR, C&A).

132. *ANJ*, May 1, 1880, p. 794. In his annual report for 1880, Miles wrote of Little Chief: "No persuasion can induce him to place his children at school, looking upon such a course as a virtual abandonment of his plans and purposes—to accept no home as permanent except on the Powder River or vicinity" (House, *Report of the Commissioner of Indian Affairs*, p. 68).

133. S.O. 93, April 27, 1880—DMO; CNFCR Post Return, April 1880.

Supplemented by a few soldiers from other units who were ill or judged unfit for the harsh conditions of the mountains, Wheaton's Company D was for the present the only one that would remain in the garrison. Six six-mule wagons carried the gear of the companies bound for Colorado as they left the post on the morning of May 7.[134]

Dodge had reason to anticipate that his new tour of duty would be filled with interest. On the day of his command's departure from Cantonment he resumed writing in his journal.

JOURNAL: MAY 7-26, 1880

May 7, 1880. Big Creek[135]

When I was in 11Worth Genl Pope told me that there was a possibility of my taking the field against the Utes, in Comd of 15 Cos.

The possibility was so remote that I scarcely allowed myself to hope.   Today it is a fixed fact & I am in Comd of 3 Cos of my Regt. en route for Fort Garland.   Ten days ago I got a letter from Dep Hd Qrs repeating the possibility.[136]   Then we heard that 2 Cos. <from> at
∧ Supply had been ordered to hold themselves in readiness to march. A week ago they got orders & started last Monday.[137]   On Saturday I knew that orders for my move had been issued but had not received them.   Expecting them to arrive by Tuesdays mail I got ready designated the Companies, expecting to start on 8th.   <About> On Tuesday morning I recd. a telegram directing me to march my command as soon as I recd orders by mail.   Two hours after the mail arrived but no order came.   Telegraphed at once to the General, & asked orders

134. S.O. 67, May 5, 1880—CNFCR.
135. The place name is written on the stub of p. [38R], above the perforated tear line, a placement unique in Dodge's journals. According to the Lockwood itinerary, a camping site on Big Creek with wood but no water was approximately twelve miles from Cantonment on the road to Pond Creek Ranch.
136. The letter of April 13 from Pope's adjutant had reached the post on April 20 (CNFCR Register LR).
137. These were Company I, Fourth Cavalry, and Company E, Twenty-third Infantry.

by telegraph & to delay march, until after my Comd was paid – On Wednesday 6, after a day of anxious suspense, got an order to march as soon as paymaster had paid the Comd. On Thursday 10 am the paymaster arrived. The Comd was paid same afternoon.[138] Orders were given for a start today 7th, at 8 am.

Visited paymaster, & called on the ladies at night. Was invited to breakfast by Mrs Wheaton. At 8 am the Comd was formed, & marched out of the post, not a man being drunk or absent, – a most remarkable, unheard of thing, only having been paid yesterday.

Cool, excellent day for marching. I got breakfast bade all good by – paid all my bills – & started about 10 oclk – overtaking the Comd after a brisk gallop about 2 miles from my camping place. Only 12 miles today. No water good wood & grass.

May 8. Walnut Creek

General at 6. Assembly & broke camp 6.30. Pleasant march though twas very hot after 12 m Long shot at an antelope and didnt get him. Bagged 3 ducks – men killed several rattlesnakes. Saw a large wild cat, but no shot. Camped where road leaves Walnut – good place Wood water & grass.[139] Henry Keeling overtook us en route to Caldwell. Replenished my ice.

Distance 16 miles –

May 9. Panther Creek[140]

Off at 6.30. Men marched splendidly. Very hot day, but cool wind. Inside my tent is now 9 pm stifling – outside it is delightful.

Boon made some excelent long shots at antelope but did not get one. A mule escaped yesterday afternoon & has evidently started for

---

138. On May 6 Dodge telegraphed to department headquarters that the command would move the next day and arrive at Wellington on May 13. The three companies on the march included 7 officers, 125 enlisted men, and 9 civilian employees (CNFCR LS). The paymaster, Major W. A. Rucker, settled accounts with the troops through April 30 (S.O. 91, April 29—DMO).

139. This was about two miles north of the Cimarron River.

140. According to the Lockwood itinerary, the road crossed this creek 47.46 miles from Cantonment.

Missouri.   We heard of it tonight beyond Pond Ck & going on the road.   Road lovely.   Fair camp.   Distance 20 miles —

May 10, 1880. Pond Creek

Cold & very windy morning.   Started 5.20 am, as we had a 20 mile march without water   I went ahead in ambulance, to look for camping place.   No water in Pond Ck, except a few small springs trickling from bank.

Wrote postals to Julia & to Mother.   Comd came in (making distance of 21 miles in 7 hours –) an hour ahead of what I expected. All well, & in good condition.   Country all burned up from lack of rain.   Nice camp, except its want of water.   The Creek now dry, is sometimes half a mile wide.   Fred opens tonight at Chicago.[141]

May 11, 1880. Bluff Creek, Near Caldwell

Broke camp 5.15.   Went ahead in ambulance.   Reached Caldwell, or rather Bluff Ck, a little after 9, & had a rousing breakfast – or lunch I suppose I ought to call it.   Went to Caldwell after – also to Camp of I. Co.[142]

Very hot day.   Commd did not get in until near 3 pm, and then very much played out.   Sent Claggett on to Wellington, & let Febiger go with him.[143]   Old Tom's head utterly gone.   Cant put a Comd in camp.[144]   Very nice camp ground, my spot in a grove of large trees.

141. The *Chicago Inter-Ocean*, a major newspaper that included coverage of dramatic performances in the city, made no mention of Frederick Paulding during this period. However, on June 14, 1880, he opened as lead actor at the Union Square Theatre, New York, in Frank Rogers's *The Love of His Life* (Odell, *Annals of the New York Stage*, 11:12).

142. Company I, under First Lieutenant Julius H. Pardee, shortly afterward changed its station to Coffeyville, Kansas (CNFCR Post Return, May 1880).

143. These were the second lieutenants of Companies C and A, respectively.

144. In recent months Captain T. M. K. Smith had continued to cause Dodge concern by his heavy drinking. After his wife had died at Cantonment in December, he had been granted a two-month leave of absence, returning to duty on February 17. While on duty in Colorado he was granted two months of sick leave (S.O. 140, June 30—DMO; S.O. 67, July 19—MDM). Smith eventually recovered, remarried, and retired from the Army in 1899 as a lieutenant colonel.

Terrible storm came up at Nightfall & still continues. Rain wind & sharp lightning. I dont know that a lovely grove is the best place, after my Pond Creek experience, six weeks ago.[145] Mail at night – nothing important Distance 24 miles.

May 12. Shoo Fly Creek[146]

Started early – 5.15 – another hard march. A dozen drunkards last night, & lots of stragglers – or those who would like to straggle. Got five out of jail. Got through town without delay. Left Lockwood to bring up all stragglers.

Camped on head ponds of Shoo Fly. Water poor & no wood, but we brought both with us. Animals drank the Creek water eagerly.

Distance 22 miles. Dr Comfort passed enroute to Ft Reno –[147]

May 13. On Cars

Received last evening by hands of Dr. Comfort, telegram from

Dept Hd Qrs prohibiting my taking any transpn except 6, ∧ 6 mule teams & wagons. Am disgusted. Sent Claggett into town with telegram.

Broke camp 5.30. Went into Wellington ahead of Comd. Found a lot of my men, who had sneaked into town last night Train all

waiting f<rom> ∧ or us. When Comd arrived about 7 a.m. went up with it – put sentinels & N.C. Officers on watch to keep the men from slipping away & went to work. Loaded in stores, took wagons to pieces loaded those, then got shoes off my mules, loaded them & finally got all the men on board by 3.30 pm. About 4 we got off. Supper for ourselves & coffee for men at Newton. Mrs Hay left for

145. See the journal entry for March 27, 1880.
146. Northwest of Caldwell, about five miles from Wellington.
147. Acting Assistant Surgeon Comfort had been on duty with the troops at Caldwell since February 28 and remained so through June.

west & old Julia for east.[148]   We are all very comfortable.   3 of
Smith's men got away in Wellington & were left.   I am not sorry for
they were miserable drunken wretches.   S's Compy is in a horrible
state of discipline – owing to his own bad habits.   I had to set on him
very heavily.

Telegram from Dep Hd Qrs refusing to let me take my horses, but
saying there is plenty of transpn. at Ft Garland   Swapped Boon <for>

with
∧   one of the 6 mule drivers, to his great delight, & take him along
I had to send his ambulance back.

May 14, 1880. On Cars

Slept pretty well – woke up about Pawnee Rock.   Got no breakfast
until we arrived at Dodge City 12 m.   Stopped here 3 hours & had
mules taken out of cars fed & watered.   Saw Bob Wright & many
other old acquaintances

The Country is absolutely burned up.   No rain for a long time, &
not a green thing to be seen.   Maj Offley & wife came to Depot by
accident.   He is ordered to join me,[149] & is all packed & ready.   I told
him I was going to wait 3 hours, & he went off for the Fort at a great
rate, to get his baggage & join us.   As he did not return, I suppose
his wife persuaded him to take regular train.   Replenished my stock
of canned stuff, & had a good lunch about six & went to bed at 8 pm,
just about Lakin on R R   Rain storm in evening

May 15, 1880. Pueblo

Woke up at daylight, after a sleep of 9 solid hours – to find that we
had made only about 75 miles since I went to bed.   Took a lunch

148. At Newton, twenty-five miles north of Wichita, the north-south spur of the
Atchison, Topeka and Santa Fe Rail Road met the main east-west line. The two ladies
were the wife of First Lieutenant Charles Hay, Company C, and quite possibly Julia,
a former servant of Dodge who at one time lived near Leavenworth. See *PNA*, p. 328;
RID to Julia R. P. Dodge, April 17, 1870 (Dodge Papers, Yale Collection).

149. Major Robert H. Offley, Nineteenth Infantry, post commander at Fort Dodge,
had received telegraphic instructions to join the Ute Expedition on May 12 (Fort
Dodge Post Return, May 1880).

breakfast, arrived at La Junta 10 am & took another.   Country all a parched desert.   Improved on our time & finally arrived at Pueblo 3 p.m.   Found telegrams of no importance   Pope passed up yesterday to Garland & is expected to go back tomorro.[150]   Got our Compy property transferred to Narrow Guage very soon but there was no end of trouble to get cars for men & animals   Govt Agent – Rankin – Head R R man[151] very obliging, but not extremely efficient.   However he finally got the cars.   Got supper in town.   Transferred the men about 8.30 pm, & went to bed, having been pumped dry by an Interviewer   Got coffee for men & had animals taken off car for food & water. Have had a tedious but very pleasant trip

May 16, 1880. Fort Garland

No man who has not tried it, can realize the difficulty of getting a good nights rest on a car of Narrow Guage.

I woke up at La Veta, & after a long delay, went up the mountain. It is simply impossible to do justice to the scenery & the engineering. It is the most remarkable work I ever saw.[152]   Just over the summit

150. Accompanied by Lieutenant Colonel J. D. Bingham, deputy quartermaster general of the Military Division of the Missouri, and his aides-de-camp Captain Dunn and Captain W. J. Volkmar, General Pope had been inspecting supplies and transportation arrangements at Fort Garland (S.O. 103, May 12—DMO).

151. The quartermaster's agent at Pueblo was D. B. Hinman (*Official Register of the United States* [1881], 1:259). Edward H. Rankin was proprietor of the Denver Freight Transfer and Storage Warehouse. (*Corbett and Ballenger's Denver City Directory*, p. 430). Dodge was transferring to the Denver and Rio Grande Rail Way, a narrow-gauge road.

152. George A. Crofutt described the train's ascent from La Veta in a manner that confirms Dodge's superlative:

"At La Veta all extra cars are left behind, an extra locomotive is added, and the train starts out on an *average grade* of 211 feet to the mile. In some places the grade is much higher, but the passenger need not fear, as the road is well built, the ties are close together and double-spiked—the engines and cars first-class, while the road-bed is blasted from the mountain side, making it as solid as the everlasting hills on which it rests.

Leaving La Veta, our course is almost due west, winding up Middle Creek, and then on to a high plateau and up Veta Creek. The old Sangre de Christo stage road can be seen on the left, soon after leaving the station, where it winds around the side of the mountain. Continuing on up the creek, eight miles from the station, we arrive at OJO—At this side-track, by looking directly ahead, away up on top of a round, flat-

we met the train going East.   On it were Genl Pope & Mackenzie.
Had a few moments conversation with Pope who went east   Mackenzie went back with us to Garland.   He tells me I must get off
tomorro.   Gives me only one wagon, says I shall not take Laura &c.,
&c.   I know him well however & am not scared.   Got my troops in
camp   Recd my orders from Mackenzie & assumed comd.   Have 11
comp[anie]s organized into 3 Bat[talio]ns.   Webb comds 1st, Brady
2d, Offley 3d.[153]   Lunched with Mackenzie.   Got an ambulance &
authority to take Joe & Laura.   Ordered everything ready to march at
2 pm tomorro.   Cant find out where we are going, nor what we are
going for.   No letters –

May 17, 1880. Springs, 7 Miles from Fort Garland

Had my wagon loaded up early.   A hard thing to cut 2 loads into
one, & decide just what I must take, & must leave.   Had to leave my

---

topped mountain . . . can be seen a lone tree in the center. Now, notice a long,
reddish line encircling that mountain near its top. Can you see it? That is our road,
and there, in front of that low tree, we will be in half an hour, looking down at this
station.

Again we proceed. Look! On your right, away up—there! That peak is Veta
Mountain, 11,512 feet above the level of the sea. Up! Up we go! Keep your eye to
the left now! See! Away up the mountain—there is the road—can our train ever get
there? We are turning gradually, the little valley is becoming a mountain gorge,
narrow, dark and gloomy. We are climbing up to the Mule Shoe. We are there; and
having run up on one side of the 'Shoe,' we will now turn to the left and roll around
on the toe of the shoe on the other side of the gorge. We are climbing the world—
higher and higher. Now look down on the *left*, what a beautiful scene! And the higher
we go the grander the view. Ah! here we are at the point of the mountain. Now look
way down that little, narrow valley, and see *little Ojo* station, where we stood only
a few minutes ago, and looked up. . . .

Now stop a moment and take a look around. 'Old Veta' just to the north—across
the chasm, has 'come down a peg'—is not near as high! The Spanish Peaks, too, look
low—in fact they are 'beneath our notice.' A lady says: 'O! O my! The air is so light
and pure'" (*Crofutt's Grip-Sack Guide to Colorado*, p. 63).

153. In Order 1, Headquarters Infantry Column, Dodge assumed command in
compliance with General Field Order 1 from Mackenzie. He divided the troops under
him into three battalions: Companies A and G, Sixteenth Infantry, and D, Twenty-
third Infantry, under Major Charles A. Webb, Sixteenth Infantry; Companies A, B, C,
and E, Twenty-third Infantry, under Captain George K. Brady, Twenty-third Infantry;
and Companies A, C, D, and E, Nineteenth Infantry, under Major Robert H. Offley.
First Lieutenant Charles Hay was Dodge's adjutant (Fort Garland Column—DMO).

desks, but when I told Mackenzie he ordered them to be sent out by first train.[154]   Had a great deal to do, but got through all, & the Comd started half hour ahead of time.   I went up to post to see Mc & write letters to Mother & Julia.   Finished & caught Comd just as[155] it was about to pass the camping place.

7 miles –

May 18. Washington Springs, 5 Miles from Alamosa

Broke camp 6.20 am.   Part of my Comd. paid yesterday so I had lots of drunkards <yesterday>, & Vance on rear guard had a hard time. He is a weak man anyhow.[156]   Today there are many big heads, but all are so much improved that the rear guard was up promply with the wagons   Beautiful day, but very warm, tho' the spring brook on which we are camped was frozen this am   Our route is through – across – the San Louis Park, & a dreary monotonous waste of sand & sage brush[157]   These Springs are a feature.   They are Artesian.[158] The water from some high elevation finds outlet here, & <the> in course of time has thrown out mud & sand enough to build elevations higher than the general level from the top of which the springs break out.   Some of my miserable drunkards who left at Wellington came up this p.m. –   How they got along the R Rs is a mystery.   I hoped I had lost them.   Seven others deserted last night.   Our pay system is a premium on desertion[159]   Distance 13 miles.

About 5 pm freight train came by, bringing wood & hay.   Keeling came in it also –[160]   Lt Hay went to town, with telegram to Mackenzie

154. The first pack train.
155. Dodge wrote "at," probably anticipating the next word.
156. Captain Duncan M. Vance, who commanded Company G, Sixteenth Infantry, had participated in the pursuit of the Northern Cheyennes in 1878.
157. The command was passing almost due north through the San Luis Valley to Saguache, sixty miles north from Alamosa, where it would turn northwest to the Cochetopa hills.
158. Dodge followed "Artesian" with a comma.
159. Dodge refers to the practice of paying soldiers at long intervals, encouraging them to binge when flush with cash and then abscond.
160. The reason for Henry C. Keeling's presence with the command has not been established. Possibly he anticipated a business opportunity as authorized trader for troops stationed in the Uncompaghre Valley.

He sent back an orderly with notice that wood & hay were to be delivered to me as I pass Alamosa tomorro.   Sent orderly back notifying him that I can not take it.

Miserable sand camp.   If there had been wind we would have suffered.   It is a good omen that the wind has stopped for us here

Wednesday, May 19, 1880. Jackson's Ranche

My 53d Birth day - & by no means a hilarious one, but not unpleasant.   Broke Camp 6.20 am.   Took ambulance & went into town (Alamosa) bought some necessaries, saw Dorst,[161] about the wood & hay I used yesterday.   He says it's all right.   River very high.[162] Quite a business little town with many good stores.   Bought all I needed.   Joined Comd before it passed.   Camped at Jacksons - short march - 11 miles

May 20, 1880. Franklin's

Broke Camp 6.20 am.   Road pretty good, & no incidents - Made a short march to last water.   From here there is no water to Lagarata[163] - 20 miles.

Mackenzie overtook me here while looking for camp.   He was in a pettish humor, & pitched into me for allowing too many men to ride on the wagons.   I told him that I was perfectly loyal to my Comdg Offr, that I would do everything exactly as he wished, as long as I could conscienciously do so, & when he wanted me to do that which I believed to be wrong, I would apply to be relieved.   That he is the responsible man, & I will do all I can to help him.   He went off in a good humor.

161. First Lieutenant Joseph H. Dorst, Fourth Cavalry, was regimental adjutant and Colonel Mackenzie's adjutant for the Fort Garland Column.

162. The Rio Grande river, in its spring flood.

163. Dodge misspells La Garita Creek, which flowed southeast into the San Luis Valley.

I have issued some orders about riding on wagons, carrying arms &c,[164] & will make the Off Day[165] hold "the boys" up a little stronger. Our mail passed us today in the stage directed to Saguache – so we are again disappointed & must wait two days more.   Some men went fishing in Rio Grande.   One trout caught 1/2 lb.   River too high Distance 10 miles – weather good.

Friday, May 21, 1880. Bedell's Ranche, Lagarita Creek
Broke camp 5.15 am.   Road excellent, but we had to make 19 miles without water.   The Lagarata a nice creek.   Many Ranches – bottoms all fenced in & no good camping places.[166]   Mr Bedell a rich & hospitable man, gave me a field to camp in.   Also got from him wood & some straw.   Hay not to be had.   Soon after Comd got to camp Mr. B. came down & invited me to his house which is the most comfortable & best furnished I have seen on the trip.   Filled Hay & I up with beer, & invited us to dinner but we had just lunched.   About

                                   a
3 pm there came up <one> ∧ furious wind & dust storm.   A great many tents were blown down.   Mine withstood the blast, but was so filled with dust, that one could scarcely see anything.   It lasted until after 5 pm   Now all is calm & peaceful –

Got a man with measels.   Ordered Hospl steward to take him to Rose Camp in ambulance tomorro.[167]   Beaumont passed us about 2 pm – went into camp on Carneros – 4 miles beyond.[168]   Pack mule

164. Order 5 from Infantry Headquarters, dated May 20, prohibited men other than the sergeant major, the headquarters clerk, and the company cooks from riding on the wagons unless by authority from the commanding officer, the battalion commanders, or one of the two surgeons (Fort Garland Column—DMO).

165. Officer of the Day.

166. William E. Pabor wrote in 1883 of the La Garita district: "No new settlements are likely to be made on this creek, the land bordering on either side being taken up" (*Colorado as an Agricultural State*, p. 127).

167. Hospital Steward Ralph Wood, the man with measles, was being transported for isolation to a supply camp established at Cochetopa Pass, northwest of Saguache, by Captain Thomas E. Rose, Sixteenth Infantry, Dodge's traveling companion on the trip to Fort Sill in 1878 (Order 6, May 21, Fort Garland Column—DMO).

168. Major Eugene B. Beaumont, Fourth Cavalry, commanded a battalion. Carnero Creek was another stream flowing southeast into the San Luis Valley.

train also along camped in next field.   Men badly used up today by the long march without water.   Mr Bedell gave me a sack of potatoes. This is a fine agricultural country[169] – also a great mining country.

Distance 23 miles

May 22. Russell Springs

Broke Camp 6.15 am   Called on Mr Beadell to thank him & wife for their kindness, & to bid good by.   Men somewhat used up by yesterdays march.   Took it easy today.   Good road & several streams of water.   Camped here at 11. am.   Good water – & bought wood and hay – very good camp.   Ben Clark came by en route to visit Mackenzie.   No news.   Pleasant day.

Distance 13 miles –

Sunday, May 23. Near Saguache (pronounced Siwatch)[170]

Broke camp 6.10.   Rode in in ambulance   Arrived town 7.30. Got mail – Letter from James[171] – Mother improving   No letter from Julia or Fred.   Bought many things.   Comd. arrived 9.50.   Rode out ahead & selected camp 2 miles from town   Beautiful Camp.   Went fishing.   Got 3 trout – Wrote to Mother Julia & Clarke[172] at night.

Distance 10 1/2 miles

Sunday, May 24. Upper Crossing, Saguache Creek

Broke Camp 6 am.   Good road & marching except the wind which blew directly in mens faces carrying great clouds of dust, making it altogether the worst day we have had.   I arrived in Camp 11 am

169. Pabor wrote that Saguache County had more acres in cultivation than any other county in southwestern Colorado, with twenty-five hundred farms on 150,000 acres of arable, pasture, and meadow lands (*Colorado as an Agricultural State*, p. 125).

170. Crofutt wrote: "(Pronounced Ci-wach)." He described the town as one of about six hundred inhabitants, built chiefly of adobe or log structures but with "a few good brick and stone buildings for business purposes." Hay was hauled from here to the mining towns, but the principal occupation of local residents was sheep and cattle raising (*Crofutt's Grip-Sack Guide to Colorado*, p. 138).

171. James Dodge Glenn (1852–1892), a son of Dodge's sister Annie.

172. First Lieutenant William L. Clarke had remained at Cantonment as post quartermaster and commissary of subsistence.

found Cavy Sergt with hay.   Tried fishing.   Could'nt get a bite –
hardly stand up for wind.   Comd. arrived 1 pm   Good camp.   Met
Paymaster

Distance 17 miles.

May 25, 1880. Cochetopa Pass

Courier from Mackenzie last night.   In accordance with my
request he authorized me to remain over one day either at Creek
or at Pass.[173]   Creek very tempting – nice camp &c but I have
numbers of barefooted mules, & so moved to this place to have
them shod.

Arrived at Mc's Camp 8.30 – had satisfactory talk with him – got
all arranged to suit me.   Beaumont & Cavalry leave tomorro, I next
day.   Visited Rose's Cantonment.   He has done a deal of work, but
not in as ship shape a manner as I like –   Quite busy today.   Mac
has kept me going with all sorts of orders.   Took McMinn my
orderly.   I took OBrien in his place, & got another man on Hd Qr
guard[174]

Very cold.   Our Camp is 10,000 feet above the sea   Snow last
night, & last winters snows not yet all gone about us   We have been
constantly on the move 19 days without a rest or break.   Tomorro is
our first days rest – & with it will close what I consider the first
chapter of this expedition –

Scenery today very wild & beautiful – roads very bad.

Distance 8 miles.

Had a glorious hot bath, & for the first time a stove in my tent –

173. Writing from Camp at Cochetopa Pass—Captain Rose's supply camp—First
Lieutenant Dorst conveyed the authorization Dodge had requested. His command
was to move early on May 26 and camp that night "some miles beyond this place"
(Fort Garland Column LR—DMO).

174. Dodge's orderly since he had left Cantonment was Private Robert McMinn,
Company A, Twenty-third Infantry. Private William O'Brien, also of Company A, was
his substitute. Dodge's headquarters guard consisted of Corporal John Janson,
Company C, Twenty-third Infantry, and two privates from each of the three infantry
battalions (Orders and Circulars, Fort Garland Column—DMO).

May 26. Cochetopa Pass

Walked up to Rose Camp.   Mackenzie had gone taken the Sub-[sisten]ce. Dept with him & my Officers have no supplies.   Wrote to Wife & Mother – at night wrote to Cop.[175]   Nothing new – pleasant day but cool –

———————————————————[176]

175. Major John J. Coppinger, at Fort Leavenworth.

176. Except as noted here, the remainder of the journal is written with the notebook in reversed position, beginning with p. [60V] and ending with p. [56R]. On p. [60V] Dodge drew a simple map that shows a trail or roadway and another perpendicular to it labeled "Trains." Also on this page are three sums—one showing a total distance of 120 miles from Cantonment to Wellington, the second, 112 1/2 miles from Fort Garland to Cochetopa, and the third, written with the notebook right-side-up, 92 miles from Cochetopa to "Agency." At the bottom of this page, also right-side-up, are the following: "<Hat>, <gloves – cuffs> with Gorm[?]."

On p. [60R] Dodge summarized "Bag of trip Jany" and "Bag of Feby," both lists referring to activities earlier in 1880. On p. [59V] he wrote memoranda of supplies to be purchased and of arrangements with Lieutenant Pardee for transportation. Two shopping lists, one with the heading "Personal" and the other "For Laura," occupy pp. [59R] and [58V]; the latter page also includes brief notes of information from Pardee about lumber illegally obtained in Indian Territory. On pages [58R] and [57V] Dodge wrote lists of topics for treatment in his work-in-progress about Indians. Pages [57R] and [56V] are blank. The following sentence, evidently a thought for inclusion in the manuscript about Indians, is on p. [56R]: "While we wisely separate Church from State in the administration of our own affairs, we are so inconsistent as to unite them for the administration of the affairs of the Indian."

Commentary on Journal Eight
The Mission of Colonel Mackenzie

DODGE'S JOURNAL ACCOUNT OF THE 1880 SUMMER campaign ends with the entry of May 26, six days before he and his command reached the site on the Uncompahgre River near Los Pinos agency that became the base of operations for the Fort Garland Column. Marching in advance of the infantry and supply train, Colonel Ranald Mackenzie had selected the position three days before, and through his adjutant he urged Dodge to complete the journey as rapidly as possible without injury to the troops.[1] Despite the distance between his battalion and the three under Dodge, Mackenzie dispatched to the rear a series of directives that revealed his careful concern with details then under his subordinate's immediate oversight. At Cochetopa Pass, Dodge was enjoined again not to permit his men to ride on the wagons. The next day he was instructed to ensure that his units kept close together on the march so as not to be separated in the unlikely event of an attack.[2] Moving his troops and escorting a hundred-man pack train with wagons that carried two Hotchkiss machine guns and tons of supplies over a primitive road was a demanding task in itself, not made easier by his commander's micromanagement. Mackenzie seemed to regard the entire operation as his own property.

Of course, as commander of the column Mackenzie did bear responsibility for its proper conduct. He took the mission seriously and, as

1. AAAG to RID, May 27, 1880 (Fort Garland Column LR—DMO); *ANJ*, June 12, 1880, p. 917. A statement of Dodge's daily marches from Cochetopa Pass to the supply camp is in Twenty-third Infantry Regimental Returns, May and June, 1880.
2. AAAG to RID, May 27 and 28, 1880 (Fort Garland Column LR—DMO); Order 9, May 28, Headquarters Infantry Battalions (Fort Garland Column—DMO).

Dodge had divined, personally. The assurance Dodge gave on May 20 that "he is the responsible man, & I will do all I can to help him" was just the message needed to ease Mackenzie away from his nervous fault-finding and into better humor. Although not yet forty years of age, this intense young officer was ambitious to win a general's star.[3] The success of the Fort Garland Column would be a further step in that direction.

Since his arrival at Fort Garland in October 1879, Mackenzie had chafed at the long delay in his being authorized to take the field. Wintering at an obscure, remote post like Fort Garland seemed to him a slight toward an officer of his rank, and he complained bitterly of it to General Pope's aide-de-camp.[4] He needed a pack train to be kept ready for service during the winter months, but Pope did not supply it; instead, he sent two companies of infantry that had not been asked for. Mackenzie objected, and at length he ruffled his departmental commander by appealing to General Sheridan for his preemptive assistance.[5] Focusing on the task before him, Mackenzie tended to discount the requirements of officers elsewhere. For example, he wished to make use of General Crook's chief civilian packer, Tom Moore, and his corps of men and animals. Crook was the Army's foremost advocate of pack mule transportation, but he was also a department commander fully occupied with the military needs of his own region. He responded tersely to an inquiry from Sheridan, observing that he had been training these men for twelve years and could not spare them now.[6] Mackenzie called for one hundred Indian

3. Mackenzie is the subject of three modern biographies: Nohl, "Bad Hand"; Pierce, *The Most Promising Young Officer*; and Robinson, *Bad Hand*.

4. Pierce, *The Most Promising Young Officer*, p. 206; Robinson, *Bad Hand*, p. 267.

5. Pope to Sheridan, October 30 and October 31, 1879; Mackenzie to AAG DMO, October 30, 1879; Pope to AAG MDM, November 5, 1879; Pope to Sheridan, November 7, 1879 (MDM Ute Campaign Special File); Sherman to Pope, January 13, 1880 (AGO LS).

6. Crook to Sheridan, November 30, 1879 (MDM Ute Campaign Special File). Crook was willing to have his men organize Mackenzie's pack train but not to be absent "for any time."

scouts, preferably to be organized under Captain George Randall, but neither was this a practicable suggestion.[7]

Restive and disposed to find fault with those who questioned his views or failed to comply with his wishes, Mackenzie gave offense to several of his superiors during the early months of 1880. In February the adjutant general objected to Mackenzie's complaint about recruits to be sent to Colorado, observing "this is not the first time in which that officer has presumed to arraign the action of this office upon his assumption of facts that do not exist."[8] Mackenzie nettled even the General of the Army. On March 17 Sherman instructed his adjutant to inform the young colonel that he himself gave attention to the assignment of all available recruits "and considers himself a better judge of the wants and necessities of each Regiment, and of each locality, than Col. Mackenzie can possibly be."[9] In his relations with other officers, Mackenzie could be a severe test of patience. His prospects for promotion would have been severely dimmed by his pertinacious presumption, except that his views on most military questions were sound and his performance in the field consistently superior.

The authorization to march from Fort Garland with a well equipped force of some seven hundred men was to Mackenzie both a relief and an anxious responsibility. For a time he remained intensely critical of Dodge,[10] but once he relented, the two officers worked well together. Early in the summer he had placed his second-in-command in an anomalous position. Although technically the infantry battalions formed a command under Dodge, Mackenzie authorized the three battalion commanders to issue orders to their units independently of Dodge's controlling oversight. On June 23 he amended this policy,

7. Mackenzie to AAG DMO, October 30, 1879 (MDM Ute Campaign Special File).
8. AG to Pope, February 19, 1880 (AGO LS).
9. AG to Pope, March 17, 1880 (AGO LS). Nohl points out that, whatever justification Mackenzie imagined he had for complaints about recruits, by June 30 his regiment had gained 313, far more than any other mounted unit ("Bad Hand," pp. 268–69).
10. The reasons for Mackenzie's disapproval are uncertain. In a journal entry for September 3, Dodge remarks only that early in the campaign Mackenzie was "down on" him.

Ranald S. Mackenzie (Western History Collections, University of Oklahoma Libraries)

ordering Dodge to assume direct command of the three organizations that earlier had been only nominally his.[11] That delegation of authority left Mackenzie more free to range away from camp, as he had orders to do. Even so, he was hard pressed for ways to pass the time. Late in June he wrote to Pope that the campaign thus far had consisted only of "quiet uneventful weeks"—almost as quiet as the time he had been forced to endure while waiting idle at Fort Garland.[12]

Although Mackenzie expected much from his troops and was not tolerant of failure to meet his standards, many officers and men were proud to accept the rigors of enrollment in what one soldier called the "McKinzie regiment."[13] On the other hand, the temptation to dispense with the discipline he imposed could be strong, especially among soldiers who could desert with little risk of capture and find employment at a good wage in mining camps and towns not many miles distant. The high desertion rate of the Fort Garland Column soon became a cause for concern. Early in July Dodge requested of the adjutant general that one hundred recruits be sent to the column.[14]

Recruits were not alone in receiving Mackenzie's correction; even the battalion commanders could be punished for behavior that other commanders might consider as cause for no more than a caution or rebuke.[15] One such incident concerned the order of June 23, by which battalion commanders retained command authority only in matters of drill and discipline, produced a demonstration both of his diplomacy

11. Order 19, June 23, 1880, Headquarters Infantry Column (Fort Garland Column—DMO).

12. Mackenzie to Pope, June 29, 1880 (Nohl, "Bad Hand," p. 272).

13. Wallace E. Bingham, "Early Days on the Frontier" (Don Rickey Papers, USAMHI). Bingham had enlisted at Cantonment on April 23, 1880; he was assigned to Company C.

14. RID to AG, June 27, 1880 (Fort Garland Column LS—DMO).

15. For example, Mackenzie referred to Dodge for review as a possible court-martial case an incident wherein an enlisted man, Private Berryman of Company C, Twenty-third Infantry, had refused to obey the orders of his sergeant. Dodge investigated, and on July 23 he reported that the man had been assigned to a detail installing poles for a telegraph line. His refusal to climb out onto a pole was not the result of insubordination but of simple fear. Dodge recommended that the man be "restored to duty without trial," which was done (Endorsement, Fort Garland Column LS and Register LR—DMO).

and of his unwillingness to tolerate insubordination. On that day Dodge's adjutant returned unapproved to First Lieutenant George K. Spencer, Nineteenth Infantry, a request that a certain private be relieved from duty in the quartermaster's department. Spencer's battalion commander, Major Offley, had approved the request, but Dodge directed that "a more specific reason" for the desired transfer be stated. In response, Spencer simply reiterated the request, observing that it had received his battalion commander's approval. On learning of this, Mackenzie replied to Spencer with wry reserve: "Taking the fact of the return of this paper to Lt. Spencer by his superior, Lt. Col. Dodge, the Commanding Officer is somewhat surprised that Lt. Spencer should have deemed it judicious on no better ground to renew his request. The Commanding Officer of the Column regrets to feel obliged to express the opinion that such course was not very well advised."[16]

Now comprehending that the published change of command structure was to be observed in practice, Major Offley requested that the order of June 23 be modified to leave him in command of his battalion or else that he be relieved from duty with the Fort Garland Column. Mackenzie replied through his adjutant, now in a less forbearing tone. Pointing out that the order Offley disliked had been promulgated by him after consultation between himself and Dodge, he considered that "under the circumstances, Major Offley's request to be relieved from his command, [was] very improper."[17] Presently it became known that Offley had protested the June 23 order in a letter to the commander of his own regiment, Colonel Charles H. Smith at Fort Leavenworth. When Mackenzie learned that an officer under his authority had communicated to his superior on a military matter without directing his statement through the proper military channels, he at once had Offley placed under arrest. In response to an appeal from Offley to

16. Endorsements, Spencer to AAAG, June 23, 1880 (Fort Garland Column LR—DMO). The heavy irony of this statement is easily accounted for. Only weeks earlier, First Lieutenant Spencer had been court-martialed at Fort Garland and judged guilty of conduct to the prejudice of good order and military discipline. See *ANJ*, May 29, 1880, p. 876.

17. Offley to AAAG, June 25, 1880; AAAG to Offley, June 26, 1880 (Fort Garland Column LS and Register LR—DMO).

talk over the matter in person, the adjutant of the column replied that since his offense could be considered conduct to the prejudice of good order and military discipline—a cause for trial by court-martial—communications on the subject had best be confined to writing. Still under arrest, Offley now made a lame attempt to characterize his letter to Colonel Smith as not a protest but "simply a request." After one more day of confinement, he was permitted to return to duty with a rebuke for "mischief making."[18] Thereafter the records of the Fort Garland Column reveal no further questioning of the commanding officer's arrangements.

Dodge's duties during the summer were of the sort that he had anticipated. Much of the construction work he oversaw was road building, essential to permit communication between the three posts General Pope thought necessary to minimize the threat of violence in the coming years.[19] Additionally, he took command of the column during Mackenzie's absences on patrol or on missions in search of a post site. After a thorough reconnaissance, Mackenzie decided that the best possible location for the cantonment and future post was the one now occupied by the supply camp. Thus on July 21 the site was designated Cantonment on the Uncompahgre, and construction was begun shortly thereafter, under First Lieutenant Calvin D. Cowles.[20] Two additional camps were established during the summer, one for the cavalry, on the Uncompahgre River seventeen miles north of Dodge's,

18. Offley to AAAG, July 9; AAAG to Offley, July 10; Offley to AAAG, July 10; AAAG to Offley, July 11, 1880 (Fort Garland Column LS and Register LR—DMO).

19. Pope favored a post on the La Plata River to the south, a second on the Uncompaghre River near the Los Pinos Agency, and a third adjacent to the White River agency. He asked an appropriation of fifty thousand dollars for road construction (Pope to AG, May 15, 1880—AGO LR; House, *Report of the Secretary of War* (1880), pp. 91–92).

20. On August 9 Cowles was named acting quartermaster and commissary of subsistence of the supply camp in the absence of Lieutenant Charles Hay, who was under subpoena to appear as a witness before a general court-martial. On August 30, Major J. S. Fletcher, Twenty-third Infantry, was designated post commander of Cantonment on the Uncompaghre, and from that time the work of construction was his responsibility (Order 49, August 9; Order 67, August 30—Fort Garland Column, DMO). See also Frazer, *Forts of the West*, p. 36.

the other for infantry and cavalry at Roubideaux's Crossing on the Gunnison River.

Congress having ratified on June 15 a modification of the proposed agreement between representatives of the confederated Ute bands and the Department of the Interior, a few days later five commissioners appointed by the president received their instructions from Secretary Schurz.[21] Their primary responsibility was to obtain in Colorado the signatures of three-fourths of the adult male Ute Indians, indicating acceptance of the treaty's terms. This was a challenging task, both because the treaty provided for displacement of one band from its ancestral home and relocation of another on farming lands yet to be specified, and also because of the physical difficulties involved. In order to seek out the widely separated members of the tribe, the commissioners would need to pass over many miles of forbidding mountain terrain. A military escort would be imperative, and accordingly arrangements were made for troops and supplies from the Fort Garland Column to be made available to members of the Ute Commission. On June 29 Agent William Berry of the Los Pinos agency received notice that the commissioners hoped to meet with the Uncompahgre Utes there on their first official stop. This was prudent, since the home of Ouray, the chief of the Uncompahgres, was only a mile from the agency and within three miles of the Army's supply camp. It was thought that Ouray, who held more authority among the tribal bands than any other Ute, would be able to sway his dubious tribespeople toward ratification and so help smooth the process from the beginning. On July 8 the commissioners reached the agency, and on July 21 they held their first council, which was attended by a large number of Uncompahgre and some White River Utes. The lengthy proceedings were orderly, but it was clear that some Indians were not ready to sign the instrument and that others remained firmly opposed. Nevertheless, thanks in part to the influence of Ouray, by July 31 a total of 145 persons had given written consent to the treaty, an encouraging first step.

21. The commissioners were John B. Bowman, George W. Manypenny, Alfred B. Meacham, Otto Mears, and John J. Russell.

Mackenzie had been impressed by the Uncompahgre Utes, for their civility and also their prosperity. Although in private he referred to commission members like George W. Manypenny and Alfred B. Meacham as "chronic commissioners" and did not appreciate their staunch opposition to Army involvement in Indian affairs,[22] Mackenzie did his part to facilitate the meetings between Indians and commissioners. However, he played no part in the formal councils. Given to understand that the presence of his cavalry troops might frighten the Indians and disrupt the proceedings, on July 24 he rode north on a long patrol, crossing the Gunnison River and passing over Grand Mesa to Buzzard's Creek, within fifty miles of the White River column of army troops. After making contact with the garrison there, he and his men returned across the range and scouted eastward for several days across the plateau above the Gunnison River. They arrived back at Camp on the Uncompahgre on August 8, having promoted the present effort to make peace with the Utes by their timely absence.[23]

The Ute Commissioners wished next to travel across country to the Southern Ute agency on the Animas River, approximately sixty miles due south from Los Pinos but accessible to them only by wagon roads over circuitous, sometimes precipitous former Indian trails that made the actual distance much greater. Dodge directed his quartermaster to issue the necessary provisions and supplies and named as escort Captain Otis Pollock's Company C, Twenty-third Infantry. In view of the still unstable state of relations between the United States government and the Indians, one hundred rounds of ammunition were issued each soldier in addition to those he carried on his person. For transportation, the infantry company received two wagons, each pulled by a six-mule team. The commissioners were provided a four-horse ambulance, a large Dougherty wagon, and two six-mule teams, with two hospital tents for use as temporary residences.[24] The caravan left Los Pinos agency on Tuesday, August 3.

22. Mackenzie to AAG MDM, May 21, 1880 (Nohl, "Bad Hand," p. 271).
23. "Indian Affairs," *ANJ*, July 24, 1880, p. 1048; August 28, 1880, p. 61.
24. Order 44, July 31, 1880 (Fort Garland Column—DMO).

On their journey the commissioners and their escort encountered no hostile Indians, but the mountain travel was a daunting enterprise nonetheless. Twelve days of intense effort were required to pass over 130 miles of terrain. Unable to pass over the San Juan Mountains using wagons, the party instead moved first eastward to the Lake Fork of the Gunnison River, then south up that stream to its head and over Engineer Mountain, and finally southeast to its destination. Ten mules were required to pull each wagon to the highest point along the trail, which was well above timberline, and one morning the soldiers awoke to find seven inches of snow covering their blankets.[25] Three days after the commissioners reached the Southern Ute agency, Ouray and a few of his subchiefs also arrived, intending to assist in the next round of meetings.

The effort to persuade the Indians to ratify an agreement that would deprive most of them of their reservation lands had now reached a delicate stage. At a preliminary meeting between the commissioners and 123 members of the Weenimuche, Muache, and Capote bands, a Weenimuche chief named Alahandra arose and delivered a powerful speech against ratification. His opinions were neither affirmed nor opposed by the others, but it was decided to adjourn the meeting and reconvene three days later, after the several parties had taken time to confer. The next meeting, on August 23, was not promising. After long discussion, the Weenimuche Utes declared that they were not inclined to accept the proposed terms, and representatives of the other bands remained silent. The success of the commission hung in the balance. Ouray, who enjoyed the respect of his tribesmen and also of the government officials, was gravely ill and all but unable to sway the result. On the morning of August 24, the day agreed upon for resumption of talks, Ouray died, and the effect was electric. The Indian tipis ranged along the river were struck at once, and as the commissioners later reported, their occupants dispersed "as from a pestilence."[26]

25. Bingham, "Early Days on the Frontier" (Don Rickey Papers, USAMHI).
26. "Report of the Ute Commission" in House, *Report of the Commissioner of Indian Affairs* (1880), p. 261.

Two days later only eight headmen met with the Ute Commissioners in the grove near their camp. In response to an invitation to sign the agreement, they were unwilling. Ignatio, head of the Weenimuche band, submitted that the tribe had already done all that could be asked. They had given up the mountains in which the valuable minerals were located, but they wished to retain what was left of their country. The meeting was then adjourned. On the following morning, August 27, the commissioners notified Pollock that they desired to move beyond the lines of the reservation for a few days to await events. Evidently their efforts had reached an impasse. However, about noon that day about seventy-five Utes rode into camp in a body and requested a council session at once. Ignatio, cautioning that he hoped the commissioners would be careful to ensure that the government kept its word, announced that he and his companions had come to sign the agreement. They then stepped forward and made their marks on the documents, and by the next morning fifty-nine more men had done the same. A breakthrough had occurred, and implementation of the pact now seemed a likelihood. A census of the adult male population of the Utes yet remained to be completed, but by September 25 the commissioners were satisfied that the 581 names by then affixed to the document exceeded the necessary number. In a rare instance of cooperation between representatives of the Department of the Interior and the Army, the Ute Commission had accomplished its difficult task. In their report to Secretary Schurz, the members gratefully acknowledged the "important and courteous aid give us by gentlemen of the Army."[27]

Miles away from this quiet drama, at the supply camp, Dodge had enjoyed time to spare from his official duties, which he put to use in hunting, fishing, and other diversions. He forwarded to Spencer Baird of the Smithsonian Institution a collection of unusual mountain herbs and flowers.[28] He had often chatted with Agent Berry or with Ouray, at whose home he was a welcome guest. From Chipeta, Ouray's wife,

27. "Report of the Ute Commission," p. 264.
28. Baird to RID, October 25, 1880 (Dodge Papers, Graff Collection).

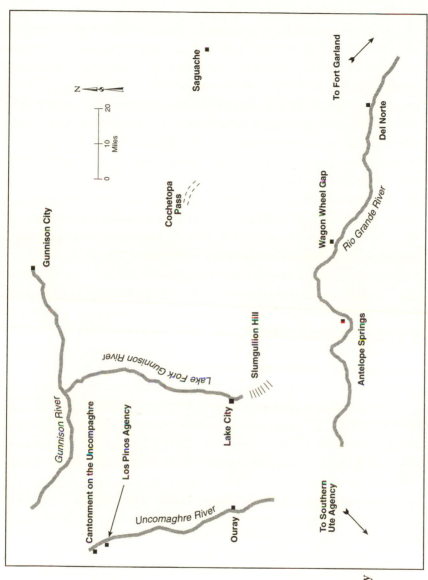

Region of
military activity
in southwest
Colorado,
summer 1880

he obtained a water jar made of grass, and from other Indians he purchased or was given other examples of Ute handcraft.[29] Exploring the vicinity of his camp, he came upon a Ute campsite where a death had recently occurred and examined closely the evidence it contained of the Indians' beliefs and funerary customs.[30] Given Dodge's long-standing interest in Indian culture, his residence near the Utes was a feast of opportunity to broaden his knowledge. Conversations with fellow officers yielded further insight. From Captain Pollock he received a thorough written account of Ouray's death, funeral, and—so far as the Utes' strict secrecy would permit—his burial. Dodge himself observed the remarkable manner in which information about the Uncompahgre chief's deteriorating condition somehow made its way almost instantaneously to the Los Pinos agency. He was on hand to see the dramatic response at the agency to the news of the chief's death.[31]

Jottings at the end of Dodge's journal made on the march to Cochetopa Pass indicate that he was then considering further work on his book about Indians and the frontier. During the summer of 1880 this ongoing project became a major outlet for his spare energy. The Indians of the western plains and mountains and the impact upon them of contact with the government and its citizenry were topics he had come to know well and at first hand. The federal laws regulating Indian reservations were germane to the treatment he now had in mind, and accordingly for reference he requested from the adjutant general's office a copy of the *Revised Statutes*.[32] He planned also to supplement his earlier published discussion of Plains Indian culture with chapters on topics he had not dealt with before, including Indian pastimes such as music, dance, and hand games. Coincidentally, at the time of Ouray's death he was drafting a discussion of burial customs.[33]

29. OWI, pp. ix-xi, 264; *Annual Report of the Board of Regents of the Smithsonian Institution* (1881), p. 138; *Annual Report of the Board of Regents of the Smithsonian Institution* (1882), pp. 46, 239.

30. *OWI*, p. 163.

31. *OWI*, p. 175-76.

32. RID to AG, August 10, 1880 (AGO Register LR).

33. *OWI*, p. 167.

By August 6 the site of Cantonment on the Uncompahgre had been selected and the Ute commissioners sent on their way under care of Captain Pollock and his men. On that day Dodge addressed to his departmental headquarters a request that he be relieved immediately from duty with the Fort Garland Column. He did not specify a reason for his request, but he made clear that it was "entirely personal to myself, and in no way connected with my duty in the field," adding that it was known to both Mackenzie and General Pope.[34] The unstated purpose was truly a personal one: he wished to return to Cantonment in order to finish his book. This project continued to occupy him in the days that followed, but for almost three weeks he received no response to his letter. The arrival in camp of General Sheridan on August 23 may have accelerated the process of approval. Sheridan was on a tour of inspection, and though a stickler for tidiness and arrangements made by the book, he was well satisfied with what he saw in "Col. Dodge's camp."[35] Perhaps coincidentally, also on August 23 General Pope's adjutant directed the commanding officer at Fort Garland to notify Dodge that he was relieved from duty with the Fort Garland Column and ordered to take post at Cantonment.[36] On August 26 Sheridan and his party left the supply camp and proceeded downriver to the cavalry camp, where he reviewed Mackenzie's troops and was much impressed. Mackenzie once again had the satisfaction of witnessing his division commander's hearty approval.

The visit of Sheridan effectively concluded Mackenzie's contribution to the work of the Fort Garland Column. Construction of the cantonment was under way, and the five companies of Dodge's regiment that would garrison it through the winter should keep the region secure. Together with two companies of his regiment as escort, Mackenzie accompanied Sheridan and other dignitaries on a hunting

34. RID to AAG DMO, August 6, 1880 (Fort Garland LS—DMO). Pope visited the region early in August, but whether Dodge saw him at that time is uncertain.

35. *ANJ*, September 11, 1880, p. 83.

36. AAG DMO to C.O. Fort Garland, August 23, 1880 (Fort Garland Column LR—DMO). This message was not received at the supply camp until August 30. Dodge's relief from duty with the Fort Garland Column was made official by S.O. 185, August 24—DMO.

expedition that eventually took them to Gunnison City, where the general boarded a train for the east. After returning to Fort Garland and appearing later in September at a court of inquiry in Washington, D.C., Mackenzie spent the last months of the year in New York, where he took steps to enlist support for his promotion to brigadier general.[37]

During the summer of 1880 Mackenzie had played a useful if not glorious part in the government's effort to establish peace on the Colorado frontier. By maintaining a more than credible military presence and then absenting himself while the commissioners worked to secure an agreement with the Indians, he did all that could reasonably be expected of him. His success was of another sort than the performance in battle that had won him fame in the Red River War and later on the Powder River Expedition, but it was success nonetheless, demonstrating versatility and prudent tact. His erratic behavior and sometimes harsh treatment of subordinates had won him few friends, but at least he had not further alienated his superiors. Though long delayed and devoid of action against an enemy, the Ute Campaign had been for Mackenzie and the Army a costly but clear success.

For Mackenzie's second-in-command, the summer campaign had also been a good one. As commander of the infantry battalions, Dodge had encountered no real difficulty, and under his superintendency, wagon roads, post construction, and progress on a telegraph line were all well advanced. Five years earlier, while in command of the Army's escort to a geological exploration party in the Black Hills, he had described his physically challenging and diplomatically delicate assignment without irony as a "delightful summer."[38] Probably he would have said much the same of the summer now drawing to a close. If his

37. Nohl, "Bad Hand," pp. 275–77; Robinson, *Bad Hand*, pp. 270–73. Mackenzie was unsuccessful at this time, the next two persons promoted to brigadier general being Colonels William B. Hazen and Nelson A. Miles. However, on November 1, 1882, he was promoted to that rank, the highest he attained in his relatively short career.

38. *BHJ*, p. 26.

proximity to Mackenzie had necessitated circumspection and even on occasion swallowed retorts, the months in Colorado had offered many compensations, not the least of which was his progress on the new book. On September 1, accompanied by Joe, Laura, and their infant daughter Ida, Dodge set out with his escort on the return to Cantonment.

Journal Eight
September 1–23, 1880

Wednesday, September 1, 1880[1]

Everything ready on time & at about 7 am I pulled out on my way to Cantonment, with Lt Febiger 2 Sergts, 9 Pvts <&> 4 prisoners, – 2 ambulances, <6>5 escort wagons, & 3 six mule teams   I feel bigger than a Lt Genl for I have all his transpn & more.[2]   Bade good by to Webb & Hay, the only people up, & rode out with Cowles to the Post. He is doing excellently & if they dont worry him, will have the post built in a little while –[3]   Rode all day, to get myself in trim for fall work, and fished all afternoon so am pretty tired.   On the very top

---

1. This manuscript journal, manufactured by Reynolds and Reynolds of Dayton, Ohio, measures 3 11/16 by 6 11/16 inches and includes sixty unnumbered sheets. It consists of brown flexible cardboard covers at front and back, secured to the pages inside by a strip of tape at the top. Its first and last leaves, the endpapers, are of light blue, unlined laid paper. The inner leaves, of plain cream-colored paper, are lined horizontally in gray ink and vertically in red ink; the vertical lines are spaced to form columns as in a ledger. On the front cover Dodge has written in black ink an identification: "Ute Campaign [/] 1880." Below, in the hand of a person other than Dodge, is a notation in pencil: "Sept 1/ 80 to [/] Sept 23/ 1880." (In fact, the journal also includes an entry dated December 18, 1880.) Pages [1], [32V]–[58R], [59V], and [60V] are blank. Pages [58V] and [60R] include text written with the notebook in reversed position. The text begins on p. [2R].

2. Dodge implicitly compares himself to Lieutenant General Sheridan. His escort consisted of Sergeant John Janson, Company C, with a private from each of companies A, B, and E, Twenty-third Infantry. Second Lieutenant Lea Febiger, with another sergeant and four privates, had charge of four convicts being transported to the military prison at Fort Leavenworth. Febiger was to accompany Dodge as far as Fort Garland (Order 68, August 31—Fort Garland Column, DMO).

3. Although officially Major Fletcher had charge of constructing the post, as its quartermaster, First Lieutenant Calvin D. Cowles supervised the actual labor. Detachments of men had been at work cutting timber since August 14 (Order 54, August 14; Order 66, August 29; Order 67, August 30—Fort Garland Column, DMO).

of a mountain I met the stage.   I stopped the driver to tell him about my train, which he had to pass, & the road is in some places too narrow.   I had hardly spoken three words when there was a scream from the Stage, & a Lady called out to me by name, & excitedly raised her veil.   "Col Dodge, dont you know me[?]" –   I looked intently on a little woman nicely dressed & gloved, rather haggard, might be from age or hard travel.   I had never seen the face before.   "No,["] I said, ["]I don't know you.["]   "Don't you remember Rosa Keim?" she said, (Mrs. Dr. Hazzard) & I immediately tumbled off my horse & kissed her I have not seen her for 17 years,[4] & as when I saw her last she was a fresh budding girl of 15 I dont blame myself for not recognizing her.

Her husband – who was on the box, is a <merchant>   ^   Doctor in Ouray,[5] and she is going to live out there.

No other adventure.   Arrived at Clines about 2 pm.[6]   Crossed Cimarron & camped opposite to his house in a good camp.   Went out fishing, would not go far from camp being tired, & it threatening rain.   Cline told me that I could get but few here & told me where to go.   I fished just around his house – not two hundred yards away & got 16.   Mrs Cline showed me a very wonderful cactus, looks like a bundle of snakes.[7]   Cline gave me some radishes, lettuce <&c>& a fine cabbage.   The radishes are marvellous.   One weighed 2 1/2 lbs & was as hard firm & sweet as possible –   I went into his garden & was astonished.   This ranch is about 8000 feet, but he has all the hardy vegetables.   Radishes Beets, turnips parsnips & Cabbages, &

4. Between 1862 and 1864 Dodge had been on duty in central Pennsylvania, where he had contact with many prominent citizens, in all likelihood including the family of William High Keim (1813–1862), of Reading, a politician who served as a brigadier general of volunteers in the early months of the Civil War. Possibly the former Rosa Keim was a member of his family.

5. Dr. Hazard, of Philadelphia, owned a crusher at Ouray, Colorado, that concentrated ten tons of mineral ore into one, making possible a great saving in transportation for processing elsewhere (Crofutt, *Crofutt's Grip-Sack Guide to Colorado*, p. 128).

6. The ranch of M. W. Cline, at Cimarron Crossing, was twenty-six miles from Cantonment on the Uncompaghre, on the same road Mackenzie's command had passed over en route to the camp in late May.

7. Possibly a cholla.

splendid crop of rutabagas.[8]   His peas will not mature & tomatoes are already killed by frost.   Heavy snow on mountains south east of us, fell this evening.   Cold & raw.   To bed early.

Thursday, September 2, 1880

Spent half an hour at Clines before the train got off.   I like him very much & he has a real nice oldfashioned work-woman of a wife, who took quite a liking to me & at the last moment insisted on my taking half a dozen eggs as a parting present.   They were extremely hospitable & kind.   Cline was a captain of scouts in the Army of the Potomac during the War.   <The>After it was over he went to Chicago, & says he was brought away on a stretcher, with scarce half hours life in him.   He was dying with consumption, when he made up his mind to make one more effort for life, & came to Colorado.   He says he would not go "across the range" for any money   "Why Col[onel]" said he, "I am as strong & well as any man.   I can hunt, fish, work, ride, & enjoy life as much as any man, & I get it all by staying here.   I can wade the river all day for fish or trudge through the snow, equal to anybody.   Yet I was as good as dead"   His wife was also nearly dead & she said, "I was pretty nigh gone Col, but I am as well as ever now, & can do more work than any two women in Colorado" –[9]

We left Clines at 7 a.m.   The night had been cold & damp & in the morning all the high peaks in the vast ampitheatre of Mountains had a covering of snow, some not to doff it again until next July.   The air was cool, crisp & bracing, & I greatly enjoyed a brisk gallop of two or three miles, which I found necessary to settle my horse for the days

8. Cline's satisfaction with his crops raised in this mountain valley reflects the optimism about prospects for agriculture in the region encouraged by advocates like William E. Pabor. According to that author, the valleys of the Uncompaghre, Gunnison, and Grand Rivers "await the coming of those who shall make an apparent wilderness bloom and blossom as the rose" (*Colorado as an Agricultural State*, p. 204).

9. The testimonials of the Clines echoed contemporary promoters who portrayed the climate of the Colorado mountains as what one called "rigorous but healthful to the end" (Strahorn, *Gunnison and San Juan*, p. 40). According to Frank Fossett, "This region possesses influences that arrest the tendency to pulmonary disease. Consumptives who do not put off their coming too long have been cured effectively" (*Colorado*, p. 103).

steady gait.   He is a splendid animal walks & canters well, is gentle as a dog, but the most awful shyer I ever backed.   I think he can turn end for end in a road, quicker than any horse I ever saw.   I do not mind a shying horse ordinarily, & have never been unseated by one, but this rascale shies at the most inopportune moments, & without regard to position.   He once came very near going down the side of a mountain with me, where we could not have stopped short of 500 feet, & many times he has put his life & mine in jeopardy by his foolishness –   By dint of severe thrashing I have almost cured him, but my confidence is not sufficient to enable me to ride with perfect comfort, when a return of his "little vice" might send us 50 to 500 feet, & numberless such places occur in the road.

My pups have been a constant trouble, & today I determined to let them run & tire themselves out.   They ran, but did not tire worth a cent.   Just before arriving at Barnums[10] they flushed three black or dusky grouse.   I went after the birds got two & missed the third by a most shameful shot.   Came about 2 miles on the Lake City Road from Barnum – & went into camp.

Located Camp & then went fishing – & had one of the worst days luck I ever had.   Everything went wrong.   The fish would'nt bite, but came up & looked at the flies, & retired in disgust.   By dint of extra skill, I finally got bites, but continually lost my fish.   Sometimes they would go off with the hook at others I'd get them to the bank & they'd flop back.   I determined to work off the bad luck, & kept my temper.   Was rewarded at last by bagging ten – of from 1/4 to 1/2 lb each.   But the crowning piece of bad luck came.   I let my flies float down under thick branches of bushes to a deep pool.   I saw a monster, near two feet in length come leisurely out.   He took my fly & I pulled – a quick flip & he went back taking the fly with him.   I was terribly disgusted sat down & put on another much stronger, let it slide down the same way.   He came out again took it & I pulled   A flirt, the line came back to me, & the fish went off, this time with my leader & two

10. A stage station on the Lake Fork of the Gunnison River, forty miles south of Gunnison City and twenty miles north of Lake City by post road.

flies.   Of course he would'nt come any more, & is probably by this time drowned –

My tackle is nearly all too old.   Most of my flies, I have had since the War, & though they appear as good as ever, they wont stand a big fish.   I had on my hook this afternoon at least 12 lbs of fish.   I brought to bag about 4 lbs.   I'll try to change this next time.   This is the finest trout stream I have ever seen – but the trout stay only in spots.   I happened to strike an extra good spot.

Am off the road by which Mackenzie might return to the Uncompagre, & feel better, as I feared he might interfere with me.[11]   Nice camp.   Ice in camp last night, & cold tonight.   Scared up a deer very close to camp, but he got away.   Ida quite sick.   Glorious fish supper & to bed almost as soon as dark.   About 24 miles today.

Friday, September 3, 1880

Got out of camp a little after 7 am.   Cold – ice plenty in camp, this am.   Road today very good considering the country, which is an extra difficult one.   The canon of Lake fork is a very curious one. There is no "bottom" to the Creek – that is no low lands on each side. From top to top of mountains on each side, <is>will average scarcely

three miles, & these summits are from <1 to 5000> ^ 1000 to 5000 feet above the water.   The bed of this huge gulch was sometime nearly level, and about 200 ft above the present bed of the stream.   Through this old bed the present stream has cut a channel, with almost perpendicular sides – indeed, they may with truth be called perpendicular for 4/5ths of the entire cañon is abrupt rock.   The road has to find its way through such difficulties as best it may, & though a good road it is certainly an excentric one – going up or down, east west north or south just as it pleases.   I did think of taking the ambulance and pushing in to Lake City but when I had gone over a few miles of the road, I preferred all the chances of a shying horse, to riding over it in

11. If Mackenzie traveled south on the post road from Gunnison City, in order to return to the supply camp he would turn west at Barnum's Station, a few miles north of Dodge's present position.

any vehicle.   Not that it is actually dangerous, but that it looks so, when cooped up in an ambulance, where any one can see that a refractory mule or losing of a linch pin might send the whole "outfit" tumbling two hundred feet into the Creek ——

Everything arrived without accident at Lake City a little after 12 m. It is a town of 1000 people, huddled into a small space given by the mountains which rise abruptly on every side - some far above timber line.   Unless the tenement house system is introduced, "the City" can never be a large one, the whole available building space, being scarcely sufficient for a closely packed city of 10,000 inhabitants   It is essentially a mining town   Everybody owns mines, everybody talks mines. There are a few pretty well built houses (none over 2 stories -) of wood & brick.   Saloons & cigar stores have the monopoly of numbers, & one would suppose of cash since the poorest 2 cent cigar, or glass of bad beer, is 25 cents.[12]

There are some well dressed people (tho'I find the best dressed are gamblers, & ————[)] & there are said to be some very wealthy & cultivated persons residing here.   I met Lee & Reynolds, who, since I interfered with them as "Kings of the Territory" have turned their attention to mining.[13]   It seems a very thriving busy town.   There are three smelters doing full business, & I saw some new Charcoal Pits

12. Crofutt described Lake City as "very pleasantly situated on the west bank of the river [the Lake Fork], beyond which the mountains rise, sloping to the height of about three thousand feet. The stranger visiting here will be surprised to see the great number of stores, hotels, livery stables, saloons, and shops of all kinds, all of which appear to be doing an unusual amount of business for the size of the place. The explanation can be found in the fact, that the city is located in the centre of a score or more of small mining camps, numbering all along up to 300 population each. These people . . . find it the best and most convenient place to purchase their supplies, spend their money, and sojourn for a season of recreation" (*Crofutt's Grip-Sack Guide to Colorado*, p. 114).

13. W. M. D. Lee and A. E. Reynolds had purchased mines near Lake City and Ouray that were to prove highly successful. The Belle of the West near Lake City, owned by Reynolds, became one of the great mines of the state (Hall, *History of the State of Colorado*, 3:549). After purchasing Lee's interest in the huge LE Ranch in Texas, in 1881, Reynolds and his brothers continued to operate the property until 1902, when they sold it in order to focus on their mining interests (Haywood, *Trails South*, pp. 123, 127).

(at least new to me) built of brick.   "Lake Fork" here divides – two beautiful streams uniting to form it, in neither of which can a trout be found, & no one knows why, for they say there were none before mining might have injured or tainted the water.   No grass, bought hay at 5. c. or $100 per ton for my animals.[14]

I had hardly got into Camp till Hugh Patton came up   Hugh was butcher at Fort Hays, & has followed me around ever since as Boon does. <but> When I was ordered on this campaign, he begged to come with me & I told him that if he <c>would drive a team I would give him one.   He took the team &, though I doubt if he ever drove before, made a pretty fair driver.   In the early part of the Campaign, when Mackenzie was "down on" me, he was also "down on" every body who he suspected of having a liking for me. All the teamsters that came with me, came in for a share of this – & Old Hugh got mad & quit.   Mackenzie acted like a pig to him, tried to keep him from getting his pay, (tho' Lawton was too just for that)[15] refused to let him accept a situation with Post Trader, who offered him $60 per month – refused to permit him to come back to camp with a load of vegetables after I had given him permission – in fact acted out a very contemptible nature.   So old Hugh in disgust came to Lake City, got a place on the very day of his arrival as butcher, at $65, & found everything.   Hugh is a most excellent & reliable man, a hard worker, & makes lots of money, but cant keep it.   It goes like water in every way, & I have abused him &, he says, effected a reformation.

Ida was very sick & I went after a Doctor.   High fever & nausea, vomiting – in short – indigestion.   At night I went up to town. (We are really right in the town for there are homes all around us) Hugh, I find is well liked & treated.   He took me around introduced

14. Five dollars per hundredweight or one hundred dollars per ton was an outrageous price for hay, but according to Robert E. Strahorn, it was only slightly above the going rate in 1881 in the Gunnison and Lake City district. Mining operations required the use of animals, and purchasers were glad to find hay at almost any price (*Gunnison and San Juan*, p. 36).

15. Captain Henry W. Lawton, quartermaster of the Fort Garland Column, in whose department Hugh Patton had been employed.

me to all his acquaintances & friends (some of the best people in town) & afterwards insisted on my going to the billiard room at the "American Hotel",[16] to beat the best player in town.   And by the by a singular confirmation of a dream comes in here.   Five days ago, I got my order from Mackenzie, & no one here could by any possibility have heard of it or of its likelihood.   Five nights ago Hugh dreamed that I was coming to Lake City, & was so convinced of it that next day he told everybody that I was coming, & arranged to beat[17] the best billiard player —   He told me that as soon as he heard that <we>soldiers had come he knew it was me, & came down at once to see me.

Well, I went to the billiard room tackled the marker,[18] who I was led to believe the best player.   In spite of my lack of practice, composition balls, small table & bad light from lamps, I "walloped" him four straight games   He gave it up & handed the cue to another man, who I afterwards discovered could beat the marker & give him a third.   As my games with the marker had been close, he thought he had an easy thing.   We played one, very tight, but I beat him   He proposed another, & the drinks on it.   Tight again but I beat him.   Then he proposed a third, which I told him would be my last as I had to start early.   I made <2>two bad miscues in the start of the game, so we stood his 20 to my nothing.   I felt sure he would beat me but I buckled myself to it, made two good runs, leaving me only one point to go.   He had but 3 to go, & playing safe left me what he thought an almost impossible shot.   I made it by cushion, & "busted" my evening to the delight of Hugh, & many spectators. So my evenings entertainment cost me nothing.   I was invited to a party, but was too lazy to dress for it, so declined   Febiger went & danced til morning almost.   Hugh came back to my tent with me, & in a most earnest way, asked me whom to vote for as President. He is a republican, but was in Hancocks Corps.   His principles

16. Crofutt names this as one of Lake City's two principal hotels, the other being the Occidental (*Crofutt's Grip-Sack Guide to Colorado*, p. 114).
17. Perhaps Dodge intended "meet."
18. The scorekeeper.

were about to be sacrificed to his loyalty to his Comdr but I settled him, & Garfield is stronger by one, than when I came to town.[19]

Saturday, September 4, 1880

I only took two drinks last night yet woke up with a big head, showing Lake City Whiskey to be bad – as might be expected   Ida very sick.   Had a spasm just after daybreak.   Joe went after the Dr. who said she is dangerously ill, & must not be moved today.   I am disgusted, but must care for the dear baby.   She is a great comfort to her "Grand-pap" & I would feel her loss, as severely as if she were my own child.

Sent Febiger off with all the train, except my wagons with directions to wait for me on Clear Creek,[20] where the fishing is good.   After the Drs visit I walked up town with him, & find that I would have done just right had I treated her myself.   He gave some aconite for the fever[21] & ordered an injection of starch & Laudanum.   The trouble with the baby is simply indigestion – (raw cabbage stalks & trash of all kinds, which, as Laura can eat herself, she gives to the baby) & she will not begin to get well until this is all out of her.   So I stopped the injection, & am giving Aconite & Mix,[22] to break the fever, & work off the stuff.   It is now near noon, & she is doing fairly well. I hope to have her all right by morning.

10 p.m.   The longest & most tiresome of long days.   After lunch I took a nap & when I had slept enough woke up to find it only 1 1/2 pm.   Read the newspapers, & loafed, attending to baby, who had

19. Dodge's reasons for supporting James A. Garfield in the coming presidential election are unknown, but his preference is not surprising. Though a respected military man, Major General Winfield Scott Hancock, commander of the Department of the East, was a relative novice in politics. Moreover, he was the candidate of the Democratic party, whose members in Congress had been stingy supporters of the Army. Hancock narrowly lost the election.

20. A stage station about twenty miles south of Lake City, over difficult mountain trails.

21. "The root or leaves of Aconitum Napellus. . . . As an internal remedy aconite is very valuable in sthenic fever from any cause. . . . May be administered in powder, extract, or tincture" (Wood and Bache, *Dispensatory*, p. 128).

22. The *Dispensatory* defined *mix* as "those preparations in which unsoluble substances whether solid or liquid, are suspended in watery fluids, by intervention of gum arabic, sugar, the yolk of eggs, or other viscid matter" (pp. 977–78).

several threatened convulsions, but we got her out of them by rubbing & mustard baths   The Dr. came down in the afternoon.   I told him very frankly that I had been using Homeopathic, Aconite & Mix & he told me he could do no better, and recommend[ed] me to continue. Gave her a starch & laudanum injection tonight at dark, & she has been sleeping nicely since, tho occasionally restless.

Went up town at dusk receipted for hay for my animals.   Found Hugh & went the rounds of all the billiard tables looking for an antagonist, but they had all heard of my beating the best man & I could find no one to fight.   Came back & went to bed – where I do this writing.

Sunday, September 5, 1880. Lake City, Colorado

Baby so much better this am that I determined to start.   When I came back last night she seemed to have arrived at that stage of the disease that her medecines ought to be changed.   I commenced with Mer. Cor.[23] – continuing the aconite.   Joe called me in the night & I found her without fever, but suffering from gripes.   Threw out the acon<y>ite and substituted Colycinth[?] in attenuation with the mercury.[24]   Got off late – got a dozen beer in town.   Bade good by to Hugh, & several others, & started.   Made a blunder at start by taking old, instead of new road – or rather by sending my wagons ahead of me, & they did it.   Sent O'Brien after & brought them back.

The common name of the *gentle* ascent by which the road rises from Lake City to the summit is "Slumgullion Hill."   I dont know the meaning of the term, but if it is a superlative of all hugeness the hill is rightly named –   Rising always sometimes gradually, sometimes,

23. Coriander was an aromatic "almost exclusively employed in combination with other medicines, either to cover their taste, or to correct their griping qualities" (Wood and Bache, *Dispensatory*, p. 508). Dodge administered it with mercury, "a powerful and universal stimulant" when used with other drugs, according to the *Dispensatory* (p. 793).

24. The *Dispensatory* described colocynth , the fruit of Citrullis Colocynthis, as a powerful cathartic, seldom prescribed alone. Dodge combined it with more mercury, which "in functional derangements of the digestive organs . . . in minute doses often exert[s] a salutary operation, by subverting the morbid action" (p. 793).

very abruptly, in ten miles it attains an altitude of nearly 12,000 feet – rising 3500 feet in that distance.

In all my experience of travel, I have seen no such ascent in same distance.   I rode up on horseback, & was delighted with the road, for though the grade was steep, the roadbed is excellent –

On the top of the mountain we struck the corduroy.   <f>For miles every foot is composed of poles laid down – sometimes one end on the side of the mountain & the other supported on a sort of bridge frame –[25]

It is a terribly tiresome road to ride over, & though I intended to go to Clear Creek, I had thought of the baby & stopped at Sevoya or White Earth – about 1<2>4 miles from Lake City, where I made a camp with excellent wood water & grass.   The Stage Station man told me that there were plenty of trout in the Sevoya, *below the falls*, about 3 miles below my camp.   I rode down near 4 miles without a sign of falls, & came back disgusted.   Ground Hogs, or wood chucks more plentiful than I have ever seen them elsewhere.   Killed 3, & might have killed lots —

Monday, September 6, 1880. Rio Grande River Near Antelope Springs

Baby still improving.   The dysentery greatly checked, & every indication of imp[rove]m[en]t.   I left Camp immediately after breakfast & came on to notify Febiger & the main train to be up & moving. Found it encamped about 1 1/2 miles east of Clear Ck Station.   They had had poor luck fishing.   Started them out & we all came on to Antelope Spgs.[26]   Found no grass, & came on 1 1/2 miles to the river

25. Slumgullion Mountain was named for bright yellow dirt on its northern face, which according to Crofutt, "seems to have no bottom" when wet and sticks to the footsoles like glue. The toll road over the mountain, completed in 1877, was celebrated locally as a feat of engineering. Crofutt reported that nine miles of it was "'corduroyed' with logs, *alternating*, from six to twenty inches in diameter. . . . The effect of riding over the road is much like walking backwards up stairs, and then sliding down with the feet slightly elevated" (*Crofutt's Grip-Sack Guide to Colorado*, p. 143).

26. An inn and post office one-half mile north of the Rio Grande River, at the junction of roads leading northwest to Lake City, west to Silverton, and east to Del Norte.

& encamped   A rain came on before we got our tents pitched & made it uncomfortable.   When baby was taken sick I gave Joe & Laura my tent & stove & I have been taking it all fresco since.   Last night our camp was over 10,000 feet above sea level tonight it is over 9,000.   Ice every night of course & so cold that a fire is a necessity – Last night I was so tired & cold, that I went to bed soon after sundown, but slept comfortably until daybreak – except that Laura waked me up 2 am to come & look at the baby who seemed worse. I gave her 2 drops laudanum, & we all went to sleep again.   Passed through some lovely scenery today   When I got to Febigers camp I ordered all out, & now we are all together again.   The Rio Grande here is about 60 feet wide shallow & quiet, not much appearance of a trout stream.   Febiger says Clear Ck is lovely but it is evidently fished out –

I was tired and took a nap   After the shower was over Feb went out fishing but came back without anything except a story of having seen some sage hens.   Gave him my gun & sent him back but he could'nt find them   I tried fishing for a few minutes.   They would not touch a fly, but one took a grasshopper off for me.   He would'nt try it again.   A man came to our camp who claimed to have taken 40 lbs (with 3 friends) yesterday.   He however had only 3 little ones to show for todays work –   Very nice ride & drive today.   The country south of the range is much better than north.

Distance 20 miles – good camp – plenty of grass.

Tuesday, September 7, 1880. Wagon Wheel Gap[27]

When I woke up this am the whole valley was filled with mist, & nothing could be seen but the surrounding mountains all yet bearing traces of yesterdays snow.   It snows or rains in these high altitudes, according to altitude.   While a lovely shower was falling in our camp, the same cloud was sending a snow storm on the peaks & summits

27. A summer resort on the Rio Grande River, twenty-nine miles west from Del Norte and sixty-nine from the railroad at Alamosa. It featured hot springs "of remarkable medicinial properties" (Crofutt, *Crofutt's Grip-Sack Guide to Colorado*, p. 152).

around us.   Query – Does'nt it all start from the cloud as snow, & melt on the way down?

I started early on horseback & got six or eight miles before the ambulance overtook me.   Got in & came on rapidly arriving at Wagon Wheel Gap about 10 1/2 am   Found Hale & Reynolds.[28]   They insisted so much on my stopping here that I agreed – especially as I found very good grass, & there were other attractions –   The man who keeps the ranch store & hotel on the river promised me a good fish.   Nice camp.

Went out fishing about 1 pm, & worked like a horse   Was broken in upon by a heavy shower, took refuge under a rock, & commenced fishing when it was over.   Took twenty fish.   The largest a beauty of 1 1/2 pounds – next a fine fellow of 3/4 lbs – then near a dozen of about 1/4 or less, & tailing off to the little ones.   Had a glorious day, though a bad one for fishing – east wind – & bad water.   I did excellently well for even the crack fishermen got nothing.   Febiger <&> Hale & Reynolds went up to the Hot Springs & came back at night enchanted with all.[29]   I would like to spend a few days here, but cant do it.   Baby still improving, but not yet well by any means.

Wednesday, September 8, 1880. Rio Grande River About Four Miles Above Del Norte

Started about usual hour   Went over to ranche - paid old man for beef & potatoes, & gave him the leader he loaned me.   Road good, but a little heavy from yesterdays rain, which came down while I was out fishing, but which I escaped by getting under a huge rock.   My horse behaved abominably today shying at everything & keeping me scared.   Shied at a dove, in a narrow road, one side a precipice above, the other a sheer fall of 100 feet into the river —   Rode him

28. Captain Clayton Hale, Sixteenth Infantry, was attached to the Fort Garland Column, as was Charles Reynolds, the post chaplain at Fort Riley.

29. Just above the entrance of a gap in the range of mountains north of the Rio Grande, Hot Springs Creek flowed toward the river. Here were located the springs, with a large hotel and bathing accommodations. An engraving that depicts the resort nestled in its scenic surroundings is in Crofutt, *Crofutt's Grip-Sack Guide to Colorado*, p. 154.

nearly twelve miles, then gave him to O'Brien to lead, I going on in ambulance –

Road very good, & we came on nicely.   Civilization too frequent, almost all the good camping places being fenced in.   Arrived finally at a place my driver knew Genl Sheridan having camped for two days here.   Drove inside the fence, & went into camp, & will arrange with owner in the morning —   Lovely camp – everything as nice & convenient as can be   Went fishing.   Lost more than half an hour trying to get a big fellow out of a pool under a rock but could not get him to touch anything –   Gave him up & went down river to find Laura had taken a fellow of a pound, in a comparatively shallow place, & had got hold of six others which however had got away from her lack of skill in managing them.   She was excited, pleased & mad, & begged me to come where she was & catch some of them as she could not, & they were biting continually.   At the first cast I got a nice 1/2 lb fellow.   Landed him scientifically & telling her to do likewise I went off leaving her to finish up.   I went down the stream.   It is full of splendid trout.   In less than an hour I had taken fourteen averaging near 1/2 pound.   Then there came up a nasty wind storm, & after the first puff I could get no rise.   I think it is a shame that our only two good days on the fishing grounds (or water) should have been spoiled by bad weather.   I believe I would have got 40 or 50, if the weather had remained good.

Sent down & bought hay   Laura is very jubilant over her first trout, which is the largest caught today & bullies Joe, who caught 0.   Baby better & I think out of danger.   She was up today walking about, but is very weak.   I gave her 1/2 of a camphor & opium pill.

September 9, 1880. Franklin's Ranche, Fifteen Miles from Alamosa

Broke camp at usual hour   O'Brien's horse very lame   Gave him mine & took to ambulance.   Gave Mr South a certificate for the Hay bought – 600 lbs   In 3 miles came to Del Norte – one of the "Has Beens"[30] –   Evidences of a thriving busy town, but pretty well used

30. Dodge wrote "Has Bens."

up now – more than half the houses being unoccupied or dismantled, the woodwork having been carried off.[31]

Stoped a few moments & bought some little necessaries.   No eggs to be had, but bought a dozen from a Mexican woman at bridge, 6 miles from town, for 50 cents.

Some of my teams rather shaky, & am obliged to be easy with them. Stopped at Franklins Ranche 15 miles from Alamosa.   He is an Englishman, rich I guess – owns six or eight miles along river, & has it all fenced, to the disgust of travellers.   I am camped in the same lane that we camped in going out, & I take shame to myself in finding that by going 300 yards further, I could have had a lovely camp.   We are very well as it is but might have been better   Went out fishing as soon as I got lunch.   In four rises I got four fine trout – but then my "luck" left me.   I broke my rod by carelessness then lost a good fish, because I had put the hook on in a hurry.   Took pains after that & worked like a Trojan.   Got five after a hard struggle when the wind came up again, & stopped my fun.   I had set my heart on getting seven, for that completed my even hundred since I have been on the trip.   I was however ready to give up on 98, when in crossing river to come to camp I unexpectedly got a rise & a fish.   This put me in heart, & I went on down working hard, & at last I landed another on which I immediately took a drink —

I got 2 more making 9 today & 102 on the trip

The wind was so high that fishing became a bore & I went back to camp   I had however seen a good many ducks, so exchanging rod for gun, I started again.   Got several shots – knocked down 5 mallard & 3 teel – but having no dog I with great difficulty & walking (it seemed a hundred miles) I finally bagged 2 mallard   Old Bunk would have secured 7 instead of 2 ducks   Returned to camp before sundown – to find Franklin with hay.   Gave him a certificate.   He seems

31. First occupied in 1872, the town of Del Norte rapidly developed into a flourishing mining supply center. It aspired to become the favored distribution point for the entire region across the mountains to its north, but completion of the Denver and Rio Grande Rail Way to Alamosa in 1878 made that town the economic center of the San Luis Valley (John Dietz and Albert Larson, "Colorado's San Luis Valley," in Wyckoff and Dilsaver, *The Mountainous West*, p. 358).

a very pleasant fellow & was quite polite.   Was very tired – to bed early   Baby hardly so well, & rather beyond me

Saturday, September 10, 1880. Fort Garland, Colorado

Baby appearing to get no better, I determined to make a push for Garland & a Doctor.   Gave the necessary orders, & started at 7 am, in ambulance & two escort wagons bringing bedding & mess outfit. Drivers very sulky to which I paid no attention.

Found the roads bad but quite as good as I expected.   Arrived Washington Springs before 11 am.   Stopped an hour.   Gave my excess of lunch to the drivers, which put them all in a good humor, & I arrived here at 3 pm.   About 40 miles in 7 working hours & not a mule hurt   Found Leefe & Williams here – also, much to my surprise Dr. Brown, who got away from Mackenzie at Gunnison, & went with Sheridan to Pueblo, & was then ordered back via Ft Garland.[32]

Found a nice letter from Mother & one or two others of little importance.   Not one word of news as to the troops to stay at the Cant[onmen]t.[33]   Dr. Brown came at once to see baby, & prescribed.   I spent the afternoon sprawled around on beds & chairs thoroughly tired.   Leefe had good rooms for me & we are perfectly comfortable.

Had a very pleasant day, but tiresome.   I hate ambulance riding

32. First Lieutenant John G. Leefe, Company C, Nineteenth Infantry, and First Lieutenant William M. Williams, Company F of the same regiment were both stationed at Fort Garland, the former as post quartermaster and commissary of subsistence. Assistant Surgeon Justus M. Brown was chief medical officer of the Fort Garland Column (*ANJ*, July 3, 1880, p. 982). He had been designated a member of a general court-martial to be convened September 15 at Cantonment on the Uncompaghre (S.O. 193, August 30—DMO).

33. Dodge expresses doubt which companies, if any, currently with the Fort Garland Column would return to Cantonment North Fork Canadian River rather than remain at Cantonment on the Uncompaghre over the winter. On September 16 Second Lieutenant Febiger, then at Fort Leavenworth, received orders to proceed to Cantonment, collect all baggage and clothing belonging to the companies then in Colorado, and arrange for its transportation there. The commanding officer at Fort Supply received a similar order for the companies detached from his post (S.O. 205, September 16—DMO). See Dodge's entry for September 21. Five companies wintered at Cantonment on the Uncompaghre: A, C, and D, formerly at Cantonment, and B and E, formerly at Fort Supply.

Saturday, September 11, 1880. Fort Garland, Colorado

Woke up early, but got up late for me – about 7 am   Gave Rawlins his discharge.[34]   Had the boxes &c left here last spring brought down, & set Laura to work repacking.   She is an excellent hand always ready for work, not a lazy bone in her body.

Febiger got in about 11 – his party somewhat later.   Turned in the horses &c &c & stored all the property that is to go back to Cantonment.   Made detail to go to Ft Leavenworth 2 Sergts & 3 privates.[35] Wrote to Capt Bradford at Dodge about transp[ortatio]n.   Telegraphed to White at Topeka asking for 1/2 fare tickets for my servants. Wrote to Dept Hd Qrs asking that Febiger & party be sent to Cant[onment]. I. T. for Compy property provided 23d Cos are to remain on Uncompagre.   Wrote also to Rice about transpn from Supply to Cant[onmen]t.[36]   Have got all pretty well arranged for start tomorrow for Dodge.   Gave Febiger his orders for Leavenworth —

Took long nap in afternoon   At night visited Mrs Dr Brown, & Mrs Lt Williams both pleasant attractive ladies.   Mrs W. I knew before at 11 Worth.   Came home 10 pm & went to bed.   Baby somewhat better tonight   Williams & wife went out fishing today & got 45 trout.

Sunday, September 12, 1880. En Route

Arranged everything for a start today.   We were busy all day *diminishing*.   Gave Febiger my stove & box, a chair, all my tables &c &c &c to take back & distribute.   Wrote to Mother & to several outside parties.

34. This was Private Stephen H. Rawlins, Company D, Twenty-third Infantry, who had completed his term of service. With his discharge papers he was given a character reference of "excellent."

35. A detachment under Lieutenant Febiger, these men would accompany the military convicts.

36. Captain James H. Bradford, Nineteenth Infantry, was now in command of Fort Dodge; Dodge needed him to arrange for his transportation from Dodge City to Fort Supply. W. F. White, at Topeka, was general passenger and ticketing agent for the Atchison, Topeka and Santa Fe Rail Road (Poor, *Manual* [1880], p. 938). Through First Lieutenant William F. Rice, regimental and post quartermaster at Fort Supply, Dodge arranged for transportation from there to Cantonment.

A terribly long day, as is always the case when one waits – & Ft G. is a wonderfully stupid place.   All as kind as can be but when the *all* is two or three quiet men, the effect is not hilarious –

Got everybody & everything to depot in time – got all my baggage on train without paying extra.   Half fare tickets for self Joe & Laura & Rawlins to Pueblo & at 5.30 pm we left on train all comfortable & baby better.

Monday, September 13, 1880. Bluff Creek Ranche, Kansas

Woke up this am after a glorious nights sleep in cars, at 9 am & was told that we were near Lakin the Breakfast place.[37]   Dressed, had a good drink & a good breakfast.

We arrived 12 pm at Pueblo where I found orders for half fare tickets for Joe & Laura.   We remained in that villa scarce long enough to change baggage.   Found all the baggage people very clever, no extra charge, & got everything checked to Dodge.   Arrived Dodge City 12 m.   Gave Sgt Janson $5. for his care of me.   Bade good-by to Febiger.   Found all the Officers of Ft Dodge at Dodge City.   Bradford had recd my letter & supposing I was in a great hurry, brought up ambulance & escort wagon so I could start at once.

This suited me exactly – though I was greatly surprised at it.   A Corpl & 2 men also reported, & in an hour ∧ all my things were
                                                                    or two
loaded.   Joe & Laura went shopping.   I went to get a drink & to call on some of my old friends.   Found only two or three.   Bradford & his Offs stuck to me however.   Bought some beer for the trip – also some watermelon & cantelopes, the first we have had for the season.

At 1.40 we "lit out", for Bluff Creek.   The team was poor, & driver execrable, but roads good, so we made the distance 25 miles by sundown.   Had a fair supper & went to bed early – Joe & L Baby & I, all in same room

37. A train stop about fifty miles east of the Colorado-Kansas state line.

Tuesday, September 14, 1880. Cimarron Ranche

Started about 7.30 am   A most utterly miserable & disgusting day. The wind blew continuously, but varied its power by puffs every few moments, keeping the air full of dust.   It was direct in our faces all day.   Arrived at Cimarron Ranch 1.30 pm.   Saw several lots of ducks along road, & fired four times – getting however only 2 ducks – teel. I am shooting away a remnant of miserable cartridges loaded with Hazard powder[38] which will not stick shot in a spring snipe at twenty yards

Last night's ranche & this both alive with fleas & bed bugs.

September 15, 1880. Fort Supply, I. T.

Got off at 7.30 am.   It is a long road, stopped for lunch at Buffalo Springs & got into post 3.45 p.m.   Col Haller met me very cordially. Had 2 rooms fixed up for me, in a vacant house.   Find so little tranportation that I am obliged to wait until the arrival of the Paymaster from Cantonment.   He will not be here until Sunday.   It is a nuisance to have to wait so long but there is no help for it.

Met nearly all the Ladies.   Dined at Col. H, where I am to take my meals, during my stay.   Joe and Laura also provided for at same "<p>Hospitable B[oar]d"   No news.   Played a game of billiards with Broderick & went to bed 10 pm

Thursday, September 16, 1880. Fort Supply, I. T.

Up at 7 am.   Beautiful day but warm.   Haller took me all around post, & nearly busted me, specially as I have made the same tour lots of times before.   Played billiards with Goodale, & got beat, giving him discount.

Col Haller got up a reception for me at night –   Excellent music. There are about 17 Ladies at the Post & about 7 gentlemen   Beaux at a premium –   Danced flirted, talked sense & nonsense drank ale whiskey et al until 12 pm, then went to bed.   Dined with Rice & had

---

38. The Hazard Powder Company of New York had been for many years a major manufacturer and distributor of gunpowder.

3 square meals today breakfast, lunch & dinner & a good stagger at a fourth in the supper tonight

Friday, September 17, 1880. Fort Supply

Breakfasted with Col Haller   Lunched with Broderick   Dined with Goodale, & am stuffed like a Bologna.   Have eaten more yesterday & today, than I have in any one week this summer.

Rawlins went on to Cant[onmen]t.   Got a wife there, & could'nt wait.

Tried to get Berninger to go to Cant. with me to write up the Indian Songs.[39]   He says he cannot do it – nor can any man of band. A d— pretty band say I –   I fear I'll have to lose a splendid chapter. Played two or three games of billiards but it was too hot to enjoy them.

Spent evening at Col. H.s listening to music, & gassing.

Saturday, September 18, 1880. Fort Supply

Pretty dilapidated this a.m.   Had attack of diaroeha.   Felt very weak but played billiards in am.   Took no lunch – & at 1.30 went out with Rice on a hunt.   I Bagged 14 quail.   Rice got 10 quail one yellow leg, one dove & 1 coon, & the dog bagged 1 quail – & Rice & I had one in common.

It was excessively hot, & I was weak, so that my hunt was an awful labor.   I could walk scarcely a hundred yds at a time.   Paymaster left Cant[onmen]t. today – so I calculate to get off on Monday.

Sunday, September 19. Fort Supply

Found to my disgust this am that the paymaster did not start from Cantont until this morning.   So I cannot possibly get off before Tuesday

Before I found it out, I had got everything ready – so I will have nothing more to do.

---

39. Sebastian Berninger was principal musician of the regimental band. Dodge hoped for his assistance in preparing a discussion of Indian music.

Paid all my bills.   Not very well took it easy.   Had a nap in after-noon   Bought my old riding horse Buster.[40]

Monday, September 20. Fort Supply

Paymaster arrived about noon.   Gave all my orders, & got every-thing ready to leave tomorro.   At night made the rounds visited & bade good by to all the Ladies.   Twas quite a job, & not feeling very well since I've been here, I put it off to the last moment

I have had a real pleasant visit, tho' it was involuntary   Col. Haller, his family, & all have been just as kind as they could be.   Went to bed late all ready to start early —

Tuesday, September 21, 1880. Cedar Bluffs, I. T.

The wagons reported at 7 am & by 8 were loaded and en route. - It being right after payday, about half my escort is drunk.   Our pay system is utterly abominable.   Just after Breakfast Col H. came down to my Qrs with the order, directing the heavy baggage of all the Co[mpanie]s at Los Pinos, to be sent to them –   Grand Commotion among the women.   Saw most of them & they took it like the good Army women that they are –.   Mrs Brady, & Cowles will go out with the baggage   Mrs Pollock doubtful[41] & Mrs Hinton will not, as she wants to keep her children at school.   Bade every-body good by.   Took a Tustanegge[?][42] with Col H, invited him & his family to visit me at Cantonment.   Rice & Broderick came to suttlers store to see me off, & about 10.30 am, sailed away in ambulance.

Tried a new road – one not at all used, a mere trail in fact, which I discovered when out hunting with Rice last Saturday   Found it considerably further, but a very great improvement on the old road.

40. See the journal entry for February 19, 1880.
41. She chose to go to the new cantonment. Years afterward, her daughter Winifred wrote a brief but vivid recollection of the winter that followed. See Nankivell, "Fort Crawford," pp. 59–60.
42. Probably "tostinate" or a variant, referring to a parting drink. See the *Oxford English Dictionary*, sb. *tosticate*.

Bagged nine (9) teel, & one yellow legged snipe.   Road (after we got into the regular route) heavy & slow, & only arrived at Cedar B[l]uffs 18 miles at 3 pm.   Went into camp.[43]   Some of my escort yet drunk. Will have to go for them if they dont stop.

The whole country here tracked up by deer and Turkeys.   Must be hundreds of them.   I took a long walk hoping to meet some of them, but saw nothing – but tracks.   Saw an immense number of quail today, but had no time to stop for them   Very little water in North Fork – & no fishing.   To bed early – tired but feeling first rate.

Wednesday, September 22, 1880. Caticum Creek[44]

Broke Camp 7. am.   Before breakfast I discovered a small flight of ducks – & bagged them all (six).   Saw a fine covey of Grouse but got no shot.   Got three more ducks at Caticum – making (9) today all I have seen.   Tried fishing but got only 2 small cats.   Creek almost dry.   Cold & raw this am but lovely afternoon.   Had a huge camp fire.   Joe Laura & I sat around & gassed until nearly 11 pm. The beauty of negro servants is that they do not presume on such familiarity.

Distance about 25 miles.   In all likelyhood, this is the last camp of the Campaign.

Thursday, September 23, 1880. Cantonment, I. T.

Broke camp at 7 am but before leaving bagged 2 teel, that had the temerity to come near camp.   Thousands of cattle all along here.[45] On road home saw a flock of Turkeys & bagged three.   Arrived before 12 m – all apparently glad to see me, & Old Sgt Leonard so delighted that he got on a moderate drunk – much to my surprise &

---

43. Dodge wrote "came."

44. A stream that flows northeast, joining the North Fork from the south at a point about halfway between Fort Supply and Cantonment.

45. Dodge took particular note of these herds and shortly after his return to Cantonment reported their presence to Agent Miles. See below, p. 415.

his wife's disgust.[46]   Dined with Clarke.   Found everybody well –
post in good condition – no sickness – but everything parched up
by dry weather —

So Ended the Grand Campaign[47]

46. This was Sergeant Patrick Leonard, Company A; his wife, Mrs. Ellen Leonard, was one of the two authorized laundresses of the company.

47. This day's entry concludes at the bottom of p. [30V] in the journal. One more entry, dated December 18, follows on pp. [31] and [32R]; it appears on p. 435 below. Pages [32V]-[58R] are blank. On p. [58V], written in a hand not Dodge's and with the notebook reversed, is a name and address: "Thos C F Tillson [/] 2d Lt 1st Infy [/] Fort Keogh [/] Montana." At the top of p. [59R], in Dodge's hand, is another: "Gussie Morrow [/] 177 West 12." The remainder of that page is Dodge's daily summary, with brief commentary, of the 102 trout he caught in seven days of fishing during the summer. Page [59V] is blank; on p. [60R], with the notebook reversed, Dodge wrote "93"; p. [60V] is blank.

Afterword
Missions Accomplished

CANTONMENT: A DIMINISHED MISSION

In June 1880 Captain Charles Wheaton commanded a garrison at Cantonment numbering only forty-six men, three officers, and the post surgeon. Early in that month General Pope directed Wheaton to suspend for the present "all labor of construction," limiting his efforts to maintaining in good repair the buildings and government property already in place; but even this task was beyond what the post commander could hope to accomplish with the resources he had at hand. In July, reporting on health conditions at the post, Assistant Surgeon La Garde drew attention to the already deteriorating temporary quarters. Floored with loose boards set on bare earth and roofed with an agglomeration of makeshifts that now leaked badly, they were drafty, bug-ridden, and unhealthful. The post quartermaster could only respond that construction material, laborers, and skilled craftsmen were not available to attempt repairs.[1] Shortly after Dodge returned to Cantonment in September, he reported to departmental headquarters that work on the post must remain suspended until additional troops and transportation became available.[2]

In the summer and fall of 1880, Cantonment conformed in most respects to De Benneville Randolph Keim's suggestive analogy between a frontier military post and an isolated ship at sea.[3] The post was in a

1. AAG DMO to C.O., June 2, 1880 (CNFCR Unregistered LR); Louis La Garde to C.O., July 8, 1880 (CNFCR LR); William L. Clarke, endorsement to La Garde report, July 6, 1880 (CNFCR Endorsement Book).
2. RID to AAG DMO, October 11, 1880 (CNFCR LS).
3. Keim, *Sheridan's Troopers on the Borders*, p. 59.

406 AFTERWORD

sense autonomous, a rigorously organized little world by itself. Military forms and usages continued to be observed, and the days were sub-divided as before by trumpet calls, drills, guard mountings, inspections, and other benchmarks of Army routine. But this ship was becalmed, without a destination or mission, other than to remain afloat. Proposed as a permanent post only a few months before, Cantonment was in danger of becoming—to change the figure—a blank spot on the map, and almost literally so.

Early in July an inquiry was received from the departmental quarter-master whether the more advantageous depot for delivery of goods to be transported to the post was South Haven, Kansas, rather than Caldwell, which was twelve miles closer than South Haven and about to become a railroad terminus. Wheaton replied that Caldwell had long since been determined the most convenient point and that Colonel Dodge had personally superintended work on the road there. He added that, on a map just received from the engineer officer of the department, the road shown as passing to Cantonment did not come within four miles of its actual location. "The Cantonment," he wrote, was "in the bend of North Fork Canadian River, right bank, opposite the word 'Marsh' on the map."[4]

One company formerly at Cantonment, the mounted unit under Lieutenant Julius Pardee, saw field service throughout the summer. On May 2 David Payne slipped past Pardee's patrols with a party of 153 persons and proceeded south, intending to set up a colony deep within Indian Territory. In a dispatch the following day these intrepid folk proclaimed themselves "here to stay" and then hurried on to set up camp in a locale that now forms part of Oklahoma City.[5] Con-

4. Endorsement, July 8, 1880 (CNFCR Endorsement Book).
5. Rister, *Land Hunger*, pp. 55–64. An article entitled "Invasion" in the Kansas City *Times* for April 28, 1880, described the several "squads" of men who had crossed into Indian Territory four days before, determined to travel south for the next twenty-four hours without stopping. "Captain D. L. Payne, the commander of this expedition, is personally in command, and his heart is in the work to that extent that nothing but actual force can turn him from his purpose. [¶] From where they cross the line of the territory the selected town site is about one hundred miles—as beautiful a spot, and surrounded on all sides by as fine a country as can be found on this continent" (OIA LR, C&A).

fronted by Pardee on May 5, Payne somehow managed to convince him that the lands he occupied were not on Indian reservations—as was true—but had been "ceded" for use by citizens—as was not true. A few days later another officer forced Payne to surrender and escorted him and the followers still with him to Fort Reno. Pardee and a detachment of his men then returned the intruders to Kansas and released them, no further legal action being taken. However, in July Payne made another attempt, and upon being captured he and five associates were transported to Fort Smith, Arkansas, to be turned over to the United States marshal there.[6] Of course, the publicity for his cause that resulted from this challenge to federal authority suited Payne's wishes exactly. He was soon released, and by late October he was back in Wichita, designating himself "President, Oklahoma Colony" and preparing for yet another incursion. Pardee was there to watch him, now with Company D and twenty-five Indian scouts.[7]

That same spring, a crisis erupted at the Cheyenne and Arapaho agency, occurring in two parts. The first, a portion of which Dodge had witnessed, was the failed attempt by Agent Miles to enroll children of Little Chief and other Northern Cheyennes in school. A month later the second emergency developed when it became clear that the appropriated supply of beef would be exhausted by June 11, three weeks before additional amounts could be issued at the beginning of the new fiscal year.[8] This was a matter of more than administrative concern, both to the affected Indians and to the military who were expected to help preserve the peace. On May 26 Pope informed Sheridan of "this most urgent matter," passing along Agent Miles's estimate that 350,000 pounds of cattle would be necessary to tide him over.[9] On June 2 Randall telegraphed directly to the Commissioner of Indian Affairs warning of "serious trouble" should the usual weekly rations not be distributed. Additional anxious messages were

6. *ANJ*, August 14, 1880, p. 30.
7. *ANJ*, November 13, 1880, p. 281.
8. SW to SI, June 1, 1880 (OIA LR, C&A).
9. The quoted phrase is from a follow-up telegram by Pope to AAG MDM, June 3, 1880, wherein he refers to the message of May 26 (OIA LR, C&A).

exchanged in the next few days, and Randall hurried Pardee's company back to Fort Reno.[10] Fortunately, on June 5 the secretary of the interior informed the secretary of war that arrangements had been made to make available a supplementary supply of beef.[11] Apprehensions were eased, and after a brief renewal of anxiety when the beef contractor was late in making delivery, by June 17 the ration for that almost expired week had been issued, and the crisis was past.

Late in July, Randall was granted a month's leave of absence, to be taken whenever he thought it safe to leave Fort Reno,[12] but he delayed his departure. A narrow brush with disaster on August 16 affords some insight into the tense conditions that dictated his delay. The precipitating cause of this incident was another disagreement over beef rations. According to Agent Miles, an Indian man[13] demanded a ration of beef in addition to the one he had just received, claiming the second as due him from an earlier week's allotment that he had not received. Upon being informed that the Indian Bureau forbade distributing back rations, the man leapt into the corral and aimed his rifle at a steer, evidently intending to kill it. Miles hurried after him and ordered him out of the shed. Later, as Miles and two employees were driving his carriage back to the agency office, five of the seven Indian men who had been present at the disruption formed a line across the road in front of them, stopping the carriage while the other two began beating the horses over their heads. The Indians demanded that the back issue beef be given their aggrieved tribesman at once; and Miles, defenseless and fearing for his own and his companions' lives, gave the order.

Consulting with Randall immediately afterward, the agent directed his Indian police to arrest the two "ringleaders" of the assault so as to

10. Randall to Commissioner of Indian Affairs, June 2, 1880 (OIA LR, C&A); ANJ, June 5, 1880, p. 897; AG to Sheridan, June 5, 1880 (AGO LS).
11. AG to Sheridan, June 7, 1880 (AGO LS).
12. S.O. 166, July 31, DMO; Fort Reno Post Return, August 1880.
13. According to Berthrong, this was a young Southern Cheyenne named Hippy (*The Cheyenne and Arapaho Ordeal*, p. 45). John H. Seger characterized Hippy as "a foolhardy man [who] delighted in doing desperate things that he might be talked about . . . always having adventures" (*Early Days Among the Cheyenne and Arapahoe Indians*, p. 56).

quell any notion that their behavior would be tolerated. But the captain of police soon informed him that the two men, Bull Coming Up and Little Coyote, would die fighting rather than be taken. At this point Miles called upon Randall to make the arrest, and together with two companies of cavalry and his interpreter, George Bent, the post commander moved toward the sand hills south and east of Fort Reno where the offenders were said to have entrenched themselves. Randall discovered awaiting him a large body of hostile Indians that one observer estimated at between fifteen hundred and two thousand persons and that Miles described as "the whole Cheyenne tribe."[14] A master at dealing with Indians, Randall understood the importance of appearance and due demeanor at moments of confrontation like this. Over six feet in height and wearing a mustache "so ferocious it would mesmerize an Indian at one sitting,"[15] he stood at his ease for a moment, surveying the crowd and allowing himself to be observed. Then, removing the cigar from his mouth, he ordered Bent to climb onto a box and translate to the crowd, coolly delivering an ultimatum. One of the two instigators had already come in to the agency, he said; he was here now for the other. If that man came, or was brought in, his purpose here would be accomplished. If not, he and his men would take him themselves. More soldiers than the blades of grass on the hills were already on the march from Caldwell, and if the Indians chose to fight they would be wiped off the earth.

This was mendacity, but it served the turn. Wise heads among the Cheyennes calmed the ire of the soldier element, and a probable tragedy was narrowly averted. Shortly thereafter a few Indians were brought to the agency office where, anticlimactically, they were informed that their coming in was all Miles required, since he had wished to explain to them officially the impossibility of issuing back rations. This too was not the truth, but Miles was convinced that no arrest could have been made that day without support from a full regiment of troops. "As it was," he wrote, "had a gun been accidentally

14. The other witness was Henry C. Keeling, whose account of the incident is in "My Experience with the Cheyenne Indians," pp. 67-68.

15. *ANJ*, November 19, 1889, p. 139.

George M. Randall (Roger D. Hunt Collection, U.S. Army Military History Institute)

discharged nothing could have prevented a general fight and massacre of all whites."[16] The Indians had superior strength and knew it, as did Miles, Randall, and many another. A reporter for the *Wellington Press* submitted that the garrison of Fort Reno, "the most important post in the Territory," was "far too weak."[17] Shortly afterward Randall was granted one month of sick leave with permission to apply for an additional month if he required it, and this relief from duty he accepted at once.[18]

Little Chief and his band had recently kept to themselves, playing no major role in either of the emergencies over beef rations. Opinion was building that the interests of all parties would be served best if the old chieftain were allowed to return north. Major Mizner had predicted in August 1879 that so long as Little Chief remained at the agency he would remain a source of "constant anxiety." By November of that year Mizner had concluded that, as a matter of prudence and "common justice," he and his people should be permitted to join their relations in their former home.[19] In February 1880 General Pope wondered what good could possibly accrue to the Indians or the government by keeping them in a place distasteful to them, and from which they continually spent time devising ways to escape. If they were allowed to return north, their absence would enable him to use elsewhere the forces now deployed to prevent their outbreak. Enumerating other military situations his troops were expected to deal with in Indian Territory and in New Mexico, Colorado, and along the border with Mexico, Pope made clear that the removal of the Northern

16. Miles to R. E. Trowbridge, August 18, 1880 (OIA LR, C&A). Colonel Edwin P. Pendleton, who in 1880 was a second lieutenant with Randall's Company I, Twenty-third Infantry, recalled that Agent Miles owed his life on this occasion to Randall and an old Cheyenne, Wild Hog (Shirk, "Military Duty on the Western Frontier," p. 123).

17. Reprinted in *ANJ*, September 25, 1880, p. 141. Although this writer praised Miles and Randall for their discretion, he wondered how they could submit to such insults and honorably retain their positions. The crisis they had survived argued the need for more military strength to support brave persons such as they.

18. *ANJ*, September 18, 1880, p. 122. On September 24 Randall's month of sick leave was extended one month (Fort Reno Post Return, September 1880).

19. Senate, *Report . . . on the Removal of the Northern Cheyennes*, p. 122; Mizner to Pope, November 17, 1879 (OIA LR, C&A).

Cheyennes from Indian Territory would be both "an immense boon to them" and also a benefit to himself.[20]

Colonel Nelson A. Miles, a steady advocate of Little Chief and his people, also urged compliance with their wishes, asserting that it would be "humane, just and wise to allow them to return north." He elaborated his views in testimony before the Senate committee on the Northern Cheyennes, and upon its publication in June 1880 the committee's report showed that his opinions had received careful attention.[21] The first of its five recommendations was that Little Chief's band be returned to the vicinity of Fort Keogh, Montana Territory, where it had earlier rendered valuable service to Colonel Miles, and that its competent men be employed again as police, as scouts, or in other capacities.[22] The Northern Cheyennes had not yet realized their hopes, but Little Chief's policy of firm but usually civil inacquiescence had proved effective thus far.

Agent Miles formed a smooth working relationship with Captain Randall, as he had done with Major Mizner. He worked less amiably with officers like Dodge at Cantonment, whose very presence he considered an unwarranted intrusion, and during the summer of 1880 he crossed swords with a troublesome Army man even further afield, Colonel Granville Haller at Fort Supply. On July 5, following his usual practice when he learned of an objectionable activity, he complained of Haller to the new Commissioner of Indian Affairs, W. E. Trowbridge. According to Miles, the post commander at Fort Supply had recently written a pass granting Big Horse and twelve other Southern Cheyennes permission to hunt for a few days in the vicinity of his post. However, he continued, those Indians were absent with-

20. Pope to Sherman, February 12, 1880 (AGO LR). Pope enclosed a report he had received from Ben Clarke, dated January 23. Clarke considered that most of the Northern Cheyennes who had come south with Little Chief and many of those who had come earlier with Dull Knife were "determined . . . to be unreconciled" to life in Indian Territory.

21. Endorsement, January 26, 1880, of Ben Clarke to Nelson A. Miles, January 14, 1880 (OIA LR, C&A); Senate, *Report . . . on the Removal of the Northern Cheyennes*, pp. 202–16. Miles's testimony figures prominently in the Senate committee's summary of its findings; see *Report*, pp. xxi–xxiv.

22. Senate, *Report . . . on the Removal of the Northern Cheyennes*, p. xxvi.

out permission from their reservation and "should have been sent back" at once.[23]

On receipt of Miles's complaint, Trowbridge protested to the secretary of war about Haller's "interference . . . with prerogatives of the Agent," asking that he be instructed not to issue further passes "or in any other way interfere with the Agent in the discharge of his official duties."[24] But instead, Haller was sent the commissioner's letter and the earlier one from Miles, with a request for a report on the matter. In his response, dated August 6, Haller made no reference to the implication by Miles that he had willfully usurped the agent's powers. Instead, describing the incident when the Indians had presented themselves at the fort, he mentioned that, having no interpreter at hand, he could barely communicate with them and so had no clear idea of where they came from. From their manner of straightforward confidence he had no reason to believe they might have reached his post without authorization. Referring to a post order of February 1879 that required all strangers visiting Fort Supply to be issued permits to pursue their business, he certified that an entry for the Indians had been made in the post's pass book and that they had been duly issued a pass.[25]

This explanation proved unsatisfactory to the Commissioner of Indian Affairs and prompted a renewed complaint. Citing Miles's assertion that the thirteen truants should have been sent back to their reservation as soon as they appeared at Fort Supply, Trowbridge insisted that Haller had acted improperly.[26] His accusation provoked Haller to a rebuttal in which he deftly hoisted Agent Miles on his own petard of prerogative. Borrowing a line from Shakespeare, he declared "baseless as the fabric of a vision" the commissioner's presumption that he had known the Indians lacked permission to be where he

23. SI to AG, July 19, 1880 (AGO Register LR); Haller to AG, September 14, 1880 (OIA LR, C&A).

24. Quoted in Haller to AG, September 14, 1880 (OIA LR, C&A); see also SW to SI, July 23, 1880 (OIA LR, C&A).

25. Haller to AAG DMO, August 6, 1880, with SW to SI, August 21, 1880 (SW LS).

26. R. E. Trowbridge to SI, August 27, 1880 (AGO Register LR); Haller to AG, September 14, 1880 (OIA LR, C&A).

encountered them. Next, he proceeded to set forth a few material facts he had not mentioned earlier. Big Horse, he wrote, had in his possession a paper, signed by Agent Miles, authorizing him to arrest any person who had stolen Indian stock in his possession. This warrant signed by Miles, he continued, had seemed to him "a *standing pass* to move through the Indian Territory, without regard to Reservation limits," and he invited anyone to differ with that interpretation. On the other hand, had Agent Miles only informed officials at Cantonment and Fort Supply by telegraph when he discovered the Cheyennes absent without permission, the military could have complied with his request for assistance. This he had not done, but now he and Trowbridge were "discourteously" dictating to the commanding officer of an Army post what course he should have followed, a liberty "at all times more or less offensive—and which under the circumstances, I respectfully submit, was gratuitous."

Haller turned the tables on the complainants, requesting that the secretary of war ask the secretary of the interior to direct Indian agents always to telegraph post commanders whenever Indians left their reservations. In that way, he wrote, when they sought assistance from the military they would be conforming to the provisions of General Order 28, Department of the Missouri, September 26, 1870—the very order Agent Miles habitually relied upon to assert his authority.[27] Haller's letter brought discussion of his shortcomings as a post commander to an abrupt end.[28] He dated it September 14, 1880, the day before the arrival of Dodge at Fort Supply on his return from Colorado. Discussion of his recent bout with Miles and his master in Washington, D.C., surely occurred between the two senior officers, and it may well have contributed to the obvious good feeling that prevailed between them during Dodge's five-day visit.

In the summer and fall of 1880 events occurred within fewer than one hundred miles north, east, and west of Cantonment that required a military presence and that, in the case of the Cheyenne and Arapaho

27. Haller to AG, September 14, 1880 (OIA LR, C&A). For the Shakespeare quotation, see *The Tempest* IV.1.151.
28. SW to SI, September 27, 1880 (OIA LR, C&A).

agency, twice approached violence. However, as if somehow hidden, the post itself remained a place of relative calm. Except for its location near trails being created by cattlemen, it was at least two days' march from the centers of concern. When in June one of the Cheyenne scouts complained that cattle driven across the reservation had destroyed his cornfield west of the post, the provost marshal wrote Agent Miles asking whether, to avoid trouble, something should be done to prevent a repetition. Miles replied that, while the Indians had no individual rights to the plots of land they farmed, cattlemen were prohibited from crossing the reservation without permission from the Indian Bureau. He did not ask the post commander to correct the problem, and Captain Wheaton was without the manpower to do so even if he had received such a request. Wheaton therefore concluded that as matters stood, the matter of trespass by cattle herds "is in the hands of the Indian Department now to manage."[29]

The garrison maintained its minimal staffing after Dodge's return, mustering in November forty-four enlisted men, and of these only sixteen available for general duty. When Second Lieutenant Febiger was about to leave for Colorado, taking with him the property of the companies now stationed there and the men attached to those units who had earlier remained behind, Dodge petitioned his departmental headquarters on behalf of two old soldiers who he thought ought not to go. Sergeant Leonard, who had celebrated his commander's return by a moderate drunk, he characterized as old, unfit for the field, and

29. Endorsement, n.d. [after June 21, 1880] (Endorsement Book, CNFCR). See also Pennington, "Government Policy and Indian Farming on the Cheyenne and Arapaho Reservation, 1869–1880," p. 189. Shortly after his return to the post, Dodge alerted Miles to a related problem. Between Cantonment and Persimmon Creek, about twenty-five miles upriver, he had seen approximately five thousand cattle set out to graze. They were owned by various concerns—Tony Day, the Dicky Brothers, Lee and Reynolds, Volz and Wells. The Indians had complained of their herders as trespassers, but the cattlemen claimed they were on Cherokee lands and with permission, having paid taxes to the tribe. Dodge volunteered to eject the men and their cattle if they were within the bounds of the Cheyenne and Arapaho reservation, but since he could not interfere if they were there legally he required Miles's advice (RID to Miles, September 28, 1880—CNFCR LS). The question of the cattlemen's location and legal status was still unclear, and the matter was not pursued during the remainder of 1880.

within three months of his discharge. Sergeant Sommer was a married man and the only soldier at the post capable of attending to the quartermaster's property and papers.[30] The leniency he proposed for these regimental stalwarts was quickly approved, and the garrison settled into a routine something like domestic peace. Though without a family of his own at hand, Dodge enjoyed a close relationship with his servants Joe and Laura, who had served him for several years and to whose daughter he was "Grandpap."

The location of Cantonment away from the swirl of affairs was exactly what Dodge required during the final months of 1880. Like many another intending author, he needed the opportunity to address himself in comfortable circumstances to an extended bout of desk work. Fortunately for him, Amos Chapman was still at hand as post interpreter. Should Cheyennes like Stone Calf drop in for a chat, as was their habit, Chapman was on hand to translate, and so perhaps might help gather new material for the book. Private Alexander Van Buren, formerly sergeant major of the regiment and a very able man, was available to serve as copyist.[31] After October 1 few special orders were issued from post headquarters to break the daily routine. Cantonment remained in touch with the world by telegraph, the postal service, and occasional visitors, but it had become a quiet place. The time was propitious for work on a book whose topic warranted Dodge's best effort.

COLONEL DODGE AND *OUR WILD INDIANS*

After his arrival at Cantonment in September 1880, Dodge worked almost without interruption on his book project, grinding away at what he called "the description Mill." Of all possible topics, the one he was best qualified to write about was the Indians of the American plains—not only from firsthand experience but also from study of other authorities. Following the publication of *The Plains of North America and Their Inhabitants*, he had acquired copies of works by

---

30. RID to AAG DMO, October 7, 1880 (CNFCR LS).
31. S.O. 113, November 3, 1880; S.O. 115, November 29, 1880—CNFCR. In later years Van Buren again rose to the rank of sergeant major; see *ANJ*, April 16, 1887, p. 755.

students of the Indians like Henry Rowe Schoolcraft, George Catlin, and Prince Maximilian of Wied and had studied them to compare their views with his own. Now, having ready access to his personal library, his notes and drafts written at intervals in recent years, and a succession of Indian visitors to whom he could put queries, he pushed ahead. By December 12 he had completed a manuscript, and Private Van Buren had prepared a fair copy for submission to a publisher. In the preface he described his work as "a detailed account of the characteristics, habits, and—what I particularly desire to invite attention to,—a minute and careful study of the social or inner life of the wild Indian of the present day."[32]

The manuscript was lengthy, almost 150,000 words, and comprised fifty-one chapters and a "L'Envoi."[33] Although at some points in this work Dodge referred to the earlier writers whose works he had perused, as also to more popular figures like James Fenimore Cooper and George Belden,[34] his comments on them were of a general nature and

32. "Author's Preface," *OWI*, p. vi. Except for a few pages of material omitted from the published work or else included in fragmentary form, Dodge's manuscript has not survived. However, the available evidence makes clear that by December 1880 he considered the text of his work complete, ready for review by informed persons, and ready for publication. By March 1881 it had been seen by a Professor Angel in Washington, D.C., who then induced Senator Henry A. Dawes to ask Dodge that it be loaned to him also. After reading through it, Dawes assured the author that "it will be a valuable contribution to Indian literature" (Dawes to RID, March 27, 1881, and April 4, 1881—Dodge Papers, Graff Collection; Priest, *Uncle Sam's Stepchildren*, p. 196). Only one sentence in the printed text of *Our Wild Indians* was certainly written after December 1880, a detail added to a longer discussion (p. 86). Dodge's attention to his book in 1881 consisted chiefly of arranging with the Smithsonian Institution for production of the color illustrations included in it, reading proofsheets, and deleting twelve initial chapters that his publisher considered too argumentative in a work intended for a general audience. (Much of this latter material he simply moved to the other end of the manuscript. The controversial passages were later issued together in a pamphlet, *A Living Issue*.) It is therefore assumed here that, except as noted, the contents and organization of the manuscript he completed in December 1880 were the same as appear in the published book, *Our Wild Indians*.

33. Dodge's may be the only book ever written by a United States Army officer that concludes with a L'Envoi, a convention derived from medieval lyric poetry.

34. Though little remembered now, George P. Belden's *Belden, The White Chief; or, Twelve Years Among the Wild Indians of the Plains*, edited by Major James S. Brisbin, Second Cavalry, was a popular work at the time of its issue in 1870, selling over twenty thousand copies.

unsupported by documentation. He also acknowledged the assistance of other persons, chiefly on the basis of their unpublished observations. Among these were Major Robert S. Neighbors, a former agent to the Comanche Indians; William H. Berry, agent to the Uncompahgre Utes; Ben Clarke, the Cheyenne interpreter at Fort Reno; George Aschmann, a musician with the regimental band; Captains Pollock and Randall of his regiment; and probably the most helpful of all, Amos Chapman, his employee and frequent companion.[35] When a conflict of opinion arose between himself and some printed authority, Chapman could sometimes help Dodge to take the matter in dispute to the Indians themselves. "My position as commanding officer—'Big Chief'—enabled me always to get a hearing and an answer on any subject," he wrote; "and my well-known friendship for the race caused the Indians to give me more frank confidence than a white man usually obtains."[36] As his Indian collaborators he named several Indians attached to the Cheyenne and Arapaho agency, but those who appear to have given him the most valued assistance were Buffalo (or Running Buffaloes), one of the post's scouts, and Stone Calf, a wise old Southern Cheyenne.[37] Other material incorporated in the manuscript included facts gleaned from private correspondence with Army officers like Major Mauck and Captain Pollock and also from unpublished official reports.[38]

The preponderance of material in the work derived, however, from Dodge's own experiences. Examples abound, but a few will suffice to suggest that, while he drew upon observations that went back over many years, recent experience was the source of some of his most vivid descriptions. He sketched the scenes, recorded in his journals, of a young Indian man interrupted by soldiers while in his devotions atop a mountain and of an Indian woman cutting meat from a horse that had drowned in the Cimarron River. Elsewhere he described from memory the Indians begging for food or picking through offal at the

35. *OWI*, pp. 99, 128, 163, 353, 608.
36. "Author's Preface," OWI, p. v.
37. *OWI*, pp. 74, 95, 202, 214, 279, 310, 345, 398, 540, 581.
38. *OWI*, pp. 122, 164, 446, 484, 582, 628.

post.[39] Despite its many references to published and unpublished sources, Dodge's book manuscript was not a scholarly discussion but a personal statement by a uniquely well-qualified amateur, based largely on first-hand observation.

Dodge expressed his intention to portray the Indian "exactly as he is," judging Indian people necessarily "from the civilized stand-point" but otherwise without bias. As steadily as his perceptions would permit, he sought to occupy a middle ground between two influential views of the Indian, both erroneous: on one side, "enthusiastic admiration for the 'noble Red Man,'" held by uninformed idealists; on the other, "prejudice against the ignoble savage," held by tacit exterminationists.[40] Writing as a friend to Indian people, he nonetheless portrayed them as real creatures, as "at least partially civilized" fellow human beings.[41] He submitted that earlier writers had failed to represent the Indian accurately and completely. Catlin, primarily a painter, produced vivid prose sketches of Indian life and costume but confined himself to external surfaces only, failing to comprehend even a basic but essential Indian term like medicine. The "ideal Indians" of Cooper were a conscious fiction, just as his fiendish Mingoes were also fantasies.[42] Those who credited the portrayals of Cooper and Catlin as representing real persons would turn with "loathing and disgust" from a glimpse at Indian life in the present: "The peerless warrior with 'eye like the eagle,' whose name a few short years ago was a terror, and whose swoop destruction, may be found patiently plodding between the handles of a plough. The tender maiden,—wont in fiction to sacrifice herself to save her lover, or, reduced to despair, to fling herself from 'tallest cliff into the raging flood beneath,'—may now be seen following the plough of the father, nimbly plying the sportive hoe, intent only on getting through with a square day's work, and thinking fondly of the square meal that is to follow it."[43] Dodge proposed to

39. *OWI*, pp. 79–80, 279–80. See the journal entries for March 25 and May 31, 1879.
40. *OWI*, p. 41.
41. *OWI*, p. 67.
42. *OWI*, pp. 43, 54.
43. *OWI*, p. 258.

strip away the veil of romance that obscured some readers' perception of Indians, exposing to view the reality of their everyday existence.

Early in the work Dodge pointed out that the great diversity of customs and character among Indian peoples made easy generalizations about them always doubtful.[44] In his chapters he referred to a great many tribes—Algonquins, Apaches, Arapahos, Bannocks, Cherokees, Cheyennes, Chickasaws, Chippewas, Choctaws, Comanches, Dakotas, Delawares, Diggers, Gros Ventres, Hidatsas, Kickapoos, Kiowas, Minneconjou Sioux, Moquis, Navajos, Nez Perces, Ogallala Sioux, Omahas, Osages, Pawnees, Poncas, Shoshonis, Snakes, Tonkaways, Utes, Winnebagoes, and Zunis—but he did not pretend that his portrayal of Indian life was comprehensive. The tribes he described the most fully were the native inhabitants of the western plains. His most fruitful source of examples was the Cheyenne Indians, as it had been in *Plains*. Contact with members of this tribe while at Cantonment had enriched his understanding of their culture, even though that comprehension remained far from complete. He presented his work as a general commentary, dealing primarily with the Plains tribes and focusing most often on the Cheyennes.

The most fruitful published source of material for the new manuscript was Dodge's own book, *The Plains of North America and Their Inhabitants*. Of the fifty-one chapters in the final draft, nineteen were essentially identical to passages in the earlier work, sometimes rephrased or reorganized but otherwise unchanged.[45] Lest he be accused of covertly plagiarizing from himself or representing as original a book that contained sections that had previously appeared in print, in the preface he made clear his concerns on just those issues. Friends had overruled his scruples, he added, and he therefore contented himself with a general acknowledgment of self-indebtedness.[46] Eleven other chapters of the new work also derived from *Plains* but

44. *OWI*, p. 53. In a preliminary jab at federal Indian policy, Dodge wrote that the various Indian tribes shared in common only that "all are savage, all are swindled, starved, and imposed upon."

45. Chapters 3, 4, 5, 6, 9, 10, 13, 15, 16, 22, 25, 26, 33, 34, 38, 40, 41, 43, and 44.

46. "Author's Preface," *OWI*, p. v.

contained a large majority of fresh material. Several of these were three thousand–word treatments of topics that earlier had been dealt with in a paragraph or two.[47] Twenty-one other chapters and the "L'Envoi" were without precedent in *Plains*.[48]

The general manner in which Dodge went about incorporating passages from *Plains* is evident from comparison of the two books. Of the first sixteen chapters in the book manuscript, roughly one-third its length, nine included lengthy passages from *Plains*.[49] However, of the thirty-five chapters that remained, all but ten were almost entirely or entirely new.[50] That is, after writing two initial chapters expressly for the new book, through chapter 16 Dodge drew extensively upon *Plains*. After that point it served him only to supplement discussions that he was drafting for the first time.[51]

Not surprisingly, then, the two works shared many features, in subject matter and also in style. The straightforward ease of Dodge's commentary in *Plains* had won praise from several reviewers. The *Atlantic Monthly* likened his writing to conversation, "the talk of a man who has a good deal to say and knows how to say it," and the *Nation* found in its wealth of anecdotes "all the charm of oral narrative."[52] The new manuscript also warranted comment of this sort, its easy movement from example to example suggesting a deep reservoir of information. Dodge's disinclination to shape each chapter according to an inflexible pattern was actually a source of interest in itself, for a reader could not be certain what new material he might encounter on the next turn of a page. The work gave pleasure even as it conveyed its

47. Chapters 1, 17, 23, 24, 28, 32, 39, 42, 45, 46, and 47.

48. Chapters 2, 7, 8, 11, 12, 14, 18, 19, 20, 21, 27, 29, 30, 31, 35, 36, 37, 48, 49, 50, and 51.

49. Chapters 1, 3, 4, 6, 9, 10, 13, 15, and 16.

50. Chapters 17, 18, 19, 20, 21, 23, 24, 27, 28, 29, 30, 31, 32, 35, 36, 37, 39, 42, 45, 46, 47, 48, 49, 50, and 51.

51. Eight of the new chapters dealt with subjects Dodge had intended to cover in *Plains*. These were chapters 35–37, on Army life on the plains; chapters 48–50, on frontiersmen; and chapters 29 and 30, on sign language and chronological measurement, the latter two being topics his friend and editor, William Blackmore, had planned to discuss.

52. Quoted in *PNA*, p. 29.

information. It was published in 1882 as *Our Wild Indians*, followed by a lengthy subtitle that included the apt phrase *A Popular Account*.[53]

Dodge hoped *Our Wild Indians* would reach a larger audience than *Plains*, and the style of the later work manifests his effort to appeal to popular taste. At the time he wrote *Plains*, in 1874 and 1875, he was still something of a novice author, but that was no longer the case. Assured of his abilities and engaged in a process of composition that he enjoyed, he now wrote with easy confidence, occasionally reaching after some happy effect or permitting himself little elegancies of style. Wishing to evoke the pre-dawn moments on November 25, 1876, when Colonel Mackenzie and his force of cavalry and Indians were about to begin their attack on the village of Dull Knife, he began with an exclamation—"Imagine the scene!"[54] From time to time he alluded to passages from the Bible and the writings of Shakespeare and later authors, including Laurence Sterne, William Hazlitt, Wordsworth, Dickens, and Bulwer-Lytton, often quoting a line or two. He delivered himself of neatly crafted, sometimes pungent phrases (Indian chiefs "suave as a crossroads politician"; "the Great American Buffalo Destroyer, fearless as Bayard, unsavory as a skunk") and maxims that ring like Rochefoucauld's.[55] The playful tone of observations like these conveys his awareness that the book was, after all, a performance.

Naturally Dodge portrayed himself in the manuscript, both implicitly through his narrative manner and explicitly through description of scenes and events he had observed. However, he rarely represented

53. The full title of the book was probably the work of Dodge's publisher, A. D. Worthington, who employed verbal grandiloquence as a marketing tool. It was *Our Wild Indians: Thirty-three Years' Personal Experience Among the Red Men of the Great West. A Popular Account of Their Social Life, Religion, Habits, Traits, Customs, Exploits, etc. With Thrilling Adventures and Experiences on the Great Plains and in the Mountains of Our Wide Frontier.*

54. *OWI*, p. 492. At some points Dodge presented narrative material in monologue or dialogue form, as when he portrayed Amos Chapman describing his adventures in the Buffalo Wallow fight, pp. 631–32.

55. *OWI*, pp. 76, 608. Among the apothegms were these: "Religious faith (or what we call superstition when applied to any religion but the one we happen to believe in) is strongest among the uneducated" (p. 149); "In all ages and climes the blessed sex have arrogated to themselves the right of exaggeration in all matters of sentiment or affection" (p. 171).

himself as a participant in the events he recounted. For example, he introduced the outbreak and flight of the Northern Cheyennes in 1878 as "the most extraordinary feat of travel and pursuit within my knowledge," but in the pages that follow he said nothing of the part he had played in the effort to capture the Indians.[56] Similarly, he referred several times to events in the Black Hills in recent years but said nothing of the important role he had played there in 1875. On the other hand, he paid generous tribute to several other Army officers with whom he had shared experiences. General George Crook received praise for his courage and independence of mind, especially in his willingness to employ Indian scouts in campaigns against other Indians. Captain George Randall was described as "a man who, in knowledge of Indians and success of their management, is second to no man on the frontier." Dodge introduced Amos Chapman as "One of the best and bravest, the most sober, quiet and genial of all scouts I have ever known."[57] He described the deeds of certain other officers without divulging their names but in a manner that would make their identities recognizable at once to informed readers.[58] Because he was confining himself to topics always in some way connected with Indians, he refrained from presenting detailed accounts of the Army's performances in battle. Narratives of that stirring sort might easily be multiplied, he wrote, "but grateful as is the task of recording such noble deeds, I will leave it to other pens."[59]

Our Wild Indians touches upon a wide range of topics relating to Plains Indians—tribal government, warrior societies, medicine chiefs, rites and ceremonies, burial and mourning, training in childhood, the life of women, names and epithets, music, and cooks and cooking, to name only a few. In the diversity of its coverage it is a continuously interesting book. Some of its engaging character is owing to the

56. *OWI*, pp. 572-73.
57. *OWI*, pp. 492-93, 111, and 628, respectively.
58. For example, see *OWI*, p. 164 (Captain Pollock), 310 (Captain Randall).
59. *OWI*, p. 472. In the first of his three chapters describing Army life on the plains, Dodge did write a brief tribute to the United States Army for its contributions to the nation's century of unexampled progress. See *OWI*, pp. 469-70.

author's genial assurances that, however outlandish some beliefs and practices of the Indians might seem, they are at bottom human beings like everyone else. Ordinarily he offered manifestations of this truth with irony directed simultaneously toward his "savage" subjects and his "civilized" audience. For example, in describing the great authority enjoyed by Indian soothsayers, he wrote: "Be he civilized or be he savage, man delights in being humbugged, and any pretender to mysteries, either medical or spiritual, is sure to find some one to believe him."[60] Elsewhere, discussing items of personal decoration, he mentioned that the fortunate few who can ornament their war-bonnets with eagle's quills "value them as a millionaire his estate, and they serve exactly the same purpose, often pushing forward a man who has no other claim to distinction."[61] Recounting a conversation between himself and Stone Calf wherein the old chief expressed his will to die fighting rather than submit to starvation, he recalled the admiration he felt for his friend's manly self-respect. "Were I an Indian," he concludes, "I fear that, with their provocations, I should be a bad Indian."[62]

At many points in *Our Wild Indians* Dodge wrote of the great changes that had occurred in Indian life in recent years. Exposure to new conditions brought on by the advance of modern civilization had of course inevitably affected some Indian customs and beliefs. The tomahawk, for example, was once a prime weapon of a warrior, but it had become a mere ceremonial ornament, like a lady's fan. The medicine dance, once swathed in secrecy and mandatory for all young men as a rite of initiation into warrior status, had become optional, with the ceremony open even to casual observers from outside the tribe. The good old times of hunting for food were almost gone, for the buffalo and many other game animals had been all but exterminated.[63]

Dodge itemized developments like these with some regret, for they marked a departure from customs in times when the Cheyennes and

60. *OWI*, p. 125.
61. *OWI*, p. 305.
62. *OWI*, p. 280.
63. *OWI*, pp. 143, 153, 420, and 578.

other tribes had functioned splendidly as independent societies. Yet he also described changes of an even graver character that were directly attributable to the effects on Indians of reservation life. In describing these developments, his tone was not that of a detached anthropological observer or of a genial fellow human being attuned to our mutual folly. Instead, he wrote as an advocate of the Indian and a scandalized United States citizen.

According to Dodge, the most visible alteration in Indian life since their relocation onto reservations was the new importance necessarily given by them to food. As late as 1872 the question of access to food was of small concern, but it had since become "the paramount, and . . . I may say, the only question."[64] He painted a grim picture of the poverty suffered by Indians placed on reservations and forced to live there as effective prisoners. He pictured men and women at military posts examining the contents of slop-barrels and dump piles, carrying off "stuff that a cur would disdain." At Fort Reno, where naive citizens in the eastern states might suppose hunger could never occur, "a dead horse or mule is no sooner dragged away from the vicinity of the post, than it is pounced upon, cut up and carried off by the starved Indians. They ask no questions, and meat is meat, even though it was killed for farcy or glanders. Nothing is too disgustingly filthy to come amiss to the starving Indian."[65]

Matter of this kind was painful to read, and intentionally so. By his insistent use of words like *starved*, Dodge was portraying dramatically the abject state of Indians as the result of their treatment by the United States government. The varied tones of *Our Wild Indians* thus expressed a double purpose. As an informal account of Indian beliefs, pastimes, and customs it was a comfortable work to peruse; as a critique of the nation's policy toward Indians it was not comfortable, for it resonated with angry frustration. Perhaps disconcertingly to casual readers, within a single chapter it often modulated from one tone and purpose to the other, invariably passing from inoffensiveness to corrosive

64. *OWI*, p. 279.
65. *OWI*, pp. 280–81.

criticism.[66] Viewed as a whole, the book itself developed in the same direction. Moving in general from topics without political overtones, it became in its later chapters a tract for the times—an indictment of federal Indian policy and a call for reform.

In Dodge's view the historical source of the government's disastrous record of official contact with the Indians was its absurd reliance on a treaty system that equated savage bands with sovereign states, as if they possessed the power to enter into legal relationships with nations around the world. Often as the consequence of defeat in war, in recent decades tribes had unwillingly entered into treaty agreements with the United States. In return for possession of the tribe's ancestral range, the government had undertaken to provide its members a new home in Indian Territory and supply them regular rations, annuity goods, and perhaps other benefits. Professing a will to fair play, it then moved the defeated people to locations far from their tribal homes and forcibly confined them there. Gnawed by homesickness and unable to grow accustomed to the new mode of life being imposed on them, many of the Indian people grew ill and died. This was the consequence of treating Indian tribes as sovereign nations—a result "ludicrous, were it not so sad."[67]

To complicate the wrong, the government had failed repeatedly to abide by the terms of its solemn covenants with Indian tribes. As examples, Dodge cited provisions in the *Revised Statutes* designed to protect Indians by prohibiting entry onto their reservations by commercial hunters and others who might victimize them. These laws were not rigorously enforced and were thus in effect misrepresentations of the national will. The statute prohibiting hunting and trapping on Indian lands "is and has always been a dead letter, the whole of that country having been constantly overrun by white men, who made their living by killing game and trapping the fur-bearing animals."

66. For example, see chapter 15, entitled "Love-Making in an Indian Camp—Courtship and Marriage," pp. 194–203; chapter 22, "The Buffalo and its Destruction," pp. 282–96.

67. *OWI*, pp. 89–91, 267. Dodge returns to this theme on several occasions, invariably labeling the government's treaty system "absurd."

The slaughter of five million buffalo on the southern plains in the early 1870s was a violation of federal law and a contravention of Indian treaties, but Congress chose not to interfere. That lax enforcement resulted in the almost complete loss of the tribes' traditional mode of subsistence by hunting.[68] By then appropriating too few funds to purchase food and other supplies for the Indians, again guaranteed by treaty, the United States government had tacitly condemned tribes on reservations to slow starvation. Little wonder, Dodge observed, that the hopeless vision of their future drove some Indians to "aggressive desperation." They resolved "to die fighting rather than by the slow torture of starvation to which the government condemns them."[69]

Dodge argued that the reservation system harmed the Indians not only by failing to satisfy their physical needs but by providing an inadequate system of law enforcement. Having undermined tribal government by dispossessing the chiefs and intratribal organizations of their despotic powers, the United States had made all tribespeople equally subject to the will of the Indian agent. That substitution had perhaps benefited the Indians as a first step toward democratic rule, but it left almost no provision for the control of criminal behavior that was earlier exerted by the chiefs and tribal councils. Dodge described several instances of the lawless conditions that grew unchecked within this legal vacuum, but the most dramatic was an incident recounted to him by Stone Calf. The chief's thirteen-year-old daughter, "his pet and jewel," was sent one day with another girl to deliver a message to a sub-chief seven miles away. The girls performed the errand, but on their return they were waylaid by a renegade member of Stone Calf's band who, pistol in hand, ordered the companion away. He then took the chief's daughter to his lodge and in the presence of his wives raped her repeatedly. Fearing reprisal, after two days he went in search of Stone Calf and took the girl to Cantonment, where she managed to escape to the tipi of one of the Indian scouts.

68. *OWI*, pp. 265, 296.
69. *OWI*, pp. 259, 313.

Later that day Stone Calf sought out Dodge and "begged for vengeance":

> "Have you among yourselves no remedy for such outrages?" I asked.
>
> "Yes," he replied, "I can kill him, and I ought to kill him, but the agent is not my friend, and if I do kill this scoundrel, the agent will put me in the guardhouse, and when I get out not only my daughter, but my wives and family will all be gone or outraged."
>
> "I am truly sorry for you, my friend," I said, "but I can do absolutely nothing. If this were a white villain I would put him in my guard-house, and turn him over to the civil authorities for trial, but he is an Indian, and there is no law to punish such acts when committed by Indians."
>
> Covering his face with his hands, the old man was bent and racked with emotion. Recovering himself he placed his hand on my arm, and in a quivering voice, said:
>
> "I am sick of the Indian road, it is not good;" then raising his eyes to Heaven, he added:
>
> "I hope the Good God will give us the white man's road before we are all destroyed."[70]

The predicament of Stone Calf was essentially that of any Indian man or woman on the reservation who, when mistreated in any way, was without recourse through a code of law.

An axiom of Dodge's conception of Indian character had long been that, unlike civilized persons, Indians lacked a moral sense. Although in civilized society a code of morality articulated the mutual obligations of individuals, the Indian had no conception of right and wrong as abstract realities. "All is right that he wishes to do, all is wrong that opposes him."[71] In the absence of social control, lawlessness must therefore prevail. As Dodge portrayed it, life on an Indian reservation was far from being a benign modification of traditional ways that gradually acclimated tribesmen to more progressive modes of living. Instead, quoting Wordsworth, he represented it as often vicious and predatory, where "he shall take who has the power, and he shall keep who can."[72]

70. *OWI*, pp. 95–97.
71. *OWI*, pp. 57–58. The Indian's lack of a moral sense had been a theme of *Plains*; see, for example, pp. 247–48.
72. *OWI*, p. 601. See Wordsworth, "Rob Roy's Grave."

In making his case against the reservation system, Dodge reserved the most bitter denunciation for its cruelest fixture, the authorized Indian trader. A trader's monopoly, he explained, was complete, enabling him to cheat at will the persons whom he was appointed to serve. As an instance of the treatment suffered by Indians at the hands of traders he recounted an experience recently reported to him by the victim. This man had cut twenty cords of wood for a contractor at $1.25 per cord, and on delivering the wood he received an order on the authorized trader for the agreed amount. But on presenting the warrant he received, not money, but supplies in kind amounting to one pint of brown sugar for each cord of wood. He had been grossly cheated, but he could do nothing since the trader was without competition and supervision. Dodge likened merchants like this one to harpies that, "under the guise of friendship," devour their helpless victims.[73]

In the incident of cordwood and brown sugar the unscrupulous trader was almost certainly George A. Reynolds, whose practices Dodge had interfered with to the extent he could. However, in *Our Wild Indians* he did not name Reynolds or any other abuser of delegated power, for after all, the problem was widespread, and ultimate responsibility lay with the government that sustained the system. Similarly, when discussing the necessity of stationing "a force of troops to watch and guard" the Indians on reservations, he clearly had in mind posts like Cantonment.[74] But in this context he did not name it or other particular posts, for the situation was endemic to much of Indian Territory.

73. *OWI*, pp. 269, 296. Elsewhere Dodge refers to the Indian trader in equally strong terms, denominating him "the monster devised by the government to keep the Indian in abject penury" (p. 281).

74. Dodge was here describing the fate of the Nez Perces, a tribe "which for generations has lived in the most amicable relations with white men, [but] is, for a single outbreak, forced on it by injustice, greed and aggression, exiled to a strange land. Despairing and desperate, men who have been our life-long friends are converted into unforgiving enemies. Hoping, almost praying, for an excuse for outbreak, willing to risk death for even the slightest chance of regaining their loved homes, these fragments of bands are a constant source of anxiety to States containing over two millions of inhabitants, and require a force of troops to watch and control them, at an expense ten times greater than would feed, clothe, house, and make them valuable citizens in the countries for which they yearn" (*OWI*, p. 314).

In concluding *Our Wild Indians* Dodge expressed his desire as a citizen to preserve the honor of his nation. Americans, he maintained, were honorable, merciful, and readily aroused to sympathy for the plight of oppressed peoples elsewhere in the world. Yet, owing chiefly to the remoteness of Indian territory and their ignorance of conditions there, they had thus far permitted the Indians to suffer without sympathy. Dodge called upon his compatriots to consider the nation's treatment of the Indians in its full enormity and recognize their complicity in the wrong. Next to slavery, he held, "the foulest blot on the escutcheon of the Government of the United States is its treatment of the so-called 'Wards of the Nation.'"[75] By denying citizenship to the Indian and refusing him the right to possess land in severalty, the nation was condemning him to a cycle of degradation, impoverishment, and despair.

The "L'Envoi," far from an elegant coda to a neatly framed literary exercise, was a passionate call to reform. In it, Dodge affirmed his awareness that in the body of the book he had seriously offended certain classes of readers. Those good men and women who, misled by Cooper, Catlin, and others, chose to embrace as reality a fanciful conception of the Indian, had been painfully disabused. They preferred their supposed Indians to continue existing in some pristine state, but the laws of progress and the Indians' actual nature made that wish impossible. Another group, the professional humanitarians, served and were served by the status quo, providing for themselves while victimizing the Indian whose plight they professed a wish to alleviate. To those persons Dodge offered no apology. Rather, he declared his "unalterable hostility" to them and expressed determination "to use every faculty with which I am endowed to wrench the Indian from their sordid grasp."[76]

As a proponent of reform, Dodge addressed himself to a third group of readers, the great mass of Americans who, passing through life with their own preoccupations, had known little and cared less about the Indian. Only a few decades before, he pointed out, the

75. *OWI*, pp. 639–40.
76. *OWI*, p. 652.

term *Abolitionist* had been one of bitter reproach. Many honorable persons had doubted the wisdom of emancipating Negro slaves and extending to them the rights and duties of citizenship. Yet the Negro race had already justified the nation's commitment to it, swelling the number of its valuable citizens. The same prospect lay open to the Indian, if only the energy of "a few true men" could be brought to bear in his behalf. Like the Abolitionists, the future friends of the Indian must steel themselves to endure a long and sometimes desperate struggle, retaining unshakable faith in the wise humanity of the American people. Dodge appealed to the press, the pulpit, "every lover of humanity": "Arouse to this grand work. No slave now treads the soil of this noble land. Force your representatives to release the Indian from an official bondage more remorseless, more hideous than slavery itself. Deliver him from his pretended friends, and lift him into fellowship with the citizens of our loved and glorious country."[77]

Clearly the composition of *Our Wild Indians* had become for Dodge more than an ambitious project of authorship. It was also a private mission, an appeal for action on behalf of American Indians, many of whom he had come to know, respect, and pity. He included in his book a list of policy changes that he believed would ameliorate the status of the tribes on reservations.[78] Not all of these proposals would be acted upon in the near future, but at least he had used his status as a known author to set forth a program for reform of the sorry arrangements that prevailed. Of course, his recommendations would be discounted by some as merely a partisan appeal, as indeed it was. The first two of his ten policy suggestions were to turn over the care of Indians to the War Department and to abolish the Indian Bureau as then constituted, proposals already long debated and with entrenched adherents on both sides. What gave his book unique power was the connection it estab-lished between his own experience of actual conditions and the ideas he advanced to root out their underlying causes. *Our Wild Indians* was an authoritative report and recommendation from the field.

77. *OWI*, p. 653.
78. *OWI*, pp. 646–47.

The completion of his book manuscript was in several respects a time of fulfillment for Dodge. He could look back at the past two years as among the most eventful of his career. He had been called upon to serve in a variety of capacities and had in every instance acquitted himself ably, to the satisfaction of himself and almost all others. As a field commander against the Northern Cheyennes he had faithfully followed orders that ran counter to his better judgment and, when challenged, had vindicated himself from imputation otherwise. His report of the midwinter reconnaissance mission had won full approval, even though it had yielded a recommendation somewhat different from what General Pope had anticipated. The move from Fort Hays and the establishment of the new post had been conspicuously successful. As post commander at Cantonment he had directed an ambitious construction program, effectively parried the attacks of Agent Miles, and promoted the welfare of the Indians living around him. He had been a factor in deposing Lee and Reynolds from their role as Kings of the Indian Territory, and if his stewardship of Keeling and Co. had not been a complete success, the result was not for lack of high principle and due effort. Later he had proved a faithful subaltern under the exacting eye of Colonel Mackenzie, and in the past three months he had drafted a substantial book on a topic that concerned him deeply. Certainly as a professional soldier and an author he had reason to reflect with satisfaction on the past two years. And as a father and husband he had been hardly less fortunate. Fred was well launched on a stage career,[79] and Julia seemed more inclined than in recent years toward a reconciliation.[80]

79. Frederick Paulding continued for many years as an actor, writer, and lecturer. He never achieved star stature on the New York stage, but he participated in some celebrated productions, including a long run in 1885–86 as Romeo opposite Margaret Mather's Juliet. His activities in New York are detailed in Odell's *Annals of the New York Stage*, volumes 10–14, *passim*; see also Bordman, *American Theatre*, pp. 132, 161, 317, 576, 639–40. After 1910 Paulding devoted his energies to readings and dramatic recitals, giving one-man performances in New York hotels and in schools, colleges, and clubs across the country. For his contributions to the drama he was awarded an honorary Doctor of Letters degree from Holy Cross College. He died in 1937 (*New York Times*, September 8, 1937, p. 23).

80. A partial reconciliation eventually did occur between Dodge and his wife. In 1884 he wrote to Fred, who hoped to reunite his parents: "At present we do not

The closing months of 1880 also brought to Dodge hopeful antici-
pations for the future. Legislation then under review in Congress
would make mandatory the retirement from active duty of Army
officers sixty-two years of age and over. Enactment of that law would
help break the logjam for promotion that had demoralized the service
for years, and Dodge knew well that it would make him a full colonel
at once.[81] What was more, General Pope had privately informed him
early in November of another wholly unanticipated development.
General Sherman had requested him to supply the name of an officer
to replace the late Colonel Joseph C. Audenried, Sixth Cavalry, as a
member of his personal staff. He had named Dodge, and as he wrote
in strict confidence, he had just done so again.[82] Service as aide-de-
camp to the General of the Army carried with it the rank and salary
of colonel, but to military men it was yet more valuable as a mark of

---

quarrel, & there is nothing on my part to keep alive the animosity that she has
exhibited towards me for some years. If you now begin to *urge reconciliation* she
will in true womanly perversity revive in her own mind those old animosities—now
dormant—or she will conclude that I am at the bottom of your appeal, will hate me
worse than ever, & you may possibly come in for ill feeling as a dupe & tool of mine.
Be assured my dear boy, that I understand this matter better than you possibly can.
The only hope for future peace & reconciled life between us, *is to let her entirely
alone.* I believe she has a strong womanly attachment for me, now & of late years
obscured by diseased imaginings. If not *fixed* in her by trying to turn her too suddenly,
these ill-feelings will probably wear away with the disease. . . . I dont want her until
she can come to me an affectionate wife, happy in me & contented with her lot. I
dont want her to come from love & deference to you or your wishes" (RID to
Frederick Paulding, July 17, 1884—Dodge Papers, Graff Collection).

Dodge continued to support his wife in the years afterward, and the two corre-
sponded and exchanged visits. The last letter he is known to have written, dated three
weeks before his death on June 16, 1895, was an affectionate note addressed to "Julia"
from Sackett's Harbor, New York, his chief place of residence following his retirement in 1891. He had just returned from the home she then shared with Fred in New
Rochelle, New York (RID to Julia R. P. Dodge, May 25, 1895—Dodge Papers, Yale
Collection). Julia died in 1926 at the home of her son in Rutherford, New Jersey; Fred
had never married (*New York Times*, January 7, 1926, p. 25).

81. Evidence of junior officers' desire for brighter prospects of advancement in
rank appeared regularly in the *Army and Navy Journal*, especially during this period.
For example, see the issues for August 21, 1880, p. 49; November 6, pp. 268–69;
December 11, p. 377. In June 1882 Congress mandated the retirement of Army
officers at the age of sixty-four (Coffman, *The Old Army*, pp. 232–33).

82. Pope to RID, November 2, 1880 (Dodge Papers, Graff Collection). Audenried
had died on June 3, 1880; for a summary of his career see *ANJ*, June 5, 1880, p. 897.

recognition by the Army for the merits of one of its own. To have been nominated by Pope for such a position was to Dodge a gratifying mark of his department commander's regard.

As he had done with his two earlier books, Dodge planned a trip to New York to find a publisher once he had a copy of the completed manuscript in hand for review. He therefore applied for a four-month leave of absence that would afford him time also to correct proofs, collect illustrations, and attend to details of production that he regretted not being able to oversee before *Plains* was issued. Early in December an authorization for the requested period arrived,[83] and he began his preparations for a long absence. He was packed and ready to depart from Cantonment when, on December 15, he received notice by telegraph that General Pope had been directed to order him to report in person to the General of the Army.[84] Sherman had selected him as the senior member of his staff, to replace Colonel Alexander McD. McCook, who had just been promoted to command the Sixth Infantry. On December 16 Pope ordered Dodge by telegraph to report to Fort Leavenworth,[85] and Dodge therefore dismissed without regret his leave of absence, gathering his possessions for a permanent departure from the post.[86] On December 17 he issued his final order

83. S.O. 257, November 24, 1880—DMO, granted Dodge one month's leave of absence, with permission to apply for an extension of three months.

84. William D. Whipple, AAG MDM, to RID, December 15, 1880 (Dodge Papers, Graff Collection).

85. Pope to RID, December 16, 1880 (Dodge Papers, Graff Collection). Sherman's new aides-de-camp were announced in G.O. 82, Headquarters of the Army, December 17, 1880. His had appointed one officer from each of three arms of the regular army. The appointees included Dodge, representing the infantry; Major John C. Tidball, Second Artillery; and Major Albert P. Morrow, Ninth Cavalry. See also *ANJ*, December 18, 1880, p. 394.

86. Dodge never returned to Cantonment, and the history of the post after his departure was brief. In August 1881 the Commissioner of Indian Affairs approved the removal of Little Chief and his people to Pine Ridge agency, in Dakota Territory, and on October 6 of that year the band began the march north. See Powell, *Sweet Medicine*, 1:282–84. With their departure a major reason for Cantonment's continued existence was removed. Company G, Twenty-third Infantry, had left the post in January 1881 to take post at Fort Reno, and thereafter Cantonment was garrisoned by units of the Twenty-second Infantry and Fourth Cavalry. For a time as many as three companies were stationed there, but in May 1882 Company K, Fourth Cavalry,

as commander of Cantonment, directing a sergeant and three privates to proceed to Caldwell, Kansas, the next day "as escort to public transportation."[87]

On his return to Cantonment from Colorado three months before, Dodge had laid aside his journal, devoting his daily energies to the quiet labor of writing his book manuscript. But on the evening of December 18, camped twenty-five miles from Cantonment on the Pond Creek road, he took out his small pocket notebook and wrote a final summary entry:

December 18, 1880. Walnut Creek

With the exception of a little flyer to Ft Reno, & various little hunts I have been "Cabbin'd Cribbd, Confin'd"[88] hard at work.   Van Buren did my copying.

The "description[89] Mill" had to grind out a certain amount each day. About end of Novr. I applied for a leave of absence for 4 mos, & got it. In the mean time however I got a letter from Genl Pope telling me that Genl Sherman had asked him to recommend an Officer to take Audenrieds place on his staff – & he had recommended me – I wrote thanking him & to say I would accept the position if offered.   Then came the great excitement about the retirement of Officer[s] of & over 62 years, which if carried out would make me a Colonel at once, & in anticipation of my promotion I gave up all idea of the staff position.

---

was transferred to Fort Supply, and a month later Companies B and F, Twenty-Second Infantry, were transferred to Fort Elliott, leaving the post without a garrison (CNFCR Post Returns, January 1881–June 1882; ANJ, June 3, 1882, p. 1010).

Later in 1882 the post property was transferred to the Department of the Interior, which contracted with the Mennonite church to run a school for Indians. See Kaufman, "Mennonite Missions among the Oklahoma Indians," pp. 41–44. In 1898 the United States government assumed direct supervision of the property, which housed both a school and a mental hospital until 1949 (Frazer, *Forts of the West*, pp. 118–19). In recent years the original headquarters building, constructed under Dodge's supervision, has been restored. It is in use as the home of a Head Start program for local children, a function he would surely approve.

87. S.O. 119, December 17, 1880—CNFCR.

88. A quotation from *Macbeth* III.iv.24.

89. Dodge wrote "descrintion."

My book was finished on 12th, & I began packing – boxing every-thing carefully, to be stored until I send for it.   When nearly done (on 1<7>6th) received a telegram from Genl Pope directing me to report to him, before Jany 1 – that I would not return to Cant[onmen]t. but would be ordered to Washington.   Being all ready, I did not in any way change my programme – but started on Saturday 18th, the only difference being that I go under orders, instead of on leave.

Cold, disagreeable day, & commenced to snow after we got in Camp on Walnut Ck, but am very comfortable.   Letter from Mother, today, also tel[egra]m. from Whipple, notifying me that I am ordered to Washington.[90]

All has happened admirably & I am a truly fortunate man.

90. The transcribed telegram containing the information referred to here is dated December 16 (Dodge Papers, Graff Collection). The last official document pertaining to Dodge's four years of service in the Department of the Missouri between 1876 and 1880 was paragraph two, Special Order 283, issued at Fort Leavenworth on December 24: "Lieutenant-Colonel *R. I. Dodge*, 23d Infantry, having reported at these Head-quarters in compliance with paragraph 2 of Special Orders No. 276, current series, from these Headquarters, is relieved from duty in this Department, and will proceed to comply with orders received from the General of the Army."

Appendix A
Dodge's Manuscript Account of the Northern Cheyennes, November 1876–October 1878

[UNFORTUNATELY, THE PRECEDING NIGHT HAD BEEN intensely cold, not less than twenty degrees below zero. Indians when in camp, and unsuspicious of danger, habitually sleep naked.[1] The Cheyennes were so, and aroused as they were, had no time to clothe themselves; some few had seized a blanket or robe in their flight, but the large majority had no covering whatever. Human

---

1. Drawing upon information received from Captain Clarence Mauck, Fourth Cavalry, from official reports, and from hearsay, Dodge composed this account a few days after returning to Fort Hays, Kansas, after his participation in the effort to capture the fleeing Northern Cheyennes. The concluding paragraphs register his erroneous belief that, having reached the sand hills of northern Nebraska, the Indians would elude capture. In fact, the part of the band under Dull Knife was taken captive on October 23. Despite this and other errors of fact, the narrative conveys vividly Dodge's mixed reactions to the Northern Cheyennes: pity for their plight, respect for their fighting ability, admiration for their indomitable will, and horror at the enormities they had perpetrated.

The manuscript text is written in black ink on pages numbered 31–47 (Dodge Papers, Graff Collection). A pencilled line down the left margin of pp. 31–33 suggests editorial attention, by Dodge or another person. The three pages so marked were originally numbered pp. 28–30 and have been renumbered by Dodge. They include the text printed in *Our Wild Indians* at the close of chapter 37, pp. 498–500 ("build fires . . . inevitable."), where they are preceded by the material presented here within square brackets. Dodge's published account of the Dull Knife battle of November 25, 1876, emphasizes the tactical genius of General George Crook, who as commander of the Powder River Expedition had enlisted 350 Indian auxiliaries as members of his fighting force.

nature could not stand it, and notwithstanding their favorable tactical position, they were compelled to get back into the main cañon, and retreat to a position where they could] build fires and procure food. Collecting their herds of ponies they left during the night. Early next morning <scouts reported their> ∧ their departure ∧ was discovered , but Mackenzie's attempt at pursuit was frustrated in the first few miles, by a strong and determined rear guard posted as before in the rocks and summits of almost inaccessible cliffs.[2]

Our loss in this battle was one officer and five soldiers <and one enlisted Indian killed and tw> killed, twenty five soldiers and one enlisted Indian wounded. The <Indian> ∧ Cheyenne loss in killed and wounded was probably about fifty. Insignificant as it appears, this battle was a death-blow to the independence of a tribe of men as brave as ever trod the soil of Greece.

The sufferings of these Indians during the <next> three months ∧ succeeding the battle can never be known<,>. Numbers perished, principally women and children. With no food but the flesh of their ponies, no covering but the green hides of the same faithful animals, the survivors with indomitable determination made their way across the bleak and snow covered summit of the Big Horn Mountains, and after a long and most terrible march, presented themselves to Crazy Horse, then encamped on Mizpah Creek. At no time previous had the Cheyennes been otherwise than welcome visitors to the Sioux, but here was a band of near fifteen hundred people, absolutely impoverished, in want of tepees, clothing, food, everything. The warriors still possessed their gallant spirit, and burned for an opportunity for revenge against their white enemies, but their arms were in poor condition, their ammunition expended.

2. At this point on p. 31 in the manuscript Dodge wrote a reference mark signaling that a passage on the reverse side of that page was to be inserted. The paragraph that follows is the passage he wished to interpolate.

It was too great a tax on the Sioux chieftain, and he received the newcomers so coldly and with so scant a charity that they soon left his inhospitable camp.

They had not been defeated, yet they had received a blow far worse than a bloody defeat, and from which it would take years to recover. Their women were suffering, their children dying. Crazy Horse, their last hope, had failed them. Struggle as they might their fate was too hard for them. One cannot but feel sympathy for any people however savage, which after displays of desperate courage in battle, of fortitude
$\wedge$ under <, after> untold hardship and misery, is forced at last to yield to the inevitable.

In 1877 the Cheyennes came in and surrendered. Offered a home in the Indian Territory, with fair promises of food and other necessaries, they accepted gladly, as they would have accepted any terms which promised peace plenty and comfort —

It is not proposed to enquire into the treatment of the Cheyennes after they arrived in the Indian Territory, nor to take sides in the rather bitter controversy on this subject <now being> waged between the Indian department and the Army. Suffice to say, that after a residence there of but little over a year, a number of them became so intensely dissatisfied that they determined not to remain, preferring rather to incur all the dangers of an attempt to escape, with a possible repetition of many of the horrors of the Big Horn experience. The Cheyenne and Arrapahoe Reservation is situated on the Canadian River in the very heart of the Indian Territory. Near the

Agency is the Military Post of Fort Reno, garrisoned by two $\overset{2}{\wedge}$ Companies of Cavalry and two $\overset{2}{\wedge}$ of Infantry, numbering all told, scarcely one hundred and fifty effective men, with which formidable force, the Commanding Officer, (by some grand fiction of the elastic Governmental brain), is expected to keep in subjection and control some four thousand of the best fighting men in this or any country.

About the 1st September it began to be rumored about the garrison that some of the Cheyennes were preparing to leave, and that the disaffected were collecting in the sand-hills some twelve miles from the post.   A force was sent out to investigate, but no sooner had it arrived in the vecinity of the Indians, than they silently decamped in the night, leaving their tepees standing, and abandoning all but the most portable and absolutely necessary of their property.   So far as can be ascertained, this recalcitrant force numbered not more than one hundred warriors, led by Dull Knife.   They were encumbered with more than two hundred and fifty women and children.

All the disposable force at Fort Reno was at once ordered in pursuit. The movements and actions of the Indians for the next twenty days evidenced the most utter contempt for the forces which could be brought against them.   Moving most leisurely, averaging less than fifteen miles a day, they were on 13th Sepr. overtaken by their pursuers on the Cimarron River, near the mouth of Bluff Creek.

A demand to surrender being met by abrupt defiance, the Cavalry at once attacked, but, though nearly equal in number to their enemies, they were in an instant surrounded, forced to seek cover, <and> held as in a prison without water for thirty six hours, at the end of which time they were glad to escape and get back to Camp Supply with a loss of three killed and four wounded.   On the 18th in the breaks of Bear Creek, scarcely twenty five miles from the battle ground of the 13th the Indians were again overtaken, this time by a single small company of Cavalry.   The resulting conflict was not a desperate one; the soldiers prudently withdrawing with the loss of one man wounded. On the 23d the Indians crossed the Arkansas.   Up to this time nothing could exceed their contemptuous audacity.   They had marched but about one hundred and seventy-five miles in twenty days.   From the 13th to the 23d they were at no time further than 40 miles from Fort Dodge.   The attacks of the scanty force of troops were repulsed as a magnanimous mastiff might shake off the attacks of a tiny cur, no effort being made to pursue the beaten troops.

Moving up into the great plains around the sink of Poison Creek (the only section between the Arkansas and the Platte where buffalo could then

<may yet>   ∧   be found) they were enjoying themselves at
their favorite sport and at the same time laying in a good supply of
food, when their rear guards discovered an enemy more formidable
than they had yet encountered.   They were evidently not at all frightened, but this persistent pursuit annoyed them, and they determined
to rid themselves of the annoyance.

Poison Creek takes its rise on the high plains, cutting many cañons,
not remarkable for depth, but for the abruptness of their walls.   A
box-cañon is one, the sides and upper end of which are [per]pen-
dicular, the only outlet being from below.   Such a cañon was selected
as the trap into which Lewis and his command was to be enticed and
slaughtered at pleasure.   A heavy trail was made directly up this
cañon indicating, apparently, that the whole body of Indians had
passed that way.   All along the top of the cañon rifle-pits were constructed, ingeniously, in that from the outside they were unnoticeable.
In a lateral cañon just below the point where the *box* of the main
cañon commenced, nearly half the fighting force of the band were
assembled on horseback, ready to dash in and close up the mouth of
the box when the last soldier had entered, and thus assure the destruction of the entire command.   Lewis had several Pawnee Indian guides

somewhat

who were <considerably>   ∧   in advance of the column.
These, with the precaution natural to all Indians, looked carefully
around before entering the box, and discovering the mounted Indians
in ambush in their rear, at once gave the alarm.   Immediately the
ambushed Indians charged with vigor and gallantry attempting to force
the command into the cañon.   Realizing the situation, Lewis immediately faced his command to its flank, and scaled the side of the ravine,
fortunately not yet too steep for such manoevre.   The country was so
broken, the Cavalry could do nothing as cavalry.   They were dismounted and ordered into the fight.   The moment the heights were
scaled the Infantry were deployed as skirmishers, and wheeling
around the rear of the rifle pits dislodged the defenders, and drove
them into the cañon below.   In a very few moments the affair was

over, the Cheyennes disappearing entirely, not however until they had inflicted an irreparable loss on the Army and Country, in mortally wounding the gallant Lewis.   One soldier was mortally, another slightly wounded.   The Cheyenne loss is unknown but must have been considerable.   Sixteen ponies were left wounded on the field, and over seventy were captured.   The Indians had laid an ingenious and fatal trap, and the command was saved from Custer's fate, only by the fortunate discovery made by the Pawnee guides, and by the prompt action and soldierly skill of Lewis.

Up to this time the Cheyennes had seemed to act on a "laisser faire" policy.[3]   They had done no special damage to settlers or others; had moved slowly and easily, contenting themselves with shaking off their pursuers when too pertinacious.   This blow changed their whole action.   Escaping as best they might from the field of battle, they pushed north-east for about twenty miles and went into camp, late at night, on the head waters of Chalk Creek.   Here they remained until late next morning, and here were matured their plans for future movement.   Not only were the mode and speed of the march entirely changed, but also its direction.   The loss of nearly a thousand ponies made a detour into the settlements, where they could obtain a remount, almost an imperative necessity.   Hitherto they had all travelled together, taking no pains to conceal their trail.   Henceforth they were apart, no two ponies following each other, the trail of the whole band

<being from three>   covering a space   from three to five miles wide.
                         ∧

Hitherto they had marched at their leisure, now they are to travel like the wind.   Hitherto they had been a pic-nic party pleasantly sauntering through the country, taking what they wanted, but doing no wanton damage; henceforth they are to be a scourge and a terror revenging on the innocent and unarmed settlers, the miseries they themselves have suffered at the hands of the whiteman —

The line of the Kansas Pacific R.R. was guarded by an ample force of troops.   Everything had been fully matured, and it was confidently

3. Here, a live-and-let-live policy.

believed that the Indians could not possibly escape from the toils spread for them.   Sheridan seemed to be the point for which they were aiming, and Mauck (now in command of Lewis' column) so notified the officer in command of the line.   But the Indians, acting on their new tactics, had swung in a broad band down Chalk Creek to its junction with Beaver down Beaver to its junction with Smoky then due North, and crossing the R. R. on the night of the 28th (with extra precautions as to their trail) had gone into camp, somewhere in the "wee sma'hours"[4] on the Saline, not more than six miles from Carlisle, having made the extraordinary march of at least seventy miles without a halt, and in about twenty six hours.   On the Saline they remained until the afternoon of the 29th, when a march of forty five miles brought them to the Prairie Dog.   Early on the morning of Monday the 30th, they commenced their depradations on the South Sappa.

Mauck arrived at Carlisle on the trail at 11 am on Sunday, 29th, but so careful had been the Cheyennes, that with all his astuteness, his Pawnee guides were unable to fix the direction of the trail until late that afternoon.   His report set all the troops in motion, and on Monday morning no less than four columns, each fully capable of coping successfully with the enemy in fight, pushed from the R. R. in pursuit, with confident hope of success.   The feeling of these troops can be better imagined than described, when after tremendous marches they reached the scenes of outrage, to find that they were being perpetrated, at the moment the columns were leaving the R R. from fifty to eighty miles away.

The outrages themselves are not to be voluntarily thought of, much less described.   Suffice to say that murder rape arson and pillage went hand in hand, no man who fell into the power of the savages, escaping death, no female of ten years or over, escaping outrage. Every house was pillaged, to an excess of wantonness, some were burned.   No murdered man was scalped or mutilated, no woman or child killed.   The perpetration of these crimes does not seem to have delayed in the least the onward march of the savage horde.   Mauck

4. See Robert Burns, "Death and Dr. Hornbook."

with the most strenuous efforts, and with all the advantage of Indian guides, could never overtake the enemy.   His proximity to them was ever dependant on their will, not his.   One day he would be almost

upon them, the next,   _^ however he exerted himself   they would be full thirty miles ahead.

But the escaping Cheyennes had yet another enemy.   The line of the Union Pacific R.R. was to be passed, and on it Genl Crook had concentrated ample forces.   The Indians crossed near Ogallala at about 1 Oclk p.m. and pushing on crossed the North Platte before dark.   It is said that these fresh troops were on the trail within three

3
_^   hours after the Indians had crossed the R. R.   But once across the North Platte the Cheyennes were masters of the situation.   An Indian can subsist comfortably for five days on the food & drink that the white man requires for one day.   Plunging at once into the Sand-hills, the great waterless wastes between the Platte and the Niobrara, the Cheyennes not only distanced their pursuers, but came near being the cause of their destruction, the country passed over being an abso-

lute desert.   The troops   _^ in following the trail   travelled for seventy five miles without a drop of water.

From that time there has been no authentic account of the escaped Cheyennes, but it is safe to predict that they crossed the Missouri somewhere in the neighborhood of Fort Sully, and keeping the divide between the great stream and the Dacotah River, are now well on their way to the Brittish Possessions, having successfully and triumphantly accomplished a feat more marvellous than the "Retreat of the Ten Thousand."[5]

5. Dodge compares the odyssey of the Northern Cheyennes to the Greeks' arduous return home under Xenophon after the death of their former leader, the younger Cyrus, in 401–400 B.C.

Appendix B
General Order No. 28.
Headquarters Department of the Missouri, Fort Leavenworth, Kansas, September 26, 1870

IN ORDER THAT THE EXACT RELATIONS BETWEEN officers commanding troops and the agents of the Indians on Reservations in this Department may be clearly understood, the following rules are published and will be carefully observed by all officers in the Department of the Missouri.[1]

I. . . . Indian reservations and the Indians upon them are wholly under the jurisdiction of the agents in charge who are alone responsible for the conduct of the Indians, and for the protection of the rights of person and property both of Indians and of white men on Indian reservations.

---

1. Issued shortly after Brigadier General John Pope replaced Major General John M. Schofield in command of the Department of the Missouri, this order was intended to delimit the responsibilities of Army personnel in Indian Territory and to regulate their interaction with representatives of the Indian Bureau, especially in times of emergency. Though not always observed in the years that followed, during Pope's tenure General Order 28 was understood by Army officers and Indian agents alike as defining the formal protocol for cooperation in Indian Territory between their respective agencies of the federal government.

The military forces on or near such Indian reservations are placed there solely to assist the Indian agents to preserve good order on the Reservations.

II. . . . Under no circumstances except specific orders from Department Headquarters or higher authority will any commander of troops assume jurisdiction or exercise control over reservation Indians or their agents, nor originate nor execute any act of their own volition in regard to affairs on such reservations. Whenever the services of troops are needed it will be necessary for the Indian agent so to state in writing to the nearest commander of troops, setting forth the reasons why troops are needed and the specific object to be accomplished. Upon the receipt of such written statement the military commander will furnish the required military force, always if possible to be commanded by a commissioned officer, who will be instructed to report with his detachment to the Indian agent and to act under his orders. No commander of a detachment will of his own motion take any action whatever in relation to affairs in Indian reservations even under the orders of an Indian agent unless the agent himself or some properly authorized subordinate is present with him and gives the necessary orders.

III. . . . From the foregoing rules it will be clearly understood that Indian agents must in all cases accompany the troops whose aid they apply for and point out to the commander of such troops the acts to be done and the persons to be interfered with. Troops cannot be used to expel unauthorized traders or intruders upon Indian Reservations, or to seize the goods or other property of such persons except as a posse to act under the orders and in the presence of some proper officer or agent of the Indian Department.

IV. . . . By closely observing the foregoing rules the necessary military aid can always be had and no occasion can arise for controversy or misunderstanding between the Indian Department and the military authorities.

By command of Brevet Major General POPE:

W. G. MITCHELL,
Brevet Colonel, U.S.A.
Acting Assistant Adjutant General

Bibliography

MANUSCRIPT MATERIALS

Blackmore, William. Papers. Manuscript Division, Museum of New Mexico, Santa Fe.

Crook, George. Papers. U.S. Army Military History Institute, Carlisle Barracks, Pa.

Crook-Kennan Papers. U.S. Army Military History Institute, Carlisle Barracks, Pa.

Dodge, Richard Irving. Papers, 1865–1949. Everett D. Graff Collection of Western Americana, Newberry Library, Chicago.

———. Papers, 1867–1895. Yale Collection of Western Americana. Beinecke Library, Yale University, New Haven, Conn.

Indian Wars Miscellaneous Collection. U.S. Army Military History Institute, Carlisle Barracks, Pa.

Mackenzie, Ranald S. Papers. United States Military History Institute, Carlisle Barracks, Pa.

Office of Indian Affairs. Annual Reports from Field Jurisdictions. Canton School and Insane Asylum, 1907–1938; Cheyenne and Arapahoe Agency, 1907–1938. National Archives and Records Administration. Record Group 75. Microcopy No. M1011, Rolls 7, 8, 14.

———. Letters Received, Central Superintendency, 1878–1880. National Archives and Records Administration. Record Group 75. Microcopy No. M234, Rolls 69–70.

———. Letters Received, Cheyenne and Arapahoe Agency, 1878–1880. National Archives and Records Administration. Record Group 75. Microcopy No. M234, Rolls 123–26.

———. Records of Inspection, Cheyenne and Arapahoe Agency, 1873–1900. National Archives and Records Administration. Record Group 48. Microcopy No. M1070, Roll 4.

Office of the Secretary of War. Letters Sent, 1878-1880. National Archives and Records Administration. Record Group 107. Microcopy No. M6, Rolls 76-81.

Order of the Indian Wars Collection. U.S. Army Military History Institute, Carlisle Barracks, Pa.

Ovenshine, Samuel J. Papers. United States Army Military History Institute, Carlisle Barracks, Pa.

Rickey, Don. Papers. United States Army Military History Institute, Carlisle Barracks, Pa.

Sherman, William T. Papers. Manuscript Division, Library of Congress, Washington, D.C.

Thoburn, Joseph C. Papers. Oklahoma Historical Society, Oklahoma City, Oklahoma.

United States Army. Cantonment North Fork Canadian River. Endorsements. General Orders and Circulars. Letters Received. Letters Sent. Monthly Report of Schools in Operation. Monthly Statement of Persons in Arrest or Confinement. Pass Book: Descriptive List of Civilian Employees. Register of Letters Received. Special Orders. Unregistered Letters Received. National Archives and Records Administration. Record Group 393.

———. Cantonment North Fork Canadian River Post Returns, 1879-1882. National Archives and Records Administration. Record Group 94. Microcopy No. 617, Roll 870.

———. Department of the Missouri. Endorsements. Fort Garland Column Field Records. Letters Received. Letters Sent. Special Orders. National Archives and Records Administration. Record Group 393.

———. Fort Crawford Post Returns, 1880-1890. National Archives and Records Administration. Record Group 94. Microcopy No. M617, Roll 263.

———. Fort Dodge Post Returns, 1866-1882. National Archives and Records Administration. Record Group 94. Microcopy No. M617, Roll 319.

———. Fort Garland Post Returns, 1873-1883. National Archives and Records Administration. Record Group 94. Microcopy No. M617, Roll 395.

———. Fort Hays. Letters Received, 1876-1880. Letters Sent, 1874-1883. Orders and Circulars, 1871-1889. National Archives and Records Administration. Record Group 393. Microcopy No. T713, Rolls 2, 11-12, 21.

———. Fort Hays Post Returns, 1876–1889. National Archives and Records Administration. Record Group 94. Microcopy No. M617, Roll 470.

———. Fort Leavenworth Post Returns, 1870–1890. National Archives and Records Administration. Record Group 94. Microcopy No. M617, Roll 612.

———. Fort Reno Post Returns, 1874–1884. National Archives and Records Administration. Record Group 94. Microcopy No. M617, Roll 998.

———. Fort Riley Post Returns, 1872–1884. National Archives and Records Administration. Record Group 94. Microcopy No. M617, Roll 1013.

———. Fort Sill Post Returns, 1876–1887. National Archives and Records Administration. Record Group 94. Microcopy No. M617, Roll 1174.

———. Fort Supply Post Returns, 1868–1894. National Archives and Records Administration. Record Group 94. Microcopy No. M617, Rolls 1243, 1244.

———. Fourth Cavalry Regimental Returns, 1877–1883. National Archives and Records Administration. Record Group 94. Microcopy No. M744, Roll 43.

———. Headquarters. Letters Sent, 1873–1883. National Archives and Records Administration. Record Group 108. Microcopy No. M857, Roll 8.

———. Letters Received (Main Series), 1871–1880. National Archives and Records Administration. Record Group 94. Microcopy No. M666, Rolls 4, 335, 428–30, 459, 463, 539, 541, 550, 552, 558.

———. Letters Sent (Main Series), 1878–1881. National Archives and Records Administration. Record Group 94. Microcopy No. M565, Rolls 49–52.

———. Military Division of the Missouri. Field Records. Fort Garland Column, 1880. National Archives and Records Administration. Record Group 393.

———. Military Division of the Missouri. Cheyenne Outbreak Special File, 1878–1879. National Archives and Records Administration. Record Group 393. Microcopy No. 1495, Roll 6.

———. Military Division of the Missouri. Indian Territory Operations Special File, May–December 1879. National Archives and Records Administration. Record Group 393. Microcopy No. M1495, Roll 10.

———. Military Division of the Missouri. Ute Campaign Special File, 1879–1880. National Archives and Records Administration. Record Group 393. Microcopy No. 1495, Roll 7.

————. Nineteenth Infantry Regimental Returns, 1871–1888. National Archives and Records Administration. Record Group 94. Microcopy No. 665, Rolls 204, 205.

————. Omaha Barracks Post Returns, 1874–1885. National Archives and Records Administration. Record Group 94. Microcopy No. M617, Roll 880.

————. Office of the Adjutant General. Richard Irving Dodge Personnel File. National Archives and Records Administration. Record Group 94.

————. Office of the Adjutant General. Registers of Letters Received, 1878–1880. National Archives and Records Administration. Record Group 94. Microcopy No. 711, Rolls 66–70.

————. Sixteenth Infantry Regimental Returns, 1870–1889. National Archives and Records Administration. Record Group 94. Microcopy No. M665, Rolls 175, 176.

————. Twenty-third Infantry Regimental Returns, 1874–1882. National Archives and Records Administration. Record Group 94. Microcopy No. M665, Roll 237.

War Department. Office of the Judge-Advocate General. Registers of Army General Courts-Martial, 1869–1883. National Archives and Records Administration. Record Group 153. Microcopy No. M1105, Roll 7.

GOVERNMENT PUBLICATIONS

Annual Report of the Board of Regents of the Smithsonian Institution . . . for the Year 1881. Washington, D.C.: Government Printing Office, 1883.

Annual Report of the Board of Regents of the Smithsonian Institution . . . for the Year 1882. Washington, D.C.: Government Printing Office, 1884.

First Annual Report of the Bureau of Ethnology to the Secretary of the Smithsonian Institution 1879–'80. Washington, D.C.: Government Printing Office, 1881.

Headquarters of the Army. Office of the Adjutant General. *General Court-Martial Orders,* 1878–1881.

Official Army Register. Washington, D.C.: Government Printing Office, 1877–1882.

Official Register of the United States, Containing a List of Officers and Employés in the Civil, Military, and Naval Service. 2 vols. Washington, D.C.: Government Printing Office, 1879, 1880, 1881.

Revised Statutes of the United States. Second edition. Washington, D.C.: Government Printing Office, 1878.

The Statutes at Large of the United States of America, from October, 1877, to March, 1879, and Recent Treaties, Postal Conventions, and Executive Proclamations. Volume 20. Washington, D.C.: Government Printing Office, 1879.

The Statutes at Large of the United States of America, from April, 1879, to March, 1881, and Recent Treaties, Postal Conventions, and Executive Proclamations. Volume 21. Washington, D.C.: Government Printing Office, 1881.

U.S. Army. *Regulations of the Army of the United States and General Orders in Force on the 17th of February 1881*. Washington, D.C.: Government Printing Office, 1881.

————. *Revised United States Army Regulations of 1861. With an Appendix Containing the Changes and Laws Affecting Army Regulations and Articles of War to June 25, 1863*. Washington, D.C.: Government Printing Office, 1863.

————. Department of the Missouri. *Roster of Troops Serving in the Department of the Missouri*. Fort Leavenworth: Departmental Headquarters, 1878, 1879.

U.S. Congress. House. Committee on Military Affairs. *Reorganization of the Army*. Misc. Document No. 56, 45th Congress, 2nd Session. Serial 1818.

————. House. *Report of the Commissioner of Indian Affairs* (1877). Executive Documents No. 1, Part 5, 45th Congress, 2nd Session. Serial 1800.

————. House. *Report of the Commissioner of Indian Affairs* (1878). Executive Documents No. 1, Part 5, 45th Congress, 3rd Session. Serial 1850.

————. House. *Report of the Commissioner of Indian Affairs* (1879). Executive Documents No. 1, Part 5, 46th Congress, 2nd Session. Serial 1910.

————. House. *Report of the Commissioner of Indian Affairs* (1880). Executive Documents No. 1, Part 5, 47th Congress, 1st Session. Serial 2018.

————. House. *Report of the Secretary of War* (1878). Executive Documents No. 1, Part 2, 45th Congress, 3rd Session. Serial 1843.

————. House. *Report of the Secretary of War* (1879). Executive Documents No. 1, Part 2, 46th Congress, 2nd Session. Serial 1903.

————. House. *Report of the Secretary of War* (1880). Executive Documents No. 1, Part 2, 46th Congress, 3rd Session. Serial 1952.

————. House. *Report of the Secretary of War* (1881). Executive Documents No. 1, Part 2, 47th Congress, 1st Session. Serial 2010.

————. House. *Revised Army Regulations.* Report No. 85, 42nd Congress, 3rd Session (1873). Serial 1576.

————. House. *Testimony in Relation to the Ute Indian Outbreak, Taken by the Committee on Indian Affairs.* Miscellaneous Documents No. 38, 46th Congress, 2nd Session. Serial 1931.

————. Senate. *Letter from the Secretary of the Interior, Transmitting in Compliance with a Resolution of the Senate of December 8, 1879, Correspondence Concerning the Ute Indians in Colorado.* Executive Documents No. 31, 46th Congress, 2nd Session. Serial 1882.

————. Senate. *Letter from the Secretary of War to the Chairman of the Committee on Indian Affairs Communicating Information in Relation to the Escape of the Northern Cheyenne Indians from Fort Robinson.* Miscellaneous Documents No. 64, 45th Congress, 3rd Session. Serial 1833.

————. Senate. *Message from the President of the United States Communicating . . . Information in Relation to an Alleged Occupation of a Portion of Indian Territory by White Settlers.* Executive Documents No. 20, 46th Congress, 1st Session. Serial 1869.

————. Senate. *Report of the Select Committee on the Removal of the Northern Cheyennes.* Report No. 708, 46th Congress, 2nd Session. Serial 1899.

NEWSPAPERS AND PERIODICALS

Army and Navy Journal, 1878–1895.

Atchison (Kansas) Globe, 1879–1880.

Caldwell (Kansas) Post, 1879–1880.

Chicago Inter-Ocean, 1878–1880.

Harper's Weekly, 1878–1880.

Iowa State Register (Des Moines), 1880.

Leavenworth (Kansas) Times, 1879–1880.

New York Daily Tribune, 1879–1880.

New York Dramatic Mirror, 1879–1880.

New York Herald, 1878–1880.

New York Times, 1878–1880.

Omaha Herald, 1880.

Topeka (Kansas) Weekly Commonwealth, 1880.

ARTICLES

Ayres, Mary C. "History of Fort Lewis, Colorado." *Colorado Magazine* 8, no. 3 (May 1931): 81–90.

Clapsaddle, David K. "The Fort Hays-Fort Dodge Road." *Kansas History* 14, no. 2 (Summer 1991): 100–12.

Collins, Herbert E. "Ben Williams, Frontier Peace Officer." *Chronicles of Oklahoma* 10, no. 4 (December 1932): 520–39.

Covington, James Warren. "Causes of the Dull Knife Raid." *Chronicles of Oklahoma* 26, no. 1 (March 1948): 13–22.

Dale, Edward Everett. "The Cheyenne-Arapaho Country." *Chronicles of Oklahoma* 20, no. 4 (December 1942): 360–71.

———. "Ranching on the Cheyenne-Arapaho Reservation, 1880–1885." *Chronicles of Oklahoma* 6, no. 1 (March 1928): 35–59.

Dodge, Richard Irving. "The Enlisted Soldier." *Journal of the Military Service Institution of the United States* 8 (May 1886): 259–318.

Johnson, Walter A. "Brief History of the Missouri-Kansas-Texas Railroad Lines." *Chronicles of Oklahoma* 24, no. 3 (Autumn 1946): 340–58.

Kaufman, Edmund G. "Mennonite Missions Among the Oklahoma Indians." *Chronicles of Oklahoma* 40 (March 1962): 40–52.

Keeling, Henry C. "My Experience with the Cheyenne Indians." *Chronicles of Oklahoma* 3 (March 1925): 59–68.

Kelley, E. H. "When Oklahoma City Was Seymour and Verbeck." *Chronicles of Oklahoma* 27 (December 1949): 347–53.

Kime, Wayne R. "'Not Coarse . . . But Not Delicate': Richard Irving Dodge's Portrayal of Plains Indians in *The Plains of the Great West and Their Inhabitants*." *Platte Valley Review* 17, no. 1 (Winter 1989): 69–83.

Le Van, Sandra W. "The Quaker Agents at Darlington." *Chronicles of Oklahoma* 51, no. 1 (Spring 1973): 92–99.

McDermott, John D. "Were They Really Rogues: Desertion in the Nineteenth Century U.S. Army." *Nebraska History* 78 (Winter 1997): 165–74.

Nankivell, John H. "Fort Crawford, Colorado, 1880–1890." *Colorado Magazine* 11 (March 1934): 54–64.

Osborne, Alan. "The Exile of the Nez Percé in Indian Territory, 1878–1885." *Chronicles of Oklahoma* 56, no. 4 (Winter 1978–1979): 450–71.

Peery, Dan W. "The Indians' Friend: John H. Seger." *Chronicles of Oklahoma* 10, no. 3 (September 1932): 348–68; no. 4 (December 1932): 570–91.

Pennington, William D. "Government Policy and Indian Farming on the Cheyenne and Arapaho Reservation, 1869–1880." *Chronicles of Oklahoma* 57, no. 2 (Summer 1979): 171–89.

Reade, Philip. "Chronicles of the Twenty-third Regiment of Infantry." *Journal of the Military Service Institution of the United States* 35 (1904): 422–27.

Shirk, George H. "Military Duty on the Western Frontier." *Chronicles of Oklahoma* 47, no. 2 (Summer 1969): 118–25.

Thoburn, Joseph B. "The Story of Cantonment." *Chronicles of Oklahoma* 3 (1925): 68–73.

Wright, Peter M. "The Pursuit of Dull Knife from Fort Reno in 1878–1879." *Chronicles of Oklahoma* 46, no. 2 (June 1968): 141–54.

BOOKS

Aderman, Alice R. *A Genealogy of the Irvings of New York: Washington Irving, His Brothers and Sisters, and Their Dependents.* N.p.: privately printed, 1981.

Aldridge, Reginald. *Life on a Ranch: Ranch Notes in Kansas, Colorado, the Indian Territory, and Northern Texas.* New York: D. Appleton, 1884.

Athearn, Robert G. *Rebel of the Rockies: A History of the Denver and Rio Grande Western Railroad.* New Haven: Yale University Press, 1962.

Bancroft, Hubert Howe. *History of Nevada, Colorado, and Wyoming, 1540–1888.* San Francisco: History Company, 1890. Volume 25 of Bancroft's Works (39 vols., 1882–1890).

Belden, George P. *Belden, The White Chief: or, Twelve Years Among the Wild Indians of the Plains.* Edited by Gen. James S. Brisbin, U.S.A. Cincinnati: C. F. Vent, 1870.

Berthrong, Donald J. *The Cheyenne and Arapaho Ordeal: Reservation and Agency Life in the Indian Territory, 1875–1907.* Norman: University of Oklahoma Press, 1976.

———. *The Southern Cheyennes.* Norman: University of Oklahoma Press, 1963.

Billings, John D. *Hardtack and Coffee: or, The Unwritten Story of Army Life.* Philadelphia: Thompson Publishing Co., 1888.

Bordman, Gerald. *American Theatre: A Chronicle of Comedy and Drama, 1869-1914*. New York: Oxford University Press, 1994.

Brandes, T. Donald. *Military Posts of Colorado*. Fort Collins, Colo.: Old Army Press, 1973.

Brayer, Herbert Oliver. *William Blackmore: A Case Study in the Economic Development of the West*. 2 vols. Denver: Bradford-Robinson, 1949.

Bryant, Keith L., Jr. *History of the Atchison, Topeka and Santa Fe Railway*. Lincoln: University of Nebraska Press, 1974.

Burton, Jeffrey. *Indian Territory and the United States, 1866-1906*. Norman: University of Oklahoma Press, 1995.

Butler, David F. *United States Firearms: The First Century, 1776-1875*. New York: Winchester Press, 1971.

Butterfield, Consul W. *History of the City of Omaha, Nebraska*. New York: Munsell and Co., 1894.

Carriker, Robert C. *Fort Supply, Indian Territory: Frontier Outpost on the Plains*. Norman: University of Oklahoma Press, 1970.

Catlin, George. *Last Rambles Amongst the Indians of the Rocky Mountains*. London: Sampson, Low, Son, and Marston, 1868.

The Centennial of the United States Military Academy at West Point, New York, 1802-1902. 2 vols. Washington, D.C.: Government Printing Office, 1904.

Chalfant, William Y. *Cheyennes at Dark Water Creek: The Last Fight of the Red River War*. Foreword by Father Peter John Powell. Norman: University of Oklahoma Press, 1997.

Check List of Publications of the Smithsonian Institution. Smithsonian Miscellaneous Collections, No. 745. Washington, D.C.: Government Printing Office, 1890.

City Directories of the United States, 1860-1901: Guide to the Microfilm Collection. Woodbridge, Conn.: Research Publications, 1983.

Coffman, Edward M. *The Old Army: A Portrait of the American Army in Peacetime, 1784-1898*. New York: Oxford University Press, 1986.

Connelly, William E. *A Standard History of Kansas and Kansans*. 5 vols. Chicago and New York: Lewis Publishing Co., 1918.

Corbett and Ballenger's Denver City Directory for 1881. Denver: Rocky Mountain News Printing Co., 1881.

Crofutt, George A. *Crofutt's Grip-Sack Guide to Colorado*. Denver: Alvord & Co., 1881.

Cullum, George W. *Biographical Register of the Officers and Graduates of the U.S. Military Academy from 1802 to 1890*. Boston: Houghton Mifflin, 1891.

Dale, Edward Everett, and Morris L. Wardell. *History of Oklahoma*. Englewood Cliffs, N.J.: Prentice-Hall, 1948.

Delo, David Michael. *Peddlers and Post Traders: The Army Sutler on the Frontier*. Salt Lake City: University of Utah Press, 1992.

Dodge, Richard Irving. *The Black Hills Journals of Colonel Richard Irving Dodge*. Edited by Wayne R. Kime. Norman: University of Oklahoma Press, 1996.

——. *A Living Issue*. Washington, D.C.: F. B. Mohun, 1882.

——. *Our Wild Indians: Thirty-three Years' Personal Experience among the Red Men of the Great West. A Popular Account of Their Social Life, Religion, Habits, Traits, Customs, Exploits, Etc. With Thrilling Adventures and Experiences on the Great Plains and in the Mountains of Our Wide Frontier*. Hartford, Conn.: A. D. Worthington and Co., 1882.

——. *The Plains of North America and Their Inhabitants*. Edited by Wayne R. Kime. Newark: University of Delaware Press, 1989.

——. *The Powder River Expedition Journals of Colonel Richard Irving Dodge*. Edited by Wayne R. Kime. Norman: University of Oklahoma Press, 1997.

Dunlay, Thomas W. *Wolves for the Blue Soldiers: Indian Scouts and Auxiliaries with the United States Army*. Lincoln: University of Nebraska Press, 1982.

Dyer, Mrs. D. B. *Fort Reno: or, Picturesque Cheyenne and Arapahoe Army Life Before the Opening of "Oklahoma."* New York: G. W. Dillingham, 1896.

Ellis, Richard N. *General Pope and U. S. Indian Policy*. Albuquerque: New Mexico University Press, 1970.

Emmitt, Robert. *The Last War Trail: The Utes and the Settlement of Colorado*. Norman: University of Oklahoma Press, 1972.

Farrow, Edward S. F*arrow's Military Encyclopedia: A Dictionary of Military Knowledge*. Second edition. 3 vols. New York: Military-Naval Publishing Co., 1895.

Faulk, Odie B., Kenny A. Franks, and Paul F. Lambert, eds. *Early Military Forts and Posts in Oklahoma*. Oklahoma City: Oklahoma Historical Society, 1978.

Foner, Jack D. *The United States Soldier Between Two Wars: Army Life and Reforms, 1865-1898*. New York: Humanities Press, 1970.

Fossett, Frank. *Colorado: Its Gold and Silver Mines and Health and Pleasure Resorts*. Second edition. New York: C. G. Crawford, 1880.

Frazer, Robert W. *Forts of the West: Military Forts and Presidios and Posts Commonly Called Forts West of the Mississippi River to 1898*. Norman: University of Oklahoma Press, 1965.

Freeman, George D. *Midnight and Noonday: or, The Incidental History of Southern Kansas and the Indian Territory, 1871-1890*. Edited by Richard L. Lane. Norman: University of Oklahoma Press, 1984.

Fry, James B. *Army Sacrifices, or Briefs from Official Pigeon-Holes. Sketches Based on Official Reports—Grouped Together for the Purpose of Illustrating the Services and Experiences of the Regular Army of the United States on the Indian Frontier*. New York: Van Nostrand, 1879.

———. *Military Miscellanies*. New York: Brentano's, 1889.

Greene, Jerome A. *Yellowstone Command: Colonel Nelson A. Miles and the Great Sioux War, 1876-1877*. Lincoln: University of Nebraska Press, 1991.

Grinnell, George Bird. *The Fighting Cheyennes*. Norman: University of Oklahoma Press, 1956.

Hall, Frank. *History of the State of Colorado*. 4 vols. Chicago: Blakely Printing Co., 1895.

Hamersley, L. R., comp. *Records of Living Officers of the United States Army*. Philadelphia: L. R. Hamersley and Co., 1884.

Hamersley, Thomas H., comp. *Complete Army Register of the United States: For One Hundred Years (1779 to 1879)*. 2 vols. Washington, D.C.: T. Hamersley, 1880.

Haywood, C. Robert. *Cowtown Lawyers: Dodge City and Its Attorneys, 1876-1886*. Norman: University of Oklahoma Press, 1988.

———. *Trails South: The Wagon Road Economy in the Dodge City-Panhandle Region*. Norman: University of Oklahoma Press, 1986.

Heitman, Francis B. *Historical Register and Dictionary of the United States Army*. 2 vols. Washington, D.C.: Government Printing Office, 1903.

Hewes, Leslie. *Occupying the Cherokee Country of Oklahoma*. Lincoln: University of Nebraska Press, 1978.

Hill, Edward E. *The Office of Indian Affairs, 1874-1880: Historical Sketches*. New York: Clearwater Publishing Co., 1974.

Hoig, Stan. *The Peace Chiefs of the Cheyennes*. Foreword by Boyce D. Timmons. Norman: University of Oklahoma Press, 1980.

Hunt, Elvid, and Walter E. Lorence. *History of Fort Leavenworth, 1827–1937*. Second edition. Fort Leavenworth: Command and General Staff School Press, 1937.

Hutton, Paul A. *Phil Sheridan and His Army*. Lincoln: University of Nebraska Press, 1985.

Hutton, Paul A., ed. *Soldiers West: Biographies from the Military Frontier*. Introduction by Robert M. Utley. Lincoln: University of Nebraska Press, 1987.

Hyde, George E. *A Life of George Bent, Written from His Letters*. Edited by Savoie Lottinville. Norman: University of Oklahoma Press, 1968.

Irving, John Duer. *Geology and Ore Deposits Near Lake City, Colorado*. U.S. Geological Survey Bulletin No. 478. Washington: Government Printing Office, 1911.

Johnson, Harrison. *Johnson's History of Nebraska*. Omaha: Henry Gibson, 1880.

Kappler, Charles, ed. *Indian Affairs: Laws and Treaties*. 3 vols. Washington, D.C.: Government Printing Office, 1904.

Keim, De Benneville Randolph. *Sheridan's Troopers on the Border: A Winter Campaign on the Plains*. Philadelphia: Claxton, Remses and Haffelflinger, 1870.

Kime, Wayne R. *Pierre M. Irving and Washington Irving: A Collaboration in Life and Letters*. Waterloo, Ontario: Wilfrid Laurier University Press, 1978.

Knight, Oliver. *Life and Manners in the Frontier Army*. Foreword by Paul L. Hedren. Norman: University of Oklahoma Press, 1993.

Ladies and Officers of the United States Army; or, American Aristocracy. A Sketch of the Social Life and Character of the Army. Chicago: Central Publishing Co., 1880.

Laidley, T. T. S. *A Course of Instruction in Rifle Firing*. Philadelphia: J. B. Lippincott, 1879.

Leckie, William H. *The Military Conquest of the Southern Plains*. Norman: University of Oklahoma Press, 1963.

Lowie, Robert H. *Indians of the Plains*. Preface by Raymond J. DeMallie. Lincoln: University of Nebraska Press, 1982.

McChristian, Douglas C. *An Army of Marksmen: The Development of United States Army Marksmanship in the Nineteenth Century*. Fort Collins, Col.: Old Army Press, 1981.

————. *The United States Army in the West, 1870–1880: Uniforms, Weapons, and Equipment*. Norman: University of Oklahoma Press, 1995.

McNitt, Frank. *The Indian Traders*. Norman: University of Oklahoma Press, 1962.

Marszalek, John F. *Sherman: A Soldier's Passion for Order*. New York: Vintage Books, 1994.

Mathews, Mitford M., ed. *A Dictionary of Americanisms*. 2 vols. Chicago: University of Chicago Press, 1951.

Mattes, Merrill J. *Indians, Infants, and Infantry: Andrew and Elizabeth Burt on the Frontier*. Lincoln: University of Nebraska Press, 1988.

Matthews, Washington. *Ethnography and Philology of the Hidatsa Indians*. Washington, D.C.: Government Printing Office, 1877.

Miles, Nelson A. *Personal Recollections and Observations of General Nelson A. Miles*. Introduction by Robert M. Utley. New York: Da Capo Press, 1969.

Miller, William H. *The History of Kansas City. Together with a Sketch of the Commercial Resources with Which It Is Surrounded*. Kansas City: Birdsall & Miller, 1881.

Miner, H. Craig. *West of Wichita: Settling the High Plains of Kansas, 1865–1890*. Lawrence: University Press of Kansas, 1986.

————. *Wichita: The Early Years, 1865–80*. Lincoln: University of Nebraska Press, 1982.

Moore, John W. *History of North Carolina*. 2 vols. Raleigh: Alfred Williams, 1888.

Morris, John W., Charles R. Goins, and Edwin C. McReynolds. *Historical Atlas of Oklahoma*. Third edition. Norman: University of Oklahoma Press, 1986.

Morton, J. Sterling. *Illustrated History of Nebraska*. 3 vols. Lincoln: J. North, 1905–1913.

Noel, Thomas J., Paul F. Mahoney, and Richard E. Stevens. *Historical Atlas of Colorado*. Norman: University of Oklahoma Press, 1994.

Nohl, Lessing J. "Bad Hand: The Military Career of Ranald Slidell Mackenzie, 1871–1889." Ph.D. dissertation, University of New Mexico, 1962.

Nye, Wilbur S. *Carbine and Lance: The Story of Old Fort Sill*. Norman: University of Oklahoma Press, 1937.

————. *Plains Indian Raiders: The Final Phases of Warfare from the Arkansas to the Red River. With Original Photographs by William S. Soule*. Norman: University of Oklahoma Press, 1968.

Odell, George C. D. *Annals of the New York Stage*. 15 vols. New York: Columbia University Press, 1939.

Oliva, Leo E. *Fort Hays, Frontier Army Post, 1865–1889*. Topeka: Kansas State Historical Society, 1980.

Pabor, William W. *Colorado as an Agricultural State: Its Farms, Fields, and Garden Lands*. New York: Orange Judd, 1883.

The Papers of the Order of Indian Wars. Introduction by John M. Carroll. Fort Collins, Colo.: Old Army Press, 1975.

Parker, James. *The Old Army: Memories, 1872–1918*. Philadelphia: Dorrance, 1929.

Pierce, Michael D. *The Most Promising Young Officer: A Life of Ranald Slidell Mackenzie*. Norman: University of Oklahoma Press, 1993.

Poor, Henry V. *Manual of the Railroads of the United States*. New York: Poor, 1878–1883.

Powell, Cuthbert. *Twenty Years of Kansas City's Live Stock Trade and Traders*. Kansas City: Pearl Publishing Co., 1893.

Powell, Peter J. *People of the Sacred Mountain: A History of the Northern Cheyenne Chiefs and Warrior Societies*. 2 vols. San Francisco: Harper and Row, 1979.

————. *Sweet Medicine: The Continuing Role of the Sacred Arrows, the Sun Dance, and the Sacred Buffalo Hat in Northern Cheyenne History*. 2 vols. Norman: University of Oklahoma Press, 1969.

Powell, William S. *A North Carolina Gazetteer*. Chapel Hill: University of North Carolina Press, 1968.

Pride, Woodbury F. *History of Fort Riley*. Fort Riley, Kans.: Cavalry School, 1926.

Priest, Loring Benson. *Uncle Sam's Stepchildren: The Reformation of United States Indian Policy, 1865–1887*. New Brunswick, N.J.: Rutgers University Press, 1942.

Prucha, Francis Paul. *American Indian Policy in Crisis: Christian Reformers and the Indian, 1865–1900*. Norman: University of Oklahoma Press, 1976.

Reber, Bruce. *The United States Army and the Indian Wars in the Trans-Mississippi West, 1860–1898*. Special Bibliography 17. Carlisle Barracks, Pa.: U.S. Army Military History Institute, 1978.

Record of Engagements with Hostile Indians within the Military Division of the Missouri, from 1868 to 1882, Lieutenant-General P. H. Sheridan, Commanding. Washington, D.C.: Government Printing Office, 1882.

Rickey, Don, Jr. *Forty Miles a Day on Beans and Hay: The Enlisted Soldier Fighting the Indian Wars*. Norman: University of Oklahoma Press, 1963.

Rister, Carl Coke. *Land Hunger: David L. Payne and the Oklahoma Boomers*. Norman: University of Oklahoma Press, 1942.

Roberts, Robert B. *Encyclopedia of Historic Forts: The Military, Pioneer, and Trading Posts of the United States*. New York: Macmillan, 1988.

Robinson, Charles M., III. *Bad Hand: A Biography of General Ranald S. Mackenzie*. Foreword by Stan Hoig. Austin, Tex.: State House Press, 1993.

Rockwell, Wilson. *The Utes: A Forgotten People*. Denver: Sage Books, 1956.

Roe, Frances Marie Antoinette. *Army Letters from an Officer's Wife, 1871–1888*. New York: D. Appleton & Co., 1909.

Sandoz, Mari. *Cheyenne Autumn*. Lincoln: University of Nebraska Press, 1953.

Savage, James Woodruff. *History of Omaha, Nebraska*. New York: Munsell, 1894.

Schindler, Henry. *Fort Leavenworth, Its Churches and Schools, 1827–1912*. Fort Leavenworth: Army Service School Press, 1912.

Schindler, Henry, comp. *A Guide. Description of Fort Leavenworth, Kansas, and the U.S. School of Application for Cavalry and Infantry, and the U.S. Military Prison, Together with Other Useful Information About the Army, and a Directory of Fort Leavenworth, Kansas*. Leavenworth: The Compiler, 1884.

Schmeckebier, Laurence F. *The Office of Indian Affairs: Its History, Activities, and Organization*. Baltimore: Johns Hopkins University Press, 1927.

Schorger, Arlie W. *The Wild Turkey: Its History and Domestication*. Norman: University of Oklahoma Press, 1966.

Schutz, Wallace J., and Walter N. Trenerry. *Abandoned by Lincoln: A Military Biography of General John Pope*. Urbana: University of Illinois Press, 1990.

Seger, John H. *Early Days Among the Cheyenne and Arapahoe Indians*. Edited by Stanley Vestal. Norman: University of Oklahoma Press, 1956.

Skaggs, Jimmy M. *The Cattle-Trailing Industry: Between Supply and Demand, 1866–1890*. Norman: University of Oklahoma Press, 1991.

Smith, Sherry L. *The View from Officers' Row: Army Perceptions of Western Indians*. Tucson: University of Arizona Press, 1990.

Socolofsky, Homer E., and Huber Self. *Historical Atlas of Kansas*. Second edition. Norman: University of Oklahoma Press, 1988.

Sorensen, Alfred R. *History of Omaha from the Pioneer Days to the Present Time*. Omaha: Gibson, Miller, and Richardson, 1889.

Sprague, Marshall. *Massacre: The Tragedy at White River*. Lincoln: University of Nebraska Press, 1957.

Stallard, Patricia Y. *Glittering Misery: Dependents of the Indian-Fighting Army*. Norman: University of Oklahoma Press, 1992.

Stands in Timber, John, and Margot Liberty. With the assistance of Robert M. Utley. *Cheyenne Memories*. Lincoln: University of Nebraska Press, 1967.

Starita, Joe. *The Dull Knifes of Pine Ridge: A Lakota Odyssey*. New York: Berkley Publishing Co., 1995.

Stone, Wilbur Fiske. *History of Colorado*. 4 vols. Chicago: J. Clarke, 1918–1919.

Storm, Colton. *A Catalogue of the Everett D. Graff Collection of Western Americana*. Chicago: University of Chicago Press for the Newberry Library, 1968.

Strahorn, Robert E. *Gunnison and San Juan. A Late and Reliable Description*. Omaha: The New West, 1881.

Strong, William Emerson. *Canadian River Hunt*. Norman: University of Oklahoma Press, 1960.

Sutton, George M. *Oklahoma Birds: Their Ecology and Distribution, with Comments on the Avifauna of the Southern Great Plains*. Norman: University of Oklahoma Press, 1967.

Thornton, Richard H. *An American Glossary*. 3 vols. New York: Frederick Ungar, 1962.

Tillinghast, B. F. *Three Cities, and Their Industrial Interests, with a Historical and Descriptive Sketch of the National Army and Arsenal*. Davenport, Iowa: Glass and Hoover, 1883.

Trenholm, Virginia Cole. *The Arapahoes, Our People*. Norman: University of Oklahoma Press, 1970.

U.S. Army. Military Division of the Missouri. *Outline Descriptions of the Posts in the Military Division of the Missouri*. Chicago: Headquarters, Military Division of the Missouri, 1876.

U.S. Bureau of Indian Affairs. *Biographical and Historical Index of American Indians and Persons Involved in Indian Affairs*. 8 vols. Boston: G. K. Hall, 1966.

Upton, Emory. *A New System of Infantry Tactics, Double and Single Rank: Adapted to American Topography and Improved Fire-Arms*. New York: D. Appleton, 1873.

Utley, Robert M. *Frontier Regulars: The United States Army and the Indian, 1866-1891*. New York: Macmillan, 1973.

Walker, Henry Pickering. T*he Wagonmasters: High Plains Freighting from the Earliest Days of the Santa Fe Trail to 1880*. Norman: University of Oklahoma Press, 1966.

Wellman, Paul I. *Death on the Prairie: The Thirty Years' Struggle for the Western Plains*. Lincoln: University of Nebraska Press, 1987.

Welsh, Jack D. *Medical Histories of Union Generals*. Kent, Ohio: Kent State University Press, 1996.

Wheeler, John H. *Reminiscences and Memoirs of North Carolina and Eminent North Carolinians*. Baltimore: Genealogical Publishing Co., 1966.

Wilder, Daniel Webster. *The Annals of Kansas*. Topeka: T. Dwight Thatcher, 1885.

Wood, George B., and Franklin Bache. *The Dispensatory of the United States of America*. Sixteenth edition. Philadelphia: J. B. Lippincott, 1892.

Wooster, Robert. *The Military and United States Indian Policy, 1865-1903*. New Haven: Yale University Press, 1988.

Wright, Muriel H. *A Guide to the Indian Tribes of Oklahoma*. Foreword by Arrell Morgan Gibson. Norman: University of Oklahoma Press, 1986.

Wyckoff, William, and Lary M. Dilsaver, eds. *The Mountainous West: Explorations in Historical Geography*. Lincoln: University of Nebraska Press, 1995.

Index